A
Mustard Seed
Life

Jill McIlreavy

Copyright

A Mustard Seed Life. By Jill McIlreavy.

No part of this publication may be reproduced or transmitted in any form or by any means, electronic or mechanical, including photocopy, recording or any information storage and retrieval system, without permission in writing from the author.

Preface

All You Need Is Faith The Size of A Mustard Seed.

When God called Moses, He asked him the question, *"What's in your hand?"* All Moses had in his hand was an ordinary, everyday shepherds' staff; but surrendered in faith to the God of miracles, that staff became the staff of God!

Jesus said that all that is required to move mountains is faith the size of a mustard seed. He also said, *"Without me, you can do nothing."* *A Mustard Seed Life* is a series of daily devotional style studies and thoughts, with a theme for each week, covering a six-month period. We will delve into some well known stories of ordinary people in the Bible who became God's movers and shakers; and remind ourselves of what happens when ordinary people put their faith in an *EXTRAORDINARY* God!

I hope that as you read the topics that I have only lightly covered, you will be enticed to deeper study. And it is my sincere prayer that, as you daily immerse yourself in the Word of God your heart and mind will be awakened to His presence; your ears opened to your Shepherd's voice. May you be refreshed and strengthened in your daily walk with God.

My own mustard seed story

Over twenty years ago God promised me that He was going to lead me into writing. Apart from keeping a personal Bible study journal, almost nothing happened, or so it seemed, with regard to writing for over two decades. Finally three years ago the Lord began to remind me of that long forgotten promise.

On the very morning that I said *yes* to God regarding the call to write, my friend Alice Stewart came to speak to me. Knowing nothing about my plans to write nor how daunted I felt about it, she pressed a single mustard seed into my hand, saying *"the Lord says that's all it takes Jill"*.

I took that seed home, planted it in a tiny five millimetre measuring cup on my kitchen window sill and started a blog that very afternoon called *Mustard Seed Blog*.
As the seed grew I had to keep transferring it to bigger pots to give it space to grow. Now a shoulder-high thriving tree, it resides in a heavy earthenware pot at our front door; a daily visual reminder of God's faithfulness to His promises.
I have recently learned that these type of mustard plants rarely grow on our side of the world; they thrive in hot, dry arid conditions ~not quite how one would describe Northern Ireland!

My blog has grown too, almost as rapidly as my 'mustard tree'. I recently sensed that the Lord was leading me to *'transfer it to a bigger pot'* too. This book is the bigger pot!

Writing, both my blog and this book, is a joy! I have been a follower of Jesus for forty years, yet I have found a deeper intimacy with Him in the last three years years than ever. The reality of His presence has been so real and tangible as I have searched the Word of God.

I believe this book contains an invitation from the heart of God to you His child, to come, sit with him awhile, and listen; not to what I have to say, because my words are merely my opinions; but to listen to the wonderful truths contained in His Word, that you will discover for yourself when you take time to open up your Bible and study further. It is my dearest hope that you will hear your Father's invitation.

Jill McIlreavy

About The Author

Jill McIlreavy was born in Belfast, Northern Ireland and lives in the small coastal town of Whitehead, County Antrim, with her Husband David and two miniature schnauzers. Jill is Mum to four adult children and has two grandchildren. Jill is an artist, jewellery designer and faith-lifestyle blogger. After graduating from Bible college in the early 1980s, Jill felt led by God to go to South Africa. A three-week trip became a twenty-year journey and Jill was involved in various church related ministries, before returning to Northern Ireland in 2005. A 'Mustard Seed Life' is Jill McIlreavy's first book.

Contents

Dedication

For David, my beloved husband and best friend.
All that is needed is faith the size of a mustard seed.

The Great Escape

Monday - Free To Go

"Yet it was our weaknesses he carried; it was our sorrows that weighed him down. And we thought his troubles were a punishment from God, a punishment for his own sins! But he was pierced for our rebellion, crushed for our sins. He was beaten so we could be whole. He was whipped so we could be healed." Isaiah 53:4-5 (NLT)

Isaiah paints a powerful, prophetic picture in this scripture, of Jesus taking our sin, shame and sickness upon himself. I recently watched a documentary about an infamous court case in 1989 known as *The Central Park Five.* Five teenagers were wrongfully accused of a heinous crime, and despite many 'holes' in the case and an alarming lack of evidence, they were convicted. The boys spend several years in a juvenile centre before being transferred to a federal prison; innocent young men mixed in with hardened criminals.

Because of the sensitive racial issues surrounding the crime, the boys suffered terrible abuse, bullying and threats for the duration of their internment. The awful tragedy is that the real perpetrator of the crime kept silent for thirteen years. Eventually, his conscience caused him to give himself up, and the young men were exonerated, but this was after the boys had endured indescribable suffering for a crime they had not committed.

* * *

I wondered, as I watched the documentary, what had gone through the real perpetrator's mind as he had followed the very public trial. How did he feel, seeing the innocent boys convicted, their lives forever changed?

Jesus was innocent

"He was oppressed and treated harshly, yet he never said a word. He was led like a lamb to the slaughter. And as a sheep is silent before the shearers, he did not open his mouth." Isaiah 53:7 (NLT)
"He had done no wrong and had never deceived anyone. But he was buried like a criminal; he was put in a rich man's grave." Isaiah 53:9 (NLT)

Jesus was tried and convicted of crimes He did not commit, *our* crimes; *our* sin. He was given the death sentence. But Jesus was not led kicking and screaming into the dock, protesting His innocence; His love compelled Him, He went willingly, choosing to take our guilt upon himself. He died in our place so that we could go free. Jesus died not only *for* you, but literally *as* you.

Jesus chose to die

Jesus *chose* to die. His life was not taken, it was freely given. Keep in mind that although Jesus was fully God, He was also fully man. He felt pain, He experienced emotions just as you and I do, but His choice to die in place of us was motivated by both His love for us and obedience to the Father, knowing that this was part of His father's perfect plan. We see this in these two Messianic prophesies:

"But it was the Lord's good plan to crush him and cause him grief. Yet when his life is made an offering for sin, he will have many descendants. He will enjoy a long life, and the Lord's good plan will prosper in his hands." Isaiah 53:10 (NLT)

* * *

3

"Because the Sovereign Lord helps me, I will not be disgraced. Therefore, I have set my face like a stone, determined to do his will. And I know that I will not be put to shame." Isaiah 50:7 (NLT)

Jesus could have evaded crucifixion had he wanted to; after all, He was the Miracle worker. The crowd who had bayed for His death had this same thought, and jeered at Jesus to *"come down off the cross"* (Mark 15:30)

Even His own disciples didn't really understand why Jesus was choosing this path, and when Jesus, in that compassionate way of His, began to prepare them for His imminent suffering and death, Peter actually rebuked Jesus for saying such things! (Matthew 16:14) But, Jesus had *"set His face like a stone"* to go to Jerusalem and carry out God's purposes.

We, the real perpetrators, are free to go!

The real perpetrator in the opening story got to a place where he could no longer live with himself and the knowledge of his crime, he felt compelled to own up to his crime and pay the price he deserved. And so it was with you and me, when we acknowledged our sin and need of a saviour; *The* Saviour. We 'handed ourselves in,' acknowledging that it was in fact we who were the guilty ones.

The all-important difference in the stories is that in accordance with the world's judicial system the true perpetrator in the first story, upon confessing, was then required to pay the price for his crimes. In our story, according to God's judicial system the Judge looked at us with such love and mercy upon our confession and said, *"The price has already been paid".*

Jesus has paid it all! As we saw earlier, He died both *for* us, and *as* us. In other words as if *He were us,* with the full weight of our

4

sin and shame heaped upon Him. And now, because of the price Jesus paid, we are declared righteous before God. We have a *'not guilty'* verdict in the eyes of God: *"God made him who had no sin to be sin for us, so that in him we might become the righteousness of God."* 2 Corinthians 5:21 (NIVUK)

See also: 1 Peter 2:24; Ephesians 1:7; Romans 5:8; 1 John 2:2

Tuesday - Living Free

"We have escaped like a bird from the fowler's snare; the snare has been broken, and we have escaped." Psalms 124:7 (NIVUK)

We reminded ourselves yesterday that Jesus paid the price for our sin, and that as a result we are 'free to go'. There are several ways a pardoned prisoner could respond when given those release papers. He could remain exactly where he is, having become so used to being a prisoner that he has become institutionalised, so that even though his prison door is wide open he finds he cannot leave. He could leave prison and go straight back to his old way of life, running with the old crowd and ending up back in prison. Or he could leave prison, grateful to be given a new opportunity to start life with a clean slate, and live the rest of his days making the most of the freedom granted to him.

The ex prisoner who won't leave

"If you hold to my teaching, you are really my disciples. Then you will know the truth, and the truth will set you free." John 8:31-32 (NIVUK)
"So if the Son sets you free, you will be free indeed." John 8:36 (NIVUK)

The clearest illustration I have of this is something that happened with our dog Maisie. We have double glass doors in our living room, opening onto the back garden. We seldom use these doors, and in her five years of life (at that time) Maisie had never seen them open. One particularly hot summer's day, we decided to open the doors. As we stood in the garden enjoying the sun, we heard a sad, lonely whine. We turned to see Maisie looking at us from the open doorway. She sat just behind the line of the doorframe. Maisie was so used to looking out through the glass but being unable to go through, that now, even though the doors were wide open she still believed that she couldn't go through.

The moment Maisie 'broke free' is forever imprinted in my memory. In response to our calling and coaxing, she stood on her hind legs to press her front paws against the non-existent glass, and tumbled head first out onto the patio. Many Christians, just like Maisie, cannot see that the door is wide open. And so they choose to continue living imprisoned.

The ex prisoner who returns

Paul wrote to the church at Galatia, "It is for freedom that Christ has set us free. Stand firm, then, and do not let yourselves be burdened again by a yoke of slavery." Galatians 5:1 (NIVUK)

Paul addresses the issue of people who have received the gift of freedom from God, and then go straight out and try to somehow earn righteousness and favour with God by other means - namely by being religious. Without pulling any punches, Paul says to them, if you're going to be circumcised, then you'd better make sure you keep the whole law! In other words, you can't pick and choose which parts of the law you want to obey and which you'd rather leave. Jesus came in order that we would be set free from the old law. His righteousness is a freeing gift.

The moment we start trying to earn what God has already graciously given, we start getting ourselves all tied up in knots, or as Paul put it: *"burdened again by a yoke of slavery" (NIV)*

* * *

Our enjoyment of freedom, and our resultant relationship with Him, is far important to God than those many other things we concern, and distract ourselves with. This scripture is a clear command, not a suggestion: *"stand firm, then and do not let yourselves be burdened again by a yoke of slavery."* We need to ask ourselves the question, "What diligence do I apply in my own life to ensure that I *stay* free, and enjoy the freedom given to me?"

The grateful free

It's good to be grateful for what Jesus has done for us, however, there is a very fine line that we need to be cautious of. It is the line between devotion to Him - working for Him out of a heart filled with love, that I will call *Devotion-Gratitude,* and something close to that - it may even appear from the outside to be the former, but it falls just short. I will call it *Obligation-Gratitude.*

Obligation-Gratitude says, "I'm indebted, I will devote my whole life to 'repaying' Jesus for all He has done for me." The Christian who lives out of this way of thinking, walks a fine line between accepting God's free gift of salvation and trying to earn it, as some kind of loan that has to be repaid. It makes that person become like a prisoner on parole - free but not <u>really</u> free, because he still has to report to his parole officer, and earn his place in society.

Obligation-Gratitude is a very subtle shift of your position from son or daughter, to slave. We could never, if we lived for a million years, repay Jesus for the freedom He has purchased for us. To try and do so is to enter into a debtor relationship, weighing ourselves down with a yoke of slavery.

<u>Devotion-Gratitude </u>is a joy-filled sense of indebtedness. It isn't a

burdensome sense of 'you have done this for me, therefore I feel <u>must</u> do something in return'. It is a delight in Jesus' presence and companionship. The Psalmist captured this sense so well when he said:"Compared to all this cosmic glory, why would you bother with puny, mortal man or be infatuated with Adam's sons? Yet what honor you have given to men, created only a little lower than Elohim, crowned like kings and queens with glory and magnificence. You have delegated to them mastery over all you have made, making everything subservient to their authority, placing earth itself under the feet of your image-bearers." Psalms 8:4-6 (TPT)

It's when this delight in the Lord *Himself;* in His goodness, awesomeness, kindness, and generosity, takes on just the smallest hint of a burden to 'repay,' that we need to check our hearts and remind ourselves again of Galatians 5:1. We are free, truly free, let's enjoy that freedom!

Wednesday - Free From The Bully Named Fear

"For God will never give you the spirit of fear, but the Holy Spirit who gives you mighty power, love, and self-control." 2 Timothy 1:7 (TPT)

Something you learn about bullies, as you grow older, is that they are usually very insecure people. They control with fear, and threats, (and sometimes physical violence) but in most cases when their victim stand up to them, the bully stands down.

A Bully Named Fear

Many Christians are bullied, day in and day out for years. The name of the bully? Fear. His playground? The mind. We allow ourselves to be dominated and controlled by fear; fear of the future, fear of getting hurt, fear of rejection, fear of failure. Fear of illness. Fear of job loss. The list could go on for pages.

Fear, if you allow it to, grips hold of you, plagues your mind, wakes you up night with a pounding heart for what tomorrow might bring. Fear taunts, filling your mind with thoughts such as, *God has deserted you, you're all on your own, No one cares about you.*

Like most bullies, fear bides its time, until you have isolated yourself from your usual support structures; having listened and taken to heart the lies fear has whispered to you that you're unloved and alone, fear pounces like a playground bully; pinning you down, squeezing the air from your lungs till you can barely breathe. However much you struggle, you can't move. You feel immobilised by this bully.

It seems easier to just give in. You've got to the point where you can't remember what it was like not to have fear robbing you of so much in your life. Fear doesn't even have to work that hard to keep you where it wants you. You've become so used to fear limiting your life that you don't even bother to fight it any more! And so you live the limited life you believe is your lot, robbed by a bully named fear. If this is you, there is hope: There is good news! You don't have to live under the tyranny of fear for one moment longer.

Robbed No More!

Imagine the school child who is robbed of his lunch money by a bully. Every day the school canteen prepares an excellent menu that the child could have enjoyed along with his classmates. His parents had provided the *means,* by giving him lunch money. But he had allowed the bully to steal that means from him, so he went hungry, day after day, for years.

Many Christians go without what God has provided the means for because they are robbed by fear. It isn't that God hasn't provided; He has given us everything we need, and fully equipped us for life. But we let ourselves be robbed. Jesus said: "The thief's purpose is to steal and kill and destroy. My purpose is to give them a rich and satisfying life." John 10:10 (NLT)

God did not design you and me to live under fear's tyranny. Jesus came to give us an abundant life. I looked up the word 'abundant' in the dictionary. A few definitions are, *fruitful, plentiful, profuse, overflowing, inexhaustible, generous, prolific.* These are the characteristics that flow out of the heart of God.

He's the God of abundance; a generous Father who lavishes his love and goodness on His children.

Knowing the truth

Fear has no voice when we know what the Bible says about who Jesus is, and when we are confident of our position in Him. Here are a few little reminders:

* There is no name higher and no authority greater than Jesus (Philippians 2:9-11)
* There is no one more powerful than Jesus. And He lives in you! (John 4:4)
* You are more than a conqueror (Romans 8:37)
* You are God's beloved child, as well as being more than a conqueror, you cannot be separated from God's love, by anything or anyone. You belong to Him (Romans 8:31)
* God's presence is always with you. (Deuteronomy 31:6) (Matthew 28:20)

Fear is a liar

As for who our *enemy* is, we've already seen that he's a thief. He's also a liar. Jesus describes Satan as "the father of lies" (John 8:44) The devil uses the spirit of fear and its side-kick anxiety to spread his lying, fearful propaganda. But a bully only has power over the one who gives them that power. When you stand up to fear from the position of confident knowledge and *belief* in who you are in Christ, like all bullies, fear will back down.

Make the choice - ditch the victim image

Choose to ditch the victim image. When I was bullied at school, from the *first* time I complied to the bullies' demands, I made the decision to be a victim. Sure, it may have been a subconscious decision but it was still a decision. I gave them permission to bully me.

* * *

12

The way I see it, you can't stop a bully from targeting you, but until you actually *comply* with a bully's demands, that's all you are, simply a target. In a similar way, we are *targets* of Satan's evil schemes and bully tactics. But we don't have to fall victim to them. Being, and remaining a victim is a choice.

The moment you choose faith over fear, you take away fear's power over you. The second you choose to believe what God says about you, you take your first step towards victory over fear.

Every now and then fear will still come up to you and taunt you; but once you have made the decision not to allow fear to bully and dominate you, then with each subsequent encounter, you will grow in faith, confidence and in your understanding of God's great love for you, and you will realise that the bully fear has no hold on you, and that you are indeed free of the bully named fear.

Thursday - Legally Dead

"For you died, and your life is now hidden with Christ in God."
Colossians 3:3 (NIVUK)

I recently read an article (a true story) about a man in the United States, who was very much alive and physically well, but was declared legally dead by the court judge he stood before. The man had walked out on his wife and children twenty-seven years earlier and had gone into hiding. He hadn't been heard of again until he reappeared trying to obtain a driving license. It was then that the man learned of his own sad demise.

The man went to court to try to have the court ruling reversed and failed. The judge referred to a three-year time limit for changing a death ruling, and is reported to have told the man "I don't know where that leaves you personally, but as far as the law is concerned you are deceased."
What could that man do, other than go on to live the rest of his life as a new person? After all, the old 'him' was technically dead! What a great opportunity to start life with a brand new slate!

But, hold on a moment! Does this true-life story ring any bells for you? It did for me. It's exactly what we have been given, as followers of Jesus. The old Jill is dead. The old you is dead. And we have been granted the wonderful freedom of a brand new life.

Sin, you are not the boss of me!

"For we died and were buried with Christ by baptism. And just as Christ was raised from the dead by the glorious power of the Father, now we also may live new lives." Romans 6:3 (NLT)

This verse tells us that the old us is dead; that we no longer live under sin's rule. So why is it that we still struggle with sin? The message of Romans six is not that we won't sin anymore. The message of this chapter in Romans is that sin no longer has *jurisdiction* over us. In other words, it is our sinful *nature* that is dead.

Perhaps I could put it another way; we are no longer sinners, but 'followers of Jesus who sin.' The sinful habits we find so hard to shake are no longer an integral part of us. In that way, sin's power over us is broken: *"We know that our old sinful selves were crucified with Christ so that sin might lose its power in our lives. We are no longer slaves to sin. For when we died with Christ we were set free from the power of sin."* Romans 6:6-7 (NLT)

We don't have to try to fix ourselves. We don't have to beat ourselves or wear metaphorical sackcloth and ashes; We also, importantly, must not try to hide or cover up our sin. I love this verse in 1 John in the The Amplified version: "If we say we have no sin [refusing to admit that we are sinners], we delude ourselves and the truth is not in us. [His word does not live in our hearts.] If we [freely] admit that we have sinned and confess our sins, He is faithful and just [true to His own nature and promises], and will forgive our sins and cleanse us continually from all unrighteousness [our wrongdoing, everything not in conformity with His will and purpose]. 1 John 1:8-9 (AMP)

Living life as a new creation

"And just as Christ was raised from the dead by the glorious power of the Father, now we also may live new lives." Romans 6:4 (NLT)

Brand new lives! This doesn't give us free licence to live as we please. Paul starts off Romans six by saying, "Well then, should we keep on sinning so that God can show us more and more of his wonderful grace? Of course not! Since we have died to sin, how can we continue to live in it? Romans 6:1-3 (NLT)

Paul, led by the Spirit of God, describes this process by using the simple metaphor of 'taking off' the old nature as if it were clothing and dressing yourself in the new:"throw off your old sinful nature and your former way of life, which is corrupted by lust and deception. Put on your new nature, created to be like God—truly righteous and holy." Ephesians 4:22-24 (NLT)
Also: *"Don't lie to each other, for you have stripped off your old sinful nature and all its wicked deeds. Put on your new nature, and be renewed as you learn to know your Creator and become like him."* Colossians 3:9-10 (NLT)

Like that court judge's decision in Ohio, God's decision will not be reversed. The old You is *dead*. The old Me is *dead*. Let's be thankful for the life of victory that Jesus secured for us by His death, and live our new lives. Let's leave for dead those people that we used to be and stop trying to persuade Heaven's judicial system that there must have been some mistake!

We are now free to live brand new lives, 'sold out' for the One who sold out his whole life for us, in order to purchase our freedom: "And since we died with Christ, we know we will also live with him. We are sure of this because Christ was raised from the dead, and he will never die again. Death no longer has any power over him. When he died, he died once to break the power of sin. But now that he lives, he lives for the glory of God. So you also should consider yourselves to be dead to the power of sin and alive to God through Christ Jesus." Romans 6:8-11 (NLT)

Jill McIlreavy

Friday - Don't Look Back

"Forget the former things; do not dwell on the past." Isaiah 43:18 (NIVUK)

Do not dwell on the past

As we have been reminded throughout this week, God has rescued us from our "spiritual Egypt," a place of bondage and slavery. We have a whole new and exciting life before us, of walking with our Saviour and Redeemer. The Lord spoke through Isaiah in chapter forty-three, reminding the people of their release from captivity and then, prophetically to the freedom that is to come through His incredible plan! The plan? To redeem mankind to Himself through His own precious Son.

We so often become bogged down by our pasts. We forget that the past belongs in the past and that the Lord our God is the One who keeps and sustains us. We allow the (forgiven) sins of our past to overwhelm us, causing us to feel unworthy in His presence when He has declared us righteous and worthy through His Son. We dwell on sins perpetrated against us, forgetting that we have been forgiven so much and are required therefore to forgive.

A rear view mirror

We have the past as a 'rear view mirror,' meant only for glancing in to see what has gone before, so that we can avoid certain dangers. Now and then in the New Testament we are told to look at the past, in order to learn from our spiritual forefathers. We can also glimpse at our own past and learn from it. We are never to <u>dwell</u> in the past. Think of this way; if you were to drive your car with your eyes fixed on the road *behind* you in the rear view mirror, instead of the view through the wide, clear windscreen in front of you, how soon would it be before you crashed? We can't go forward in life while gazing into the past.

A glance in the rear view mirror

In Luke's Gospel (Luke 17:32) Jesus gives us an example of glancing in the rear view mirror - He told His followers to *remember Lot's wife* (Luke 17:32). As Lot and his family were being led out of the city before its destruction, Lot's wife looked back in direct disobedience to God, who had told them expressly not to look back. Lot's wife became a pillar of salt. We won't go into all of that now, but I want to look at why Jesus told His followers to remember her.

This is only my theory, but I wonder if Jesus wanted, not only to draw our attention to the point that she looked back, but also to think about the <u>way</u> in which she looked back. I don't think it was merely a glance; I think she <u>really</u> looked - it was a longing look. A pining sort of look. Perhaps her heart was in Sodom; she liked it there, and didn't really want to leave.
Or was it that some of her family were still there - some of her children, brothers, sisters - and her heart went out to them? Did she just want to go back? Was her heart really in Sodom? The terrible tragedy in her story is that she was almost there. She had been led out of that dreadful place, only by God's mercy and grace, and given the incredible opportunity to move on and start afresh....and what did she do? She looked back. It's almost

incomprehensible. Except for the fact that we very often do the same thing, don't we?

When Jesus calls we have to be willing to forsake everything to follow Him (Luke 14:33). This doesn't mean <u>everyone</u> will be required to sell up everything, give away all our money and possessions, and cut ties with our families; (unless any one of those things is more important to us than Jesus) but it's the <u>willingness</u> of heart to completely surrender that Jesus looks for. Have a look at what Jesus said in Luke chapter nine: *"Why do you keep looking backward to your past and have second thoughts about following me? When you turn back you are useless to God's kingdom realm."* Luke 9:62 (TPT)

By looking back, Lot's wife demonstrated that she wasn't really willing to forsake all in order to obey God. Perhaps she hadn't really counted the cost. Have we counted the cost? Are you and I attempting to go forward with God while constantly looking back? If so, while we probably won't turn into a pillar of salt, we may find our lives crashing! Let's keep going forward, forgetting those things that are behind us.

Saturday - A Way Of Escape

"We all experience times of testing, which is normal for every human being. But God will be faithful to you. He will screen and filter the severity, nature, and timing of every test or trial you face so that you can bear it. And each test is an opportunity to trust him more, for along with every trial God has provided for you a way of escape that will bring you out of it victoriously." 1 Corinthians 10:13 (TPT)

I like the way the Amplified version puts this: *"No temptation [regardless of its source] has overtaken or enticed you that is not common to human experience"* 1 Corinthians 10:13a (AMP). Temptation is something we all face as Christians, no matter how long we have been following Christ. This verse reminds us of these things:

God is faithful

God is faithful in these two specific ways: 1) He won't allow us to be tested or tempted beyond our ability to resist. 2) God Himself does not tempt us.

When tempted, no one should say, "God is tempting me." For God cannot be tempted by evil, nor does he tempt anyone." James 1:13 (NIVUK)

God cares about His children

The Lord is not a spectator, merely watching us from a distance as we fumble our way through life. He cares about our affairs, and he doesn't want us to be overcome by sin. He wants us to win our battles against temptation and sin because He loves us.

God provides a way of escape.

God is so faithful, so good to us, and loves us so much that He provides a way of escape for us in the heat of the heaviest temptation. The trouble is that when we are faced with temptation, we often aren't looking for an escape route, because sin, or the temptation to sin, is usually dressed in an attractive looking package. We *want* what's on offer! If it didn't *look* attractive enough to grab our attention, it would be easy to turn down. So the question we need to ask ourselves first is, "Do I *want* God's way of escape?"

Paul wrote this regarding the children of Israel and their time in the wilderness: *"All the tests they endured on their way through the wilderness are a symbolic picture, an example that provides us with a warning so that we can learn through what they experienced."*
1 Corinthians 10:11 (TPT) *"So beware"*, Paul continues, *"if you think it could never happen to you, lest your pride becomes your downfall."* 1 Corinthians 10:12 (TPT). One could never accuse Paul of mincing his words!

Beware equals 'Be- Aware'

Carrickfergus, where we live, has a lovely spot where I like to stop the car sometimes and just sit and look at the sea and our town's thousand-year old castle, right on the edge of the water. It's a funny shoreline though; when the tide is in, you would never suspect that under the beautiful, still water of the lough, close to shore, the seabed is covered with rocks. Some are big and jagged, others smaller rounded boulders. If anyone not knowing the area were to come along in a small boat when the tide was at just the right level to cover the tops of these rocks, they could find themselves in big trouble.

When the tide is low, you can see the tops of the bigger rocks above the surface, and any experienced sailor would see the danger and avoid it. When the tide is out, every rock is exposed. This reminds me of Paul's admonishment not to allow ourselves to be "*exploited by the adversary, Satan, for we know his clever schemes*" 2 Corinthians 2:11 (TPT)

Satan's scheme is to 'raise the tide', covering up temptation and its dangers. The unaware, non-alert Christian will find themselves on the jagged rocks. It's important to remember that God is not the one who tempts us, but He both limits our temptation and provides a way of escape. It's our choice then whether or not to take that way of escape, God doesn't force us to.

The way of escape isn't necessarily an easy way.

I'm always encouraged by the great escape plan God had for the Israelites, pursued by the Egyptian army. They were trapped on the shores of the Red Sea, with the mountains behind them, the Egyptians hot on their heels. They were afraid and more than a little discouraged.

This incredible plan of God's required obedience and trust from the people. (Read the story in Exodus and remind yourself.) First of all they had to turn back and start walking towards the enemy who were gaining ground on them, and then, trapped on the shore, nowhere to run, they had to wait until the Egyptians were within sight, trusting that God was going to do something! *They* didn't know He was going to part the sea. They had no idea what the future held; they had to put their trust in God: "*But Moses told the people, 'Don't be afraid. Just stand still and watch the Lord rescue you today. The Egyptians you see today will never be seen again. The Lord himself will fight for you. Just stay calm.'* Exodus 14:13-14 (NLT)

* * *

So, we see from this story the way of escape isn't necessarily an *easy* way. But it's the way that will lead us to a place where we are *'able to bear it.'* Also, the way of escape doesn't give us a way out of temptation altogether; that won't happen until we get to heaven. The Lord provided a way out of that situation for Children of Israel, but they still faced many more trials and temptations, and God continued to show His faithfulness towards them in the wilderness.

Sunday - Restored, refilled and reloaded

"May he work perfection into every part of you giving you all that you need to fulfil your destiny. And may he express through you all that is excellent and pleasing to him through your life-union with Jesus the Anointed One who is to receive all glory forever! Amen!" Hebrews 13:21 (TPT)

A few years ago, my attention was captivated by an advertisement in a magazine for a very striking necklace made from empty bullet shells. It amazed me that something so beautiful could have been made from something as horrible as a bullet.

Ethiopian farmers are plagued with these casings that litter their fields. Not only because they are a constant reminder of the country's many past conflicts, but because they contaminate the soil, damage farm equipment and harm grazing livestock.

One day, someone had the brilliant idea of collecting these bullet casings, and taking them to local women, who transform them into beautiful jewellery. These spent, once forgotten casings, found half buried in the dirt, now raise an income that supports families and communities all over Ethiopia. In a way, you could say that these bullets have been recomissioned and are being re-used to fight a new war - a war on poverty. Does this sound familiar?

Restored, refilled and reloaded

"And provide for those who grieve in Zion – to bestow on them a crown of beauty instead of ashes, the oil of joy instead of mourning, and a garment of praise instead of a spirit of despair. They will be called oaks of righteousness, a planting of the LORD for the display of his splendour." Isaiah 61:3 (NIVUK)

Those bullets littering Ethiopia once destroyed life and brought harm. Now they have been transformed and recommissioned to bring life and hope to communities. We were like those spent shell casings. We lay broken in the dust and dirt, after so many past battles. But God is in the business of restoration. He puts our spent shell lives back into service and in His hand we become something beautiful; transformed by the power of His might, into vessels of honour for His Kingdom.

Isaiah continues in chapter sixty-one, to proclaim God's words: *"And you will be called priests of the LORD, you will be named ministers of our God. You will feed on the wealth of nations, and in their riches you will boast. Instead of your shame you will receive a double portion, and instead of disgrace you will rejoice in your inheritance. And so you will inherit a double portion in your land, and everlasting joy will be yours." Isaiah 61:6-7 (NIVUK)*

"Instead of your shame," What a promise of transformation by the Spirit of God! No more shame, instead, a double portion of honour. What an inheritance! Called 'ministers of our God', we are anointed and commissioned for His Kingdom purposes, to bring light and Hope everywhere we go.

Jesus commissions every one of His disciples: *"Now wherever you go, make disciples of all nations, baptizing them in the name of the Father, the Son, and the Holy Spirit. And teach them to faithfully follow all that I have commanded you. And never forget that I am with you every day, even to the completion of this age."* Matthew 28:19-20 TPT

"And he said to them, "As you go into all the world, preach openly the wonderful news of the gospel to the entire human race! Whoever believes the good news and is baptized will be saved, and whoever does not believe the good news will be condemned. And these miracle signs will accompany those who believe: They will drive out demons in the power of my name. They will speak in tongues. They will be supernaturally protected from snakes and from drinking anything poisonous. And they will lay hands on the sick and heal them. And the apostles went out announcing the good news everywhere, as the Lord himself consistently worked with them, validating the message they preached with miracle-signs that accompanied them!" Mark 16:15-18, 20 (TPT)

Truly Free

Monday - Shame Is A Liar

"Forever I will lift up my soul into your presence, Lord. Be there for me, God, for I keep trusting in you. Don't allow my foes to gloat over me or the shame of defeat to overtake me. <u>For how could anyone be disgraced when he has entwined his heart with you</u>? But they will all be defeated and ashamed when they harm the innocent." Psalms 25:1-3 (TPT)

We all have a story, don't we? We all come from somewhere, and have done things in the past, or had things perpetrated against us. Many Christians have hidden, 'no-go' areas of their lives; little secret pockets into which those things have been stashed; never dealt with, never spoken of, because even now, years later, they have the capacity to induce shame. *What would people think of me if they knew?* So these no-go areas stay buttoned tightly closed, shrouded in shame.

Sexual abuse, divorce, addiction, eating disorders, all manner of things from Satan's bag of nasties, all part of his onslaught against humanity. Somewhere, deep down, you may hold the belief that God has forgiven every sin - except *that* one; He can heal every hurt perpetrated against you - except *that* one.
But here's a thought…perhaps that which you feel too ashamed to share is the very thing that God wants someone else to hear in order to bring *their* breakthrough.

* * *

Silence the propaganda, not your own lips
As we know, we have an enemy, Satan, who seeks every opportunity to "kill, steal and destroy." One of the ways he does this is through a weapon called shame; whether this shame is associated with something that happened to you, or something you have done. Shame is not from God. God doesn't shame His children.

Look at how God views your future in the light of your forgiven past, as you 'entwine your heart' with His: "*Forgive my failures as a young man, and overlook the sins of my immaturity. Give me grace, Lord! Always look at me through your eyes of love— your forgiving eyes of mercy and compassion. When you think of me, see me as one you love and care for. How good you are to me! Escort me along the way; take me by the hand and teach me. For you are the God of my increasing salvation; I have wrapped my heart into yours! When people turn to you, they discover how easy you are to please—so faithful and true! Joyfully you teach them the proper path, even when they go astray.*" Psalms 25:5-8 (TPT)

Still, the enemy seeks to spread his nasty, twisted anti - Jesus propaganda, totally opposed to what the Lord says about you, by telling you things such as, "you are tainted," "you deserved what happened to you," or worse, "God didn't care, when it happened." He will try to convince you that you couldn't possibly be a Christian, *look at how you've hurt other people.* "You're, worthless, a loser." Do agree with his lies?

Shame is a Liar.
Shame spreads its insidious lies against precious, forgiven sons and daughters, declared "*white as snow*" by our Father. It tries to tell us we are unworthy, tarnished, irredeemable. We have a choice: To believe and live in agreement with what God says about us, or to live in agreement, and take on board this enemy 'propaganda.'

* * *

When Jesus rescued and redeemed us from our old life, it was total. His said on the cross *"It is finished,"* '*it'* being the work of redemption that He came to accomplish. He did not say, "It is partially finished."

God says you are:
* Sons and Daughters: "And I will be your Father, and you will be my sons and daughters, says the Lord Almighty. " 2 Corinthians 6:18 (NLT)
* Forgiven: "I will never again remember their sins" Hebrews 8:12 (NLT)
* A Brand New Person: "My old self has been crucified with Christ. It is no longer I who live, but Christ lives in me. So I live in this earthly body by trusting in the Son of God, who loved me and gave himself for me." Galatians 2:20 (NLT)

The shame associated with the past is over
"Fear not; you will no longer live in shame. Don't be afraid; there is no more disgrace for you. You will no longer remember the shame of your youth and the sorrows of widowhood." Isaiah 54:4 (NLT)

In Christ, there is no part of your past that you need to feel ashamed of. This includes things perpetrated *against* you, as well as those things you have done. Jesus is a Mighty Redeemer who transformed and is still transforming your life and mine.

We are beautiful works in progress. Jesus Christ, by whose own blood you have been ransomed, stands in between you and the enemy and therefore no charge or condemnation the enemy of your soul tries to hurl your way can stand against you.

Your testimony is powerful, don't let shame's lies silence you. Jesus has won!
"It has come at last— salvation and power and the Kingdom of

our God, and the authority of his Christ. For the accuser of our brothers and sisters has been thrown down to earth— the one who accuses them before our God day and night. And they have defeated him by the blood of the Lamb and by their testimony." Revelation 12:11 (NLT)

Tuesday - Free Of Shame

Yesterday we looked at shame, and the effects it can have on us when it isn't put in its place. Shame is that little voice inside that constantly whispers: *I wish I hadn't done that, If people really knew me they'd walk away, My sins are too big to be forgiven, God couldn't really love me.* It's an underlying feeling that you're 'tainted' in some way. When we entertain these thoughts, they take root and start to grow, until they affect every area of our lives and our relationships.

Shame is a Liar
"We can't escape the constant humiliation; shame is written across our faces." Psalm 44:15 (NLT)

This is an outpouring of feelings; of abandonment, humiliation and a sense shame of the people, collectively, at the hand of their enemy. They've forgotten about the love and faithful care of the Lord their God.

Just as these beloved ones of God in Psalm 44 had very real enemies, so do we, as His beloved children, have an enemy; The enemy of our soul, Satan, whose great desire is to keep us in that sense of shame.

We start accumulating shame from childhood. Often it involves trauma, abuse or neglect. Sometimes it's caused by events at school: an insensitive comment by a teacher, a classmate making fun of the way you spoke. Some have had a 'wild' past, involving drugs, or multiple sexual partners. I grew up in "a household of shame." My father was an alcoholic and we were told constantly, *"don't tell anyone."* We were not allowed to talk about what went on at home, and as a result, for many years I carried a deep sense of shame.

I'll let you in on another 'shameful secret,' my first marriage of 15 years failed, and ended in divorce in 2001. Even 'worse;' even *more* 'shameful,' we were in full time Christian ministry at the time. Does that make either of us failures as Christians? Does it disqualify either of us from further ministry? Only if we allow it to by listening to and agreeing with, the propaganda that shame continually declares. But shame is a liar.

Declared white as snow

"Come now, let's settle this," says the Lord. "Though your sins are like scarlet, I will make them as white as snow. Though they are red like crimson, I will make them as white as wool." Isaiah 1:18 (NLT)

If you are being held captive for a past that you have repented of, and have been redeemed from, then your 'captivity' is a lie! God declares you as "white as snow."
Are you a disciple of Jesus? Do you know in your heart of hearts that you belong to Him, yet every now and again, when you least expect it, that nasty little voice of shame whispers into your ear: 'God couldn't really love you, after what you've done?'

Do you agree with shame? The moment we start to entertain those thoughts, we are standing in agreement with the enemy. We're giving permission for shame to set up camp in our hearts. *Shame is your enemy! I definitely do not want to be aligning myself with the enemy.*

What your Father says about shame

"Everyone who believes in him will not be put to shame."
Romans 10:11 (NLT)
Every time you or I entertain thoughts of shame, we declare
ourselves unworthy, despite all The Bible says about our position
in Christ. And when we do this, we reject God's precious gift,
freedom from shame: *"Fear not; you will no longer live in
shame. Don't be afraid; there is no more disgrace for you. You
will no longer remember the shame of your youth and the
sorrows of widowhood."* Isaiah 54:4 (NLT)

Staying Free
Isaiah 1:18, which I quoted earlier, is one of those most quoted
and loved verses. Who doesn't need to be reminded that, "you
will white as snow?"
However, read on and you'll noticed this: Yes, there is freedom
from shame. There is also an "If" and a "But" (all the following
quotes are from Isaiah 1:18-20 NLT)

"**If** ...you will only obey me, you will have plenty to eat. **But** ...if
you turn away and refuse to listen, you will be devoured by the
sword of your enemies. I, the Lord, have spoken!"

Remember when you were little, and your mother would smack
your hand for poking your fingers into the electrical sockets?
Was it because she didn't love you or the opposite? Though it
broke her heart to smack your little baby hand, she couldn't bear
to think of her child being hurt through disobedience. There are
natural consequences for our actions. God's commands are
always motivated by His great love for us. I take from this a
warning of the Lord's to obey Him by *listening what He says*,
otherwise the *consequences will be that our enemy will get the
better of us.*

We need to soak ourselves in the truths of The Word of God –
He says so in verse nineteen "**if** you will only obey me, you will
have plenty to eat".

This brings to mind Jesus, being tempted in the wilderness by Satan; He said, *"man shall not live by bread alone but by every word that comes from the mouth of God".*
God's Word nourishes us from the inside out, giving us everything we could possibly need.

Jesus Disregarded Shame

In Hebrews 12:2 we are told that Jesus *"endured the cross, disregarding its shame".*
A big part of crucifixion was the public shaming and humiliation of the one being crucified. People stood around and jeered, mocked, shouted insults and spat on the condemned one.
Jesus *endured* the suffering of the physical pain on the cross. But as for the shame, He *disregarded* it! The shame Satan that hoped to pour on Jesus had *absolutely no power over Jesus.*
Jesus defeated shame, once and for all, for you, and for me. Let's live in that victory over shame that Jesus won for us!

Wednesday - Don't Bully Yourself

"I thank you, God, for making me so mysteriously complex! Everything you do is marvellously breathtaking. It simply amazes me to think about it! How thoroughly you know me, Lord! You even formed every bone in my body when you created me in the secret place, carefully, skilfully shaping me from nothing to something."Psalms 139:14-15 (TPT)

Do you know that you can be your own worst enemy or your own best friend?

Do you bully yourself?
Whether it's about the way we look, what we do for a living, our parenting skills, performance as a spouse, or our role at church, many of us verbally bully ourselves.
We compare and measure ourselves unfavourably to others, and then give ourselves a hard time for not measuring up. Do you find yourself saying things such as, "I'm so clumsy, so stupid, I'm never picked, I'm too old, too young, too fat, too skinny, I have no friends, I'm no good at anything?" When someone pays you a compliment, instead of just smiling and thanking them, do you respond with a self put-down?

It's not okay!
Would you speak to anyone else the way you speak to or about yourself? Most of us would walk away from someone who was being verbally abusive, yet we think it's okay to speak to and

about ourselves in the negative way that we do.

If I were to wake up in the morning and my kind, gentle husband greeted me with the words, "Look at the state of you! Look at your hair! You really, can't get away with not wearing makeup, those wrinkles are getting worse," I don't think I could get out of bed in the mornings. Yet I say those things to my reflection in the mirror on a regular basis! I know I'm not alone in this and it is really not okay that we speak to ourselves this way.

How to stop being your own worst enemy

We need to change our speech habits. Most of us don't mean to bully to ourselves. It isn't something one consciously decides to do. But if we do it all the time, it can become a habit.

1. Speak the "Right Things"

Habits can be unlearned. You can teach yourself the new habit of declaring what God says about you, every time you feel a tirade of verbal self deprecating remarks on the tip of your tongue, even if you mean to say them in jest. We can start by asking God to teach us right habits: *"Teach me your ways, O Lord, that I may live according to your truth! Grant me purity of heart, so that I may honour you."* Psalm 86:11 (NLT)

Does my speech honour God when I say nasty things about myself, the one He created and loves? The very next verse says, *"for your love for me is very great"* When God deems you and me so greatly loved, why do we declare anything less over ourselves?

2. Fill your heart with the right things

The Bible says *"What you say flows from what is in your heart."* Luke 6:45 (NLT)

We need to fill our hearts with the right things, (God's Word) to replace the wrong thinking. This means real, 'meaty' Bible reading and study. How can we speak the 'right things' if we don't know what those things are?

* * *

3. Ask God to help you 'zip it'

"Take control of what I say, O Lord, and guard my lips." Psalm 141:3 (NLT)

A leader in a church I belonged to years ago, a man by the name of Alwyn Miles, used to say that if you feel the urge to pass on a bit of gossip, or say anything nasty about anyone, first ask yourself the questions: *"is it true, is it kind, is it necessary?"* We could apply this principle to self-deprecating comments too. Better still, we could do what David did and thank God for creating us so beautifully! (Have another look at that verse in Psalm 139 that we opened with) It isn't big-headed to thank God for the incredible, intricate way in which He has designed and put you together.

Something else that David says in this Psalm, after thanking God for making him so wonderfully, is that he *knows* it full well. He has a 'handle' on it; a firm grasp on the truth of who he is as God's unique and beautiful creation.

4. Know what God says about you

"Your workmanship is marvellous—how well I know it." Psalm *139:14 (NLT)*

How well do you know it? How comfortable are you with thanking God - *for you*? As I've written before, our God isn't a generic, one-size-fits-all God. Each one of us is made with unique detail, love and care. Every hair on your head is numbered, (Luke 12:7) and isn't incredible that of all the billions of people on the planet, no one has the same fingerprints as you? *You* are absolutely beautiful! Why not look in the mirror this morning and say, "Thank you Lord, for me!"

Thursday - The Poisonous Weed of Bitterness

"In your anger do not sin': do not let the sun go down while you are still angry, and do not give the devil a foothold." Ephesians 4:26-27 (NIVUK)

Although there are other types of bitterness, today I want to look at a very common and insidious issue, bitterness towards the Lord.

A poisonous weed

Bitterness usually happens when we are angry or disappointed and, rather than dealing with those normal human emotions right away with God, we allow an *experience* to become a *belief system*. Like a noxious weed, bitterness needs to be uprooted and destroyed, or it will destroy the person who nurtures it.

"Watch out that no bitter root of unbelief rises up among you, for whenever it springs up, many are corrupted by its poison." Hebrews 12:15 (NLT) We see from this verse that bitterness does not only affect the person in whom it grows, but those close to them.

Bitter towards God

In the book of Ruth we read about Naomi (which means *pleasant*). Her husband and both her sons had died in Moab, leaving Naomi and her daughters-in-law alone in a foreign country, to fend for themselves. News arrived from home that the famine in Judah had lifted and Naomi decided to go back to her own people. The three set out together, but as they walked Naomi offered her daughters-in-law the freedom to return to their own people.

At first they insisted on staying with Naomi. It is here that Naomi's bitterness becomes evident. She asks them why they would want to stay with her? After all, she can't give them more sons to marry. It seems to me that her question is loaded with sarcasm, and springs from a well of deep bitterness; a belief that the Lord has let her down. Look at the sting, in the last sentence. *"Things are far more bitter for me than for you, because the LORD himself has caused me to suffer."* Ruth 1:14 (NLT)

Our bitter speech effects and infects others

Notice that Naomi's bitterness had a deep effect on Orpah, who did turn back then. I wonder what impression Orpah was left with, of Naomi's God? The sad thing is, that Orpah had wanted to go with Naomi, a woman who knew the One True God, yet in her own bitterness towards God, Naomi sent Orpah back to her false gods. She then set to work on Ruth: *"Look," Naomi said to her, "your sister-in-law has gone back to her people and to her gods. You should do the same."* Ruth 1:15 (NLT)

This is what happens; when bitterness sets in; we become so consumed by it that we don't think about, or even care about, the words we say and the effect they might be having on unbelievers or new Christians. It becomes 'all about me.'

Bitterness shows on our countenance

"So the two of them continued on their journey. When they came to Bethlehem, the entire town was excited by their arrival. "Is it really Naomi?" the women asked." Ruth 1:19 (NLT)

'Is it really Naomi?' I wonder what prompted this rhetorical question. Was it only that Naomi had been away for years, or was it because her once 'Pleasant' countenance was hard to recognise, because it was etched with the bitterness that scarred her heart?

We see Naomi's bitterness again in her response to her old friends, *"Don't call me Naomi," she told them. "Instead, call me Mara, [meaning bitter] for the Almighty has made life very bitter for me. I went away full, but the LORD has brought me home empty. Why should you call me Naomi when the LORD has caused me to suffer and the Almighty has sent such tragedy?"* Ruth 1:19-21 (NLT)

Breaking free from bitterness

Hard as it may be to acknowledge, bitterness towards God springs from a sense of entitlement - 'You owe me God.' We feel we have 'done so much for Him,' 'served Him faithfully,' and yet 'God has not held up His end of the bargain.' Paul wrote: *"Get rid of all bitterness, rage, anger, harsh words, and slander, as well as all types of malicious behavior."* Ephesians 4:31 (NLT)

I am aware that this scripture is an instruction for 'doing life' together as Believers, but how can we have these heart attitudes towards other people and at the same time hold 'bitterness, rage, anger, harsh words and slander' in our hearts towards God Himself? It is impossible, and Paul says, *"Get rid of it!"*

The healing process begins with humbling ourselves before the Lord, asking Him to shine His bright light on the contents of our hearts. It is in repentance and a spirit contrite for where we have hurt and damaged others with our bitter words and actions, and for where we have sinned against God by slandering His name and character.

"Search me, O God, and know my heart; test me and know my thoughts. Point out anything in me that offends you, and lead me

along the path of everlasting life". Psalm 139:23-24 (NLT)

"Humble yourselves before the Lord, and he will lift you up in honor." James 4:10 (NLT)

A change of perspective

The person who is bitter towards God usually believes that God did not care, when they went through the experience that has made them bitter. Nothing could be further from the truth. God is intimately involved in the lives of His children and has good plans and purposes for each and every one. (Jeremiah 29:11)

Where was God in the 'big picture' of Naomi's pain of having lost her husband and both sons? Had God forgotten about this little family? Well, look at it this way: If Naomi's son have lived, Ruth would not have been free to meet and marry Boaz. She would not have given birth to their son, Obed, who became the father of Jesse, who is the father of David, from whose lineage came Jesus. What a wonderful example of God causing *"everything to work together for the good of those who love God and are called according to his purpose for them.* Romans 8:28 (NLT)

Friday - Anxious For Nothing

"Then Jesus said to his disciples: 'Therefore I tell you, do not worry about your life, what you will eat; or about your body, what you will wear.'" Luke 12:22 (NIVUK)

Be anxious for nothing

Do you ever feel overwhelmed with anxiety? I'm not talking about the medical condition of anxiety, linked to depression. What I want to address today are two common types of anxiety that come to our doors like unsolicited salesmen.

This concept of your heart and mind being accessible via a door is found in several places in the Bible. The greatest example of course is Jesus: *"Here I am! I stand at the door and knock. If anyone hears my voice and opens the door, I will come in and eat with that person, and they with me."* Revelation 3:20 (NIVUK)

Our enemy, Satan, and his evil forces also come knocking and we have the choice whether or not to open the door. The Lord said these words to Cain: *"If you do what is right, will you not be accepted? But if you do not do what is right, sin is crouching at your door; it desires to have you, but you must rule over it."* Genesis 4:7 (NIVUK)

* * *

Sudden Anxiety

Sudden Anxiety's favourite time to appear is when you're faced with an unexpected crisis. Sudden Anxiety doesn't knock, but pushes open the door and loudly shouts its fear-filled threats, drowning out all your usually calm, reasonable thoughts. Everything Sudden Anxiety spews will contradict the Word of God. Its words come at you like rapid machine-gun fire; phrases such as, *God has abandoned me, He won't answer my prayer, how am I going to fix this?* Threaten to overwhelm your mind. But the good news about this type of 'intruder' is that it's the quickest and easiest to deal with and evict.

Stealth Anxiety

This type of anxiety is far sneakier and more dangerous than its loud, big mouthed counterpart. Stealth Anxiety 'politely' knocks at the door of your mind, with the tiniest thought. It might sound a little bit like *'what if?'* You may ignore the first few knocks, but then you give in and entertain the *what if* thought for a moment. As you ponder this thought and allow it to stay, Stealth Anxiety quickly slithers in through the crack in the door, and thoughts such *it could happen* very quietly join *what if.* Suddenly you're thinking, *it probably will happen* and then, before you know it, *"it is going to happen!"*

Once in the door, Stealth Anxiety sets up camp and then invites its best friend Chronic Worry to keep it company. Chronic Worry, like a squatter, is not going to be shifted unless you exercise your legal rights - remember those ones you have as a Child of the Living God?

Control versus humility

The reason we feel anxious is because we feel a loss of control. When we're anxious about a situation, the need to take control can be strong. But this is when we have to watch out for pride. By taking over, we tell God through our actions that we don't trust Him; that we could do a better job than He can. This is what The Lord has to say about it:*"Don't let the wise brag of their wisdom. Don't let heroes brag of their exploits. Don't let the rich brag of their riches. If you brag, brag of this and this only: That you understand and know me. I'm God , and I act in loyal love. I do what's right and set things right and fair, and delight in those who do the same things. These are my trademarks."* Jeremiah 9:23 (NLT).

There is something we <u>can</u> control, and that is our initial response.

Initial response

What are the *first* words that come out of your mouth in a threatened crisis? Remember that your words are important; fear-filled words can affect and *infect* the people around you, and very importantly, your own heart 'listens' to the words you speak. On the other hand, faith-filled words can turn a situation around within minutes, even seconds.

King David understood this and addressed his own heart: *"Why, my soul, are you downcast? Why so disturbed within me? Put your hope in God, for I will yet praise him, my Saviour and my God."* Psalms 42:5 (NIVUK)

In our initial response, we can make the conscious decision to *"put your hope in God."* We can hand over complete control of every circumstance to God, trusting in His faithfulness and ability to handle it.

Pray

Even though the Bible commands us not to be anxious, and to cast all our cares upon Jesus, we do still have an important part to play. Our role is to <u>pray</u>. *"Do not be anxious about anything, but in every situation, by prayer and petition, with thanksgiving, present your requests to God. And the peace of God, which transcends all understanding, will guard your hearts and your minds in Christ Jesus."* Philippians 4:6-7 (NIVUK)

Notice that it is in <u>every</u> situation. It's a lifestyle of prayer, not quick *help me* prayers to a God whom we ignore the rest of the time.

1 Thessalonians 5:17(NIV) tells us, *"Pray continually."* That's it; just two words make up this verse! Do you think this might be because Paul really wanted to impress upon us the importance of a <u>lifestyle</u> of prayer?

In closing, the Word of God tells us,*"Humble yourselves, therefore, under God's mighty hand, that he may lift you up in due time. Cast all your anxiety on him because he cares for you."*

1 Peter 5:6-7 (NIVUK) Why entertain anxiety and try to control potentially stress-inducing situations in our own ways when we have a God who lovingly cares for us right down to the minuscule detail of our lives? (See Luke 12:24-31)

Saturday - Restraining Order

"Little children, you can be certain that you belong to God and have conquered them, for the One who is living in you is far greater than the one who is in the world." 1 John 4:4 (TPT)

Do you know anyone who has had to take out a restraining order against an abusive ex partner? The one against whom the restraining order is in place, nearly always attempts to cross the line in some way, by intimidation and threats. Many more have the audacity to ignore the order altogether and barge in uninvited, wreaking havoc and instilling fear in the newly found peaceful environment.

You're probably wondering where I'm going with this. Well, if you are a child of God, there is type of Heavenly restraining order in place against someone. This restraining order is legally binding and unbreakable. Who is it that this restraining order is against?

It's Satan, the enemy of our souls, who looks for every opportunity to rob you of your joy and peace. Like that ex who ignores the restraining order, the devil starts by attempting to get over the threshold. He stands outside, trying to get you to open the door, hoping to get his foot in the door with a thought; perhaps something like *"God couldn't love you. You are unworthy."*

* * *

He will constantly seek to remind you of your past, trying to rob you of your abundant future.

As we've already seen, the Bible describes him as the thief, who comes only to kill, steal and destroy. (John 10:10)

Jesus described him as a Liar - in fact the father of lies, *"He's been a murderer right from the start! He never stood with the truth, for he's full of nothing but lies—lying is his native tongue. He is a master of deception and the father of lies!"* John 8:44 (TPT). You do not have to put up with it!

Know your legal standing

When a person who has taken out a restraining order is being plagued by the 'restrained' person, all she needs to do is to remember her legal standing, call the police, and allow them to deal with the bully. She does not have to open that door! So it is with the Child of God.

"So then, surrender to God. Stand up to the devil and resist him and he will turn and run away from you." James 4:7 (TPT)

If you are being bullied by thoughts that *you don't measure up, God couldn't possibly love you after what you've done this week,* then perhaps you need to study the Word of God and learn what He says about you. The Christian who knows and believes the word of God is a force to be reckoned with!

Satan also knows God's Word, he knows what it says about him and his *ultimate* demise. He knows he's defeated. But it doesn't stop him (for the time being) He also knows what it says about you; how deeply and passionately God loves you. His nightmare is the Christian who not only reads the Word of God, but absolutely believes it, *all of it!*

We are not told to fight the devil, only to resist him.
Jesus has already fought and secured the victory. We are to know

our legal standing as Children of God, and then *stand* in the armour that God has provided for us. (See Ephesians 6: 10 -11 and Ephesians 6:14-18)

Our God is true to His Word; He doesn't make promises lightly. When He says you have been given the '*right to be called a child of God*.' (John 1:12) It is a legally binding, unbreakable contract, signed in blood - Jesus' blood - and it serves as the best restraining order against our enemy.

Sunday - The Comparison Trap

Theodore Roosevelt is credited with the quote 'comparison is the thief of joy,' a very true and wise saying, founded on Biblical truths. Paul spoke about the folly of comparison: *"Of course, we wouldn't dare to put ourselves in the same class or compare ourselves with those who rate themselves so highly. They compare themselves to one another and make up their own standards to measure themselves by, and then they judge themselves by their own standards. What self-delusion!"* 2 Corinthians 10:12 (TPT)

The person caught in the comparison trap feels they lack in some way, where others have been blessed. Some compare themselves constantly with others, believing they don't measure up, and this drives them to an unhealthy pursuit of the esteem and acclaim of others, when the only esteem that really matters is the Lord's.

The Performance Trap

This trap compares and measures our efforts and success to others.' It's exhausting, like a hamster's wheel, it saps all your energy, uses maximum effort while taking you absolutely nowhere. The person caught in the performance trap strives to be better than others rather than being our personal best for the glory of God. *"And whatever you do or say, do it as a representative of the Lord Jesus, giving thanks through him to God the Father." Colossians 3:17 (NLT)*

* * *

The Pride Trap

This trap compares who we are, with who we judge *others* to be. It works in two ways, and both are destructive. We build ourselves up at the expense of others; those we deem of less value, or with less to contribute than us. Alternatively, we tear ourselves down at the elevation of others, calling unworthy that which God has deemed worthy, nullifying the one Jesus died to justify (ourselves) Either of these attitudes has the prisoner constantly striving for recognition, and acceptance, from others instead of just resting in the acceptance and recognition they already have, as God's child. There's a way to combat the pride trap. It's found in Romans chapter twelve: *"Be devoted to tenderly loving your fellow believers as members of one family. Try to outdo yourselves in respect and honor of one another."* Romans 12:10 (TPT)

The Insecurity Trap

This is similar to the first pride trap. This trap could be compared to a fairground house of distorted mirrors; the person caught in this painful trap constantly sees their own weakness distorted out of proportion, while the strength of others seem alarmingly distorted, mocking their weakness. However hard they try, they cannot see that this is an illusion, a distorted view, a trick! They long to be like those 'stronger' people.

Sadly, part of them secretly hopes for the other person's downfall and gloats when it happens. But the truth is, our strength and power is not our own. All our strength comes from the Lord! *"It is God who arms me with strength and keeps my way secure."* Psalms 18:32 (NIVUK)

So yes, comparison is the thief of joy. Satan is a thief - the thief of joy! And one of the ways he does this is through comparison. It's time to walk right out of those traps: *"if the Son sets you free, you are truly free."* John 8:36 (NLT)

Jill McIlreavy

The Exchange

Monday - Surrendering The Mirrors

"Bezalel made the bronze washbasin and its bronze stand from bronze mirrors donated by the women who served at the entrance of the tabernacle." Exodus 38:8 (NLT)

Still in keeping with yesterday's theme of comparison, what are your thoughts when you look at your reflection in a mirror? Do your eyes zone in on every wrinkle, blemish, roll and saggy bit? The problem is, we *feel* younger, slimmer or taller in our own heads, and then, one glance in the mirror brings us right back to reality with a sharp bump.
We are our own harshest critics, constantly comparing ourselves with others and feeling we fall short. This attitude to ourselves is not limited to our physical appearance, but creeps into how we view our 'performance' as church members, how we measure our levels of productivity at work, and judge our effectiveness as parents.

In light of this, imagine giving up every single mirror in your house; both literally and metaphorically. No reflection anymore to concern yourself with, no more harsh criticism of yourself, no more comparing. Could you do it? For those of us who default to self criticism this would be no easy task! The above scripture gives a brief glimpse of a group of women who did that very thing. This story which is summed up in a single sentence, which to me is rich in symbolism and prophetic meaning.

* * *

The serving women

Not much is said about these women. We don't even know their names, but that in itself says so much about them. Bezalel, the gifted artisan working on the tabernacle needed bronze to make the Bronze Laver; the basin in which the priests would wash their hands. The women *willingly* surrendered their mirrors for this purpose.

In our modern culture you don't get many anonymous givers. Most people like to be acknowledged in some way: their name on a plaque on the hospital wing that they paid for, a mention on Social Media for a 'sacrificial act of kindness.' Yet these generous women have gone down collectively in history as merely 'The serving women.' Completely anonymous, all lumped together. But the Lord knows who they were, each one!

Their sacrifice might not seem much to us. We take mirrors for granted; they can be picked up fairly cheaply, and most modern houses have several. But in those days, a mirror was a status symbol and prized possession. Only the well-off could afford such a frivolity, and most houses would only have one. The ordinary woman had to be satisfied with seeing her reflection only occasionally, and even then, not a very clear one, perhaps in the stream as she did the family washing.

A Divine exchange

The women willingly surrendered their ability to measure their own physical beauty, so that the basin for ritual cleansing could be made. These mirrors, once items for vanity, comparison, probably harsh self-criticism - because that's what we women (and many men), do - are now reshaped by this God-appointed craftsman into a basin, to be filled with water with which the priests could cleanse themselves in preparation to go into God's presence.

There's a beautiful analogy in this; a picture of the Divine exchange to which Jesus calls you and me. Are we willing to make that exchange? Will we give up our mirrors of attitude, thought and judgement, concerning ourselves and others, in exchange for God's perfect mirror and Bronze Laver: "*He [Jesus] gave up his life for her [the church] to make her holy and clean, washed by the cleansing of God's word.*" Ephesians 5:25-26 (NLT)

Gaze into God's mirror

The Word of God is a mirror that shows us our true selves - the way God sees us. Not the distorted way in which we see ourselves (and others). The Bible says that we become like that which we spend time gazing at. "*We all, with unveiled face, beholding as in a mirror the glory of the Lord, are being transformed into the same image from glory to glory, just as from the Lord, the Spirit.*" 2 Corinthians 3:18 (NLT)
"*But don't just listen to God's word. You must do what it says. Otherwise, you are only fooling yourselves. For if you listen to the word and don't obey, it is like glancing at your face in a mirror. You see yourself, walk away, and forget what you look like. But if you look carefully into the perfect law that sets you free, and if you do what it says and don't forget what you heard, then God will bless you for doing it*". James 1:22-25 (NLT)

If you or I were to stand in front of the bedroom mirror for half the day gazing at our reflections, we could rightfully be considered vain, but the more we 'gaze' into God's mirror, the Bible, absorbing, taking in, *believing* and *living* every word He says, the more clearly we will see Him and the more like Him (in character and nature) we will become. So let's keep surrendering the murky mirrors of our attitudes and beliefs, and gaze instead into His.

Tuesday - Beauty From Brokenness

"O Israel, can I not do to you as this potter has done to his clay? As the clay is in the potter's hand, so are you in my hand. Jeremiah 18:6 (NLT)

We live in a consumer society and the principle of 'make do and mend' has become antiquated. Some even see it as a stinginess. It's easier to just discard and replace the broken or old, to *buy-new* rather than *re-new*. God doesn't discard, He renews! God places a high value on His vessels, even those we would deem broken, spoiled or of no more use.

Our God is in the renewal business.

I love this story in Jeremiah: "This is the word that came to Jeremiah from the Lord: 'Go down to the potter's house, and there I will give you my message.' So I went down to the potter's house, and I saw him working at the wheel. But the pot he was shaping from the clay was marred in his hands; so the potter formed it into another pot, shaping it as seemed best to him." Jeremiah 18:1-4 (NIVUK)

What a lovely picture of what God, the Master Potter, can do with a life, even a broken one, that is completely surrendered to Him.

Do you believe you are too broken for God to use? Do you think you've 'messed up' one too many times and He couldn't possibly use a person like you to fulfil His purposes? The pot in Jeremiah's story was 'marred,' but rather than discard it, the potter continued to work with it, patiently and expertly perfecting and shaping it into something beautiful and useable.

Marred 'in the Potters hands'

Here's another thought. The pot become 'marred' *in* the Potter's hands.

How could this happen? Was it the potter's fault? Was he not skilled enough? On the contrary, I think God wanted Jeremiah to see a very skilled craftsman at work, one who could take a lump of clay that had become uncooperative in his hands, as clay does sometimes, and form it into something beautiful.

It wasn't the potter who changed his mind halfway through and decided to make something else instead.

God doesn't make mistakes. He doesn't start things and give up halfway through, and He doesn't change His mind. (Numbers 23:19; James 1:17; Hebrews 13:8)

God doesn't force us into obedience, we have free choice. Sometimes we fight God, instead of surrendering to His leading, and then when our lives go skew as a result, we wonder if we are still in His hands. The wonderful imagery in this story is of how our gracious God, the Master Potter, can reshape us into His vessels of beauty, even when we have made a 'hash' of things.

We are never too broken for God to restore and reshape.

"My sacrifice, O God, is a broken spirit; a broken and contrite heart you, God, will not despise."Psalms 51:17 (NIVUK).

The brokenness this Psalm speaks of is a 'heart attitude.' The Psalmist isn't saying that the Lord desires to 'break' us. It speaks rather, of humility; acknowledging to the Lord that in our pride, stubbornness, and unwillingness to listen properly, we have sinned against Him, and then humbly, sincerely repenting.

* * *

When we're humble, submitting our brokenness to Him instead of attempting to hide it, we offer to the Potter clay that is workable. Have you ever tried to work with clay that's become unworkable? I have, and it isn't easy! But the moment the piece of clay has some water worked through it to make it soft again, it becomes like a brand new, fresh piece of clay, ready for the craftsman to make something lovely from it.

When we humbly submit, and let the Holy Spirit work Living Water from Heaven into our hearts, we become wonderfully 'workable' in the Master Potter skilful hands.

Beauty from brokenness

What sort of vessel could the Master Potter be making from you? We are just humble vessels of clay, but remember, we are also His image bearers. Remember who lives in you! Our bodies are temples of God's Holy Spirit - that's a very weighty and incredible truth.

You and I are only 'jars of clay,' but we contain the most indescribably beautiful fragrance of Heaven itself, that of Jesus. God chose us to be His vessels! *"We are like common clay jars that carry this glorious treasure within, so that the extraordinary overflow of power will be seen as God's, not ours."*2 Corinthians 4:7 (TPT)

Wednesday - Check Yourself Out

"Anyone who listens to the word but does not do what it says is like someone who looks at his face in a mirror and, after looking at himself, goes away and immediately forgets what he looks like." James 1:23-24 (NIVUK)

How many times a day do you think the average person checks his or her appearance in a mirror? I was surprised to learn, according to the brief study I did, that it's eight to ten times a day. This accounts for only the use of 'made for purpose' mirrors. When you take into consideration all the other places we see our reflections, such as shop windows, smart phones or tablet screens, that figure could easily quadruple.
It isn't only vanity that induces us to regularly check our appearance. More often than not, people have a last minute check before an important business meeting, meeting up with friends, or before walking up to the podium to make that all-important speech. Nobody wants to discover, halfway through an event, that they have been walking around with spinach stuck in their front teeth!

Now, imagine if, during the course of the event, you caught a glimpse of your reflection, noticed spinach in your teeth, and decided to leave it where it was and just carry on. What would have been the point in checking your reflection in the first place if you weren't going to do anything about it?

* * *

Spinach in your teeth

In our spiritual lives we can have those 'spinach-in-my-teeth' times. James says that reading or hearing the Word of God without acting on it is like looking into a mirror and then immediately forgetting what we've seen.

God has given us a mirror, which is His Word, to check ourselves in. How many of us have ever read something in the Bible and seen something about ourselves that we know we need to do something about, and then, in the end, have done nothing. We just put it off, for a while longer.

James exhorts us to look closely and *take action* on what we see. He goes on to say that when we hear or read God's Word without taking action, we are *fooling ourselves.* What's the first thing you do when you see something amiss in your appearance in the mirror? You put it right, it's instinctive. James exhorts us to develop this kind of attention to detail in our spiritual 'grooming.'

Checking ourselves in God's 'Mirror'

If I read the Word of God and see something in me that needs to change, it's got to change *now.* I cannot go 'back out there,' having seen myself in God's mirror and having done nothing about it. Practically speaking, when I see something awry with my appearance; my mascara has run, I have lipstick on my teeth, I clean it off and carry on. It's as simple as that spiritually speaking too. John tells us: *"if we confess our sins to him, he is faithful and just to forgive us our sins and to cleanse us from all wickedness"* 1 John 1:9 (NLT)

It's God who brings the change, not our own striving, and trying to 'be good'. He does this through His Word. The more we look at ourselves in His mirror through the day, (you can never check yourself too much in God's mirror) and ask Him, *'Lord how does my heart look in the light of your Word?'* The more we will change to be like Him, and reflect His beauty.

Thursday - Exchange Your Labels

I recently watched a documentary about the rise of cyber bullying. The very beautiful Jesy Nelson of the girl band Little Mix was terrorised and driven almost to the point of suicide by the inner turmoil and pain of the hateful things said about her by online bullies. In her interview she wept and candidly described how she had battled for years to shake off these 'labels' and stop seeing herself the way those bullies had described her.

From the moment we are born, labels are placed upon us, both negative and positive. A tiny baby might be labelled as 'a good feeder,' a 'cryer' a 'good sleeper,' 'the image of his daddy'. As we grow, we and other people add to these labels. Labels accumulate through school, such as loser, popular, bully, loner, cool, pretty, victim, sporty, *un*-sporty, introvert, clever, drama-queen, outgoing, skinny, chubby - these are unwittingly stuck onto us in childhood by teachers, classmates and parents and can cling for years, long into adulthood.

What labels do you remember wearing? Are you still wearing them?
Maybe the labels you wore were good ones! Perhaps you were the popular, good looking one at school and now you fear you're losing your looks? Maybe you were successful in business or ministry and things went wrong? Did you subconsciously stick a post-it note on your own heart saying, 'Failure?' Maybe your

marriage failed. Do you wear labels such as 'Divorcee' 'Rejected' 'Discarded' 'Disqualified'?

Many of us spend much of our adult lives dealing with labels. Some are trying to peel off labels, and this isn't always easy. Sometimes not all of a label comes away, but instead leaves bits behind on our heart, like those hard-to-remove labels on jars. Here's a thought: the only way to remove those last clinging bits of labels on jam jars is to totally immerse the jar in water. In much the same way, the only way we are truly going to get rid of those hard to remove heart-labels is to completely immerse our hearts in the Living Water that Jesus gives. Will you let Him completely *soak* your heart, washing every last scrap of label away with His Word?

Some are hoping to paste back on 'successful' labels of the past; those labels that made them feel valuable, worthy and significant. But we are not defined by this world's view of position or title; only by our position and title before God. If you are a child of God, then you are *His*, that's the only position and title that matters. The past is gone, but the future, *your* future - your story that God has written, stretches out before you!

God is the only one who has the authority to label you. Labels other people place on us are nothing more than man's opinion. God has placed the ultimate, most important label on your heart. His label says, *"Mine."* You have been bought at great price. You're highly valued and treasured. You are redeemed, justified, forgiven, adopted into the family of God.

Here are a just few more labels that God has especially designed for us, His beloved children (actually that's one of the labels)
* God's Beloved Child - Ephesians 5:18
* Beloved - Colossians 3:12
* Forgiven - Colossians 3:13

* Chosen -   John 15:16
* God's workmanship - Ephesians 2:10

Today, if you find yourself looking at labels you wear, and any one of them was not placed upon you by God, take it off, right now. It may sound a bit simplistic but that's because it is! Here's something to ponder in closing: If that label you are wearing comes from any other source than your Creator God, it is <u>not</u> just a label, it is a price tag, and you are paying for something unnecessary.

Friday - Grace For Regret

"But go, tell his disciples and Peter, "He is going ahead of you into Galilee. There you will see him, just as he told you." Mark 16:7 (NIVUK)

These were the words of the angel that appeared to the women at Jesus' tomb. Two words in the angel's message immediately stand out to me: *"And Peter."*

And Peter

Why *the disciples and Peter*? Surely Peter *was* one of the disciples? These two small words are jam-packed with powerful truths about the nature of Jesus. The Passion Translation puts it like this: *"Run and tell his disciples, even Peter"* Mark 16:7 (TPT). And the New Living Translation: *"Now go and tell his disciples, including Peter,* (NLT)

If Peter had been feeling, 'out of fellowship,' unworthy to be a disciple, excluded, or on the outside, it was an exile of his own making; the Lord had not rejected him. I believe that there was a reason the angel singled out Peter: it was because Peter had singled himself out. So the Lord made certain that Peter knew he was included in the message.

* * *

Peter's last sight of his Lord had been as Jesus was led away for trial. We all know how Peter had denied Jesus. Not just once, but *three* times, just as Jesus had prophesied and Peter had vehemently dismissed as impossible. How devastated Peter must have been by his own unfaithfulness and desertion of Jesus, how filled with regret, self-loathing and anguish.

From Peter's point of view, there was nothing left for him. Now having denied Jesus, surely Jesus would deny Peter before the Father in heaven? After all, Peter had heard Jesus speak words to this effect not long before. *"Everyone who acknowledges me publicly here on earth, I will also acknowledge before my Father in heaven. But everyone who denies me here on earth, I will also deny before my Father in heaven."* Matthew 10:32-33 (NLT)

Then came the astounding news. Jesus had risen! He wanted to meet with His disciples and, incredibly, His invitation had made special mention of Peter. This could mean only one thing - Jesus was assuring Peter that He still loved him and *counted him as one of His disciples!* Jesus had not disowned Peter after all, but still claimed him as His own. Can you imagine the balm these two small words must have been to Peter's soul? Peter had a new and fresh opportunity to stand up and say *yes, I belong to Jesus.*

Regret

Have you done things that cause you to cringe with regret and perhaps shame every time you remember them? God is not surprised by our failures, He knows our shortcomings. He *knows* we will let Him down. He is our Father who continues to love us and restore us. His Holy Spirit never gives up on teaching and training the one who, despite repeated failure and subsequent regret, remains steadfast and teachable.

* * *

Actually, if you think about it, we have all denied Jesus in one way or another. In essence Peter denied that he was Jesus' disciple. We may never say the words, *I am not a follower of Jesus,* but how often do our actions declare these very words without our having to speak a word? Our actions can effectively contradict everything we say with our lips.

Restoration

Those words, *"And Peter"* indicate that Peter was very much on Jesus' mind. Jesus *knew* Peter, He knew what made him tick. Jesus could have sent a message through the angel saying, merely, *"go and tell the disciples,"* but it's my belief that if Jesus' message had been conveyed that way, Peter in all likelihood, would have excluded himself from the invitation. Jesus knew this. Jesus knew Peter needed that affirmation. More than the other disciples, devastated as they all were, Peter was the one who was in the greatest need of reassurance and restoration from Jesus. And Jesus knew exactly how to restore Him. Peter certainly was restored; he played a very major role through the book of Acts. We will come back to Peter a bit later in the book.

God doesn't rescind His call

I wonder how Peter viewed his calling, his *citizenship* in the Kingdom, in those first days after denying Jesus. Jesus had seen something special in Peter; yes, Peter had his flaws, he could be impulsive at times and didn't always think before he spoke, but Jesus saw past all of that to Peter's true potential. *"You are favored and privileged Simeon, son of Jonah! For you didn't discover this on your own, but my Father in heaven has supernaturally revealed it to you. I give you the name Peter, a stone. And this truth of who I am will be the bedrock foundation on which I will build my church—my legislative assembly, and the power of death will not be able to overpower it! I will give you the keys of heaven's kingdom realm to forbid on earth that which is forbidden in heaven, and to release on earth that which is released in heaven."* Matthew 16:15-19 (TPT)

In John's Gospel chapter twenty-one, we read Jesus' challenge to Peter; *"do you love me? Then feed my lambs."* The reason *(I believe)* for Peter's specific inclusion in Jesus' post-resurrection invitation to meet Him in Galilee starts to become clear. Jesus does two things in this conversation with Peter. (John 21:15-18) First, He affirms Peter's calling to be His disciple. Secondly, Jesus gives Peter the chance to affirm three times that which he had denied three times. If there were any last clinging vestiges of guilt and shame on Peter's heart, he could now say, right to Jesus face, three times, 'I love you Jesus.'

Saturday- My Weakness His Strength

"Oh, the joys of those who trust the Lord, who have no confidence in the proud or in those who worship idols." Psalms 40:4 (NLT)

Confidence

There are many books available on the subject of confidence and self confidence. But what does the Bible say about confidence? David had confidence; he was brimming with it. But David's confidence was not *self*-confidence, his confidence was in the Lord. He had absolute confidence in God's faithfulness to come through for him; to be his Strong Deliver in any situation. This is evident time and time again throughout David's life.

"The Lord is my light and my salvation, so why should I be afraid? The Lord is my fortress, protecting me from danger, so why should I tremble? When evil people come to devour me, when my enemies and foes attack me, they will stumble and fall.Though a mighty army surrounds me, my heart will not be afraid. Even if I am attacked, I will remain confident". Psalm 27:1-3 (NLT)

David, the shepherd boy destined to be king, had the heart of a strong warrior since boyhood. As a teenager he had fought a lion and a bear that threatened the sheep he was guarding, but David didn't take the credit, he attributed his victories to the Lord.

Later, still only a very young man, he killed a giant with just a stone and sling: a giant that the entire army had been unable to take down! Again David acknowledged that God was the source of his strength: *"David said to the Philistine, 'You come against me with sword and spear and javelin, but I come against you in the name of the LORD Almighty, the God of the armies of Israel, whom you have defied."* 1 Samuel 17:45 (NIVUK)

Much later, after years of running from Saul, David wrote these beautiful words to honour the Lord, attributing all his strength to Him, *"I love you, Lord; you are my strength. The Lord is my rock, my fortress, and my saviour; my God is my rock, in whom I find protection. He is my shield, the power that saves me, and my place of safety. I called on the Lord, who is worthy of praise, and he saved me from my enemies."* Psalm 18:1-3 (NLT)

A legacy

David's legacy of faith and devotion was passed down to his son, Solomon, the man God handpicked to write most of the book of Proverbs. Sounding so much like his father before him, Solomon penned these words, *"Confidence and strength flood the hearts of the lovers of God who live in awe of him, and their devotion provides their children with a place of shelter and security."* Proverbs 14:26 (TPT)

What was their secret?

The awe Solomon speaks of here, translated as *"fear of the Lord"* in most other translations of the Bible, is not speaking about being afraid of God, but echoes the heart of his father David's writing throughout the Psalms. It means fearing God as in *acknowledging* Him in every aspect of our lives, being *devoted* to Him. The secret to David's great confidence in the Lord was his lifestyle of devotion. The clearest indication of David's devoted heart is in the twenty-seventh Psalm, where he writes, *"One thing I ask from the LORD, this only do I seek: that I may dwell in the house of the LORD all the days of my life, to gaze on the beauty of the LORD and to seek him in his temple."* Psalms 27:4 (NIVUK)

After stating that the deepest longing of his heart, in fact the *only* thing he seeks, is to spend his days in the presence of God, David writes in the next two verses, *"For in the day of trouble he will keep me safe in his dwelling; he will hide me in the shelter of his sacred tent and set me high upon a rock. Then my head will be exalted above the enemies who surround me; at his sacred tent I will sacrifice with shouts of joy; I will sing and make music to the LORD."* Psalms 27:5-6 NIVUK

Paul too knew the secret

Someone else who knew that his strength and confidence rested solely in the Lord, was the Apostle Paul. He wrote these well known words, which may look a little different to what you're used to because I have quoted them from the Passion Translation: "My grace is always more than enough for you, and my power finds its full expression through your weakness." So I will celebrate my weaknesses, for when I'm weak I sense more deeply the mighty power of Christ living in me. So I'm not defeated by my weakness, but delighted! For when I feel my weakness and endure mistreatment—when I'm surrounded with troubles on every side and face persecution because of my love for Christ—I am made yet stronger. For my weakness becomes a portal to God's power." 2 Corinthians 12:9-10 (TPT)

In Philippians 4:13 he says, "I know what it means to lack, and I know what it means to experience overwhelming abundance. For I'm trained in the secret of overcoming all things, whether in fullness or in hunger. And I find that the strength of Christ's explosive power infuses me to conquer every difficulty." (TPT)

Paul, like David, had been schooled in the 'secret' of relying solely on the Lord for strength. This flowed out of a heart that pressed into God, and sought His presence in hard times, rather than trying to get through on his own strength. We too can know this secret!

Sunday - A Soul Re-Set

"Yet this I call to mind and therefore I have hope:"
Lamentations 3:21 (NIVUK)

What's your default?

The prophet Jeremiah had a way of re-setting his heart when he felt down or discouraged. One could say it was his 'default setting;' that of *"God is faithful."* Jeremiah faced some pretty hard times. We read in Jeremiah 16:1-5, 8-9 that God told him not to marry or have children. Reading this today and seeing the whole picture, we know that God had good reason for this. It saved Jeremiah from even greater heartache further 'down the road' of life. But sometimes, when we read about these Old Testament 'Greats' we can forget that they were just people, like us. Jeremiah felt loneliness at times. He felt unloved. He was an unpopular prophet in his time, with a *very* unpopular message and the people let him know this. He felt the sting of their rejection. He was just an ordinary guy, but he loved the Lord!

In Lamentations chapter three, we read an outpouring of Jeremiah's heart. At first it feels almost too painful to read; you feel as though you're reading somebody's private journal. Here are some of the things he was feeling: *"He has led me into darkness, shutting out all light." "He has buried me in a dark place, like those long dead." "He shot his arrows deep into my heart. My own people laugh at me. All day long they sing their*

*mocking songs. He has filled me with bitterness and given me a
bitter cup of sorrow to drink."*
*"The thought of my suffering and homelessness is bitter beyond
words. I will never forget this awful time, as I grieve over my
loss."* Lamentations 3:2, 6, 13-15, 19-20 (NLT)

Then Jeremiah seems to catch hold of himself. He does an about
turn, abruptly breaking this cycle of despair. He remembers
God's goodness and faithfulness and His unfailing mercy.
Jeremiah starts to focus on God's attributes, reminding his heart
of the Truths that he already knows but had temporarily forgotten
to focus on. In doing so, he 'hits the re-set button', of his heart,
instantly changing his outlook. He says, '*Yet I still dare to hope
when I remember this: The faithful love of the Lord never ends!
His mercies never cease. Great is his faithfulness; his mercies
begin afresh each morning. I say to myself, "The Lord is my
inheritance; therefore, I will hope in him!"* Lamentations
3:21-24 (NLT)

When I remember this

Jeremiah forces himself to bring truth to the forefront of his mind
and these truths sink into his heart and 're-set' him. It's a
powerful lesson for us. Jeremiah needed to bring other things to
mind to replace the 'virus,' as it were, that had got into his
system. Notice, Jeremiah says, '*when I remember this,*' or as
other versions have it '*this I call to mind.*' We can't call to mind
what wasn't there to begin with. We need to fill our hearts and
minds with the truths of who God is, what He says, (and doesn't
say) and what His Kingdom his purposes are.

In times of discouragement and despair, it's so tempting to just
let rip with a good old 'complain fest' and we've all done that at
times, haven't we? What we need is to engage our will, and
purposely, deliberately focus on things other than our problems.
To force ourselves to *remember truth,* recall an encouraging

scripture, remember a time when God demonstrated His grace and mercy to us.

If I push God's faithfulness and goodness to the forefront of my mind, even when I don't feel like doing so, I will feel hope begin to rise and my heart re-sets. Jeremiah didn't stop there; I would encourage you to read the rest of that chapter in Lamentations and you will see how his heart was completely re-set!

Living Rescued (Promised Land Living!)

Monday- What Is God's Will For My Life?

The question' *what is God's will for my life?'* Is possibly 'up there' among the top ten questions Christians ask. I believe with all my heart that our Heavenly Father has a plan for us, corporately and individually.

During a season when my own future felt uncertain, God reminded me, in that patient way He has, that His will for me is clearly laid out in scripture. It's written as plain as day in Micah 6:8 where God speaks to His people through the prophet Micah.

At that time the people had walked away from God and as a result had downward-spiralled into idolatry, corruption, violence, poor civil government and dead religion - the belief that sacrifice would be enough to 'keep God appeased'. Micah spoke the word of the Lord to them: *"He has shown you, O man, what is good; And what does the Lord require of you But to do justly, To love mercy, And to walk humbly with your God?"* Micah 6:8 (NKJV)

To do justly. To love mercy (kindness). To walk humbly with God; <u>This</u> is God's will for His people; it's what He requires of us.

I really like the way the Amplified Version translates this same verse: *"He has told you, O man, what is good; And what does the Lord require of you except to be just, and to love [and to diligently practice] kindness (compassion), And to walk humbly with your God [setting aside any overblown sense of importance or self-righteousness]?"* Micah 6:8 (AMP)

To do justly

Our God is a <u>just</u> God - He is just in all His ways: *"Everything he does is just and fair. He is a faithful God who does no wrong; how just and upright he is!"* Deuteronomy 32:4 (NLT)

Jesus tells a story about injustice in Matthew 18:21-35. The man at the centre of this story had been shown unmerited mercy and released from a great debt. You'd think then, that he in turn would have had a heart filled with gratitude and mercy. But, sadly he went straight out and demonstrated exactly the opposite towards someone who owed him *far less* than his own debt had been.

Before I am horrified by this man's attitude, I need to take a long hard look at myself. Every time I harbour unforgiveness, or think judgemental, critical thoughts towards another person, even if they know nothing about it, I am failing to show mercy and justice, and like the man in the parable, I forget the great debt from which I have been released. My own debt has been cancelled by God. I can *more* than afford to be extravagantly generous with justice and mercy towards others!

To love kindness

Our God is a kind God. The Bible is absolutely saturated with His compassion and loving kindness. God's kindness seeps through the pages of the Old Testament, where time and time again we read about His great compassion for His people. It pours out of the Gospels in the life of Jesus. The kindness of God is part of the fruit of the Spirit, who lives in us His followers, and we're called to walk in kindness and to live a life of compassion.

It's a conscious choice: *"Since God chose you to be the holy*

people he loves, you must <u>clothe yourselves</u> with tenderhearted mercy, kindness, humility, gentleness, and patience. Make allowance for each other's faults, and forgive anyone who offends you. Remember, the Lord forgave you, so you must forgive others." Colossians 3:12-13 (NLT)
I have to actively, consciously choose to *'put on' kindness"* like an item of clothing.

To walk humbly (it's not actually all about me)

God calls us to walk with Him. To partner with Him in what He is doing. That's incredible! Walking humbly doesn't fit well into our modern culture. We feel a need to post our accomplishments on social media and measure our 'success' and that of others by how many 'likes' we get (or don't get).

When He walked this earth, Jesus performed some wonderful miracles. If Jesus had come to earth during this century I do not believe for one minute that He would have felt any need or desire to post His accomplishments all over Instagram or Facebook, saying, "Look who I healed today."

Jesus had no problem in saying that He was utterly dependent upon His Father. He walked in close connection with his Father, close enough to watch what the Father was doing, and to partner with Him in that. Jesus was a model for us of humble obedience and total reliance on God. He said, *"I tell you the truth, the Son can do nothing by himself. He does only what he sees the Father doing. Whatever the Father does, the Son also does". John 5:19 (NLT)*

We so often want that pat on the back; the 'well done,' for our accomplishments. When God moves in and through us to touch the life of another person, we *hog the glory,* when really it belongs to Him!

So, in closing...

Finding God's will for your life is really quite simple. All God calls each and every one of us to do and to be, is as Jesus was, an imitator of Himself! *"Imitate God, therefore, in everything you do, because you are his dear children." Ephesians 5:1 (NLT)*

And as we walk in step with Him, He empowers, enables and equips us to 'do justly, to love mercy and to walk humbly' with Him.

Tuesday - Temporary Paralysis

Have you ever been so caught up with the circumstances of your life that even though the answer to your problem was right in front of you, you could not see it? It's a bit like staring at one of those picture puzzles where you have to spot an image within an abstract design, and then when you've stared at the design for what seems like ages, suddenly, your eyes seem to do a little adjustment and the image you were searching for is so clear that you think; "how did I not see that before?" I think this is what happened to this Aeneas, in this story in Acts:

"Peter traveled from place to place, and he came down to visit the believers in the town of Lydda. There he met a man named Aeneas, who had been paralysed and bedridden for eight years. Peter said to him, "Aeneas, Jesus Christ heals you! Get up, and roll up your sleeping mat!" And he was healed instantly. Then the whole population of Lydda and Sharon saw Aeneas walking around, and they turned to the Lord." Acts 9:32-35 (NLT)

A State of Temporary Paralysis

The Bible doesn't tell us what had caused Aeneas' paralysis, only that he had been paralysed for eight years. It is assumed that he was a Believer, because he was in the place where Peter was visiting the Believers; the scripture doesn't say he was sitting out in the street somewhere. It seems his predicament had grown to the point where he was now bedridden and even brought to church meetings on his sleeping mat. It's as if Aeneas had accepted his state and was just lying there.

Notice the words Peter said to him: *Aeneas, Jesus Christ heals you.* Not Jesus *can* heal you, or *will* heal you. Peter's words are present tense; this short sentence is packed with the simple but powerful truth that Jesus Christ does heal and is healing, present continuous.

Get Up!

Then Peter gives Aeneas an instruction that seems an outrageous thing to say to a man in Aeneas' predicament - *'Get up and roll up your mat.'* It's as if Peter, having reminded Aeneas of who Jesus is, *The One who is healing people*, then gives him the extra little (loving) kick in the rear Aeneas needed by telling him to just get up, and roll up his sleeping mat.

Three decisive actions: remember who Jesus is. Get up. Stop wallowing.In other words, 'Aeneas, roll up the sleeping mat you have been lying on - the misplaced beliefs, the lack of faith and trust, the discouragement.' By 'rolling it up' Aeneas would demonstrate that he *believed* that no longer needed it.

There are times when we need to remind ourselves or be reminded, just like Aeneas.

David, when he was tempted to "wallow" in self pity or distress reminded himself who God is and of all His ongoing goodness!: *"Let all that I am praise the Lord; may I never forget the good things he does for me. He forgives all my sins and heals all my diseases. He redeems me from death and crowns me with love and tender mercies. He fills my life with good things. My youth is renewed like the eagle's!"* Psalm 103:2-5 (NLT)

Peter's simple, outrageous instruction reminded Aeneas that the healing he longed for was already his by faith - all he had to do was stop lying there, get up and grab hold if it!

Are you spiritually bed-ridden?

We can become *spiritually bedridden* as Aeneas was physically bedridden, when we focus on our problems and our circumstances instead of fixing our eyes on Jesus. Or when we become spiritually lazy. Do you ever have days where you just feel spiritually dry? When we feel that way, we need to draw water from the *well that never runs dry:* John 4:13; Isaiah 44:3-4; Matthew 5:6; John 7:37

There's a scripture in Revelation that reminds me of the sort of *wake up call* that Peter gave Aeneas: *"Wake up! Strengthen what little remains, for even what is left is almost dead. I find that your actions do not meet the requirements of my God."* Revelation 3:2 (NLT). This is written to the church of Sardis, who looked outwardly fine but on the inside, spiritually, they were falling asleep. John goes on to write these strong words from the Lord in verse 3: *"Go back to what you heard and believed at first; hold to it firmly. Repent and turn to me again"* Revelation 3:3 (NLT)

To get back to Aeneas; in response to Peter's words he got up! He rolled up his sleeping mat and his transformation became the talk of the whole region! Make no mistake, people had been watching Aeneas all along; they'd seen his paralysis. When he suddenly got up and started walking around again, it triggered a ripple effect that went out and started to break the power of spiritual paralysis in others as well.

Remember Who He is!

If you feel paralysed by your circumstances today; whether it has been eight hours, eight days, eight weeks or, like Aeneas eight years, and whether the healing you long for is physical, emotional or spiritual, I believe this word is for you right now; *"Jesus Christ heals you! Get up, and roll up your sleeping mat!" Acts 9:34 (NLT)*
See also: Revelation 3:2 (NLT): *"Go back to what you heard and believed at first; hold to it firmly.*

Wednesday - Built On The Rock

"Therefore everyone who hears these words of mine and puts them into practice is like a wise man who built his house on the rock. The rain came down, the streams rose, and the winds blew and beat against that house; yet it did not fall, because it had its foundation on the rock. But everyone who hears these words of mine and does not put them into practice is like a foolish man who built his house on sand. The rain came down, the streams rose, and the winds blew and beat against that house, and it fell with a great crash."
Matthew 7:24-27 (NIVUK)

Storms of life

No matter who we are, we will face 'storms of life', and how we fare in these life-storms will depend on our foundations. Most houses, look fine from the outside; You could look a row of similar looking houses and presume every one of them was perfectly sound. The real test would come only when they were battered by a heavy storm. The ones built on a good, solid foundations would stand.

Jesus uses the metaphor of two men building houses. Both houses probably looked great from the outside, but their foundations were very different and so was the outcome when a storm came along. I'm sure you know that Jesus was speaking about the men's lives, rather than bricks and mortar houses.

A Rock-foundation builder listens and applies, hears and obeys

A person who builds their house on the rock foundation is someone who <u>hears</u> and <u>applies</u> the Word of God to their life. Jesus said it clearly; He began the parable by saying: *"everyone who hears these words of mine and puts them into practice is like a wise man who built his house on the rock..."*. James also impresses on us the importance of being not only hearers but doers of the Word. (James 1:22)

Throughout the Gospels Jesus teaches us to <u>listen</u> and <u>obey</u>. I have listed just two; you may want to study this topic further for yourself: *"blessed rather are those who hear the word of God and obey it."* Luke 11:28 (NIVUK)
"Jesus answered, 'It is written: "Man shall not live on bread alone, but on every word that comes from the mouth of God." Matthew 4:4 (NIVUK)

The one whose life is built on the rock foundation of God's Word will remain unshakable when the storms come. Here's what Jeremiah, David and Solomon, inspired by the Spirit of God, wrote about it: "blessed is the one who trusts in the LORD, whose confidence is in him. They will be like a tree planted by the water that sends out its roots by the stream. It does not fear when heat comes; its leaves are always green. It has no worries in a year of drought and never fails to bear fruit." Jeremiah 17:7-8 (NIVUK)

"Blessed is the one who does not walk in step with the wicked or stand in the way that sinners take or sit in the company of mockers, but whose delight is in the law of the LORD, and who

meditates on his law day and night. That person is like a tree planted by streams of water, which yields its fruit in season and whose leaf does not wither – whatever they do prospers."
Psalm1:1-3 (NIVUK)

"Take hold of my words with all your heart; keep my commands, and you will live."
  Proverbs 4:4 (NIVUK)

When the storm came, was this man's house battered? Probably; storms occur, but the important thing is that his house stood strong and secure, on a foundation that could not be moved!

Hearing-believing: the mortar that holds your house together!

Life-storms are those life-shaking events that we all face at times in our lives; sudden financial trouble, family conflicts, parenting issues, health scares, the list could go on. The thought of a storm on the horizon could be frightening. But if I have *taken hold of* the word of God; if I am both a *listener and a doer,* then I have nothing to fear! After all, what does God say about life's storms? He made some promises to us through Isaiah:
"Though the mountains be shaken and the hills be removed, yet my unfailing love for you will not be shaken nor my covenant of peace be removed,' says the LORD, who has compassion on you." Isaiah 54:10 (NIVUK)
"When you pass through the waters, I will be with you; and when you pass through the rivers, they will not sweep over you. When you walk through the fire, you will not be burned; the flames will not set you ablaze." Isaiah 43:2 (NIVUK)

It's all very well reading and quoting these scriptures, but what I really need is to *believe* them; to *build my life on them*, to let them seep right in and become the very mortar that holds the bricks of my life together! <u>Then</u> I will stand in any life storm. Tomorrow we'll have look at the man who built his house on a sandy foundation.

Thursday - A Sandy Foundation

"Therefore everyone who hears these words of mine and puts them into practice is like a wise man who built his house on the rock. The rain came down, the streams rose, and the winds blew and beat against that house; yet it did not fall, because it had its foundation on the rock. But everyone who hears these words of mine and does not put them into practice is like a foolish man who built his house on sand. The rain came down, the streams rose, and the winds blew and beat against that house, and it fell with a great crash." Matthew 7:24-27 (NIVUK)

The sandy-foundation builder

Jesus explains very simply and directly who the sandy-foundation builder is. He is someone who chooses to do life in his own way, rather than according to God's instruction; somebody who hears Jesus' words and fails to put them into practice. Christians can also be sandy-foundation builders.

Storms of disobedience - hearing but not paying attention

Sometimes the problem is not wilful, deliberate disobedience, it is that we hear, but we don't really *listen*. But the way I see it, if God has given an instruction and I have failed to listen properly, that's still a form of disobedience on my part. God tells me clearly in His Word to listen, to *pay attention* to His instructions. There are times in life when we face storms that are merely the consequence of our own disobedience and *failure to pay attention*. There's an example of this in Mark 4:35-41 where the disciples were caught in a storm at sea.

* * *

The first thing to note is that Jesus was not cause off-guard by the storm. He continued to sleep peacefully in the stern of the boat. That's because Jesus' foundation was rock solid; He was a living, breathing example of what it is to live not by bread alone but by *every word that comes from the mouth of God.*

The second thing to note is this: The disciples panicked. Why? Because *They had missed a key part of Jesus' instruction.* Perhaps they were just excited about this new venture, we don't really know why they collectively didn't listen properly, but I do know that I myself have done this many a time! So, having heard Jesus instruction regarding taking the boat out, they did so and suddenly they found themselves facing a terrifying storm, with Jesus snoozing through it all! Jesus had told them to take the boat out! Had He taken them out there into the deepest part of the sea to let them drown?

They had heard Jesus correctly. They were 'in His will' so to speak. So why was this happening? Well, the thing is, they hadn't listened to *everything* Jesus had said. What else did Jesus say? Let's go back to Jesus' instruction: *"That day when evening came, he said to his disciples, 'Let us go over to the other side."* Mark 4:35 (NIVUK)

It had been Jesus' intention all along to go to the shore on the other side! How had the disciples missed this? If they had listened properly they would have remembered this out there in the deep water. They could have quickly silenced their fears in the storm with that reminder; they were not going to drown because Jesus, the miracle worker had a purpose in this journey - it was to go to the other side.

* * *

It would be easy for us to marvel at the disciples' lack of faith, but in truth each one of us could say the same of ourselves. How many promises of God do we need to read and hear preached before we really *listen*, take heed and become doers of God's Word?

Our God is intentional

Nothing Jesus ever did was on a whim. He acted with intent, in obedience to the Father. Our God is not hap-hazard, He is the God who says, *"For I know the plans I have for you,' [declares the LORD], 'plans to prosper you and not to harm you, plans to give you hope and a future."* Jeremiah 29:11 (NIVUK)

Are you facing a life-storm, a storm of disobedience or storm due to lack of listening as you read this? Remind yourself of Jesus' very important words in John 14: "Do not let your hearts be troubled. You believe in God; believe also in me. And if I go and prepare a place for you, I will come back and take you to be with me that you also may be where I am. You know the way to the place where I am going." John 14:3-4 (NIVUK)

In this story of Jesus with His disciples, His intention had been to go to the *other* side. In a similar way, He says to us that He has gone to prepare a Place for us on the 'other side'. Our lives are a journey with Jesus toward a wonderful destination, He won't leave us to drown in the storms of life! He is with us in those storms.

Friday - Taking off The Blindfold

"Don't be afraid!" Elisha told him. "For there are more on our side than on theirs!" Then Elisha prayed, "O Lord, open his eyes and let him see!" The Lord opened the young man's eyes, and when he looked up, he saw that the hillside around Elisha was filled with horses and chariots of fire." 2 Kings 6:16-17 (NLT)

The king of Aram was at war against Israel. God had been supernaturally giving Elisha inside knowledge regarding the Aramean army, and Elisha had passed this information to Israel's king, warning Israel of planned attacks. This infuriated the Aramean king. Thinking he had a mole among his own officials, he called them in and grilled them, hoping to find out which among them had betrayed him. He was enraged to discover that it was the prophet Elisha who had got hold of the sensitive information and the king commanded his army to go and get Elisha. (2 Kings 6:13)

Elisha's prayer

Elisha's servant had got up that morning and taken a look outside the city walls; what he saw filled him with terror! The Aramean army were positioned around the city, waiting to attack. As Elisha and his servant stood looking at this terrifying sight, all the servant could see was the notoriously vicious army; Elisha told him to not be afraid; *'those who are with us are more than those who are with them.'*

Elisha saw by faith what his servant could not, and he prayed for the servant's eyes to be opened to the spiritual reality of the situation. Notice something interesting here: apart from saying that one sentence to his servant, Elisha didn't try to convince or persuade his servant any further regarding the heavenly army surrounding them. When he saw that his servant still couldn't see, Elisha prayed.

When a person is blind to spiritual reality, God is the only one who can open that person's eyes. God may do it through the words that you speak, but the work of spiritually opening eyes belongs to God. We can have our persuasive arguments, but prayer - inviting the Spirit of God into a situation like this - is vital.

God answered

At Elisha's prayer, the servant of Elisha suddenly saw with the eyes of faith. The Spirit of God opened his eyes to see that this fierce army that was threatening them was *nothing* compared with the vast Heavenly army of horses and chariots of fire that surrounded them!

Notice too, that Elisha didn't pray that God would change anything about the circumstances. His prayer was that the Lord would open his servant's eyes, so that he see the *spiritual* reality of the situation. When we understand our spiritual position, and just who we are surrounded by, every moment of every day, we can stand and face any situation.

Paul's prayer

God answered Elisha's prayer for his servant and the Apostle Paul prayed a similar prayer for us: *"I keep asking that the God of our Lord Jesus Christ, the glorious Father, may give you the Spirit of wisdom and revelation, so that you may know him better. I pray that the eyes of your heart may be enlightened in order that you may know the hope to which he has called you, the riches of his glorious inheritance in his holy people, and his incomparably great power for us who believe. That power is the same as the mighty strength"* Ephesians 1:17-19 (NIVUK)

Paul is praying for Christians who are struggling to feel the power of God in their lives. It is similar to Elisha's prayer for his servant. Paul, too, knew that *only God* can open the eyes of our hearts to really see that we have the resurrection power of Jesus Christ in us. What is Paul praying for? Paul's prayer is that God would give us The Spirit of wisdom and revelation so that we will know Him better.
That the eyes of our hearts would be enlightened
* that we would know (understand) the hope to which He has called us*
**riches of his glorious inheritance*
**the immeasurable greatness of his power toward us who believe.*

Note that Paul didn't pray that we <u>receive</u> these things, because they are already ours! Paul prayed that God would open our eyes to that truth!

Saturday - Live In God's Land Of 'Now'

"I focus on this one thing: Forgetting the past and looking forward to what lies ahead," Philippians 3:13 (NLT)

The land of The Past

Do you ever find yourself wandering into The Land of The Past? For most of us it's not a good idea to visit the past, even for a day trip. The Land of The Past for some is filled with deep valleys of regret, grief, abuse, guilt and shame. For others The Land of The Past is the opposite; it's filled with mountain peaks of happy family life, a successful career, powerful ministry, a beautiful home. Both can be hard to forget and leave behind. Either way, Paul urges us to forget what's behind us and press on to what's ahead.

We do not have a visa for the past

"Forget the former things; do not dwell on the past." Isaiah 43:18 (NIVUK) God expressly told Israel to "forget the past". It's not a suggestion, it's a command. Why? Simply put, because of His great love and because He had a plan for their future that was for their good.

It isn't memory itself that poses a problem, it is the way we use those memories that will determine the here and now. Memories are a precious gift from God for seeing what He has done and how He brought us through, not for wallowing in the past.

* * *

Look at it this way; If I try to visit a country to which I have not been granted a visa, I might be able to sneak in, thinking I'm very clever to get past security, but it is far more likely that I'll end up in jail. This is what happens when we visit The Past without a visa. God has not granted us a visa for The Past. When we repeatedly go there, or try to live part-time there, *we will end up in a prison of our own making.*

Live in the 'Land of the Present'

Maybe your Present is not what you were expecting? If your 'Now' feels like a Wasteland; a desert place, this is God's promise to you: He will *provide streams in your wasteland and will make a way in the desert"* Isaiah 43:19 (NIVUK)
Psalm 46:4-5 tells us *"There is a river whose streams make glad the city of God, the holy habitation of the Most High. God is in the midst of her; she shall not be moved; God will help her when morning dawns"*

For something that is so freeing, forgetting 'the former things' and moving on can be one of the hardest things to do. No matter what it is you are trying to move on from. Some people are not trying to shake off painful memories, but are trying to let go of a past that they perceive as brighter and happier than where they find themselves now.

It all starts in the mind. We can't stop thoughts from coming into our heads, but we don't have to dwell on those thoughts, mulling over memories until we feel as though they happened yesterday.We need to nip those thoughts in the bud immediately and replace them with the Word of God: *"Fix your thoughts on what is true, and honorable, and right, and pure, and lovely, and admirable. Think about things that are excellent and worthy of praise."* Philippians 4:8 (NLT)

"Don't copy the behavior and customs of this world, but let God

transform you into a new person by changing the way you think. Then you will learn to know God's will for you, which is good and pleasing and perfect." Romans' 12:2 (NLT)

Celebrate God's new place, its called Today

"This is the day the Lord has made. We will rejoice and be glad in it." Psalms 118:24 (NLT)

This verse is often quoted in a general sort of way, which isn't wrong, but in its context, it was speaking of celebrating 'The Day of deliverance.' Let's choose to forget that old Land of The Past, and love The Land of Today, *This* Day, whatever it looks like, because it is where God has brought us to. The past has gone and needs to stay gone. The present is now and for living with God, who made you, and who promises to give you a "hope and a future" (Jeremiah 29:11)

Sunday - Overcomer

"And they overcame him by the blood of the Lamb and by the word of their testimony, and they did not love their lives to the death." Revelation 12:11 (NKJV)

What is an Overcomer?

The verb 'overcome' is defined in the English dictionary as *"dealing with a problem or difficulty."* A few synonyms are then listed: *get the better of a struggle or conflict, bring under control, bridle, master, conquer, triumph over, defeat.*

1 Peter 5:8 says that we have an enemy that prowls around, looking for those he can destroy. We also see, reading through Revelation that the clock is ticking for this enemy Satan, and he knows he is defeated. He is literally fighting a losing battle. Chapter twelve tells us that *"he is filled with fury, because he knows that his time is short."* Revelation 12:12 (NIVUK)

This enemy works in every way he can to try and hinder our effectiveness for the Kingdom of God. This is why it is vital for us to read and put into practice what the Lord teaches us through His Word. The principles we find in the Word of God are anchors that keep us steady in every storm: *"Every word of God proves true. He is a shield to all who come to him for protection."* Proverbs 30:5 (NLT)
"Such things were written in the Scriptures long ago to teach us.

And the Scriptures give us hope and encouragement as we wait patiently for God's promises to be fulfilled." Romans 15:4 (NLT)

Overcomers know Who their help comes from!
Overcomers face struggles the same everyone, but they don't allow their troubles to become bigger than the Lord. An overcomer knows that the *Lord* is their source of help:
"I will lift up my eyes to the hills— From whence comes my help? My help comes from the LORD, Who made heaven and earth." Psalms 121:1-2 (NKJV)

Something even more important than knowing where their help comes <u>from</u>, overcomers know the <u>Helper</u>; they know without doubt that He is who He says He is and is greater than anything they face.

David was an overcomer

He knew both his source of help and the Helper, on a very deeply personal level, and he declares it again and again throughout the Psalms. David had learned from a young age that he could rely on the Lord for strength and enabling power in life-threatening situations or in heartbreak.
He wrote this in the face of a fierce battle, after The Lord had shown His faithfulness yet again: *"Now I know that the LORD saves His anointed; He will answer him from His holy heaven With the saving strength of His right hand. Some trust in chariots, and some in horses; But we will remember the name of the LORD our God."* Psalms 20:6-7 (NKJV)
"To You, O LORD, I lift up my soul. O my God, I trust in You;" Psalms 25:1-2a (NKJV)

Paul was an overcomer

Paul faced persecution, prison and the kind of adversity that you and I will probably never have to face, yet he was able to say with absolute conviction, "I <u>know</u> whom I have believed and am persuaded that He is able to keep what I have committed to Him until that Day." 2 Timothy 1:12 (NKJV)

I love the way The Passion Translation captures the essence of this verse: "The confidence of my calling enables me to overcome every difficulty without shame, for <u>I have an intimate revelation of this God.</u> And my faith in him convinces me that he is more than able to keep all that I've placed in his hands safe and secure until the fullness of his appearing." 2 Timothy 1:12 (TPT)

We are created to overcome

2 Corinthians 5:17 says that we are *new* creations. The old you no longer exists! This new person that you are is *more than a conqueror* through Christ (see Romans 8:37) This truth isn't dependent on how we *feel,* but on what the Word of God says. We are a work in progress, and we learn to overcome through trials by lifting our eyes to our Source of help, drawing closer to God, remembering His nature and character and like Paul knowing that God's strength is made perfect in our weakness.

Overcomers help others to overcome
"He comforts us in all our troubles so that we can comfort others. When they are troubled, we will be able to give them the same comfort God has given us." 2 Corinthians 1:4 (NLT)

Overcomers receive comfort and strength from the Lord and then look around to see who they, in turn, can comfort and strengthen. I don't know about you but when I'm struggling with my own issues, life becomes *'all about me.'* I sometimes wonder what I'd be like if we were to face persecution in the West, as the early Church faced and many Christians are facing in the world today.

When reading the New Testament and the life of Paul and his peers, I'm always amazed at this man; so unconcerned for his own material or physical needs; totally focussed on Jesus and on caring for people in the face of every hardship, every beating and whipping, every prison term, every long and arduous journey in the searing heat. It was all motivated by love. Love for his Saviour, and for the people he knew God had called him to serve.

David and Paul were overcomers, not because they were 'great,' (although they were great examples for us) they were not overcomers because they were strong (in themselves); what they have in common and what made them both overcomers, is that they *knew* the One to whom they looked for strength!

Seen and Known

Monday - Obedient Faith

'As he arrived at the gates of the village, he saw a widow gathering sticks, and he asked her, "Would you please bring me a little water in a cup?" As she was going to get it, he called to her, "Bring me a bite of bread, too." But she said, "I swear by the Lord your God that I don't have a single piece of bread in the house. And I have only a handful of flour left in the jar and a little cooking oil in the bottom of the jug. I was just gathering a few sticks to cook this last meal, and then my son and I will die." But Elijah said to her, "Don't be afraid! Go ahead and do just what you've said, but make a little bread for me first. Then use what's left to prepare a meal for yourself and your son. For this is what the Lord, the God of Israel, says: There will always be flour and olive oil left in your containers until the time when the Lord sends rain and the crops grow again!" So she did as Elijah said, and she and Elijah and her family continued to eat for many days. There was always enough flour and olive oil left in the containers, just as the Lord had promised through Elijah.' 2 Kings 17:12-16 (NLT)

Everything that happened in this story required obedient faith from both parties involved. Over the next two days I would like to look at this story from both parties' points of view.

Elijah's side of the story

God told Elijah "Go and live in the village of Zarephath, near the city of Sidon. I have instructed a widow there to feed you." 1 Kings 17:9 (NLT)

Why did God choose a widow, living in extreme poverty to provide food and shelter for Elijah? Why not someone rich with a larder overflowing with good food? I can't help wondering how Elijah felt, not as a prophet of God, but just as a man, about asking her for food. Not only was she obviously very poor, but she had told him that all she had was a few scraps to scrape together, enough to make a last meal for herself and her son, before they both died of hunger. However, undaunted, Elijah obeyed God and told her *"Don't be afraid! Go ahead and do just what you've said, but make a little bread for me first. Then use what's left to prepare a meal for yourself and your son."* 1 Kings 17:13 (NLT)

The thing about Elijah that comes through so clearly in this story is that he had learned to know and more importantly to obey, the voice of God. Despite the widow having explained her dire circumstances Elijah knew that God had *told* him this widow would feed him. To Elijah that was the end of it, no debate in his head. God had *said* it, Elijah *believed*, and that was it. Whether it made sense or not didn't factor into the equation.

We can become overly concerned about how others might view us. Deep down we all want to be liked and well thought of. But in God's agenda, more often than not it isn't about us. God sees the bigger picture, and requires our obedient faith in following Him.

God provided for Elijah's hunger as promised, but that was not His only purpose. The <u>much</u> bigger picture in this story is the miracle that our wondrous, compassionate God did in the life of this struggling single mother and her child, when in faith, she gave what little she had for the sake of another.

* * *

Sometimes God asks us to do things that seem strange to us, daring even; things that take us out of our comfort zones. Will we obey Him, as Elijah did, or will we let fear of what other people may think of us hold us back? The outcome to obedient faith is always the same; God turns impossible situations around. He opens seas, enables a teenage boy to take down a giant with a stone, miraculously heals 'incurable' diseases, and provides food for a widow and her child, as we will see tomorrow.

Tuesday - Release The Lack To The Miracle Worker

"As he arrived at the gates of the village, he saw a widow gathering sticks, and he asked her, "Would you please bring me a little water in a cup?" As she was going to get it, he called to her, "Bring me a bite of bread, too." But she said, "I swear by the Lord your God that I don't have a single piece of bread in the house. And I have only a handful of flour left in the jar and a little cooking oil in the bottom of the jug. I was just gathering a few sticks to cook this last meal, and then my son and I will die." But Elijah said to her, "Don't be afraid! Go ahead and do just what you've said, but make a little bread for me first. Then use what's left to prepare a meal for yourself and your son. For this is what the Lord, the God of Israel, says: There will always be flour and olive oil left in your containers until the time when the Lord sends rain and the crops grow again!" So she did as Elijah said, and she and Elijah and her family continued to eat for many days. There was always enough flour and olive oil left in the containers, just as the Lord had promised through Elijah." 2 Kings 17:12-16 (NLT)

Yesterday we looked at this account from Elijah's perspective, or perhaps it would be more accurate to say, how <u>we</u> might feel in Elijah's shoes, to be led by God as he was. I'd now like to look at this story from the widow's perspective.

A woman who listened to God

Two things that stood out to me in this story are; the woman must have had a relationship of sorts with God, because God spoke to her. And she had faith. Sure, her faith may have been shaky, perhaps it needed a bit of encouragement, but it was there. The Lord had said to Elijah, *"I have instructed a widow there to feed you."* 1 Kings 17:9 (NLT) - notice He didn't say "tell the widow that the Lord says." I conclude from this that God spoke directly to the woman.

Her name isn't mentioned, she's just referred to as "the widow," but we don't need to know her name - God knew her name. He had seen her predicament and He had a plan for her beyond her wildest expectations. The plan God had in mind, tailor made for her, involved so much more than feeding a hungry prophet. This woman had no idea how her life was about to change!

Focused on the lack

It seems that by the time Elijah arrived, the woman had become totally focused on and consumed by her lack. So much so that she had resolved that this was to be the last meal for herself and her son and then it was all over; she and her son were going to starve to death. Thankfully the Lord had a better plan in sending Elijah to her; not just an extra mouth to feed, but an opportunity for God to move! As the woman started to tell Elijah all about her lack and her 'last meal plan,' Elijah resolutely said to her *"Don't be afraid! Go ahead and do just what you've said, but make a little bread for me first. Then use what's left to prepare a meal for yourself and your son."* 1 Kings 17:13 (NLT) Elijah then assured her that meal she would make would multiply supernaturally, to feed not only Elijah, but the household, and that her supplies would continue to miraculously replenish even after Elijah had gone. She must have made the decision to believe God then, and take that step of faith, because she did as Elijah asked, and we know what happened!

Releasing our lack to the Miracle Worker

Does this remind you of another account in the Bible of miraculous multiplication from a seemingly hopeless lack? In John 6:1-13 is the story of a boy with a little basket of bread and fish for his lunch. Something to note in the story is that Jesus didn't miraculously multiply the bread and fish *first* and then tell the disciples to distribute it to the people. It was as they, in faith, *obeyed Jesus' instructions* to start giving out this tiny portion to over five thousand people, that the bread and fish multiplied and kept multiplying until everyone had been fed and there were even leftovers!

The miracle in both of these stories is in the letting go of the lack and releasing it in faith, in handing it to The God of Miracles and saying "I choose to believe you."

It was when this woman released her *little* that the miracle happened. She had to make that choice, 'release my tiny portion in faith and see God's supernatural increase, or tighten my grip on my 'lack' and stay right where I am.
Sometimes we see what we have as little or insignificant; whether materially or spiritually. No portion given in obedient faith is too small for our God to do something miraculous with!

Wednesday - The God Who Sees Me

"She gave this name to the Lord who spoke to her: 'You are the God who sees me,' for she said, 'I have now seen the One who sees me.' Genesis 16:13 (NIVUK)

El Roi

This is the only place in the Bible where God is called *El Roi* - meaning, *"The God who sees me."* It is also the only place where a person names God, rather than God telling a person His name, or one of His names.

It was (and is) no secret that God sees and cares for His people, and there are accounts in the Bible where He tells individuals *'I have seen'*. However He didn't ever *call* Himself 'The God Who Sees' [you]. There's a lovely example of God seeing a man in distress in 2 Kings:

King Hezekiah had contracted a terminally illness. He was devastated, of course, and became deeply depressed; the Bible says, "He turned his face to the wall and wept bitterly". Who wouldn't? He also prayed, asking God to heal him. God responded by sending Isaiah with a prophetic word: *" I have heard your prayer and seen your tears; I will heal you."* 2 Kings 20:5 (NIVUK)

'W*hat does this have to do with Hagar?'* you might be thinking.

Well, it occurred to me that this person who had the 'audacity' to name Almighty God was not a king, or a high priest, not a Levite, in fact not even a child of Israel! She was a 'mere' woman, a runaway slave, a nobody in the eyes of society. She was lost and lonely in a wilderness of despair. But God saw her. It demonstrates something of the nature of God, that He took this name that she gave Him. I don't think it mattered to God one bit that Hagar called Him a name that wasn't 'on the list' of His names. The very fact that the name, or a record of it, made it into His written Word shows that! Personally, I believe God *loved* her name for Him, that it made Him smile.

Hagar found herself pregnant and alone, having run away into the wilderness, because of the untenable situation between herself and her mistress. Although she lived in a household that worshipped the One True God, she personally had never known Him. But *God knew her,* and made Himself known to her. He 'broke' into her world with His loving kindness and mercy, when she desperately needed it.

Even before she cried out to Him, the 'Angel of the Lord' appeared. (Most agree that this was a pre-incarnation of Jesus) He called her by her name, asked where she had come from and where she was headed to. Of course, He already knew the answer, but He wanted to show Hagar that He genuinely cared for her; that her troubles mattered to Him.

Hagar knew in that moment that this God her master and mistress worshiped was real; not only that, that He *saw*. He saw what she was going through, all the pain, loneliness and uncertainty she was facing, He saw her, Hagar. And with that knowledge, she knew she could go back to her mistress. She could face anything!

Who touched Me?

We see Jesus again as *the God who sees* in Luke's Gospel, when

Jesus heals a woman shamed and ostracised because of the bleeding disorder she had battled for twelve years. The account is found in Luke chapter eight. Jesus was surrounded by a large crowd. A woman in the crowd touched just the edge of his clothing and was instantly healed.

Jesus stopped, asking 'who touched me?' Peter, ever the pragmatist, told Him, *"Master, this whole crowd is pressing up against you." Luke 8:45 (NLT)* The crowd were pressing against Jesus, probably bumping and pushing each other and Jesus, eager to see a miracle. What Peter and the rest of the crowd was oblivious to was that a quiet miracle had just taken place! Jesus kept insisting; *"Someone deliberately touched me, for I felt healing power go out from me."* Luke 8:46 (NLT)

The woman, realising she couldn't hide any longer, came forward, trembling and saying, 'it was me!' Now, I don't believe for a moment that Jesus couldn't have picked out in a second who had touched Him. But I think He wanted her to see that her faith had been rewarded. She had said, "If I could just touch the hem of his garment I'll be healed," and God had rewarded her faith. He had seen her pain, sadness and loneliness, and He had seen that in spite of it all, she had reached out to Jesus in faith. Jesus said, 'Someone touched me deliberately.' In other words, she had touched Him *with faith filled intent.*

In the presence of Jesus, we cannot possibly go unnoticed. He is the God who sees us. He sees our isolation, our broken hearts and our broken bodies, and is ready to heal us. When we feel unseen, unloved, or unlovable, He's the one who sees us.

"Gaze upon him, join your life with his, and joy will come. Your faces will glisten with glory. You'll never wear that shame-face again." Psalms 34:5 (TPT)

Thursday - The Comparison Trap

"Surely, LORD, you bless the righteous; you surround them with your favour as with a shield." Psalms 5:12 (NIVUK)

Do you feel overlooked, when it comes to God's favour? You aren't alone. Many Christians have the incorrect perception that God's favour is something they have to strive for. The very good news is that if you are *in Christ*, then you are righteous, and this Psalm says that God surrounds the righteous with His favour, like a shield!

We are all blessed with gifts from God

In Mathew's gospel Jesus told a parable of three men who were each given a sum of money. The amounts were not the same, but each man had to give account in the same way for what he had done with his money: *"Before he left on his journey, he entrusted a bag of five thousand gold coins to one of his servants, to another a bag of two thousand gold coins, and to the third a bag of one thousand gold coins, each according to his ability to manage."* Matthew 25:15 (TPT)

"Each according to his ability": The servants were given amounts of money according to their ability. One servant only received a single bag, while another was given *five*. But there is something important to keep sight of and it's this: *all three* of these servants had been shown favour by their master. He had

chosen these three to entrust his money to. The truth is, each of them had received a large amount; it was only the 'largeness' that varied, and the variation was only because the master knew them and their unique abilities, not any sort of favouritism.

God's choices

Sometimes in church, or in life in general, we can feel a bit like the man who was given 'only' one bag. We see our *one* as 'only' one and somehow less significant than the five someone else has received. But the truth is, that the servant with one bag had still been entrusted with a large sum of money, and the master had shown him favour by giving it to him. In the end he did nothing, while the other two multiplied theirs. I wonder why he did nothing. Did he compare his smaller amount with that of his two fellow servants, and did comparison become his excuse for lethargy?

Jesus has entrusted precious, Kingdom gifts to us - He expects us to *do* something with these. (See Ephesians 4:12–13, 15) His favour of another person doesn't imply his *disfavour* of me. He doesn't choose someone for a position I want, or bestow a gift I wanted on someone else because He loves that other person more than He loves me. His choice actually isn't about me at all, that position or gift just happens to be part of the other person's journey with Him, not mine.

Many times in the Bible, God set His choice on particular people, where the other 'players' in the story found God's choice hard to accept or understand. Of the twins, Jacob and Esau, God chose younger Jacob even though Esau was the older twin and according to the customs of the times, the older brother was to receive the family blessing and bigger share of the inheritance. God chose David, the youngest son and what's more a mere shepherd boy. Through the gospels, there are far more records of Peter, James and John doing great things with Jesus than the other disciples. Does this mean the other disciples were less special, less *chosen*, that Peter, James and John? Of course not; Jesus had chosen them all and invited them to follow Him. He loved His disciples. All it signifies is that Jesus had different purposes for each of them.

God's grace gift, what will you do with yours?

"Even though I am the least significant of all his holy believers, this grace-gift was imparted when the manifestation of his power came upon me. Grace alone empowers me so that I can boldly preach this wonderful message to non-Jewish people, sharing with them the unfading, inexhaustible riches of Christ, which are beyond comprehension." Ephesians 3:7-8 (TPT)

When we 'get over ourselves', as Paul did and truly understand that we are accepted by God, and grasp just what it is that He has given us, our insecurities, comparisons and striving to be seen by the One who already sees us, all melt away. Our position in Him has nothing to do with our looks, abilities, good works, natural abilities, and how (we *think*) they measure up to anyone else's. The King of kings has endowed us with His favour and entrusted to us gifts that are uniquely purposed to suit us perfectly. They are for wise *use,* for the furthering of His Kingdom. God cares about you, the person, far more than what you can *do* for Him. He <u>knows</u> you*!* He is gentle and kind, and calls you to be faithful in the stewardship of the gifts He has given you.

"Every believer has received grace gifts, so use them to serve one another as faithful stewards of the many-coloured tapestry of God's grace. For example, if you have a speaking gift, speak as though God were speaking his words through you. If you have the gift of serving, do it passionately with the strength God gives you, so that in everything God alone will be glorified through Jesus Christ. For to him belong the power and the glory forever throughout all ages! Amen." 1 Peter 4:10-11 (TPT)

Friday - Known and Loved

"You are so intimately aware of me, Lord. You read my heart like an open book and you know all the words I'm about to speak before I even start a sentence! You know every step I will take before my journey even begins. Lord, you know everything there is to know about me. You perceive every movement of my heart and soul, and you understand my every thought before it even enters my mind." Psalms 139:1-4 (TPT)

The one who matters most, knows you the most.
There's no person on this earth that really knows everything about you. We all have a little part of us that we keep private. Most of us have the secret little thought; 'if people knew *that* about me they wouldn't like me.' But with Jesus there are no secrets. He knows everything about you. You are absolutely, completely known by Him. There has never been a thought or feeling, even a fleeting one, in your entire life, that He didn't know about. No ache or pain in your body, every little twinge here or there, escapes His notice; even the things you don't know about, He does. Your Creator, Shepherd and Friend knows every cell, sinew, bone, tissue and muscle; He put it together! He is the one who matters most, and the one who knows you the most. We fear the judgement of others, yet the only one whose judgment is important knows every little detail about us. And the incredible thing is, He still loves us.

The glory of His omniscience

The glory of Jesus' omniscience grows more wondrous as we grasp hold of the truth that we are fully known; that we don't have to hide from Him (we couldn't anyway) For some people it can take years for the personal implications of this incredible truth to sink in.

It means there are no secrets. You may have been very successful in hiding your 'stuff' all your life from everyone you know, but it is not hidden from Jesus.

It means there are no masks. He knows the *real* you. Every millimetre of your soul is laid bare, utterly known. What an amazing relationship; No one else knows you the way Jesus does. Not your best friend, your mother, or even your spouse.

Completely loved

Here's the most incredible part: knowing everything about you, Jesus loves you. He doesn't recoil from your innermost thoughts, neither is He shocked or surprised by them.

Jesus gives you one hundred percent of His love, even though your own love for Him could never match His - it isn't an equal exchange.

There's an account in John's gospel (John 21) where we see this love in action. We touched briefly on this in a previous devotional.

It was the third time Jesus had appeared to His disciples after His resurrection. Peter having once proudly estimated his love and devotion to Jesus as being *more* than that of the other disciples, (Matthew 26:33) and then publicly denying Him, is now asked a very important question by Jesus.

Jesus asked Peter: "do you love me," Peter responded, "Yes, my Lord! You know that I have great affection for you!" John 21:16b (TPT)

The word for *love* that Jesus had used, and Peter's word in response were not the same. Jesus used the word *agape* which in its Biblical usage speaks of an all giving, selfless love. The Passion Translation interprets Jesus question as: 'does your heart *burn* with love for me?' (As Jesus' heart does for us) Peter answered Jesus using the word *philio*, which in Biblical usage has in mind a more a friendly affection; 'to hold affection for'. Some translations express Peter's answer as, *"I am your friend."*

Personally I don't think Peter's seemingly wishy-washy response reflected his true feelings for Jesus, but rather his feelings towards <u>himself</u> and his perception of how others, including Jesus, might view him now, in light of what he had done. Perhaps his response reflected a sense of residual shame and worthlessness. Perhaps he didn't dare say, "Yes, my heart burns with love for you Lord," because he'd said something very like that in the past and everyone knew how *that* had turned out! Jesus asked the question a second time, and again Peter respond, *"You know* I have great affection for you".

Jesus asked the question a third time. This time, Jesus used Peter's word, asking Peter if he had a *brotherly love,* and *friendly devotion* for Him. Peter was saddened at being asked a third time, but Jesus, knowing Peter so well, had good reason for His line of questioning: I believe that in asking this question three times, in front of the other disciples, Jesus offered Peter a chance to affirm publicly *three times* that which he had publicly denied *three times.*

The third time, Peter responded with the words, 'Lord you know <u>everything</u>...you *know* that I love you'. What caught my attention is that this time around, Jesus had used the words, *"do you have affection for me,"* and Peter's response shows that his heart has been restored by the realisation that Jesus absolutely <u>knows</u> him; He knows <u>everything</u> and still loves Peter, responded with the words Jesus had used at first, saying, "my heart burns with love for you Lord."

* * *

Notice too that Jesus didn't once ask Peter "Are you sorry for what you did?" Jesus challenged Peter to *love,* and revealed to Peter how intimately he was *known.* That's the way of our incredible Jesus! The primary thing Jesus requires of us, far more important than all our great promises, vows and 'sworn allegiance,' is simply our whole hearts, *because we have His.*

Saturday - Obscure Heroes

We all know and love the stories in the Bible of those 'heroes,' notable people of great faith, fearful people who put their trust in God, faithful people who stood their ground and believed God whatever their circumstances. There are many *other* heroes in the Bible who are less in the spotlight. Some of these even teeter on the edge of obscurity, but <u>God</u> saw them, each and every one. Here are three 'unsung' heroes from the Bible:

Ittai the Gittite

Ittai's story can be found in 2 Samuel 15. As far as a mention, or 'shout out' goes, Ittai the Gittite really only makes a cameo appearance, but his role was vital and shines through the pages of Biblical history. He was a native of Gath, one of David's most loyal friends during the revolution of Absalom, and eventually promoted to the position of a Commander in David's army. But there's very little mention of him.

Behind David, King of Israel's back, his own son Absalom had been plotting a coup. Slowly but surely Absalom had been wheedling his sneaky way into the affections of the people, turning them against David in order to overthrow his father's reign and steal the throne. (See 2 Samuel 15:2-6)

Can you picture the heartsore King David, clothes torn in mourning, as he fled the palace with his family, counsellors, and loyal followers, to escape Absalom's murderous coup? As they set out, David turned to Ittai a leader of the six hundred men from Gath, and kindly offered Ittai the freedom to stay. After all, he had only just arrived, what loyalty did he owe to David?: *"Why are you coming with us? Go on back to King Absalom, for you are a guest in Israel, a foreigner in exile. You arrived only recently, and should I force you today to wander with us? I don't even know where we will go. Go on back and take your kinsmen with you, and may the Lord show you his unfailing love and faithfulness."* 2 Samuel 15:19-20 (NLT)

The response of this 'foreigner' reminds me of another foreigner who responded in a similar way, when offered her freedom. The difference is that Ruth's story is more prominent, more spoken about. If you were to ask any preacher to prepare a sermon on loyalty and faithfulness, their first port of call would probably be Ruth. But Ruth's celebrated loyalty doesn't detract from Ittai's quiet, understated faithfulness. This was his response to the king: *"I vow by the Lord and by your own life that I will go wherever my lord the king goes, no matter what happens—whether it means life or death."* 2 Samuel 15:21 (NLT)

Shiphrah and Puah

It's strange really, that the names of these two Godly midwives are not instantly recognisable.

They also make only a 'cameo' appearance, by our standards, but their role in Israel's history, and indeed Biblical history, is *enormous*. These two midwives are powerful, yet obscure examples of the importance of doing what's right before God, no matter what the world says.

During Joseph's time, the Israelites had enjoyed favour with Pharaoh and his court. After Joseph died, another pharaoh came into power who knew nothing of Joseph and all that had transpired. The Israelite population had increased with the last government, and this unsettled the Egyptians. Fearing the

Israelites would take over the nation, Pharaoh came up with a chilling plan to limit their population growth. He gave midwives Shiphrah and Puah this order: *"When you help the Hebrew women as they give birth, watch as they deliver. If the baby is a boy, kill him; if it is a girl, let her live."* Exodus 1:16 (NLT)

Courageous Shiphrah and Puah refused to do as the king of Egypt had commanded. They delivered each baby, male and female, with all the skill and ability with which the Lord had gifted them. It wasn't long before their disobedience came to the attention of the king, and he summoned them, demanding to know why they had blatantly disobeyed Him. (verse 18)

Now, not only were these two women Godly, they were wise in their reply. While they knew they had a responsibility to obey their leaders, they also understood that God's law supersedes man's law; they could not sin against God by committing mass murder. We see from the end of this chapter that God honoured their courage and commitment to do what was right before Him. He blessed them with children of their own: *"So God dealt well with the midwives. And the people multiplied and grew very strong. And because the midwives feared God, he gave them families."* Exodus 1:20-21 (ESV)

It's important to remember that 'obscure' doesn't mean *insignificant* in the Kingdom of God. In these two examples we have looked at, the people involved were rewarded in the end, though they remained obscure. But that doesn't mean we can take from this that we will all be rewarded here on this earth for faithfulness, or courage. What we can learn from it is that nothing and no one escapes the notice of the Lord our God; no act of kindness in His name, no faithfulness, no step of faith, or loyal 'plodding' in the background at what He has asked us to to do.

* * *

Most of us will never have our name in written in lights, but we *do* have our names written in the Lamb's Book of life! You might never have your name tattooed on any besotted fan's arm, but your name is indelibly tattooed on the hand of God! (Isaiah 49:16)

You, reader, in God's eyes, are *not* obscure.

Sunday - God Sees The 'Real' You

If you owned a huge corporation of several thousand people, would you choose as a leader a man who was so anxious that he hid in the stockroom, argued with you, questioned you at every turn, showed very little faith in you as CEO and in the company in general? I don't think I would! But in a way that's what happened between the Lord and Gideon. (You can read the story in Judges 6:11 - 7:25)

God wanted Gideon

God could have picked anyone for His plan to rescue His precious people. But God wanted Gideon; this doubting man with anxiety issues, hiding in a wine press to escape his enemies. It may seem strange that the Angel of the Lord addressed Gideon as *'Mighty man of valour'*, before Gideon had done a single thing to indicate any sort of valour. (See Judges 6:11)

Mighty man of valour

Why did God call Gideon that? Because *"Mighty man of valour"* was who Gideon truly was, and it's who the Lord saw when He looked at Gideon; after all, it was who God created him to be! But Gideon didn't know it yet; he hadn't recognised it in himself. He was afraid. He didn't understand why God would choose him.

Control Issues

Fear, if we let allow it to, dictates our choices and sometimes causes us to do silly things. Gideon, in his fear had the audacity to argue with the Lord, expressing all his doubts about God's faithfulness! *"if the Lord is with us, why has all this happened to us? And where are all the miracles our ancestors told us about? Didn't they say, 'The Lord brought us up out of Egypt'? But now the Lord has abandoned us and handed us over to the Midianites."* Judges 6:13 (NLT)

When that approach didn't work on God, Gideon went down the self pity route: *"how can I rescue Israel? My clan is the weakest in the whole tribe of Manasseh, and I am the least in my entire family!"* Judges 6:15 (NLT)
It wasn't as if God was asking Gideon to go and singlehandedly fight the Midianites, God promised to be with him: *"The Lord said to him, "I will be with you. And you will destroy the Midianites as if you were fighting against one man."* Judges 6:16 (NLT)

What a promise! But Gideon still wasn't sure. And so we come to Gideon's famous fleece-laying episode. Still fearful and filled with doubt, his comfort zone well and truly shaken, he asked God for sign, then another and another. Gideon had control issues, and in his need to be the one in charge, he even tried to control God! It's only because God is loving and patient that He gave Gideon those signs.

Over the years I've often heard people say, they have 'laid a fleece' for God, citing Gideon as an example as if this were some sort of doctrine to live by. But this story is not an example for us to follow. It doesn't demonstrate faith, it is control at the highest level - trying to control the Lord!
In Matthew chapter four, Satan tries to tempt Jesus. He shows Jesus the highest pinnacle of the temple and says: *"If you are the Son of God, jump off! For the Scriptures say, 'He will order his*

*angels to protect you. And they will hold you up with their hands
so you won't even hurt your foot on a stone."* Matthew 4:6
(NLT)

Of course we know how Jesus responded! *"The Scriptures <u>also</u>
say, 'You must not test the Lord your God.'"*Matthew 4:7 (NLT).
Notice that Jesus said, "the scriptures *also* say." Yes, the
scriptures *do say* that God's angels protect us, but Satan's
suggestion was that Jesus should create an artificial crisis, with
the sole purpose of testing the Lord, rather than trusting God in
real life situations, while remaining obedient. We are not to test
God. His faithfulness towards us and the truth of His Word are
not on trial!

Go!

"Then the Lord turned to him and said, "Go with the strength you
have, and rescue Israel from the Midianites. I am sending you!"
Judges 6:14 (NLT)

When God said to Gideon, 'go with the strength you have,' He
wasn't saying, 'go in your own strength,' but was affirming traits He
had seen in Gideon's heart that Gideon probably hadn't recognised as
strengths. But these were strengths God could work with:

The strength of *humility*; Gideon recognised he had no strength of
his own.

The strength of the *caring*; Gideon cared about the troubles of Israel.

The strength of *knowledge*; Gideon <u>knew</u> God had done great things
in the past.

The strength of *spiritual hunger*; Gideon desperately wanted to see
God do great works again.

Just like Gideon, you have a God-designed purpose. There's no
other *you* in this whole world - there never has been and never will be
again. God sees the *real* you, the one He created you to be, whether
you recognise that person yet or not. God can work with a heart that is
filled with real humility, a love for people, and a hunger for Him.

Obedience doesn't require fearlessness, only the faith to trust God, even when we feel afraid. Corrie ten Boom famously wrote: *"Never be afraid to trust an unknown future to a known God."*

How Then, Shall We Live?

Monday - Comfort Eating

"When I discovered your words, I devoured them. They are my joy and my heart's delight, for I bear your name, O Lord God of Heaven's Armies". Jeremiah 15:16 (NLT)

I have a confession to make: when I don't feel well physically, I don't care much about healthy eating. I crave spicy crisps, and usually end up buying the biggest bag I can find and then munch my way through the entire bag, with endless cups of tea, feeling very sorry for myself indeed. Of course I know on some level that I'd feel better faster if I ate vitamin enriched fruit and vegetables, drank two litres of water, and rested properly, but somehow my brain equates those *good* things with disciple and self control, both of which seem to fly out of the window when I don't feel well. It's what's commonly known as *'comfort eating'*.

Spiritual comfort eating

One morning recently, with a summer cold and armed with my usual comfort food, I wearily opened my Bible to read and it fell open to where I had a book marker; it was Matthew chapter four where Jesus, hungry and tired after forty days the wilderness, was being tempted by Satan, and He replied *"It is written: "Man shall not live on bread alone, but on every word that comes from the mouth of God." Matthew 4:4 (NIVUK)*

Jesus' whole life was a model for us on how to draw aside and spend time with the Father. And here, in the wilderness is the perfect example. Tired and '*very hungry,*' Jesus didn't give in. It's easy to forget sometimes that even though Jesus was fully God, He had become fully man. He felt and experienced everything we do, hunger pangs, physical pain, grief and tiredness. Satan saw that He was tired and hungry and thought he was in with a chance. As if!

It's when you're at your most vulnerable that the devil strikes isn't it? He comes dripping his insidious lies, trying to convince you that God has abandoned you, that you could fill that hunger in your soul with 'stuff.' "A shopping spree will make you feel better, after all, 'you're worth it!'" 'Men, you'd feel so much better about yourself if you had a car like that man's down the road.' Or here's a good one that so many Christians fall for: "*a change of church will make you feel better. Nobody in your church likes you anyway, so they won't even notice you've gone!*" And so we 'spiritually comfort eat'. In other words, we try to fill the ache in our hearts by chasing meaningless, empty things that may give us momentary happiness and relief, but before we know it, that gnawing ache is back.

Created to crave Him

"*I am the bread of life! Your ancestors ate manna in the wilderness, but they all died. Anyone who eats the bread from heaven, however, will never die. I am the living bread that came down from heaven. Anyone who eats this bread will live forever; and this bread, which I will offer so the world may live, is my flesh.*" John 6:48-51 (NLT) Just as we need nutritious food in order for our bodies to function properly, our souls were created to be nourished by the Word of God. We are made for connection with God through His Word. When I eat the wrong foods, my body becomes sluggish, my energy levels drop dramatically and I generally become a bit of a slob. I just don't feel like doing anything. When I start to eat properly again I feel alive physically! So it is with our *'inner man.'* The Word of God is power-packed with spiritual nutrition able to produce incredible things in and through us. Only God's Word will satisfy that inner appetite and cause us to truly live and grow in strength and potential.

You are what you eat

Have you ever heard the expression, 'you are what you eat?' In other words, you become like the thing you indulge in. This applies to the things we feed our hearts and minds with too. If a person sits around all day watching junk on Television or reading trashy novels, the content and principles of that input starts to become the person's world - it becomes what they think about and talk about.

You can't over-indulge on the Word of God.

Even a few minutes a day of Bible reading will begin to show in your life. Not 'speed reading,' but slowly digesting, absorbing the written words, asking God to speak to you. I guarantee that people will start to notice a difference in you. *You* will notice a difference in yourself! You will begin to experience God's life, wisdom and power in your day-to-day living. Let's determine in our hearts today to 'comfort eat' from the of storehouse of God's rich, spiritually nutritious, incredible Word.

Tuesday - The Gift Of A Well Timed Word

"A word fitly spoken is like apples of gold in settings of silver"
Proverbs 25:11 (NKJV)

Some believe that King Solomon was referring in this verse to a royal custom of the time, whereby at the end of a magnificent feast, while the guests relaxed around the table, a silver basket was passed around filled with a gift for each guest; a solid gold apple. Solomon wanted us to grasp the importance of this - that well timed, beautiful, truth-filled words are as precious as these golden apples. As disciples of Jesus we have a responsibility to 'give *golden apples*' to everyone we come into contact with.

Fitly spoken

'Fitly spoken,' means, the right word for any occasion, delivered in the right manner, and in the right timing. A fitly spoken word has power to heal and strengthen, to guide and rescue.

In verse twelve, Solomon writes: *"Like an earring of gold or an ornament of fine gold is the rebuke of a wise judge to a listening ear."* Proverbs 25:12 NIVUK. I love this analogy Solomon uses of an earring of gold. I'm sure you've heard the phrase *words are cheap.* The person who uses this phrase has usually been hurt and let down time and time again by empty words, broken promises, or worse, Christians who have self-righteously delivered judgements and edicts and then have been exposed for doing those very things themselves. These sort of cheap words cause pain and discomfort to the ears of the listener, in much the same way that cheap, base-metal earrings do. We need to watch our words and be circumspect; choose them wisely. When our words are God-honouring, they are made from the pure gold of God's grace, and are precious to the ears of the listener.

Notice that Solomon isn't suggesting "tickling" ears with what they want to hear; he's speaking about 'a wise rebuke,' however it's the delivery of that rebuke and the spirit and heart behind it that is very important.

We have the Spirit of God living in our hearts, ready to pour out through us to touch the lives of others with our fitly spoken words, in partnership with the Holy Spirit. When we don't know what to say, or we are afraid to speak, the Spirit of God will instruct us: *"The Lord God has given me the tongue of a disciple {and} of one who is taught, that I should know how to speak a word in season to him who is weary. He wakens Me morning by morning, He wakens My ear to hear as a disciple [as one who is taught]." Isaiah 50:4 (AMP)*

This, as you might know, is one of the many 'Messianic prophesies', written long before Jesus was born, and which He fulfilled to every last detail. Jesus always knew exactly what to say, and when to say it. That's because everything Jesus did or said was in partnership with His Father. And with the Holy Spirit living in us, we are called to do the same.

Here's an idea, and this is just one small example; what if, the next time a beggar sitting on the pavement asked you for money, and instead dropping a few coins into his box and walking on, you stopped and engaged with him? What if you were to ask God right there and then for some encouraging words to speak to him? Your money might help him a bit, but a fitly spoken *word of knowledge,* (see 1 Corinthians 12:8) could be the priceless gold that changes his life forever!

A word in season

A single word can change a life. Just a word of encouragement; a *"well done, thank you, you're doing a good job, I've seen the change God's doing in you, you're not alone, I'm praying for you."* Every person has a story, we never really know what people are going through, and we have no idea of the impact a few fitly spoken words of encouragement could have. Will you give someone the precious gift of a golden apple today?

Wednesday - Leaky Hearts

"Your word I have treasured and stored in my heart, That I may not sin against You." Psalm 119:11 (AMP)

Our hearts have the capacity to both store and hide things. This ability can be a negative or positive reality, depending on what it is that we choose to store, because our lives and the lives of those around us are affected and influenced by our choices.

Information Leakage

Our hearts would not make good special agents! Although we might think we have those secret things of our heart locked up tightly; the key buried so deeply that even we can't remember where it is, our hearts will inevitably betray us and give away our best kept secrets.

Our hearts can't be trusted. The hearts is more like a colander than a safe, a strongbox, or a diplomatic bag. It leaks information! What is stored in your heart will eventually be heard on your lips and shown in your life; Jesus said it clearly: *"For the mouth speaks what the heart is full of. A good man brings good things out of the good stored up in him, and an evil man brings evil things out of the evil stored up in him."* Matthew 12:34-35 (NIVUK)
Also see: Proverbs 4:23

What goes in comes out

We see from what Jesus said that this storing of 'stuff' in our hearts applies to both the negative and positive and this is why it is important for us to store the *right* things in our hearts. When the squeeze is on, what's inside will spill out as either an unpleasant surprise or a blessing and inspiration to those around us.

Remember those twelve spies that Moses sent into the Promised Land? They went, they saw how incredible it was, how rich and lush the fruit was on the vines - they even brought some samples back. But ten of the spies brought something else back too. Fear and doubt! They had seen some frightening things in the Promised Land in addition to the good things and something had happened in the hearts of those ten men. They had stored *more fear than faith, more doubt than Divine destiny*. And when they opened their mouths to speak, all those fears and doubts spewed out, over everyone around them, spreading throughout the whole camp. This is what happens when we store the wrong things in our hearts.

A clear-out

Each of us has the potential to store and hide the *wrong* stuff in our hearts. Little 'nuggets' such as jealousy, unforgiveness, bitterness, lust and anger are easily hidden in the secret pockets of the heart. They can remain unseen by other people for years. But those things are toxic and will do serious damage in the long term. They will slowly erode your heart, even touching and infecting *good* things stored in your heart. And they will eventually come out, in your words and actions.

The good news is that it's never too late to have a clear-out. King David had stored some wrong things in his heart. It began when he looked at Bathsheba and didn't nip those lustful thoughts in the bud, right there and then. It was just a matter of time before he acted on what was in his heart. David wrote these words of true repentance after being confronted by Nathan the prophet about what he had done with Bathsheba. (You can find the events in 2 Samuel chapters 11 and 12.) *"Create in me a pure heart, O God, and renew a steadfast spirit within me."* Psalms 51:10 (NIVUK)

David starts this Psalm of repentance saying, "blot out my transgressions": *blot out*, means 'wipe away', as in blotting out writing (see Exodus 32:32; Numbers 5:23).

That's what God does, when we come to Him in humility and genuine repentance. He blots out the sin we have written all over our hearts. We have a clean slate. A fresh new page to write on! And we are commanded in several places in scripture to write, fix, or store God's Word on our hearts. See Deuteronomy 11:18; Proverbs 3:3; Proverbs 7:3.

When we store God's word in our hearts, then <u>that</u> is what will 'leak' out: *"Your word I have treasured and stored in my heart, That I may not sin against You." PSALMS 119:11 (AMP)*

Paul admonishes us to *"Let the message of Christ dwell among you richly as you teach and admonish one another with all wisdom through psalms, hymns, and songs from the Spirit, singing to God with gratitude in your hearts."* Colossians 3:16 (NIVUK)

It's a conscious choice; *"<u>Let</u> the word of Christ dwell in you richly…"*

When we choose to store the Word of God in our hearts, then whenever we need wisdom, strength or truth, we will have a ready supply to draw on in trying circumstances. It will be those things that will spill out of us. And when the pressure is on, those around us will be blessed, encouraged and built up by the things that "leak" out of our hearts and escape from our lips.

Jill McIlreavy

Thursday - God's Radical, Kingdom Generosity

"You must each decide in your heart how much to give. And don't give reluctantly or in response to pressure. "For God loves a person who gives cheerfully." 2 Corinthians 9:7 (NLT)

Generosity is a reflection of God's heart

Generosity is God's nature - it is simply who He is. God is the lavish provider of every good and perfect gift. His radical, Kingdom generosity toward us has nothing to do with our pedigree, postcode or position and <u>everything</u> to do with His goodness, abundance, loving kindness and mercy. As His children, Christians are called to be like Him.

Giving generously flows easily for many, and so it should, because the Holy Spirit lives in us. We are being changed into His image more and more as He teaches us His ways. But there are times - especially in the face of financial uncertainty, job loss and unemployment, when it can become a challenge to maintain an open handed, open hearted attitude to giving. If we aren't careful, we can develop a poverty mentality.

A Poverty Mentality

If we don't guard our hearts in times of personal financial hardship, we can slowly slide into a poverty mentality; which is a fearful waste-not-want-not way of thinking, that says *if I give away the little I have I'll have nothing for myself.* This way of thinking is a spirit of fear in operation. The sneaking little thoughts that accompany that first one are usually focused on a deeper thought of, '*God hasn't provided for me'.*

These thought patterns, if given any leeway, cause us to close our hearts and hands to the needs of other people, believing the lie that we have nothing of value to give, when the Word of God tells us we have *everything* we need. "*The Lord is my shepherd; I have all that I need."* Psalm 23:1 (NLT)

When we are battling a poverty mentality, those fearful thought patterns can be counteracted by:
* Reminding ourselves of what the Word of God teaches us regarding God's faithful provision.
* Trusting Him to do as He says He will do.
* Remembering all the times God has provided for us, and has come through for us, in times of need.

God isn't really interested in our money, it's our hearts He wants
God's radical, Kingdom generosity has nothing to do with how much money you have. (Or don't have) What God is really interested in is your heart. How much of your *heart* are you willing to give away?

Have a look at this story in Luke's Gospel: "*While Jesus was in the Temple, he watched the rich people dropping their gifts in the collection box. Then a poor widow came by and dropped in two small coins. "I tell you the truth," Jesus said, "this poor widow has given more than all the rest of them. For they have given a tiny part of their surplus, but she, poor as she is, has given everything she has."* Luke 21:1-4 (NLT)

Materially speaking this lady had very little, but she gave <u>all</u> of the little she had with her whole heart. When we give with a heart that reflects His own, God can take our 'small portion,' sown in partnership with Him, and multiply it to bless others far beyond our wildest dreams! Remember the boy with his little basket of loaves and fish that fed thousands of people?

Joy-results-in-giving-results-in-joy!

In my forty-plus years as a Christian here's something I've observed: the most generous people are very often the ones who have the least, materially. And these generous givers are always, without fail, joyful, people! Paul described a whole congregation with this kind of Radical Kingdom generosity: "Now I want you to know, dear brothers and sisters, what God in his kindness has done through the churches in Macedonia. They are being tested by many troubles, and they are very poor. But they are also filled with abundant joy, which has overflowed in rich generosity. For I can testify that they gave not only what they could afford, but far more. And they did it of their own free will." 2 Corinthians 8:1-3 (NLT)

The more you give, the more you will *have* to give!

God blesses you and me so that we can share, not cling tightly to what we have. We don't need to hold onto our possessions, God promises that He will make sure we have enough for ourselves and to go around: "And God will generously provide all you need. Then you will always have everything you need and plenty left over to share with others. As the Scriptures say, "They share freely and give generously to the poor. Their good deeds will be remembered forever." For God is the one who provides seed for the farmer and then bread to eat. In the same way, he will provide and increase your resources and then produce a great harvest of generosity in you". 2 Corinthians 9:8-10 (NLT)

Let's ditch our poverty mentalities today and share out of our blessings!

Friday - Pray For Your Enemies

"You have heard that it was said, "Love your neighbour and hate your enemy." But I tell you, love your enemies and pray for those who persecute you," Matthew 5:43-44 (NIVUK)

Love My Enemy?

We all, at some time, have people in our lives that we feel could fit the description in that scripture; *Enemies.* Jesus was talking to people who had faced very real enemies, for centuries; from their time of slavery in Egypt to their occupied state by their newest, despised enemy, the Romans. I can just imagine the shock-ripples going through the crowd as Jesus spoke. 'He wants me to love *my enemies?*' Perhaps, to put Jesus' words into perspective, we could imagine Jesus standing in the aftermath of one of our modern day terrorist attacks, perhaps a suicide bomb in a busy city, saying to the families of the dead and injured, "love your enemies, pray for them." It seems too big a command; too hard to follow, doesn't it? But we don't have the option to pick and choose!

Jesus set an example for us

Jesus doesn't expect us to do something He Himself didn't do. When someone hurts us, the natural response is to strike back. We feel justified in letting them have both barrels, even if it is only verbally. It seems a really tall order to have to love them; to *pray* for them.

* * *

Jesus set an example for us. He was persecuted, ridiculed, scorned, rejected and ultimately crucified; was He ever tempted to snipe back? We know Jesus was *tempted* just as we are, but we also know that Jesus never, ever gave in to temptation: *"For we do not have a high priest who is unable to feel sympathy for our weaknesses, but we have one who has been tempted in every way, just as we are – yet he did not sin." Hebrews 4:15 NIVUK*

Jesus' last words regarding those who had persecuted, scorned and crucified Him were in the form of a prayer: "Father, forgive them, for they don't know what they are doing." Luke 23:34 (NIVUK)

Why Pray for Our Enemies?

Why not send them a bunch of flowers, or order them a nice gift online with a hand written note? Because it's easy to paint a fake smile on our faces, show pretend kindness to someone we dislike, while in our hearts we have no real desire to see God bless them. We might be able to fool people, but we can't fool God. But when we pray it's a whole different arena; we're in the presence of God, the One who knows us and sees into the deepest recesses of our hearts. There's no pretending when it's just us and God!

Praying for someone who has hurt us, with a genuine desire to see God bless them, whether it's a terrorist, a family member or someone in church, brings healing to our own hearts. Something begins to shift, deep in our hearts. Bitterness is uprooted like the weed it is; the choke-hold it had on our lives, broken.

How Do We Pray For An Enemy?

Start by forgiving them: Have you ever been hurt and felt completely justified in being angry? You certainly don't *feel* like forgiving that person do you? But forgiveness, like love, is a command; it is a *non-negotiable* with Jesus. This is because unforgiveness is a lose-lose situation for the one carrying it.

If you're struggling to pray for someone who has deeply hurt you, talk to God about it. Ask Him to help you to forgive the person. Unlike your friends, God won't agree with you that the person who hurt you is a terrible person who deserves to be zapped by lightening, but He <u>will</u> give you the grace you need in order to forgive.

By making the conscious choice to forgive and to speak that forgiveness out loud, in the presence of God, we take the first step in Jesus' command. Forgiveness is powerful!

Stephen's prayer for his enemies left a spiritual legacy.
Here's an example of forgiveness that really challenges me: When Stephen was being stoned to death, he prayed out loud for his killers: *"Then he fell on his knees and cried out, 'Lord, do not hold this sin against them.' When he had said this, he fell asleep."* Acts 7:60 (NIVUK)

Stephen's prayer is a powerful example of blessing someone who persecutes you. There's nothing fake about his prayer. Stephen could have prayed quietly as he lay dying. Imagine the agony he experienced, as every stone struck his head and body. He could have curled up into a tight ball to protect himself; and whispered his prayer privately to God, with what little strength he had left. Surely it wouldn't have mattered?

But it was love that enabled Stephen to find the strength to shout his prayer out loud with his dying breath. He wanted those words to be heard because he wanted his killers to *know* that he'd forgiven them. His forgiveness was real and it was an act of pure love.

Stephen's loving act was to have far reaching results. There was one man in particular whom God wanted to reach; though the man was an enemy of the early Church at the time of Stephen's death, and in fact he spearheaded the persecution against the early Christians, I believe Stephen's prayer deeply affected him. It planted a seed in his hate-filled heart that he found increasingly difficult to ignore. His name was Saul: (Acts 8:1-3)

Of course we know that Saul later became the Apostle Paul, after his dramatic encounter with the risen Jesus on the road to Damascus. Who would have thought, looking at the angry young Christian-hating Saul, that he would become a champion for Jesus? - Paul later said that his deepest longing was to see his people come to know Jesus. (Romans 10:) So you see, we can never underestimate the power and legacy of praying for our enemies!

Saturday - Seeing As Jesus Saw

"There was such a swirl of activity around Jesus, with so many people coming and going, that they were unable to even eat a meal. So Jesus said to his disciples, "Come, let's take a break and find a secluded place where you can rest a while." Mark 6:31 (TPT)

The way Jesus saw people

Jesus had a way of seeing right into the hearts of people and their situations. He really *saw* them, and loved them. He was deeply moved with compassion for people. Throughout the gospels we often see the words, 'Jesus was *moved with compassion,'* just before Jesus did or said something. Here, in Mark chapter six we plainly see the beautiful, compassionate heart of Jesus in His day-to-day interaction with people.

He saw His disciples' needs

Jesus' disciples had just come back from a time of ministry that Jesus had sent them on, walking from town to town, healing the sick and casting out demons. (See Mark 6:7-13) They were tired. We come to verse thirty one; the usual crows that followed Jesus everywhere were pressing in, hoping to see and hear something. Jesus must have caught a look in the eyes of His disciples, sensed a weariness of heart and soul, because He suddenly said to them in the midst of it all: *"Come, let's take a break and find a secluded place where you can rest a while."* Mark 6:31 (TPT)

* * *

It wasn't as if Jesus wasn't tired as well, but He was thinking only of the disciples here - He didn't say, where *we* can rest, but where *you* can rest. It doesn't look as though they had much of a rest. They got into a boat to go across to the opposite shore, but the crowd guessed where they were headed to and were waiting for them in the other side!

Now, to be truthful, if I had been one of the disciples I probably would have been quite irritated. *Seriously, can we not have just an hour or two to rest?* But as the disciples and Jesus got out of the boat to face this multitude, Jesus looked at this sea of people and was <u>moved with compassion</u>: *"By the time Jesus came ashore, a massive crowd was waiting. At the sight of them, his heart was filled with compassion, because they seemed like wandering sheep who had no shepherd."* Mark 6:34 (TPT)

He saw as the Good Shepherd

It seems to me that the disciples often saw the crowds as *work;* as a constant demand, especially on this occasion, when their well-earned rest had been cut short. But not Jesus! His heart was moved with compassion when He looked at them. Every face in the crowd reflected a need, a hunger, or a hurt. Jesus was completely others-centred. He cared about the needs of others over His own needs. Where the disciples wanted to send people away (Mark 6:36), Jesus *was moved with compassion for them.* When the disciples just saw a crowd of people, Jesus saw sheep without a shepherd.

It moved Jesus' heart that these people were shepherd-less. Sheep can't defend themselves against predators, and when their food and water supplies run out they don't know how to find what they need; they wander about, lost and afraid. Yes, they were demanding, but their pressing demands were prompted by their great need. Rather than being irritated by their demands,

Jesus took care of them by feeding them. First, He took care of their most pressing need by feeding them spiritually: *"So he taught them many things."* Mark 6:34b (TPT)

He encouraged His disciples to see

Jesus taught the people <u>for a long time</u>. By now everyone was hungry and tired, but it seems nobody wanted to leave. Again, the disciples just didn't seem to be seeing things the way Jesus did. They told Jesus: *"You should send the crowds away so they can go into the surrounding villages and buy food for themselves."* Mark 6:36 (TPT)

There's a lesson we can learn from this: Jesus and His disciples saw exactly the same multitude of hungry people. The difference was in the *way* they saw. The disciples saw, and thought that the solution was to get rid of the need by getting rid of the needy. But Jesus saw a different solution and wanted the disciples to see it too. '*<u>You</u> give them something to eat'*

The disciples were really puzzled at times by the things Jesus said, and this was definitely one of those occasions! *"Are you sure?" They replied. "You really want us to go buy them supper? It would cost a small fortune to feed all these thousands of hungry people."* Mark 6:37 (TPT)

Jesus response was to encourage them, again, to *see*: *"How many loaves of bread do you have?" he asked. "Go and see." After they had looked around, they came back and said, "Five—plus a couple of fish."* Mark 6:38 (TPT)

After they had looked….

After they had looked around, they came back and said, "Five—plus a couple of fish." Mark 6:38 (TPT)

Now the disciples really looked, and saw. They were starting to 'get it.' The fact that they came back to Jesus with their find of just five loaves and two fish, with the dawning realisation that they were going to have to feed thousands of people with this tiny portion, shows that they were starting to see the way Jesus saw.

Jesus had met the needs of this crowd *spiritually* by teaching them, *physically* by multiplying that small portion of food, and then, amazingly, Jesus didn't rush off, too important to mix with the 'riff-raff.' Instead, Jesus sat and shared in a meal with them all, enjoying their company and meeting an *emotional* need as well. That's the way of our Jesus. Never rushed, never hurried, He invites us to come and sit with Him and enjoy His company, as He enjoys ours. Jesus loves people. He sees people. May we see the world around us with His eyes today, and may we hear and act on those words that Jesus spoke to His disciples: *"you give them something to eat"*.

Sunday - Servanthood

"Beloved ones, God has called us to live a life of freedom in the Holy Spirit. But don't view this wonderful freedom as an opportunity to set up a base of operations in the natural realm. Freedom means that we become so completely free of self-indulgence that we become servants of one another, expressing love in all we do." Galatians 5:13 (TPT)

Jesus knows what it means to serve with humility. He came to earth in the humblest of ways, a helpless little baby, born in a dirty animal shed. No five-star hotel for the King of Heaven. Throughout His life He served, and gave of Himself until He was physically spent. He humbled Himself to wash the feet of His disciples; one would wonder why why they did not fall over each other to wash Jesus' feet!

Jesus said these words to anyone hoping to be a leader: *"Whoever wants to be a leader among you must be your servant, and whoever wants to be first among you must be the slave of everyone else. For even the Son of Man came not to be served but to serve others and to give his life as a ransom for many."* Mark 10:43-45 (NLT)

Is this my attitude? Is it yours? How many of us are happy to serve others wherever or however God asks us to, with real humility, even if we think these things are beneath us? Paul, led by the Holy Spirit, wrote these words: *"Be devoted to tenderly loving your fellow believers as members of one family. Try to outdo yourselves in respect and honor of one another. Be enthusiastic to serve the Lord, keeping your passion toward him boiling hot! Radiate with the glow of the Holy Spirit and let him fill you with excitement as you serve him."* Romans 12:10-11 (TPT)

A lack of humility - an example

A man named Korah decided that the role he'd been given to serve God in the tabernacle wasn't enough. In his own opinion he was qualified to do much greater things. This grew into arrogance, and Korah conspired with three other men, Dathan, Abiram, and On. Together these men led a rebellion against God's chosen servant-leaders, Moses and Aaron.

Here's what they said: *"The whole community of Israel has been set apart by the Lord, and he is with all of us. What right do you have to act as though you are greater than the rest of the Lord's people?"* Numbers 16:3 (NLT)

Humility - an example

"When Moses heard what they were saying, he fell face down on the ground." Numbers 16:4 (NLT) Moses' response was to fall on his face. Moses didn't react in anger; he didn't contest his 'rights.' The thing is, Moses knew something Korah did not and it was this:

Moses hadn't *asked* to be leader of the nation. He wasn't where he was because he had clawed his way to the top, or climbed any corporate ladder. In fact he hadn't wanted to do it at all. Moses knew he could never do it in his own strength, he relied on God. Moses was only the leader he was because <u>God</u> had asked him to serve in this way.

This oversight of humility on the part of Korah and his sidekicks was to be their downfall. As Korah observed Moses serving God and leading the people in the wilderness, Korah began to believe he could do a better job. After all, were they not not all holy; set apart by the Lord? Why should Moses get all the glory? Korah was fed up being the background guy, he wanted to be the one out front with the staff doing the miracles.

When we continue reading Korah's story through to the next chapter, we find that the lack of humility in these men did not escape the notice of God, and they paid a price for thinking their privileged place of service was beneath them. God *often* chooses the most unlikely people to do great things for the Kingdom. There are certain criteria that God has laid out in His Word; none of these involve 'qualifications' as we would see them, and *all* of them involve humility towards others and surrender to God.

* Be prepared to be faithful in little things, for as long as God requires that of you: *"If you are faithful in little things, you will be faithful in large ones. But if you are dishonest in little things, you won't be honest with greater responsibilities."* Luke 16:10 (NLT)

* Remember who chose you and why you're where you are now: "Remember, dear brothers and sisters, that few of you were wise in the world's eyes or powerful or wealthy when God called you. Instead, God chose things the world considers foolish in order to shame those who think they are wise. And he chose things that are powerless to shame those who are powerful." 1 Corinthians 1:26-27 (NLT)

Our plans are pointless unless God is with us in them. Moses is such a great example for us in this, when he says to God: "If you don't personally go with us, don't make us leave this place. How will anyone know that you look favorably on me—on me and on your people—if you don't go with us? For your presence among us sets your people and me apart from all other people on the earth." Exodus 33:15-16 (NLT)

A Shepherd and His Sheep

Monday - My Shepherd

"The Lord is my shepherd" Psalm 23:1 (NLT)

He is MY Shepherd

There are many descriptions and metaphors of God in the Bible, including King, Deliverer, Rock, Fortress, Shield and Strong Tower to name a few. However the depiction in Psalm 23 of God as Shepherd is the most most special and personal of all.

A shepherd lives among his sheep. He knows his sheep and takes cares of them. From the sheep's perspective, the shepherd is everything. They need him. A sheep is an object of property; its owner sets great store by it, and often sheep are bought at great price.

David chooses the word *my*. 'The Lord is *my* Shepherd' not *a* shepherd, or even *the* Shepherd. Actually it would have been acceptable had David written "the Lord is *our* shepherd," since a shepherd keeps flocks, rather than single sheep. But then that would not have conveyed the wonderful and wondrous truth revealed in that one small word, *my*; it's in the choice of this word that David reveals the deeply intimate and personal nature of his relationship with his Shepherd. David says profoundly, through this statement; *"I belong to the Lord; I am His"*.

There's humility in David's words. Even as a king and fierce, mighty warrior, David keenly felt his *need* of a shepherd. A person who was self-sufficient wouldn't really connect with the heart of this Psalm. But the one who acutely feels and acknowledges their need of a shepherd; the *'poor in spirit,'* as described by Jesus in Matthew 5:2; those are the people who find deep comfort in this truth that God is a shepherd to them in a very personal way.

David understood this concept of God as Shepherd in a unique way, having been a shepherd himself. Now older, having known the Lord's tender care and experienced His protection and deliverance, all his days, I'm sure David remembered his own early life as a shepherd; how he himself took such tender care of the sheep. I wonder did he remember the times when he, David, had fought off a bear and a lion with his bare hands in order to protect the flock, as he once described to Saul: *"When a lion or a bear came and carried off a sheep from the flock, I went after it, struck it and rescued the sheep from its mouth. When it turned on me, I seized it by its hair, struck it and killed it."* 1 Samuel 17:34-35 (NIVUK)

God calls Himself our Shepherd

There are many other scriptures in which God is depicted as the Shepherd, including Genesis 49:24, and Psalm 80:1. In Isaiah 40:11, the tenderness of the Lord our Shepherd is so beautifully described; the way He provides care, protection and gives special attention to the more vulnerable in the flock: *"He tends his flock like a shepherd: he gathers the lambs in his arms and carries them close to his heart; he gently leads those that have young."* (NIVUK) Again, this speaks of intimacy: "[He] carries them close to his heart".

Jesus said of Himself: *"I am the good shepherd. The good shepherd lays down his life for the sheep."* John 10:11 NIVUK. He said: *"I know my sheep and my sheep know me –"* John 10:14

(NIVUK) Jesus is described as "*that great Shepherd of the sheep*, in Hebrews 13:20. 1 Peter 2:25 calls Jesus *the Shepherd and Overseer of your souls* and 1 Peter 5:4 *the Chief Shepherd.*

How incredible that the King of kings would call Himself our Shepherd. In Biblical times in Near Eastern culture, the occupation of shepherd was considered very lowly work. If a family needed a shepherd, it was always the youngest son, as in the case of David. And yet the Lord of all creation stooped to be our Shepherd and take tender care of us.

Tuesday - I Lack Nothing

"The LORD is my shepherd, I lack nothing."
Psalm 23:1 (NIVUK)

We could read this as, "because the Lord is my Shepherd, I lack nothing". My Shepherd is my all sufficiency; everything I need and will ever need is found in Him. Did David experience times of material lack? Of course he did. But he knew that even in those times, God would give him what he *needed*, which was the *Shepherd Himself*. David was secure in the knowledge that He knew God as his tender Shepherd, and that he, David, was known and beloved of God.

Faithful Provider

The most repetitive command in the Bible is "*Do not fear,*" along with its corollaries, *don't worry, don't be dismayed,* and *be anxious for nothing*. It gives the definite impression that the Lord wants us to catch hold of something important, doesn't it?: '*don't be afraid. I am your Shepherd and will take care of you.*'

Another repetitive command, throughout the Bible is "*Trust in the Lord.*" We have a Shepherd in whom we can place all our trust, because He promises to take care of us and provide all our needs. Either we believe this, or we don't, it's as simple as that.

When David wrote, "*The Lord is my shepherd, I lack nothing,*"

he was declaring that the Lord had provided, and would continue to provide for him. Paul reiterates this in Philippians 4:19 *"And my God will meet all your needs according to the riches of his glory in Christ Jesus."* Matthew 6:25-26 (NIVUK)
And Jesus said: *"Therefore I tell you, do not worry about your life, what you will eat or drink; or about your body, what you will wear. Is not life more than food, and the body more than clothes? Look at the birds of the air; they do not sow or reap or store away in barns, and yet your heavenly Father feeds them. Are you not much more valuable than they?"* (NIVUK)

The struggle for many Christians is not that God may not provide, we know He does. Many struggle to make this personal. Will He take care of <u>me</u>? God *is* our provider; this is fact. One of His names is *Jehovah Jireh* (The Lord Will Provide) This truth needs to move from a head-knowledge to a heart-knowledge.

A person with a head knowledge of God's provision, when suddenly confronted with the fear that God won't provide for *their* particular need, reacts with unbelief in the 'theories' they held dear, and begins scrabbling about in panic, trying to meet their own needs.

A person with heart knowledge on the other hand, when confronted with that same fear, responds in *faith,* based on who they know God to be!
He is our Faithful provider. We lack nothing. If we do nothing else today, let's move this knowledge from our heads to our hearts!

Wednesday - He Makes Me Lie Down in Green Pastures, He Leads Me Beside Still Waters

"He makes me lie down in green pastures, he leads me beside quiet waters," Psalm 23:2 (NIVUK)

He makes me lie down

"He makes me lie down in green pastures." The language of this is in the *causative*: Our Shepherd-King sovereignly guides us to this place of abundant provision and restoration.

In the original language, the concept is *'He causes me to lie down and lean against Him.'* David, having been a shepherd himself, knew and understood the concept of a shepherd who takes care of sheep with his heart; not just out of duty, taking care, not only of their basic needs, but tenderly caring for all their needs.

Sheep do not lie down easily. They won't lie down if they are afraid. Sheep are sensitive to one another and quickly pick up on fears or conflicts within the flock. These spread like contagion and cause the flock to huddle restlessly in a corner of their field. They also will not lie down if they are tormented by parasites and flies, that irritate their eyes and ears. And lastly, sheep will not lie down if they are hungry. A shepherd with an understanding of His flock knows these things. He meets all these needs, ensuring that the conditions are right, so that the sheep will lie down.

* * *

This is a beautiful picture of the Lord, our Shepherd. He knows His sheep, and sees when each one needs to rest. He causes you, His weary sheep to lie down and to lean into Him. His 'everlasting arm' around you *quiets* your soul as He whispers your name, speaking tender words of encouragement, hope and strength, to restore your soul. He holds you firmly and gently until your fears are quieted, your strength renewed; until you are once again resting in His love. See alsoIsaiah 40:11 (NIVUK): *"He tends his flock like a shepherd: he gathers the lambs in his arms and carries them close to his heart; he gently leads those that have young."*

In green pastures

I often see photos and paintings depicting this verse, with the scripture as a caption, and the green pastures are usually lush, rolling green hills of The United Kingdom or Ireland. Nice as this is, we can lose perspective of just what this scripture means: *'He makes me lie down in green pastures'.*
Lush, rolling green hills doesn't exactly describe the semi-arid landscape of ancient Palestine! Grazing land wasn't what you would call abundant, and 'green pastures' as we might imagine them, even less so. Shepherds had to keeping their flocks always on the move, constantly seeking out places with enough good grass to graze on. It is with this arid, dry, hot backdrop in mind that David writes of the *abundant green pastures* provided by his Shepherd.

He leads me beside still waters

He leads me beside still waters - literally: *'waters of rest,'* in the original language. The provision of water is essential for all life, especially for sheep in a dry and challenging landscape. Our Shepherd leads us beside places of *quiet* waters, not rushing waters; the perfect place to drink and be refreshed and for the tender Shepherd to wash the sheep, and clean any wounds they have sustained on their arduous journey.

This same word for *rest*, from the phrase 'waters of rest,' is found in several other places in scripture, where God promises rest to His people, and that He Himself will be our resting place. For us, rest is not a literal, physical place, but a person - *The* Person, the King of Kings Jesus Christ, who humbled Himself to become our Great Shepherd, and who said "*come to me and I will give you rest*" Matthew 11:28 (NIVUK)

For more references to God's rest see: Deuteronomy 12:9; 1 Kings 8:56; Isaiah 11:10

Thursday - He Restores My Soul and Leads Me in Paths of Righteousness

"He restores my soul; He leads me in the paths of righteousness For His name's sake." Psalms 23:3 (NKJV)

He restores my soul

I love this imagery of restoration and refreshing at the hand of, and in the presence, of our Shepherd. The tender care of the Shepherd that David wrote about in the previous verse has had its intended effect; David's soul has been restored and refreshed by the *green pastures* and *still waters* his Shepherd has brought him to.

To *'restore' can also* depict the rescue of a lost sheep; one that has strayed and been brought back. (Matthew 18:12-14) Jesus is the one who leaves the ninety-nine to go after the one lost sheep, and bring that lost one back to the fold.

And another way He *restores* is when when we come to Him in repentance and He restores us from sin.

He leads me in paths of righteousness

Yesterday we looked at how the Shepherd leads the sheep to where the green pastures and still waters are. We don't need to know, or concern ourselves with where the next green pasture is going to be, we only need to keep our eyes fixed firmly on our Shepherd who goes ahead of us, leading the way. We follow where He leads, *trusting* Him to lead. A good shepherd would guide the sheep along 'right paths'; secure, paths, because the shepherd had the sheep's best interests at heart. David uses this imagery to illustrate beautifully how God, Our Shepherd, leads us on 'right' paths - *paths of righteousness* - or, 'the way of righteousness.' Notice that the word is plural: *paths*, not path, and that He leads us, not He drives, or forces us to walk on these paths. Our Shepherd leads both by example and by love.

The paths God leads us on are narrow but straight. His paths of righteousness will *always* lead to places that meet all our needs. By contrast, the paths that lead to destruction are wide and are very easy to wander onto when we take our eyes off our Shepherd who is walking before us.

Some other scriptures that speak of God leading us on His paths are:"I have taught you in the way of wisdom; I have led you in right paths. When you walk, your steps will not be hindered, And when you run, you will not stumble." Proverbs 4:11 (NKJV)
"You will show me the path of life; In Your presence is fullness of joy; At Your right hand are pleasures forevermore." Psalms 16:11 (NKJV)
"Show me Your ways, O LORD; Teach me Your paths." Psalms 25:4 (NKJV)

Also see: Psalm 119:35; Jeremiah 6:16; 18:15; Acts:2:28

For His Name's sake

Why does the Lord lead us in paths of righteousness for His name's sake? 'For His name's sake' simply means for the reputation of God's name, or 'to bring glory to His name.'

* * *

1 Samuel 12:22 (NKJV) says: *"For the Lord will not forsake His people, for His great name's sake, because it has pleased the Lord to make you His people."*

It was God who made a perfect way for us to become His people. The *way* that God made for us, was Jesus His Son, who is 'The *way*, the truth and the life'. The Apostle John wrote *"your sins are forgiven you for His name's sake."* I John 2:12b (NKJV) All the 'credit', all the glory, belongs to God!; our salvation is only due to His mercy, His loving kindness and His grace. It pleased God to make us His own. He delights in us and takes great pleasure in leading us on paths of righteousness.

Friday - Through The Valley With My Shepherd

"Even though I walk through the darkest valley, I will fear no evil, for you are with me; your rod and your staff, they comfort me." Psalms 23:4 (NIVUK)

The Valley

We can't plan in advance for a valley; we can't pencil one into our diary for when it's convenient, and they usually seem to come at what we feel is the worst possible time, don't they? Jesus warned us to expect *many trials* in this world, and he also told us to 'take heart' because He has overcome the world. (John 16:33)

How many of us really heed the '*take heart*' bit of Jesus' instruction when we're in a valley? I've never in all my life heard a person say, "I'm rejoicing in this hard time I'm going through; God's teaching me so much!" And yet all of us, once we've come through that valley, can look back and take heart when we see all the ways in which God has walked with us every step of the way, working everything together for our good. Why do we find it so difficult to do this <u>in</u> the valley? Perhaps it would help to remind ourselves of these three things:

1. A valley isn't a dead end

The Valley is not a dead end. David speaks of 'The Valley of The Shadow of Death' and it sounds so deep and dark, doesn't it?

When you're in a place like this it can feel as though you just might never make it out again. When you're down at the deepest part of the Valley, where the rays of the sun hardly reach, it feels like a deep pit. But look at aerial views of any valley - they are not dead-ends. There's a way in and a way out. It is a valley of *the shadow* of death; not death itself.

In verses two and three David has just written about the leading of His Shepherd; "He *leads* me beside still waters." "He *leads* me in paths of righteousness". He 'leads me' speaks of walking somewhere <u>with</u> God, doesn't it? Now David's tone and style seems to change - he writes "even though I *walk* through the valley of the shadow of death," not "even thought he *leads* me through the valley..." But David doesn't envision himself walking there alone, he is acutely aware of the presence of his Shepherd, and he says *"I will fear no evil for you are with me"*

Another important thing to note is that David writes about walking <u>through</u> the valley. The valley wasn't his destination or dwelling place. He was not planning on hanging about in there for a bit of a picnic. He wasn't thinking of setting up camp there and staying a while. He envisioned himself walking through the dark valley and out the other side.

Valleys in our Christian walk are only ever to be walked through. They're a place where we truly experience God walking beside us and know what it is to be comforted by His presence and see His miraculous power at work.

2. I will fear no evil.

Even in the valley of the shadow of death, a *fearful* place, under the care of his Shepherd, David could resolutely say 'I will fear no evil'.

Evil exists, fear exists, there's no arguing this, and while the presence of the Shepherd doesn't eliminate the <u>presence</u> of evil,

His presence banishes the *fear* of evil. '*For you are with me,*' David writes, again emphasising that it's the presence (and the knowledge of this presence on the part of the sheep) that banishes all fear in the valley.

Suddenly, this Psalm changes in tone, becoming more intimate as it shifts from the third person of verses 1-3 'He,' to the first person, 'You.' It's very significant to me, that this intimate tone, and sense of closeness comes at the mention of David's valley experience.

3. *Your rod and your staff, they comfort me*

There's a lot of debate about the *rod and staff.* Some believe them to be two separate instruments, and others insist they are one. Personally I feel all that really matters is that our Shepherd's rod and staff are a great comfort to us. The staff, it seems was for walking, for guiding the sheep, by applying gentle pressure to the thigh of a wayward sheep here, a nudge to the rear of another there, to keep the sheep on the right path, and for defending the sheep from predators.

It would seem that the rod was part of the staff - the crooked part at the end, to be exact. It was an instrument of rescue; used to pull a sheep out of danger when it was caught in thick brush or had perhaps fallen into water. Our Shepherd's rod is for us an instrument of God's ongoing rescue and a symbol of His great love.

You know those times when someone says something that hurts your feelings, and you feel offence rising up in you? You want to react; everything in you wants to give that person a piece of your mind. Then, suddenly you feel the familiar prodding of the Holy Spirit inside, His voice whispers '*no, don't say it.*' And so you hold your tongue. Instead of becoming wounded, and in turning wounding, you talk to God about it, quietly forgive and move on.

This is one of the many ways, every day, that our Shepherd guides and comforts us with His rod and staff.

Another use for the rod was a means of counting sheep for tithes. There's something beautifully significant and prophetic in this imagery for us as the sheep of God's pasture. *"Every tithe of the herd and flock – every tenth animal that passes under the shepherd's rod will be holy to the LORD."* Leviticus 27:32 (NIVUK)

When you and I passed under Jesus' shepherd's rod, He counted us as His own, holy and set apart for Himself!

Saturday - The Good Shepherd

"I am the good shepherd. The good shepherd sacrifices his life for the sheep." John 10:11 (NLT)

Jesus said tis so clearly there could be no mistaking what He meant. Only Jesus perfectly fulfils the ideal of shepherd-like care for the people of God as illustrated in the Old Testament.

He gives His life *for* the sheep

Sheep are not exactly the most 'beauteous' of animals, are they? They look white and fluffy from a distance, but when you get up close you soon see that they're dirty and smelly. The detritus of their daily lives gets caught in their wool, and they're hard work. A bit like us! A really conscientious shepherd may take personal risks for the safety of his sheep, but as for a shepherd who would willingly <u>die</u> for the sheep? I'd say one like that would be hard to find. *Jesus is that Shepherd.* He showed His great love for us by leaving the splendour of Heaven, becoming a man and laying down His own life in our place. All so that we could enter into relationship with God the Father. Jesus our good Shepherd rescued us His sheep.

He gives His life <u>to</u> the sheep

"A hired hand will run when he sees a wolf coming. He will abandon the sheep because they don't belong to him and he isn't their shepherd. And so the wolf attacks them and scatters the

flock. The hired hand runs away because he's working only for the money and doesn't really care about the sheep." John 10:12-13 (NLT)

Jesus laid down His life for us, but that wasn't the end of it. Now He lives in us, He's still our Shepherd and He literally gives His life *to* us - He's our very source of life. We have a lifelong, Shepherd-sheep relationship with our Good Shepherd. He will never abandon us to fend for ourselves, but continue to take tender care of you and me. In the preceding verse, Jesus said that He came in order that we might have *abundant life.* Abundant, doesn't mean *easy*, or always *comfortable* and cushy, but what it does mean is that our Shepherd will always fill us with His real life and vitality, the ability to endure, increased stamina, joy and supernatural peace in all circumstances.

This is who our Good Shepherd is and what He has done for us!

Sunday - The Distinguishing Marks Of His Sheep

"My sheep listen to my voice; I know them, and they follow me, and I give to them eternal life and they will never perish and no-one will steal them out of my hand.' John 10:26-27 (NIVUK)

Jesus was having a discussion with the religious leaders of His time, and spoke plainly to about their condition - they didn't believe because they were not His sheep. *Ouch!* That must have angered and hurt their religious pride. Jesus went on to say '*I know them'* Jesus knows His sheep. What are the distinguishing marks of a sheep belonging to Jesus? This scripture, short as it is, lists them:

Jesus' sheep listen to his voice

One of our neighbours has sheep. I watch sometimes as he walks to the field; he starts whistling in a special way before he even gets there, and the sheep instantly start moving towards the gate to wait for him.

Once, when my husband and I were out for a walk, I thought just for fun, that I would try to copy that same whistling tone and see if the sheep would respond. They responded alright, by running as far away from me as they could, right to the opposite end of the field!

The sheep didn't know my voice. They knew instantly that my whistle was a fake, even though it was quite a close imitation of their shepherd's. My neighbour's sheep are used to keeping company with their shepherd. They know and trust him because they know all his little shepherd ways. As deeply as they trust their shepherd, they instinctively *mistrust* the interloper and stranger.

If you are His sheep, then you can rest assured that, inherently, you *do* know His voice. My Bible doesn't tell me that Jesus said "some of my sheep know my voice," does yours? The more we become used to listening *for* and *to* the voice of the Shepherd, the better we will become at hearing him and knowing the difference between His voice and that of a counterfeit.

Jesus knows his sheep

Jesus doesn't only know *about* you, He knows you by name. He knows you intimately and personally, far better even than you know yourself. You are known by the One who has seen everything you have ever done and ever will do, and He still loves you with an everlasting love. (See Jeremiah 31:3)

Jesus' sheep follow him

You can only be *called* a follower of someone if you actually *follow* them. Jesus calls to his sheep, and they willingly leave everything to follow him, like Peter and Andrew who left their nets right there on the shore and went with Jesus to learn how to be fishers of men.

Jesus' sheep are Heaven-bound and His forever!

* "I speak to you an eternal truth: if you embrace my message and believe in the One who sent me, you will never face condemnation, for in me, you have already passed from the realm of death into the realm of eternal life!"John 5:24 (TPT)
* They will never <u>perish</u>: The word perish here means 'to be destroyed', or 'to be punished in hell'. The same word is used in Matthew 18:14: *"In the same way your Father in heaven is not*

willing that any of these little ones should perish." (NIVUK);
John 3:16: "*that whoever believes in him shall not perish but
have eternal life."* (NIVUK); 1 Corinthians 1:18: "*For the
message of the cross is foolishness to those who are <u>perishing</u>,
but to us who are being saved it is the power of God."* (NIVUK)

No follower of Jesus will ever be lost in that way. Once you are
part of His flock, it is for all eternity.

No one will steal Jesus' sheep out of His hand

The word 'no-one' refers to <u>any</u> power that might attempt it. This
could apply to 'spiritual forces' or to people, such as false
teachers. In other words, no person however persuasive or
eloquent in false, attractive sounding doctrine; no plot or scheme
of Satan, however cunning. We belong to Jesus, our lives are in
His hands, and no one can steal us away. Of course we can
choose to walk away, we are not prisoners. But we cannot be
snatched. In the NIVUK, which
I have used, the word is *steal,* some versions have *pluck.* In the
original language the word was closer to *steal* - meaning to 'rob;
to seize and bear away as a robber does his prey.'

Jesus holds us so securely that no enemy can surprise us as a
robber would do, or overcome us by force. We are safe and
secure in the hand of our Shepherd!
*"For I am convinced that neither death nor life, neither angels
nor demons, neither the present nor the future, nor any powers,
neither height nor depth, nor anything else in all creation, will be
able to separate us from the love of God that is in Christ Jesus
our Lord."* Romans 8:38-39 (NIVUK)

God is Writing Your Story

Monday - The Day Of Breakthrough

"The Lord was with Joseph, so he succeeded in everything he did as he served in the home of his Egyptian master." Genesis 39:2 (NLT)

Destined for greatness

What great honour had been bestowed on Joseph, to be made second in charge over all of Egypt. This man had started out as a virtual nobody. As the youngest son, it was his job to take care of his father's sheep. As much as Joseph was adored and favoured by his father, he was resented and ignored by his brothers. *But the Lord saw Joseph!* God had given Joseph a tiny glimpse, in prophetic dreams, of what lay ahead for him, personally, and for the nation.

It was many years before Joseph was to see the fulfilment of those boyhood dreams. Joseph's brothers, who were already jealous of him, were only further infuriated by Joseph's talk of future greatness. We know what happened next. After being sold into slavery by his brothers, Joseph spent many rollercoaster-years, working as a servant and then, betrayed yet again, ended up in prison. All the while Joseph was grieved by his father, who had been told he was dead. His brothers probably thought they would never have to see Joseph again.

This story is so familiar that it is easy for us to read it from 'end to beginning,' knowing everything turns out so fantastically for Joseph in the latter chapter of his life, after the gruelling middle part. Let's just have a look today at that middle part; where was God in it all, and how did Joseph respond to his circumstances?

Joseph remained faithful

What must it have been like for Joseph, working as a lowly slave in Egypt, far away from his home and the father who adored him? What emotions and thoughts did he wrestle with? Loneliness? Despair? Rejection? Self pity? How did he feel, languishing in an Egyptian prison? Did he think, at first, that surely everything would be all right soon? Surely God would step in and rescue him in a few days, and this whole silly misunderstanding would be resolved.

We don't know how Joseph felt, but we do know this: As the days turned into weeks, the weeks into months, and the months into years, and still he remained in prison, *Joseph remained faithful to the Lord.* He didn't become bitter, either at his circumstances, or towards God. Joseph didn't know how his story would end, he just had to live it from beginning to end, trusting in God's faithfulness. God had shown him in a dream that he was destined for great leadership. I think what enabled Joseph to hold on, through it all, was that he *believed God's promises,* and held onto those dreams, no matter what his current circumstances told him. Joseph also continued to use his God-given gift of interpreting dreams, and eventually that's what got him out of prison and into the palace.

The day of breakthrough

Suddenly, one day years later, Joseph was released from prison and given the second-highest office in the land. It happened in God's perfect timing. It would probably have been a day like any other. I'm sure Joseph had no idea, when he woke up that morning in prison, that this was the day his life was going to change forever!

You don't know what today will bring, but the Lord, who created this day does. Today may be your day of breakthrough. In the meantime, while you wait for your day of breakthrough, trust that the 'author and finisher' of your faith knows *exactly* how your story will end, and is working all things together for your good.

Notice that there's a 'thread' running through Joseph's story: *"The Lord was with Joseph, so he succeeded in everything he did as he served in the home of his Egyptian master."* Genesis 39:2 (NLT)
"The Lord was with Joseph in the prison and showed him his faithful love. And the Lord made Joseph a favourite with the prison warden". Genesis 39:21 (NLT)
Do you see it? The Lord was *with Joseph*. Joseph had aligned his heart with the heart of the Lord his God. God remained steadfastly devoted to Joseph throughout that time, blessing him and giving him favour. And Joseph was never alone because the Lord was with him.

Do you feel stuck in a place, position, or circumstance, without any hope of change or escape? Do you wonder if your breakthrough will ever come? In these times it is tempting to try to fast-forward to the last chapter by trying to 'make it happen' by ourselves. But every story has a beginning and middle before getting to the end. God is writing your story. There are lessons to be learned along the way; a deepening and strengthening of your faith, renewed intimacy with Him, that would not happen if you were to fast forward to the end. Throughout your story, the Lord is with you; He sees you; trust Him with your whole story. Like Joseph, stay the course, and watch God fulfil His promises. He is with you!

Tuesday - Hannah's Heartache and God's Faithfulness

Read 1 Samuel 1:1-18.

Hannah's heartache

The account of God's faithfulness to Hannah is one of my favourite go-to stories in the Bible when I need encouragement. Hannah was just an ordinary woman, probably not very different to you or me. Her big heartache in life was her inability to have a baby. She had a husband who obviously doted on her, but she deeply longed and prayed for a child. Some things that stand out to me in this beautiful God-story are the following:

The Lord had 'closed her womb'

"But to Hannah he gave a double portion because he loved her, and the Lord had closed her womb. Because the Lord had closed Hannah's womb, her rival kept provoking her in order to irritate her." 1 Samuel 1:5-6 (NIVUK)

God *allowed* Hannah to go through this time of 'barrenness.' We too will have times in life where we may feel barren. Other people's lives, careers, families and ministries may seem so fruitful in comparison to yours. But "God knows the plans he has for you, plans to prosper you and not to harm you - plans to give you a hope and a future," (Jeremiah 29:11) and as we saw yesterday in the story of Joseph, His timing is impeccable. God had great plans for Hannah which we will see further on.

Hannah chose to seek God (see 1 Samuel 1:9)

As a family they went to Shiloh every year, to visit the temple. It was Hannah's choice, that particular day, to get up from the table and go alone into the temple, seek God's presence and present her deepest longings to Him in private. Hannah decided to focus on God and His provision instead of dwelling on her circumstances that had gone on 'year after year'.

It's a common scenario, even in our own lives; you feel so low that you have to drag yourself to church, fight with yourself to sing that worship song that has been pushed down into the recesses of your heart. It feels like an effort to pray, and to talk to God like you used to, before discouragement set in. But often it is when we make the conscious decision to stop 'wallowing' in our misery and seek God's presence, that we find the greatest breakthroughs. When we seek God, we will always find Him. Hannah sought Him, and she *definitely* found Him!

She believed God

Eli the priest arrived, and found her there. If you have read the story you'll know that at first he thought she was drunk, because of the way she was crying and praying. Then, when that misunderstanding was cleared up, Eli said to her: *"Go in peace, and may the God of Israel grant you what you have asked of him."* 1 Samuel 1:17 (NIVUK)

I believe these words Eli spoke were a *prophetic* blessing, and certainly Hannah believed it, her heart responded and we can see an immediate change in her demeanour as she left: *"Oh, thank you, sir!" she exclaimed. Then she went back and began to eat again, and she was no longer sad."* 1 Samuel 1:18 (NIVUK)

The difference was _in_ Hannah

Outwardly, her circumstances appeared unchanged; she wasn't pregnant. Not yet. She still had to wait, trust and keep believing for that. But it was enough for Hannah to know that God was 'on the case'. She absolutely believed Him. Hannah had dried her tears and left that place with a new lightness in her step, and hope in her heart.

There had been a shift on the inside; in her distress and despair, Hannah had sought solace in the presence of God. God had spoken, prophetically, right into the heart of her situation and Hannah *believed* His promise. That she believed God was going to give her a child was enough to put a smile on Hannah's face and restore her appetite. The story doesn't end with Hannah having only that one promised child, Samuel. God blessed her with *five more* children. Our God is the God of abundance! Oh I love this story!

If God has made a promise to you, you can be sure that He will fulfil His promise. He is a covenant keeping God who never breaks His promises. His timing and His delivery is not always as we might expect, but that He has promised at all, is enough. If you feel a 'barrenness' in any part of your life, remember Hannah. Stay in God's presence; wait, believing, for His answer, however long that takes. He will keep His promise to you.

Wednesday - What's In Your Hand?

When Moses was using his very ordinary shepherds' staff every day, watching his father-in-law's sheep, I wonder did he ever imagine that one day, he would raise that same staff and the sea would part. Could he have pictured striking a rock with his staff and seeing water supernaturally pour out of the rock? Even in his wildest dreams I don't think Moses could have imagined what God had in store for him, because God's dreams are far greater than anything we could ever dream up.

Choose someone else Lord!

The scene is set in Exodus chapter three with the call of Moses and his response. It continues into chapter four as Moses finds excuse after excuse as to why he feels unable to do as the Lord has asked: 'I can't speak properly, people won't accept me, they won't believe you sent me, please choose somebody else Lord.'

Something to note is that God waited until He had Moses' full attention before He spoke to him: "*When the Lord saw Moses coming to take a closer look, God called to him from the middle of the bush, "Moses! Moses!" "Here I am!" Moses replied.*"Exodus 3:4 (NLT) There are times when God's Word doesn't touch our hearts in the way that it might, because we don't give it our full attention; we don't approach the Word of God with a heart-attitude of '*here I am Lord*'.

* * *

I think we could surmise that Moses felt pretty inadequate. However arguing with God is always a lose-lose situation. It isn't that God is waiting with a big stick to beat us with if we don't do as He asks; that's not who God is. But if we refuse to do as He asks we may miss out on the greatest adventure in our personal walk with God!

If God has asked you to do something, no matter how daunting it might seem, be assured that He chose you *on purpose, with purpose*. God knows you, better than anyone ever has or ever will, and whatever it is He has called you to will be the perfect fit for you.

Even after God demonstrated His power to Moses to show him He would be with him, we see in Exodus chapter four that Moses still begged God to "send someone else." So the Lord, in His loving kindness gave him Aaron - not *instead of* Moses, but to accompany him. It was <u>Moses</u> that God wanted for this great task of delivering the Israelites from slavery in Egypt.

What's in your hand?

When the Lord asked this question, Moses had in his hand the very ordinary tool of his daily occupation – a shepherds' staff. We can learn something from this. No matter how ordinary the things we have may seem in our eyes, we will never know their full potential, until we allow God to have full control of those things.

He doesn't force, or coerce us into surrender, but when we willingly offer ourselves to Him, He will do great things with whatever we have. Moses learned to use in confident faith what was in his hand, and his life changed, as did the course of world history. Moses' simple staff was nothing special in itself, it was just a wooden stick. But surrendered to God, this staff was used to:

- confront Pharaoh's court: Exodus 7:10
- turn the waters of Egypt into blood: Exodus 7:19-20
- bring a plagues of gnats and frogs: Exodus 8:5-6,17
- bring thunder and hail throughout the land: Exodus 9:23
- bring a plague of locusts across the land: Exodus 10:13
- cause the the Red Sea to divide and stand up like a wall
Exodus: 14:15-16,21
- cause the waters of the Red Sea to fall back over Pharaoh's
armies: Exodus 14:26-27
- bring water out of the rock at Horeb to supply their needs
Exodus: 17:5-6
- bring victory to his army: Exodus: 17:8-9

Moses' staff becomes the Lord's staff

Notice something important that we could easily miss. At first,
all the references to the staff say things like "God said to *Moses
and Aaron,*" *"God told Moses, tell Aaron to stretch out his
staff,*" and *"Aaron stretched out his staff."*
Then, from Exodus 9:23, there's a change. The Lord no longer
says 'tell Aaron', He instructs *Moses* to do it. And Moses does it!
No arguing, no self-deprecating statements, he just uses what's in
his hand. Moses suddenly finds his mojo!
*"So Moses lifted his staff toward the sky, and the Lord sent
thunder and hail, and lightning flashed toward the earth. The
Lord sent a tremendous hailstorm against all the land of Egypt."
Exodus 9:23 (NLT)*

We see this repeated in Exodus 10:13, Exodus 14:15-16,21,
Exodus 14:26-27, and Exodus 17:5-6. By the time we get to
Exodus 17:8-9 Moses is confidently and adeptly using what's in
his hand. His ordinary shepherds' staff, surrendered to God has
now become the staff of God! Moses issued this command to
Joshua: *"Choose some men to go out and fight the army of
Amalek for us. Tomorrow, I will stand at the top of the hill,
holding the <u>staff of God</u> in my hand."*

What's in your hand?

If God could use something as ordinary and humble as a shepherd's staff to perform such mighty supernatural works, what could He do with the ordinary things of *your* everyday life, completely surrendered to Him?

Thursday - The Day Of Small Beginnings

"Do not despise these small beginnings, for the Lord rejoices to see the work begin, to see the plumb line in Zerubbabel's hand." Zechariah 4:10 (NLT)

Most of us could say that at some point in our lives, we have "despised the day of small beginnings." *'Despise'* in this verse could also be interpreted as 'sneer at,' or 'mock.'
Take a look at a 'small beginning' in your own life; a hope, a calling, a God-given dream. If what you see is less than encouraging, read the above scripture again, slowly, let the words of the verse take root, and then look at your hopes and dreams again in the light of God's words. See *'small'* from God's perspective.

God is not restricted by time
"But you must not forget this one thing, dear friends: A day is like a thousand years to the Lord, and a thousand years is like a day." 2 Peter 3:8 (NLT)
It had been a very long 'day' of small beginnings for Zerubbabel, the work of the restoration of the temple had lain in a state of small beginnings for almost twenty years! But God is not restricted by time, as we are. The Lord is more concerned with our hearts along the journey than with getting a task done. He cares more about working *in* you than through you.

* * *

God did not <u>need</u> Zerubbabel to carry out his purposes, and neither does He need you and me; It's because of His great love for us that He *chooses* to partner with us in His great purposes. It's our hearts that God is really interested in.

Small

Small doesn't belittle, or diminish your calling, your dream or your future. *Small* can be a precious gift. Think of a seed; tiny as it is, it is packed with unseen potential. If you're feeling stuck at a place of small beginnings, view your *'small'* as a seed. You will begin to see that from the Lord's perspective *'small'* is not keeping you <u>from</u> your dreams, rather, it is the place where your dreams are kept!

Hidden deep within that *'smallness'* is wisdom, patience, endurance, and unlocked Heavenly potential. You cannot obtain these any other way except by nurturing the seed of small beginnings, however long it takes, deep in the soil of your heart, until the seed's 'due season.'

It is in this humble place of *small*, that, if we press into God rather turn from Him, we experience the nurture of the Holy Spirit, who draws us closer to the heart of God. "Small beginnings" is a precious place for which we need to be thankful. It's important, after we have left the place of small beginnings, to remember our small beginnings, as this keeps the 'big things' in perspective.

The small place births humility

'Small' is a place for God to develop humility in us. We couldn't really learn humility if all we've ever known are the 'big things'. Yesterday, we read about Moses, Israel's great and mighty leader. Moses had a very small beginning. He spent forty years tending Jethro's sheep; an obscure shepherd in the desert of Midian. Having been Prince of Egypt, Moses' had now come to a point his life so small and humble that he didn't even have a flock of sheep to call his own, the sheep belonged to his father-in-law. But that small place was a seed packed with potential - not only for Moses' future, but the future of Israel and ultimately world history!

Our logic would tell us that surely Moses would have had more influence if God had used him while he was still a prince. Why wait until Moses was an obscure 'nobody?' Moses needed to experience 'small,' and so it is with us. If we've only ever known *big*, we would continually crave and run after *big*. We would find it very difficult to be satisfied with *small*. A heart that runs after big things, without being willing to experience humility, can become puffed up and proud. Humility is a rare quality. It doesn't feel the need to hog the limelight or take the credit, but knows that true 'big' is found before the throne of God in worship, whether in a time of small beginnings or reaping the rewards of that time.

What's next Papa?

Just a thought, in closing, perhaps you are not, presently, in a place of small beginnings. Maybe you have seen your hopes and dreams birthed, beyond even your wildest expectations. Perhaps you have skimmed through today's reading, thankful that you are not in need of encouragement in this area of your life. What a wonderful and exciting place to be! However, remember that God is *always* at work. In *every* season, God has plans and purposes and He looks to partner with you and me to carry these out. Therefore just because one particular dream has come to fruition doesn't mean God has finished with you and you can now sit back in your easy chair. I love this verse in Romans in the Message Bible: *"This resurrection life you received from God is not a timid, grave-tending life. It's adventurously expectant, greeting God with a childlike **"What's next, Papa?"** God's spirit touches our spirits and confirms who we really are. We know who he is, and we know who we are: Father and children."*

Romans 8:15-16 (MSG)

Friday - When God Closes A Door

"Trust in the Lord with all your heart; do not depend on your own understanding. Seek his will in all you do, and he will show you which path to take." Proverbs 3:5-6 NLT

Have you ever felt as though God has been leading you a certain way, when the 'door' suddenly, inexplicably closes? I was reading in the book of Acts when this caught my attention: "Next Paul and Silas traveled through the area of Phrygia and Galatia, because the Holy Spirit had prevented them from preaching the word in the province of Asia at that time. Then coming to the borders of Mysia, they headed north for the province of Bithynia, but again the Spirit of Jesus did not allow them to go there." Acts 16:6-7 NLT
Just two little verses, but they say so much about listening to, and obeying, the prompting of the Holy Spirit.

Sometimes God closes a door
In the original language the word translated here as 'prevented' is *forbidden*. This is strong terminology. The Holy Spirit had forbidden them to speak the Word in the province of Asia and He then had prevented them from entering Bithynia. *"The Spirit of Jesus did not allow them to go there."* Acts 16:7 (NLT)

This could seem strange to a Christian who was not used to listening to the voice of God. After all, they were preaching the gospel! Did God not want the gospel preached in these places? Did Jesus not command His followers to, *"go into all the world and preach the good news?"*

Yes, Jesus did, and we can see later in 1 Peter chapter one that those regions did hear the gospel at some stage, but at that particular time, The Spirit of God had a reason He chose not to disclose, for preventing the Apostles from going there.

We don't ever learn the whys and wherefores surrounding this event. We could surmise and speculate about what might have happened, had they gone there; maybe they would have been killed, perhaps Satan had hatched a plan to have them captured and imprisoned, but in the end, the truth is that God had a reason for firmly closing both those doors. He sees the entire picture, where we see only a very small part. The important thing is that they *knew* the voice of the Holy Spirit and were *obedient* to His prompting and leading.

Trusting when we don't understand

When a door inexplicably closes, or things just don't seem to be going the way we think they should, often the natural instinct is to push against the closed door, begging God to open it. We feel the intensity of the disappointment, we don't understand; "Lord how could you do this?"

We might even start to believe it's a spiritual attack put across our path by Satan to discourage us. But how often do we stop to consider that the closed door before us may simply have been closed by the Lord?

A few years ago, when a team from our church was going on a mission trip, one of our team members mislaid his passport on the very morning we were due to fly out. He pulled his house and office apart, searching for it. We all prayed. However, in the end with heavy hearts we had to leave without him. Guess what? The passport was found just hours after our plane took off! By then, the Lord had settled our friend's heart with His peace and we all believed that for reasons only God knew, He had closed the door for that team member, for that time.

We've all had times like these in our lives, and we always will. The Holy Spirit leads and guides us through life, and we can either kick against His leading, or be sensitive to His voice, and like Paul and Silas, act quickly when we hear His instruction.

We don't need to know why. We don't have to understand. We just need to learn to trust and obey Him: "*My thoughts are nothing like your thoughts," says the Lord. "And my ways are far beyond anything you could imagine.*" Isaiah 55:8 (NLT) When we look to God He promises to direct our steps- every step of the way: "*There are many plans in a man's heart, Nevertheless the Lord's counsel—that will stan*d" Proverbs 19:21 (NKJV)
"*A man's heart plans his way, But the Lord directs his steps*" Proverbs 16:9 (NKJV)

Lord, thank you that you see all, and know all. Help me to be tuned to your voice today in everything you and I do together; to recognise your prompting and be quick to respond and obey.

Saturday - All Things

"And we know that for those who love God all things work together for good, for those who are called according to his purpose. Romans 8:28 (NLT)

All things

All. Things. Two small, short words, yet the two put together become an incredibly, all encompassing powerful phrase that says: *'No exceptions'*.

When life is going well, it's easy to quote Romans 8:28, filled with faith. Then the hard times arrive and the little thought creeps in, *'can God really work this for my good?'* Yes, He can, and He will. Either *'all things'* means exactly that, or it doesn't. I have yet to come across a translation of the Bible that says, 'some things.' Further down in this chapter, Paul asks the rhetorical question *'If God is for us, who can be against us?'* Romans 8:31 (NLT)

Who can be against us?

This question holds huge implications for you and me as God's children. It's a good question to to ask yourself in the midst of a difficult time. As you answer your own question from the truths written in the Word of God you will keep your heart grounded. You are not on your own - God is by your side! God doesn't leave us to struggle along, trying to figure things out on our own, He has given us His Spirit who comes alongside as our teacher, counsellor and guide, to remind us of everything Jesus taught us.

When you truly grasp that God really is FOR you, and that His love for you is unshakable, it changes your entire perspective and shifts your focus, no matter what you go through in life. King David understood this; we see it in verses such as this: *"The Lord is on my side; I will not fear. What can man do to me?"* Psalm 118:6 (NLT)

Repeated through this whole Psalm is the refrain *"His steadfast love endures forever."* David knew, and was secure in the knowledge of, God's steadfast love for him, and that *because* of God's love, he had nothing to fear.

To get back to Romans chapter eight, Paul goes on in the next verses to list some extremely trying situations that Christians might find themselves in - just because we are Christians we aren't spared from hard times. Keep in mind that Paul *personally* experienced most of the entire list in Romans 8:35-36.

But the good news, Paul goes on to tell us, is that absolutely nothing - no circumstance and no problem can separate you from God's incredible love for you. And because He loves you, He has made you, not 'just' a conqueror, but *"more* than a conqueror!" (Romans 8:37)

Another person in the Bible who experienced incredibly trying times is Job. Like Paul, Job also understood the concept of 'All Things': *"I know that you can do <u>all things</u>, and that no purpose of yours can be thwarted."* Job 42:2 (NLT)

God is in Control

God knows exactly what He is doing. He is Sovereign. He's in charge of absolutely everything, at all times, in every situation. In those times when we can't see clear answers to our questions we can always trust in God's unfailing love and faithfulness.

Paul wrote: "*Now we see things imperfectly, like puzzling reflections in a mirror, but then we will see everything with perfect clarity. All that I know now is partial and incomplete, but then I will know everything completely, just as God now knows me completely.*" 1 Corinthians 13:12 (NLT)

We only see the tiniest glimpse of the picture, but God sees everything in its entirety. And He knows you and me more intimately than anyone else ever could. Wherever you are in life today, God says to you, "I've got this."

Sunday - Faithful In The Little Things

"His master replied, "Well done, good and faithful servant! You have been faithful with a few things; I will put you in charge of many things. Come and share your master's happiness!"
Matthew 25:23 (NIVUK)

How do you measure great success? Is it promotion to the highest possible rung on the corporate ladder? Perhaps it means leading dozens of people to Christ on a monthly basis and running a discipleship programme in your church to assist all those new believers to grow in their faith? (Both great things to aspire to, by the way)

Do you observe the lives of others and wonder how they got to where they are? Most of us plod along through life without ever making the news headlines or receiving any great awards. Most seldom lead even one person to Christ a month, let alone a dozen, many people are passed over for promotion in the workplace, time and time again, and many stay at home mums are so frazzled that we are more likely to snap at our children than have a Bible study with them!

For many people, even Christians, success is gauged by fame, bank balance, the car they drive, the level they reach on the corporate ladder, or even the leadership position they hold in their church. For many church leaders, success is measured by head count; how many people attend their churches. But is this how the Bible measures success?

It's okay to spend your <u>entire life</u> being faithful in the little things

Jesus said that those who are faithful in the small things will be entrusted with much. Some people interpret this as meaning that, if we just plod along for a while, doing those things we believe are 'beneath us,' then at some stage God will swoop in and rescue us from those unglamorous tasks. No more boring desk job, you'll be the boss! No more polishing the church pulpit, you'll be behind it, preaching! No more picking up tiny bits of Lego, making beds, cooking, cleaning, sleep deprivation, your children will be perfected overnight!

Some people spend their entire lives being *hugely* faithful in the *smallest* of things. These people don't grumble about not being picked for 'top' ministry positions in church. They never push themselves forward to try to find a little bit of limelight. They just quietly get on with whatever God has called them to do, however humble or anonymous that may be.

Store up treasure in Heaven

Paul and Silas were faithful, yet they didn't ever have a 'mega church.' They were itinerant preachers, going wherever the Holy Spirit led them. They were imprisoned, beaten, and eventually killed. John the Baptist was faithful, yet he lived like a hermit in the wilderness, eating locusts and honey. He was eventually beheaded! Millions of faithful Christians have suffered persecution and martyrdom over the centuries.

I believe that when we get to Heaven we are in for a few surprises. Many of the people we deemed successful here on earth may find themselves far down on the awards list, while headlining the Heavenly awards banquet will be the quiet anonymous, in-the-background, faithful ones. Remember the anonymous 'serving women' in Exodus 38:8?

If you are faithfully walking in whatever God has called you to, big or small, the measure of your 'success' is in your own heart's attitude towards that calling. Allow the Holy Spirit to train you to walk in true faithfulness; to teach you how to *"store up treasure in Heaven,"* (Matthew 6:19-21) where it really counts!

God Is Faithful Through Trials

Monday - God's Perfect Timing

"Then the LORD replied: 'Write down the revelation and make it plain on tablets so that a herald may run with it. For the revelation awaits an appointed time; it speaks of the end and will not prove false. Though it linger, wait for it; it will certainly come and will not delay."
Habakkuk 2:2-3 (NIVUK)

There's an appointed time

"The revelation awaits an appointed time." Have you ever waited for a long time for God to answer a prayer, show you something, or fulfil a promise He had made to you? Did you wonder in the waiting whether it was ever going to happen? Perhaps you're in a period of waiting as you read this. May I encourage you by reminding you of something? It's this: God has established the perfect moment in time for the fulfilment of His promises.

It will not delay

"Though it linger, wait for it; it will certainly come and will not delay." This refers to the <u>certainty</u> of God's promise, rather than the immediacy of its fulfilment. The particular promise that God made to Habakkuk was for the benefit of others, which is why God said, "make it plain on tablets," or, *write it down.* It didn't actually come to fruition for almost eighty years (*'it'* being the fall of Babylon). That might seem like a lifetime to us, but from

the Lord's perspective it's the blink of an eye. God doesn't work on the same timeline as us, He isn't restricted by time limits, and is not tied to our earthly timetables.

Write it down

In verse two, God told Habakkuk to write the vision down. This was for future reference, so that all who would read it later would see that God had fulfilled His promise. It's a good idea to keep a prayer journal. When God promises something to you, or speaks to you regarding a situation, write it down! I love reading back through my 'scribblings' and seeing all the answers to prayer! If I didn't write these things down in the moment, I could forget.

Sometimes, in addition to writing down something God has spoken to me, I've shared it with one or two close friends, saying, *'I'm telling you this now, so that when it happens we can remember this day.'* I had a vivid dream through which I know, without a shadow of a doubt, that God promised me He is going to answer a particular prayer of mine regarding the salvation of a loved one. I wrote it down and shared it with a few close friends. I don't know when, but I know it *will* happen, because God said it. Every now and then when I start to feel discouraged because nothing seems to be happening in that 'department,' I get out my prayer journal and read through the dream again, to remind myself of what God said.

If it seems slow, wait for it.

When we pray for something and don't see results as quickly as we want them, it's easy to become discouraged. God said to Habakkuk "if it seems slow wait for it." Waiting doesn't always come easily, or naturally in human nature, does it? But in the waiting process, God shapes character, moulds us, strengthens our faith and teaches us to trust Him.

God's timing is always perfect. He orders everything with perfect synchronicity and symmetry. Nothing escapes our

Father's notice:
"Look at the birds. They don't plant or harvest or store food in barns, for your heavenly Father feeds them. <u>And aren't you far more valuable to him than they are?</u> Can all your worries add a single moment to your life? And why worry about your clothing? Look at the lilies of the field and how they grow. They don't work or make their clothing, yet Solomon in all his glory was not dressed as beautifully as they are. And if God cares so wonderfully for wildflowers that are here today and thrown into the fire tomorrow, <u>he will certainly care for you</u>. Why do you have so little faith?" Matthew 6:26-30 (NLT)

God *always* hears every prayer instantly. Before a word is on your lips, He hears it. And He always answers prayer. However, we need to trust that He is God and that His answer *will* come at the appointed time.

It (the promise) will not lie

If God has said it, He *will* do it: *"God is not human, that he should lie, not a human being, that he should change his mind. Does he speak and then not act? Does he promise and not fulfil?"* Numbers 23:19 (NIVUK)

If God has promised you something, you can be sure of this; He will never break His promise. He does not go back on His Word. Be encouraged today, trust God to fulfil His promise in His perfect time. And in the meantime, more importantly, while you wait: *"Wait for the LORD; be strong and take heart and wait for the LORD."* Psalms 27:14 (NIVUK)

Tuesday - Believing Is Seeing

"Faith shows the reality of what we hope for; it is the evidence of things we cannot see." Hebrews 11:1 (NLT)

I often hear the quote 'seeing is believing, ' or a derivative of it: *'I'll believe it when I see it'*. To say that we have to see something before we are prepared to believe it is a very cynical way of looking at life, and runs contrary to what the Word of God teaches. Seeing something first and then believing it is easy! It requires no faith, no trust in God. It's the lazy man's option. By contrast, Christians are called to live by the principle of: *'I'll see it when I believe it!'*

Faith is our spiritual 'sense'

We opened today's devotional with Hebrews 11:1; other translations of the Bible translate this as *"faith is the substance of things hoped for."* We could say that in the same way as we have physical senses, and our physical eyesight is the sense that gives us evidence of the material world, *faith* is the 'sense,' or *spiritual eyesight* that gives us evidence of the invisible, spiritual world.

The 'seeing is believing' approach

When flying a plane, a pilot uses the horizon as his primary reference point. With the horizon before him, the ground below, and open sky above, it's unlikely he would end up flying upside down or going off course. This visual referencing is known as

VFR - *Visual Flight Rules*. The principle of *'seeing is believing'* works similarly to VFR.

No airline or airforce would employ a pilot who insisted upon daylight flights only, in clear weather conditions, so that he or she could rely on VFR. That pilot would be 'grounded' very quickly and reassessed. Who would want to get into a plane with a pilot who had no confidence in his ability to see?
Some Christians will only work with VFR; they always have to see the line on the horizon; always know exactly what the next step is, before they are willing to step out. That's not faith!

The 'believing is seeing' approach

In stormy weather conditions, when a pilot often can't see more than a couple of feet around the outside of the cockpit, it isn't just as easy to navigate using his natural sense of sight. The pilot's eyes could easily deceive him in these circumstances; he might *think* he knows for certain which way is up, but he can't rely on what his senses tell him. In these conditions the pilot doesn't rely on VFR, but on IFR - *Instrument Flight Rules*. These are the plane's built in flight navigation instruments.
Pilots are trained to trust their plane's built in instruments in bad weather conditions, whatever their own eyes and ears may tell them. This, sounds to me a lot like *"Believing is Seeing!"* Every Christian has built in IFR.

Faith is a Gift - our Built in IFR

"For we live by believing and not by seeing". 2 Corinthians 5:7 (NLT)
Paul urges us here to live by faith, not by what we see (or *think* we see). It's not easy to ignore feedback from your senses when you are convinced you know which way is up, but our natural senses can't perceive the subtleties of Heavenly realms. God has placed a sort of spiritual IFR into us - a built in navigation system that can be trusted in any storm, bad weather or darkness.

It's called FAITH.

Faith is a gift, given to us by God. But so many Christians have left theirs lying, still in its "gift wrapping" because the recipient doesn't quite know what to do with it.

Our faith won't grow, expand and develop if we won't step out of our comfort zones and use this precious gift. Faith is an added 'sense,' one that kicks in when we become believers in Jesus, and enables us to *see* and experience the truths of God that our physical senses are not able to perceive. We can't navigate through this life on our own, but we don't have to. With our mighty, All-Powerful God leading us by His Spirit, we can move forward with absolute confidence and trust.

Faith is the willingness to take that next step, and then the next, even when we can't see (*especially* when we can't see). Faith is *knowing* that God is who He says He is, and that His promises never fail.

Wednesday - Shaped By Trials

The roads all around where we live, are winding, narrow, and surprisingly busy for country roads. One day recently, while driving home, I noticed something about some of the tall hedges and trees that grow along the sides of the roads. Many of these have grown into strange shapes, curving deeply inwards, away from the road and then out again near the top, as though they have been 'carved.' This growth pattern has been shaped by the constant flow of traffic.

Little dry twigs, and even whole branches can frequently be seen lying in the road, snapped off by a passing lorry that has got a bit too close to the hedgerows. These trees and hedges are under constant 'assault.' But they're incredibly resilient and have learned to grow through, and around these assaults and be shaped by them. The seasons come and go. The rain provides the water the trees need, the sun provides the light, and they just continue to grow where they are, difficult as it may be.

The Apostle Peter wrote: "Dear friends, don't be surprised at the fiery trials you are going through, as if something strange were happening to you." 1 Peter 4:12 (NLT)

Hard times produce Godly character
We are clearly told to expect trials, yet when they come, most of us are caught off guard, aren't we? In truth, who says, "oh

yippee, a hard time, let's celebrate!" But is that what the Bible, means by rejoicing in trials?

"Dear brothers and sisters, when troubles of any kind come your way, consider it an opportunity for great joy. For you know that when your faith is tested, your endurance has a chance to grow. So let it grow, for when your endurance is fully developed, you will be perfect and complete, needing nothing." James 1:2-4 (NLT)

Here it is again, in Romans: "We can rejoice, too, when we run into problems and trials, for we know that they help us develop endurance. And endurance develops strength of character, and character strengthens our confident hope of salvation." Romans 5:3-4 (NLT)

An opportunity for God to lovingly shape us

Our hard times are opportunities for God to work! That's where the rejoicing part comes in. Every hard time is an opportunity for the King of Kings to carefully, lovingly shape us. We can choose to yield to this shaping process or not.

Through this process, we can stand strong, because Jesus, our Great Overcomer, dwells in us, therefore we have everything we need in order to triumph in trial and come through the other side of it stronger. Jesus tells us: "*I have told you all this so that you may have peace in me. Here on earth you will have many trials and sorrows. But take heart, because I have overcome the world.*" John 16:33 (NLT)

Paul wrote: "*We are pressed on every side by troubles, but we are not crushed. We are perplexed, but not driven to despair. We are hunted down, but never abandoned by God. We get knocked down, but we are not destroyed.*" 2 Corinthians 4:8-10 (NLT)

How was Paul able to write this in the face of everything he went through? Because, as he wrote in the previous verse, "*We now have this light shining in our hearts, but we ourselves are like fragile clay jars containing this great treasure. This makes it clear that our great power is from God, not from ourselves."* 2 Corinthians 4:7 (NLT)

Like those trees, we can expect a constant 'flow of traffic.' We have a spiritual enemy who will look for every opportunity to destroy our faith, using his arsenal of discouragement, fear and doubt, offence, anger, temptation, and secret sin, hoping to bring us down. But we have the Spirit of God living in us! Our great power, as Paul said, is from God! And God has promised: *"no weapon forged against you will prevail,"* (Isaiah 54:17)

If you need any encouragement with regard to your position and standing as a child of God, then Romans chapter eight is a very good place to start. Towards the end of the chapter, after describing our adoption into Gods family; freedom from our former status as slaves, the trials we can expect as God's children, Paul then talks about the great triumph we can know: *"If God is for us, who can ever be against us?"* (Romans 8:31 NLT) He goes on to say that *nothing* can ever separate us from the love of God. And because of this, we are *more* than conquerors through Christ!

You may be facing tough times at the moment. Perhaps like those trees and hedgerows, you have a constant assault of 'traffic' coming at you. But those trees, rather than being destroyed, are shaped by the traffic.
It's true that on our own, we are as fragile as clay and are easily broken. But if you belong to Jesus then you are not easily broken! You have been given the supernatural ability in Christ to get back up again, no matter how many times you are knocked down (2 Corinthians 4:7). As a child of God, you are an overcomer! (1 John 5:4,5)
We are lovingly, tenderly shaped by God's grace with each hardship we face, and we overcome in Him, enabled by His

Spirit who lives in us.

Thursday To Whom Do We Lift Our Eyes?

"I look up to the mountains— does my help come from there? My help comes from the Lord, who made heaven and earth! He will not let you stumble; the one who watches over you will not slumber. Indeed, he who watches over Israel never slumbers or sleeps. The Lord himself watches over you! The Lord stands beside you as your protective shade. The sun will not harm you by day, nor the moon at night. The Lord keeps you from all harm and watches over your life. The Lord keeps watch over you as you come and go, both now and forever. Psalm 121:1-8 (NLT)

To Whom do I lift my eyes? (Verse 1)

I have sometimes heard people quote this scripture in a way that makes it sound as though our help comes from the hills. Perhaps this was because of the way some of the older translations of the Bible have worded it. I've even seen part of the verse written on wall plaques, or book markers saying something like *"I will lift my eyes to the hills"* and ending there! But the Psalmist goes on to say that it is to the *Lord* our God, who made those very hills, that he lifts his eyes, because it is from Him his help comes.

Why do I need to lift my eyes? (Verse 2)

"My help comes from the Lord." Do you believe this? Do you feel overwhelmed by your circumstances today? Do you wonder if the season you're in is ever going to change? There's something about the action of standing, closing your eyes, focusing your heart and mind on the King of kings, that brings about a shift on the inside. We know He isn't 'up there' somewhere in the sky, but right here, beside us, so we *metaphorically* lift our eyes above our circumstances and fix them on our Father God, *believing that He will help.*

Lifting my head and fixing my eyes on God, even in trying circumstances is a heart statement in action; a statement of faith put into motion. It takes an action on my part, and God will always respond: *"When they call on me, I will answer; I will be with them in trouble. I will rescue and honor them."* Psalms 91:15 (NLT)

Tomorrow, we will continue through this Psalm and look at the *Lord who keeps us* - and what that means.

Friday - The Lord Is My Keeper

"I look up to the mountains— does my help come from there? My help comes from the Lord, who made heaven and earth! He will not let you stumble; the one who watches over you will not slumber. Indeed, he who watches over Israel never slumbers or sleeps. The Lord himself watches over you! The Lord stands beside you as your protective shade. The sun will not harm you by day, nor the moon at night. The Lord <u>keeps</u> you from all harm and watches over your life. The Lord <u>keeps</u> watch over you as you come and go, <u>both now and forever</u>. Psalm 121:1-8 (NLT)

Yesterday we read about the importance of lifting our eyes above our circumstances and fixing our gaze on our King, from whom our help comes. David goes on to describe in this Psalm, some of the ways in which the Lord is our helper and our keeper.

He never sleeps (Verse 3-4)

"He the one who watches over you will not slumber. Indeed, he who watches over Israel never slumbers or sleeps. The Lord himself watches over you! " Psalms 121:3-5 (NLT)

When my oldest son Rory was a baby, he had croup. The first two nights, I was literally afraid for his life. I listened to our tiny baby son struggling for each breath and was afraid he wouldn't take his next. So I tried to sit up and watch him all night. Of course, being only human, I couldn't manage it. I drifted off a few times and woke up to the sound of Rory's rattling, ragged breathing with my heart pounding.

God, your loving Father, watches you constantly - not in a fearful way; God isn't a fretful, worrying parent, but He's a *loving* one. He knows every hair on your head, He knows every word you are about to speak, before even you do. He knows all your thoughts. (Even the not so savoury ones!) And he loves you beyond measure. Psalm 103:11 says that His unfailing love toward you is as high as the height of the heavens above the earth!

Not only does God never fall asleep 'on the job,' but while your body is sleeping, your heart can still be awake to God, and He can speak to you in dreams, instruct you, and fill you with peace: "God speaks again and again, though people do not recognise it. He speaks in dreams, in visions of the night, when deep sleep falls on people as they lie in their beds. He whispers in their ears and terrifies them with warnings. He makes them turn from doing wrong; he keeps them from pride. He protects them from the grave, from crossing over the river of death" Job 33:14-18 (NLT)

"I will bless the Lord who guides me; even at night my heart instructs me. I know the Lord is always with me. I will not be shaken, for he is right beside me. No wonder my heart is glad, and I rejoice. My body rests in safety." Psalm 16:7-9 (NLT)

He watches over you (verses 7- 8)

Verse eight says that He *"keeps watch over you."* Imagine if you could watch over your child every second of every day! You couldn't, it's humanly impossible. Even the most vigilant parent can be distracted momentarily by ordinary, everyday things – a text message, a conversation, stirring the dinner. And typically, it's usually in those few seconds of distraction that your child falls and grazes her knee. And you end up berating yourself for "not watching her properly." But God your Father never takes His eye off you, not even for a split second. He watches over you day and night, never deterred, never distracted in His purpose of caring for you.

He keeps you (verse 7-8)

"The sun will not harm you by day, nor the moon at night. The Lord keeps you from all harm and watches over your life. The Lord keeps watch over you as you come and go, both now and forever." Psalms 121:7-8 (NLT)

I love the use of this word *keep*, and the comparison in verse five that the Psalmist draws between the shade that the high mountains offer from the heat of the day to the shelter the Lord gives us. God is our shelter and shade from the 'heat' of life. Psalm 125:2 (NLT) says: *"Just as the mountains surround Jerusalem, so the Lord surrounds his people, both now and forever."* and Isaiah wrote of the Lord: *"You are a refuge from the storm and a shelter from the heat."* Isaiah 25:4 (NLT) Where else would we go when the storms come? Why would we want to turn to anyone else? In verse eight, David describes how the Lord keeps us in our daily lives – as we *"come and go."*

What it means to be 'kept' by God

In English, to *keep* something or someone, means:
• To retain possession of, or to take into one's charge.
• To provide all necessities for – to raise and feed and care for.
• To protect and preserve .
In the original Greek *keep* is *phroureo*, as used in 1 Peter 1:4-5, where Peter writes regarding our inheritance *kept* in heaven. It is a military term, meaning: to establish a military outpost; to guard, hem in, and protect with a garrison; to establish a fortress.

* * *

This same word is used in Psalm 121 to describe the way we are *kept* by The Lord of Hosts! You, His child, are guarded by Heaven's armies, a powerful, fully equipped spiritual army of innumerable horses, chariots, and soldiers in full battle array, completely informed of every enemy plan and device in advance. *No weapon formed against you will prosper! (Isaiah 54:17)* He keeps you - fiercely and jealously guards you as His precious inheritance; *the apple of his eye.* This is the God you can lift your eyes to, and rely upon to help you.

Saturday - Fear's Storm Silenced

"Later that night, the boat was in the middle of the lake, and he was alone on land. He saw the disciples straining at the oars, because the wind was against them. Shortly before dawn he went out to them, walking on the lake. He was about to pass by them," Mark 6:47-48 (NIVUK)

I love this story of Jesus calming a storm with just the sound of His voice. How often, when we face storms of life, we react just as the disciples did that day. How many storms has He calmed in your own heart, with His voice? Fear and panic get a grip on us and we work ourselves into a tizzy. The disciples were in such a state that even when they saw Jesus walking towards them on the water - *Jesus* the one they knew and conversed with every day, they were so panic stricken that they didn't even recognise Him!

Fear set in motion

Verse fifty says the disciples were terrified. The word used here is *tarássō* - the literal translation of this word is '*to set in motion what must remain still'* and the definition is: to *agitate* (as in moving a thing backwards and forwards), *to cause inward commotion, to disquiet, to make restless, to stir up, to render anxious or distressed.*

All of those so aptly describe what fear does in our hearts when we let it in!

* * *

The most prolific command in the Bible is "fear not," and derivatives of it. God has *commanded* us, repeatedly throughout history 'Don't be afraid. Trust me. I am your provider, your healer, your safe haven in the storms of life'. But still, we fear!

The storms of fear are often sudden

The disciples were anxious and fearful; terrified! They allowed this fear to be 'set in motion' and take hold of, and 'agitate' their hearts. Not long before this 'stormy sea episode,' the disciples were riding high on a wave of faith. Jesus had sent them out in two's to preach and minister.(Mark 6:12-13) Then, just back from that mission, they'd been witnesses - and participants in - the supernatural feeding of over five thousand people. You'd think, in the light of all this, they'd be *fired up!* How quickly we open the door to fear. And how quickly Jesus silences those same fearful storms, when we trust Him.

Jesus sees you in your storms

Most people focus on the calming of the storm, but there's another aspect to this story that caught my attention; have a look at verse forty seven: *"The wind was against the disciples and he could see that they were straining at the oars, trying to make headway. When it was almost morning, Jesus came to them, walking on the surface of the water,"* Mark 6:48 (TPT)

Jesus *saw* that the wind was against them. He *saw* their struggle. And his heart was moved for them. His heart was touched that they were struggling, and long before they even cried out for Him, Jesus was striding across the water towards them. That's who our God is. He is not a far-off God, indifferent to your struggles. He sees you and everything you are up against and is vigilant in His care for you. Don't ever, for one moment, believe that God doesn't see what you're facing, or care about your circumstances. He never takes his eyes off you! Here are just three of those hundreds of 'do not be afraid' verses to give you a 'booster shot' of faith today:

"The LORD himself goes before you and will be with you; he will never leave you nor forsake you. Do not be afraid; do not be discouraged." Deuteronomy 31:8 (NIVUK)

"Have I not commanded you? Be strong and courageous. Do not be afraid; do not be discouraged, for the LORD your God will be with you wherever you go."
Joshua 1:9 (NIVUK)

"Do not be afraid, little flock, for your Father has been pleased to give you the kingdom."
Luke 12:32 (NIVUK)

Sunday - The Press Of God

"But I am like an olive tree, thriving in the house of God. I will always trust in God's unfailing love." Psalms 52:8 (NLT)

Be like the olive tree!

No matter what the conditions: hot, dry, cold, wet or rocky, the evergreen olive tree will, I'm told, produce fruit. It is said that the plucky little olive tree is extremely difficult to destroy. Even when cut down or burned, new shoots will begin to emerge from its roots.

This verse in Psalm 52 reminds us that no matter what the conditions of life may be, we can remain as steadfast as the olive tree in the presence of God. When we *always trust in God's unfailing love* we remain evergreen, faithful and bearing fruit in both adverse and good circumstances. David, hunted, exiled, and persecuted though he was at the time of writing this Psalm, still had confidence in the Lord to declare about himself: '*I am like a green olive tree in the house of God.*'

Oil from tough places

"He let them ride over the highlands and feast on the crops of the fields. He nourished them with honey from the rock and olive oil from the stony ground." Deuteronomy 32:13 (NLT)

This describes the tenacious little olive tree that continues to thrive through all sorts of climates, even in the hard, stoney ground, and produces a needed a precious commodity from its fruit - *oil*. That oil was a vital part of ancient living; it was used for anointing, for healing, for cooking and for lighting lamps. And of course it is still an important part of modern life.

Sweet fruit and rich oil through a process

If you have ever picked an olive directly from a tree and eaten it, you'll know that in their natural state they're really not very nice. To make olives into the palatable fruit and oil we take for-granted, they have to go through a certain lengthy process.

Both the east and west wind.

The olive tree needs both the east and the west wind. The east wind is the hot, dry, harsh wind of the desert. It's the wind that blew over Job's house, taking down his house, and all his sons and daughters. It is a fiery wind that can cause green grass to wither in just one day with its blast. The west wind comes from the Mediterranean. It is moist, brings rain and new life. Spiritually, we need both the east and west wind of God to blow in our lives. The east wind to consume all the dross, the west wind to refresh and fill and continually bring new life.

They need to be to be made clean

The olives need to be properly washed, soaked, and in some instances salted. In the same way, we need to be soaked, continually in the Word of God, so that sweet fruit and oil can be produced in us: "He gave up his life for her to make her holy and clean, washed by the cleansing of God's word. He did this to present her to himself as a glorious church without a spot or wrinkle or any other blemish. Instead, she will be holy and without fault." Ephesians 5:25-27 (NLT)

They have to be pressed

The only way to extract oil - the very best and most valuable part of the olive - is by pressing.

The Mount of Olives is located just east of the Old City of Jerusalem and is where the Garden of Gethsemane is located. Garden of Gethsemane - *Gat Shemen* in Hebrew, means, literally, *the place of the olive press.* Jesus spent much of His time there when he was in Jerusalem with His disciples: *"Jesus went out <u>as usual</u> to the Mount of Olives, and his disciples followed him."* Luke 22:39 NIVUK

Jesus made it his habit to pray at the 'place of the olive press,' conversing with The Father. And it was there, before his crucifixion, that He prayed those words *'not my will, but yours be done.'* Jesus was used to being pressed. Not only that, He submitted to the pressing process.

Pressed on every side

Paul wrote: *"We are pressed on every side by troubles, but we are <u>not crushed.</u> We are perplexed, but not driven to despair. We are hunted down, but never abandoned by God. We get knocked down, but we are not destroyed."* 2 Corinthians 4:8-9 (NLT)

The olive has to be pressed in order to produce the oil. In the same way, we need at times to be 'pressed,' for it is through the pressing process of life that the beauty and fragrance of Jesus inside us is revealed. But we can be confident that although we might <u>feel</u> squeezed and pressed by life sometimes, Paul writes in 2 Corinthians 4:8,9 that we will not be crushed.

Those pressing times in life seem unbearable when we're going through them. But we are never abandoned by God. And, when like David, we decide to *'trust in God's unfailing love,* rather than having a melt-down at the first sign of pressure, then like the olive when it's pressed at just the right pressure, sweet smelling, pure oil will flow from our times of pressing, that will effect and touch the lives of those around us.

Shaped by Grace

Monday - Shaped By The Master Potter

"And yet, O Lord, you are our Father. We are the clay, and you are the potter. We all are formed by your hand." Isaiah 64:8 (NLT)

I have never heard of a lump of clay becoming something else all by itself; left to its own devices a lump of clay will remain just that: a lump of clay. Shapeless and purposeless until it is picked up and skilfully shaped by the hands of a potter or sculptor. This is a wonderful picture of what God does with us. He takes our aimless, empty, meaningless lump-of-clay lives, and lovingly shapes us for His glory.

Life often has a way of not turning out the way we thought or hoped it was going to; these are times that God uses to perfect us. It is our response to these "shaping times" that is important. The tendency in most of us is kick against what's happening. Some fight and rage against God that it's not fair. But these times are opportunities for us to shaped into beautiful vessels by the loving hands of our Father the Potter.

The Lord says to us through the prophet Isaiah: "What sorrow awaits those who argue with their Creator. Does a clay pot argue with its maker? Does the clay dispute with the one who shapes it, saying, 'Stop, you're doing it wrong!' Does the pot exclaim, 'How clumsy can you be?' How terrible it would be if a newborn baby said to its father, 'Why was I born?' or if it said to its mother, 'Why did you make me this way?' Isaiah 45:9-10 (NLT)

What sorrow.

This isn't a threat from our Father God, but a loving warning. Perhaps you are a parent yourself? If so then you'll know that a loving parent will offer a warning, when they see their child about to make decisions that they, the parents know will harm that child, and possibly shipwreck their lives. The Lord does the same. He knows that only in Him will we find a life of abundance, and everything we could possibly need. Yet we yearn for and run after other things; we have the audacity to argue with the One who sees the whole picture, who has numbered our days and knows exactly where we will be next week, next month, next year.

Re-worked

Remember in chapter three, 'The Exchange', we looked at Jeremiah's encounter with God at the potter's house? The Lord gave Jeremiah a beautiful 'living picture' through a clay pot becoming marred while the potter was working on it, and how potter had skilfully reworked the clay into something new. I'm reminded of what Paul wrote to the church at Rome *"And we know that God causes everything to work together for the good of those who love God and are called according to his purpose for them.* Romans 8:28 (NLT)

In the Potter's hands

Something else that stands out in this story in Jeremiah is that the piece of clay was actually <u>in</u> the Potter's hands, when it became "spoiled." It wasn't that it had fallen off the wheel. You might think, because of your present circumstances, that everything is ruined, it's all over. Perhaps it feels as though the Lord has let go of you. But I can assure you with absolute confidence that He has not, and He never will.

I remember from my own pottery dabbling days, years ago that sometimes a piece of clay just seems to become 'resistant' to being shaped. Don't be that piece of clay. Let your heart stay soft and workable. If you are in the Potter's hands, He knows exactly what He is doing. Rest in Him and trust Him to work all things together for you, to complete what He started, with perfect precision, skill and love.

Tuesday - The Centre of The Potter's Wheel

Present your bodies as a living sacrifice, holy and acceptable to God, which is your spiritual worship. Do not be conformed to this world, but be transformed by the renewal of your mind, that by testing you may discern what is the will of God, what is good and acceptable and perfect. Romans 12:1-2 (NLT)

Staying in the centre of the potter's wheel

Before a potter even begins to shape any vessel from a piece of clay, it's important that the clay is centred on the wheel. It cannot be off centre, even by a couple of millimetres, but must be gently pressed right into the very centre.

Isaiah wrote: *"you, Lord, are our Father. We are the clay, you are the potter;"* Isaiah 64:8 (NIVUK) Nothing *ever* happens at random in our lives. Every traffic jam, every person that irritates, each time we're tempted to be critical or jealous, whenever worry threatens to overwhelm is an opportunity for God to shape and refine us into His vessels of beauty. If we are willing to work *with* God, being mouldable, pliable, willing to change, staying right in the centre of His Potter's wheel, God develops and shapes character in us.

Our problem often is that we are not really willing to work with God; we don't see the things that could shape and mould our character as opportunity for Him to move, but as stumbling blocks and hurdles. We pray, begging God to remove the people from our lives that hurt or annoy us. We beg Him to change our circumstances, when really God is far more interested in changing <u>us</u>. We attempt to 'pray away' the very things that God in His loving kindness allows in our lives to hone and perfect us.

The Israelites, plodding their way through the wilderness toward the promised land, had great opportunity to grow in character. But in the end, a journey that should have taken a few weeks took forty years! The problem was that they just kept getting off the Potter's wheel. They complained; they were tired, they were fed up with the food, the food was far better in captivity. So, God had to take them around and around the same mountain range, again and again. Sadly, that generation never did learn their lesson.

Present yourself to God

In the end, this is what it 'boils down to:' Do I want to be a beautiful vessel in the hand of God or not?: *"In a wealthy home some utensils are made of gold and silver, and some are made of wood and clay. The expensive utensils are used for special occasions, and the cheap ones are for everyday use. If you keep yourself pure, you will be a special utensil for honorable use. Your life will be clean, and you will be ready for the Master to use you for every good work."* 2 Timothy 2:20-21 NLT

As you keep presenting yourself to God, allowing Him to refine you, you will become a vessel of gold for His highest purposes: *"being confident of this, that he who began a good work in you will carry it on to completion until the day of Christ Jesus."* Philippians 1:6 (NIVUK)

May we remain ever in the centre of The Potter's wheel, willingly moulded and shaped by Him, trusting Him, even when the pressure feels uncomfortable, knowing that His skilled hands know exactly where and when to apply the right pressure to shape us into beautiful vessels for His purpose. No one knows you better than the One who formed you.

Wednesday - Beauty From Brokenness

One of my little pleasures in life is finding beautiful stones and pieces of sea glass on the beach. I have a small collection of particularly lovely ones on a shelf in our house, collected over years from beaches in various countries across the globe.
Sea glass fascinates me. What we know as sea glass is really just pieces of glass vessels; discarded broken jars and bottles that have somehow ended up in the sea. It might seem like the end for those once useful or perhaps beautiful glass items, but in fact it is there that the journey to new purpose and beauty is just beginning!

In the water, as each piece of glass is relentlessly tossed and tumbled in the surf and sand, the rough edges are smoothed off. The end result is something beautiful, sought after by costume jewellers and highly prized by collectors. I read recently of a piece of rare, red glass, sold in its natural state (in other words not set in a piece of jewellery) for four hundred American Dollars! A person with a trained eye can tell the difference between a genuine piece of sea glass, honed over many years in the sea and an imitation made by machinery. The imitations are often just a bit too smooth, too shiny. Genuine sea glass, although smooth, shows its journey in its unique shape and the deep scars embedded, which remain even when highly polished, but add to the beauty, uniqueness and character of each one, telling a story of their journey.

* * *

Shaped by rough waters

I looked at a piece of sea glass in my hand one day and it occurred to me that it had taken *years of rough seas* to create this beautiful thing. If it had simply lain at the bottom of a calm and tranquil ocean it probably would have stayed sharp-edged, as well as ordinary.

When our lives feel rough, we can take great comfort and encouragement from this beautiful promise in Isaiah: "When you go through deep waters, I will be with you. When you go through rivers of difficulty, you will not drown". Isaiah 43:2 (NLT)

Notice that the word used here is 'when' not if, you go through deep waters. We can expect to go through trials in life. How else will we be honed and shaped? However it's in and through these times that God can demonstrate to us His faithfulness and we experience first-hand his 'ever present help'. (Psalm 46:1)

You will not be overwhelmed

God's promise to us is that we will not be overwhelmed by the waves. The deep water will not drown us. He will never abandon us to flounder on our own. Don't be afraid, if you find yourself in stormy seas or deep waters at this time in life. The previous verse, verse one is a reminder that you *belong* to God. He has not forgotten, abandoned or discarded you, He cares for you: "*the one who formed you says, "Do not be afraid, for I have ransomed you. I have called you by name; you are mine."* Isaiah 43:1 (NLT)

Some people reading this may feel you've 'blown it,' messed up, and missed what God had for you. Like that original glass vessel that the piece of sea glass came from, you cannot be too badly broken for God to reshape. While you still have breath in your lungs, it's never too late to submit and allow God to create beauty from your brokenness.

Thursday - Pruning

"I am the true grapevine, and my Father is the gardener. He cuts off every branch of mine that doesn't produce fruit, and he prunes the branches that do bear fruit so they will produce even more. John 15:1-2 (NLT)

We had a rose bush at our front door that had never really thrived. It didn't help that I'm not a very good gardener. The bush had become straggly and hadn't produced a single rose for years. I knew the answer was to prune it, but because I wasn't sure how to do this, I just left it. And so it went on, year after year, growing taller, and wilder looking but never producing the beautiful fragrant yellow roses it had on it when we first bought it.

A few months ago finally, with the help of a gardening book, I pruned the bush. Actually against all my instincts, nearly crying, I cut it right down to just a few inches from the soil, so that through the wintertime there were just a few leafless dry looking stalks. I was convinced I'd overdone it; killed it for sure! Recently, with a heavy heart, I told myself that as soon as the weather warmed up a bit, I'd admit defeat and dig up the 'dead' bush. One morning I went outside to check on my other plants and to my amazement I saw new branches on the rose bush, and not only that, three tiny rosebuds!

Bearing fruit

We glorify our Father when we bear fruit and the only way for this to happen is by pruning.

When you're going through that pruning process with God it's painful; no one actually enjoys it. But God, our Father, described by Jesus as the Gardener, is skilful. God knows exactly what He's doing and His touch is tender and loving.

If you are presently being pruned, you may feel as though you've been stripped right down to just stalks, but new growth will come in 'Spring.' I think about my scraggly rose bush before pruning. When we first got it, it was covered in lovely yellow roses. Then, because it was never pruned, many new non-producing shoots started to grow, from all sorts of funny angles. All of these branches were covered in leaves but most had no roses. Gradually this became the norm. The leaves on these 'fruitless' branches started to block the sunlight from getting to the existing roses. In addition to that, most of the nutrients that should have been going to the roses were going to these non producing branches, sapping the very life out of the producing branches, until those branches stopped producing flowers too. I think the bush just gave up. It didn't have the strength to produce roses because it was too busy trying to sustain all these useless green leaves - not at all what it was created to produce.

Our activities may seem good and well intentioned. They may even seem productive. We might *think* we see growth when all the while we are merely producing 'leaves;' the non-producing things we fill our lives with clutter up our lives, blocking light from the *Son*. They sap our spiritual strength and prevent us from getting the nutrients we need in order to grow and produce fruit.

We need to let God prune those non-productive parts of our lives; those useless leaves, the dry, non-producing branches. Will it hurt? Yes, it usually does. It's never very comfortable letting go of those things we want to hold onto. But that's where trust in our Father the Gardener, the Vinedresser - comes into play. It takes courage, humility and strength. But He even gives us all of these things, to enable us to endure.

Friday - A Sweet Fragrance

"But thank God! He has made us his captives and continues to lead us along in Christ's triumphal procession. Now he uses us to spread the knowledge of Christ everywhere, like a sweet perfume." 2 Corinthians 2:14 (NLT)

When I lived in South Africa many years ago, we had a jasmine creeper growing near the house. Every evening as the sun went down, our garden and house were filled with the beautiful, powerful scent of the tiny white jasmine flowers and I loved to leave the windows wide open to allow that scent in, despite the mosquitoes and creepy crawlies.

Recently, that jasmine creeper came to mind and closing my eyes, I could almost smell that sweet fragrance. I had been feeling the weight of some personal circumstances crowding in on me, a little bit like darkness beginning to fall in the evening. I had just been reading the above-mentioned passage in 2 Corinthians, and the Spirit of God brought to mind that jasmine creeper from years ago. I suddenly remembered something: The jasmine flower only releases its fragrance *as the darkness of evening starts to fall;* most other flowers close up their petals and 'hide their faces' in the dark.

At that moment I realised I had a choice. 'Close up,' hide my face, batten down the hatches and let the darkness overwhelm me, or like the jasmine, open up to God, right there in the darkness and let the fragrance of all that Jesus Christ is in me flood out.

Writing to the church in Corinth, the Apostle Paul says that because we belong to Jesus, God *"uses us to spread the knowledge of Christ everywhere, like a sweet perfume."* 2 Corinthians 2:14 (NLT)

How does God do this?

One of the ways in which God releases the fragrance of Jesus through us is when we worship in the midst of trials. It's easy to worship in the bright, sunny times, isn't it? Not just as easy when darkness seems to close in on us. But when we worship God in those 'dark' times, even when we just don't feel like it, in the midst of pain, or heartache, doubt and loss, for no other reason than that He is worthy; reminding our hearts of His great faithfulness and love towards us, His mercy, His grace, His goodness, and the strength only He can bring in these times... our drooping heads begin to lift again and like that jasmine in the falling darkness, we release a sweet smelling fragrance that is far-reaching. It affects and touches everyone nearby.

The beautiful aroma of the jasmine flower is unmistakable and everyone nearby is touched and affected by it. You just want to be near it! You want to pick bunches of it for your home; you're drawn to it. *So it is in the life of a true worshipper-in-hard-times.* The aroma of a worshipping Christian in the dark is unmistakable and very beautiful - people want to be around someone like that.

He's worthy

"You are worthy, O Lord our God, to receive glory and honor and power. For you created all things, and they exist because

you created what you pleased." Revelation 4:11 (NLT)
We worship Jesus because He is the only one worthy. Your
hardest times are an opportunity to 'put your faith where your
mouth is' and to *strengthen yourself in the Lord*, as David did. (1
Samuel 30:6)

When you do this, you release something wonderful - a *sweet
smelling fragrance* that reaches the lives of others around you.
When we worship the Lord through our hardest times, we not
only encourage ourselves, we show unbelievers that we trust
God; that we aren't merely 'all words' in sunshine-times. This
sets you apart from the religious person and shows the unbeliever
that you have an unshakable trust in an unshakable God!

Paul wrote: *"You see, we don't go around preaching about
ourselves. We preach that Jesus Christ is Lord, and we ourselves
are your servants for Jesus' sake. For God, who said, "Let there
be light in the darkness," has made this light shine in our hearts
so we could know the glory of God that is seen in the face of
Jesus Christ."* 2 Corinthians 4:5-6 (NLT)

We are called to be both a *light* in this dark world and a *sweet
smelling fragrance*, everywhere we go, even, <u>*especially*</u>, when
things feel dark for us, proclaiming His goodness, His
faithfulness, His salvation, bringing hope! When we do this, we
are truly a sweet smelling fragrance to God. I like to picture God
throwing His windows and doors wide open, to let the sweet
smelling fragrance of His worshipping Beloved ones into the
courts of Heaven!
Let's be bringers of hope in dark places, a sweet smelling
fragrance, everywhere we go today!

Saturday - Bruised Reeds and Smouldering Wicks

"A bruised reed he will not break, and a smouldering wick he will not snuff out. In faithfulness he will bring forth justice;"
Isaiah 42:3 (NIVUK)

A bruised reed

Have you ever seen reeds growing at the edge of a river? They stand tall and strong. This is because they're near their life's source, the water, which they soak up, through their hollow stems; drinking continually from the river keeps them strong from the inside out.

Sometimes, clumsy feet come along and trample on the reeds, the wading boots of a fisherman, the hooves of cattle. Reeds that stood tall and sturdy are now bent, bowed and bruised.

Are you a bruised reed? Have you been bruised by disappointment, grief, the betrayal of a friend, a spouse's harsh words, job loss, chronic illness? You're still by the river's edge, your life-source, but somehow you feel unable to take in nourishment in the same way. Think about it though; what happens when you bend or squeeze a straw and then try to drink through it? It's quite difficult - as though there was a blockage.

In Isaiah's time, the bamboo-like reeds were used as a type of flute because of their capacity to produce a sweet sound. The bent or *bruised* ones were tossed aside. The original word used for *bruised* in this scripture is *rasas* and means 'slightly damaged,' or 'not quite perfect.'

Isn't that just the way of the world? We throw out the slightly damaged ones, the ones that don't quite, 'make the grade;' the 'mess-ups.' But that isn't the way our God works.

Our God is in the restoration business!

Shepherds, in Biblical times, would bind two reeds together to make a flute. They would while away the lonely hours playing their music on these little flutes. The reed flutes were fragile and could be easily damaged. If that happened, the shepherd would just snap it, toss it away and make a new one.

God, your Shepherd will never break and toss away his bruised little reed-flute. It doesn't matter to your loving Shepherd if the music that comes from your bruised heart is a little bit wobbly; if it is played for Him it is sweet to His ears. He tenderly binds up the broken parts until once more you're standing tall. If you feel as though you are so bruised you cannot take much more, He says to you: "*My grace is sufficient for you, for my power is made perfect in weakness.*" 2 Corinthians 12:9 (NIVUK)

A smouldering wick

"*a faintly burning wick he will not quench*" Isaiah 42:3 (NIVUK)

In Biblical times, lamps were filled with olive oil, and a small piece of cloth was used as the wick. The wick drew oil up from the base of the lamp and kept burning as long as it remained saturated with oil. If the wick wasn't inserted properly, or if it became contaminated with grime, it might begin to smoke. The easiest way to stop a smoking wick it is to snuff it out and trim it right down. Sometimes, if it was very dirty, it would need to be pulled out and replaced with a new one.

"*You are the light of the world.*" Matthew 5:14 (NIVUK)

Jesus has commanded, and commissioned, every one of us to let our light shine brightly in this dark world. It is not religion, but *relationship* with the Living God that makes us shine brightly. It isn't striving to be nice, or be better, that keeps the fire burning in our hearts, it's *relationship* with the one who ignites the flame to start with.

When Moses came down from the mountain after spending time in God's presence his face shone so brightly that the people couldn't look at him.

And Psalm 34 tells us: *"Gaze upon him, join your life with his, and joy will come. Your faces will glisten with glory."* Psalms 34:5 (TPT)

My lamp will stay brightly lit when I ensure that it is kept filled with the richest of oil, by spending time in God's Word and in His presence.

God is also a Light to us: *"God, all at once you turned on a floodlight for me! You are the revelation-light in my darkness, and in your brightness I can see the path ahead."* Psalms 18:28 (TPT). God gave His light and word to empower David, and He does the same for us.

Contrite Equals Revival

Sometimes our wicks can become 'contaminated.' We start to give off smoke that gets into other people's eyes - a smoking wick is really unpleasant to be around! Our light starts to become dimmer, even barely perceptible.When God sees that our wick is smoking and that we're 'not burning properly,' He doesn't decide to 'snuff us out' and use a lamp that burns brighter instead. Isaiah 42:3 says that He will not quench- *snuff out* a faintly burning wick. Isaiah led by the Spirit of God, writes later in chapter fifty seven, that God comes to *"the one who is contrite and lowly in spirit, to revive the spirit of the lowly and to revive the heart of the contrite."* Isaiah 57:15 (NIVUK) Rather than snuffing out the faintly burning wick, God will blow on it, His breath re-igniting the flame and causing it to burn brightly again.

* * *

Just a thought in closing: What does a person instinctively do when trying to light a candle that keeps going out because of the surroundings? They shield the candle with their hands.
Sometimes our lives don't quite turn out the way we hoped and this adversity causes our wicks to flicker and grow dim. Here's what God does, He comes alongside and shields us with His all-powerful hands. Though harsh winds might blow all around, the Lord our Light will not let our light be extinguished!

"But you, LORD, are a shield around me, my glory, the One who lifts my head high."
Psalms 3:3 (NIVUK)

Sunday - The Yoke of Jesus

"Take my yoke upon you and learn from me, for I am gentle and humble in heart, and you will find rest for your souls. For my yoke is easy and my burden is light."
Matthew 11:29-30 (NIVUK)

Yoke

The concept of yoke may be strange and foreign to modern, Western ears, but it wouldn't have sounded strange to those listening to Jesus. The ancient Jews were very familiar with the idea of yoke, in rabbinical law, poetic and prophetic writings and of course in farming.

In rabbinic (Jewish) theology the yoke was and is an important metaphor, symbolising service and servitude. The *'yoke of the kingdom of man'* is contrasted with *'the yoke of the kingdom of heaven,'* with the strong principle being taught that the Jew should be free from servitude to man, so that he can devote himself to the service of the Lord. Throughout the Old Testament, the yoke was also a symbol of servitude, oppression, slavery, and the burden of taxes that was placed on the people. To emphasise the weight of oppression it is sometimes described as *'a yoke of iron.'* In Deuteronomy 28:48 the Lord warns the Israelites that if they continued in their waywardness He would allow their enemies to fit them with a *'yoke of iron.'*

Take <u>My</u> yoke upon you

"Take my yoke upon you." This is so much more than just laying down our heavy burdens and walking away feeling light and free. The concept of having a yoke placed upon you could sound restrictive, if it weren't Jesus issuing the invitation.

By contrast to the yoke of iron; a heavy, uncomfortable, unyielding, confining restraint, Jesus' yoke, is *light*. There's an exchange of yokes that takes place. The heavy oppressive, man-made, man inflicted yokes, exchanged for Jesus' yoke. He says *"forget about all those other yokes, and take <u>Mine</u>."*

Easy and light

The word *easy* that Jesus uses here is *chrestos* in Greek, which can mean *well-fitting*. A caring farmer would carefully adjust the wooden yoke to make sure it fitted well, and didn't hurt the neck of the oxen. So it is with Jesus' yoke. It isn't a case of one size fits all; Jesus' yoke is tailor made for you. Bespoke, as are you! The heart of this statement of Jesus' is beautifully conveyed in The Message Bible: *"I won't lay anything heavy or ill-fitting on you."* Matthew 11:30 (MSG). If your yoke hurts and feels ill fitting, then perhaps you need to ask yourself whether you are shouldering a yoke that isn't His. On the other hand, perhaps you have been trying to be the one to set the direction of His yoke. But 'yoke' is about *partnership*, which is what makes Jesus' yoke easy.

Partnership with Jesus

Jesus' invitation is not to a life of sitting back, kicking off our shoes, and doing nothing while He does it all. As we saw yesterday, there is *still* a yoke and a burden to carry. Remember Jesus' words in Matthew 16:24 *"If you truly want to follow me, you should at once completely reject and disown your own life. And you must be willing to share my cross and experience it as your own, as you continually surrender to my ways."* (TPT)

* * *

We are to pick up our cross and follow Jesus. But with and *in* Jesus, our burden is easy and light, because we enter into a partnership relationship with Him. Do you know what's so wonderful about Jesus' yoke? It isn't a heavy burden placed on our shoulders that we are then expected to carry. Instead, Jesus says in the same context, *"learn from me."* We are yoked *together* with Jesus, with Him shouldering the weight of the burden, setting the direction and pace. All we have to do is follow His lead and do as He does.

Learn from me

A cattle yoke was a bar or frame by which two oxen were joined for working together. This ensured that two oxen would walk in the same direction and be partnered in their efforts. Often the loads were very heavy and a single ox would exert all its strength trying to pull a load. The yoke may have chafed against the animal's shoulders, causing sores. Two oxen yoked together would alleviate this.

When training a young ox to plow and work the fields, ancient farmers would often yoke it to an older, stronger, more experienced ox, who bore the burden, set the pace and guided the younger animal through the learning process.

It's my belief that Jesus had this imagery in mind, as He invited us to take His yoke upon ourselves. When we partner with Jesus, He shoulders all of the burden and we follow his lead. We don't need to struggle and strive to 'do our bit,' all that is required of us is obedience.

Jesus knew how to perfectly partner with His Father, and never did or said anything unless The Father told him to: *"So Jesus said, "I speak to you timeless truth. The Son is not able to do anything from himself or through my own initiative. I only do the works that I see the Father doing, for the Son does the same works as his Father."* John 5:19 (TPT)

You will find rest for your souls

This promised gift of Jesus to all His true disciples is an echo of Jeremiah 6:16: *"This is what the LORD says: 'Stand at the crossroads and look; ask for the ancient paths, ask where the good way is, and walk in it, and you will find rest for your souls."* Jeremiah 6:16 (NIVUK)

That rest for your soul could be considered the birthright of all those who come to Jesus and are His followers. After all, it's what He promises, to those who *walk with* Him.

Strong and Courageous

Monday - Courageous!

"This is my command, be strong and courageous! Do not be afraid or discouraged. For the Lord your God is with you wherever you go." Joshua 1:9 (NLT)

"The wicked run away when no one is chasing them, but the godly are as bold as lions." Proverbs 28:1 (NLT)

When I type the words 'bold' or 'courageous' into my search engine, all sorts of so-called inspirational quotes pop up. The problem with these quotes is that many of them approach boldness from the point of view of looking 'deep within yourself' and finding a giant somewhere inside the 'real' you. Since Christians have the Lord Holy Spirit living *inside* us, then I suppose in a way we do look within to find boldness and strength; but it still isn't ours, it's <u>His!</u>

Where does our courage and strength come from?
Paul was a true example of one who put his trust in the Lord. Here's one example: In his letter to Timothy, Paul wrote about his trial: *"The first time I was brought before the judge, no one came with me. Everyone abandoned me. May it not be counted against them. But the Lord stood with me and gave me strength." 2 Timothy 4:16 (NLT)*

There are times in life when we feel let down or abandoned by friends. Even family, however well meaning and loving, can't possibly be available to help twenty four hours a day, seven days a week. But the Lord can, and does! He will never abandon us. (Matthew 28:20; Deuteronomy 31:8)

There have been no doubt, people down through history who were notably courageous in their own strength. But the trouble with this kind of courage is that it fosters pride and a self-reliant attitude towards God. Every time I rely on myself to sort out life's difficulties and hardships, I'm asserting my independence from my Heavenly Father, saying, "I don't need you, I can do this by myself."

God designed us to go through life in partnership with Him; Here's what the prophet Jeremiah had to say about it, "*This is what the Lord says: "Cursed are those who put their trust in mere humans, who rely on human strength and turn their hearts away from the Lord. They are like stunted shrubs in the desert, with no hope for the future. They will live in the barren wilderness, in an uninhabited salty land.* Jeremiah 17:5-6 (NLT)

Stunted shrubs and flourishing trees

Cursed? A stunted shrub in the desert? That's pretty strong wording. One could read those words and think, "how could a loving God curse the lives of people for not trusting in Him? But that is not what God said. It isn't *God* who curses them, but they who curse themselves. The way I see it, God was saying that a life of misplaced trust; where trust is placed in people, or even in *self*, is cursed by that *choice,* and the consequence is a life that becomes stunted.

The truth is, every time we place our trust in people instead of the Lord, our hearts slip away from Him a little bit; we become a bit more self sufficient and proud of our achievements. There are natural laws, such as gravity, inertia and friction and these have consequences. Dropping something results in it plummeting to the floor, because of gravity. Similarly, there are God's Kingdom 'laws,' such as faith and trust. These too have consequences if broken. Repeatedly not putting one's trust in God results in a stunted, spiritually barren life.

So the conclusion I draw from this is that it's *because* of God's great love for us that He issues this warning through Jeremiah. It isn't a " if you do that I will do this," but rather, "Child, don't do that, it will damage and hurt you and have nasty consequences for your life."

God *wants* to be our Help, our Strength our Hope and the One who sustains us. The life He wants for us looks more like this: *"But blessed are those who trust in the Lord and have made the Lord their hope and confidence. They are like trees planted along a riverbank, with roots that reach deep into the water. Such trees are not bothered by the heat or worried by long months of drought. Their leaves stay green, and they never stop producing fruit."* Jeremiah 17:7-8 (NLT)

When God told Joshua to be strong and courageous, He didn't just give the command and then leave Joshua to get on with it. It was not up to Joshua to then try muster up some inner courage to face the battle that lay ahead. No, God wanted Joshua to remember who it was that was with him and was his source of strength and courage. This is what the Lord said to Joshua: *"This is my command, be strong and courageous! Do not be afraid or discouraged. For the Lord your God is with you wherever you go."* Joshua 1:9 (NLT)

God also promised Joshua that He would go ahead of him. *"Do not be afraid or discouraged, for the Lord will personally go ahead of you. He will be with you; he will neither fail you nor abandon you."* Deuteronomy 31:8 (NLT)

Today, whatever you may be facing, you *can* be strong and

courageous, not in your own strength but because the Lord your God is <u>with</u>, and <u>in</u> you, wherever you go!

Tuesday - The Power of His Might

"Finally, be strong in the Lord and in his mighty power."
Ephesians 6:10 (NIVUK)

Finally

Paul wrote this letter to the Ephesians to establish some
foundations for Christian living and their position in Christ.
Here, at the end of chapter six, before coming to his teaching on
the armour of God, Paul writes, *finally*. This is my understanding
of what Paul is hoping to communicate through this small word
'finally': *'in light of everything I have just taught you'*
· *Finally*: in light of all Jesus has won for us
· *Finally* : in light of God's great plan that He has made you part
of.
· *Finally*: in light of your standing in Christ Jesus.
· *Finally* : in light of the in-filling of the Holy Spirit.
· *Finally* : in light of the conduct that God has called us to live
by.

In light of *all* this, Paul says, there is a battle to fight in the
Christian life, and we are to *"be strong in the Lord and in His
mighty power"*

Be strong in the Lord and in His mighty power

The essential thing in this is it that its the *Lord's* strength and
power, not our own, as we saw yesterday. Paul says we must be

strong in the Lord and in the power of *His* might. There is an awful lot of teaching on spiritual warfare, Christian combat and the armour of God, and that's not a bad thing, but it can be a dangerous thing when we forget that this is in 'the power of His might' not our own.

If an army commander were to dress a weak person in the very best armour that the army had to offer, that person would still be easily overcome in the heat of battle. Before any soldier is given a weapon to use he or she has to go through rigorous training. The important purpose for this training is to build up the soldier's strength and stamina and sharpen their wits against enemy tactics. Without this, the soldier could be a danger to himself and to others. A loose canon! There are quite a lot of loose cannons in Christendom.

Equipping for Christian combat has to start with training in being *strong in the Lord and in the power of His might.* We <u>need</u> that foundation.

In the power of His might

Might is inherent power. Here's an example: have you ever watched one of those Strong Man competitions with those burly, muscular men who can move busses and lorries with their big strong arms? Their muscles are a physical display of their might, even when they are not using them. Those huge muscles are the Strong Man's 'reserve' of might.

Power is the exercise of might. It's when that strong muscular man is in competition and he draws on his reserve, using his might to push a double-decker bus several paces. Power is the reserve of might put into operation.

Our God has vast 'reservoirs' of might, beyond our highest expectations and His unmatchable might is realised as power in the life of a Christian. But we have to remember that His might doesn't work in us while we just sit around passively doing nothing. God doesn't have puppets! His might works in us as we *rely* on Him, and in faith step out to do whatever He calls us to.

Wednesday - Choose Faith Over Fear

"Overhearing what they said, Jesus told him, 'Don't be afraid; just believe." Mark 5:36 (NIVUK)

How many times in your you life have you faced circumstances that seemed completely hopeless, until God miraculously turned everything around? There's one such story in Mark's Gospel. Jairus, a leader in the synagogue had a daughter who was gravely ill. He went looking for Jesus to ask him to come and heal her, but it seemed he was too late! While he was actually with Jesus, he received the terrible news that his daughter had died: *"While Jesus was still speaking, some people came from the house of Jairus, the synagogue leader. 'Your daughter is dead,' they said. 'Why bother the teacher anymore?"* Mark 5:35 (NIVUK) Those words 'why bother' really struck me.

Why Bother?

Why bother? Isn't that so often the destructive little thought that niggles away at the backs of our minds when things are beginning to look hopeless? You don't get a situation more hopeless than the person you long to see healed dying! As a parent, if I close my eyes for a moment and put myself in Jairus' position, I can empathise with what I imagine he must have felt in those moments - fear, like a bucket of ice water, dousing his faith as he hears those words. *"Your daughter has died"* - *"why bother....?"*

* * *

What about you? Is there something that you know deep down in your heart that God has promised you, but nothing seems to be happening? Is there a part of your life where you had expected to see growth and increase by now, yet it *still* looks to your eyes like tumbleweed town? And the enemy sows that little seed of doubt: *"That dream has died," "why bother?"*

Bother because if God said it, He will do it! He is a Faithful God who keeps His Word. And it's not over until God says so!

Jesus' Response

Jairus had gone to Jesus believing. His faith had been shaken by the fearsome news, and fear got its foot in the door; that is, until Jesus said the words that silenced those fears *"Don't be afraid. Just believe."*

We need to take our eyes off that which *appears* to be dead, and fix them on Jesus, the One who can breathe life and hope into any situation. We need to speak to fear, when it tries to persuade us that 'it's over, there's no point in praying, it's hopeless', why bother?' and tell fear to *be quiet!* We need to listen to the Miracle Worker say to us *"Don't be afraid. Just believe."*

There's so much in this statement from Jesus. It isn't a command to just have faith, for faith's sake, but to *believe*. Believe what? I hear Jesus say through those words; *"believe in Me. Believe that I am all that I say I am."* When we know someone's character and believe that their motives towards us are good, just, merciful, kind and loving aren't we more inclined to trust and believe *in* them?

The Apostle Paul wrote *"I know whom I have believed, and am convinced that he is able to guard what I have entrusted to him until that day."* 2 Timothy 1:12 (NIVUK)

Paul knew Jesus.' He believed Jesus.

Kick fear out!

When Jairus and Jesus arrived at the house where Jairus' daughter lay, they were met by mourners and doubters. Jesus' response is interesting. He said to these so-called mourners: "*why are you making a commotion and weeping? ..The child is not dead but asleep.*" He put the whole lot of them outside and then Jesus got on with the business of transforming this seemingly hopeless situation! Jesus put the naysayers out of the house, and we need to do the same; we need to kick fear right out of the door.

Jesus wasn't being insensitive to the mourners by putting them out. Nobody empathises more deeply with us in our (real) mourning than Jesus. But He was there to do Kingdom business; it wasn't over yet for Jaisus' daughter and mere death was no hurdle for Jesus! The weeping and wailing was a distraction to those who <u>had</u> faith.

When we listen to the 'mourners' a hopeless, doubt-filled mindset can grab hold of our emotions and this leaves little room for faith. That's why Jesus put the weepers and wailers outside. If you have 'mourners,' in other words, doubters and naysayers in your life who are 'making a commotion,' weeping and wailing and proclaiming your dream, your God-given promise, dead, do as Jesus did - put them outside! And allow Jesus to get on with the business of breathing life into your seemingly hopeless situation.

Silence fear, choose faith, and see how Jesus speaks new life into those things you thought were dead!

Thursday - God My Hope

"LORD, you are my God; I will exalt you and praise your name, for in perfect faithfulness you have done wonderful things, things planned long ago." Isaiah 25:1 (NIVUK)

We watch the news most evenings in our house, and some days it's a barrage of the worst reports imaginable. I've heard it said that 'bad news sells,' and I could believe this, as good news stories become far and few between, buried under the avalanche of disasters, wars, bombings, terror attacks, cruelty, child abuse, rape, human trafficking, stabbings, and political scheming. I 've been asked by people who know I'm a Christian 'how can you still believe in a God that's good?'

I'm no great scholar but these things I do know:

God is good. He is faithful. And he is absolutely, without a shadow of a doubt, in control of everything. It may sound trite, but even though I don't know what the future holds, I *do* know the One who holds the future. And I trust Him. In Him, I have a sure and certain hope.

Isaiah knew this too

The first thing we see in the above passage, is that Isaiah had a personal relationship with God. He didn't just believe <u>in</u> God, he <u>believed</u> God. 'O Lord, You are *my* God.' Isaiah knew God and addresses the Lord as his friend as well as his Sovereign.

* * *

When you know the character of someone very well, and other people start to bad mouth that person in your company, or call their integrity into question, you can say with absolute confidence, *"No! That's not who they are. They wouldn't do that/ say that."* That's how well Isaiah knew God. He knew God's attributes and personality traits. He knew that God is good and always fulfils His promises. Do you know God that well?

A shift of focus

Reading through this chapter in Isaiah, we see Isaiah quickly moved from I and my to You, as he takes his focus off himself and what's going on around him to focus on who God is.
You are my God! I will exalt *You* in praise, I will extol *Your fame, You* have done extraordinary things, and executed plans made long ago exactly as *you decreed.*

We need to take our eyes off our circumstances and fix them on God, who is so much bigger than our problems, no matter how big they might seem to us.
Isaiah acknowledged that God is sovereign and in control. That God's plans are excellent and that they are fulfilled exactly as God has decreed. This is a recurrent theme throughout the Old Testament and many times through the book of Isaiah. Here are just three: *"The Lord of Heaven's Armies has sworn this oath: "It will all happen as I have planned. It will be as I have decided."* Isaiah 14:24 (NLT)
"I have a plan for the whole earth, a hand of judgment upon all the nations." Isaiah 14:26 NLT
"Only I can tell you the future before it even happens. Everything I plan will come to pass, for I do whatever I wish. I will call a swift bird of prey from the east— a leader from a distant land to come and do my bidding. I have said what I would do, and I will do it." Isaiah 46:10-11 (NLT)

*When we takes our eyes off ourselves and look to God - this
is what happens:*

1. <u>We see how great God is</u> (in comparison with our problems)
*"But you are a tower of refuge to the poor, O Lord, a tower of
refuge to the needy in distress. You are a refuge from the storm
and a shelter from the heat. For the oppressive acts of ruthless
people are like a storm beating against a wall,
In that day the people will proclaim, "This is our God! We
trusted in him, and he saved us! This is the Lord, in whom we
trusted. Let us rejoice in the salvation he brings!"* Isaiah 25:4, 9
(NLT)

2. <u>We remember that we have a Hope!</u>
Isaiah says in chapter 25:1 *'you have done extraordinary things'.*
When we start to remind ourselves of the things God has done in
our lives - we all have stories and testimonies of these - it boosts
our faith and lifts our hearts and encourages those around us as
we share our 'God stories'.

3. <u>We remember who we are</u>
Isaiah says in chapter 25:1 *"(you) executed plans made long ago
exactly as you decreed."*
We are a part of that plan! Does that mean we shouldn't be
affected by the news or what's going on the world? On the
contrary, I believe we *should* be. But we should not be adding
our voices to those of despair, hopelessness and complaining.
Here's a 'radical' thought: what about watching the news with a
notebook; taking notes of all the 'disasters,' and stories of real
people in real pain, and then interceding for those situations,
knowing - trusting God to answer?

Friday - The Caleb Report

"The Lord now said to Moses, "Send out men to explore the land of Canaan, the land I am giving to the Israelites. Send one leader from each of the twelve ancestral tribes."
Numbers 13:1-2 (NLT)

Who Are You Listening To?

Have you ever felt as though you just seem to be surrounded by 'naysayers;' people who say things to you or in your company such as "we can't, you can't, we'll never be able to do this, this was a bad plan, God has deserted us/you?" Maybe you've *been* the negative one, while everyone else around you is trying to stay positive?

These naysayers can come in various forms: Negative people who say discouraging things to you just when you're about to step out in faithful obedience to God; things such as "you can't do that! I don't think you thought that through very well." "You couldn't have heard God properly." The naysayers may even be your own unchecked thoughts, and more often than not, it's the enemy, the devil, who whispers insidious lies of doubt and fear.

Time spent in this type of company is potentially damaging. Negative talk chips away at your faith and wears you down. God's children need to actively avoid this kind of talk. We cannot afford to entertain it, even for a moment. (See Psalm 1:1-2)

The contagion of fear

The children of Israel could have avoided so much stress if they had just listened to and believed what God had said instead of naysayers. This story is an example of the consequences of yielding to fear. Fear wreaks havoc. In this story, unchecked fear gripped an entire community.

What did God say?

We all know this story; it's so familiar that we could easily gloss over it and miss an important point. What <u>else</u> did God say? We know He said *"send men to explore the land of Canaan,"* But He also said: <u>*which I am giving to the people*</u> of Israel." Before the scouts even left to spy out the Promised Land, God had already promised the land to the children of Israel!

What did the report say?

Why, we might ask ourselves as we read this story, did the Israelites not remember that promise? How did such a large group of people become so negatively influenced by reports of just ten men? They became overwhelmed by the seeming hopelessness of the situation, worked themselves into a tizzy, cried all night and began to take on the fearful attitude of the spies; *"we can't go there, there are giants in the land!"* Once that mindset took hold, it spread through the camp like wildfire. From there it was a downward spiral of grumbling and complaining against their leaders until they found themselves stuck.

Sadly, it's a common human story; one we're all familiar with. We can be so fickle, where God is so faithful. We're up - then we're down, and all it takes is listening to a few words from the wrong source.

What Did Caleb Say?

If only they'd listened to Caleb, the voice of faith and hope among the negative voices of doubt and fear!: *"Then Caleb quieted the people before Moses, and said, "Let us go up at once and take possession, for we are well able to overcome it."* Numbers 13:30 (NKJV)

"Caleb <u>quieted</u> the people." This brings to mind a beautiful scripture: *"He will <u>quiet you with His love,</u> He will rejoice over you with singing."* Zephaniah 3:17 (NKJV)
We aren't privy to the words Caleb used to quiet them, but he was a man acting on God's instruction, the voice of hope, faith and reason in the face of mass panic, so I have no doubt that the words he used came from the Lord. You and I can also be that voice of hope to those who have lost hope.
And when you yourself are overwhelmed you can go to the very source of those words in Zephaniah; let God's words wash over you and quiet your soul with His love.

Choose to believe what God says!

Our God is a covenant keeping God, who keeps His promises. Whether it's a specific promise God has made to you, or whether we are speaking generally about God's promises to all His children, God will never go back on His Word. Don't listen to the 'spies;' instead seek out the Calebs and Joshuas of life to form Godly friendships to 'do life' with, whereby you can encourage and 'quiet' one another.

"Two are better than one, because they have a good return for their labour: if either of them falls down, one can help the other up. But pity anyone who falls and has no-one to help them up." Ecclesiastes 4:9-10 (NIVUK)

However things may look at this moment, choose to wait for the promise. Don't look at the 'giants in the land,' but at the Lord who is so much bigger; don't listen to the naysayers along the way but to the 'report' that is agreement with what God has said!

Jill McIlreavy

Saturday - More Than Conquerors

"No, in all these things we are more than conquerors through him who loved us."
Romans 8:37 (NLT)

It would be wonderful enough to be told that through Christ you are a conqueror; but Romans 8:37 tell us that we are *more* that conquerors! Whatever comes against you today, isn't it good to know that you can rest in this knowledge?

Christ-Confidence, not Self confidence!

The phrase "more than conquerors" in this verse comes from the Greek words *nikao*, meaning 'to overcome,' or 'to conquer,' and *huper*, meaning 'beyond,' 'over and above,' or 'to prevail completely over.' In joining these two words *huper* and *nikao* together, Paul makes an incredible power-statement about you and me.

Jesus triumphed over sin, death, sickness and hell; leaving not one enemy unsubdued or undefeated, and because of His absolute victory we, as His disciples, prevail completely!

The battle has already been won!

Romans 8:37 is not about being <u>self</u>-confident; it's about being '<u>Christ</u> -confident.' To put it another way: in Jesus Christ, *together with Him*, you are a paramount victor, a phenomenal overcomer and a conquering force to be reckoned with!

* * *

And because you are Christ-Confident, you can rest assured that even though these things may happen to you that Paul lists in Romans 8:35,38,39, things such as trouble, calamity, persecution, hunger, destitution, danger, or the threat of death; absolutely nothing can separate you from the love of God. These verses go on to affirm this by reminding us that not even angels, demons, our fears for today or worries about tomorrow, can separate us from God's love! For you and I are *more than conquerors,* through Christ, who loved us, and gave Himself for us.

Sunday - Who is In Charge Around Here?

"Yours, LORD, is the greatness and the power and the glory and the majesty and the splendour, for everything in heaven and earth is yours. Yours, LORD, is the kingdom; you are exalted as head over all." 1 Chronicles 29:11 (NIVUK)

God is Sovereign over everything.

God is in charge of all things at all times, in every situation. He knows what he is doing and why He is doing it. God's sovereignty is the answer to the biggest question of all: *Who's in charge here?* The sovereignty of God isn't just an idea, it is probably the most important thing we need to acknowledge and believe in our approach to Him.

God's sovereignty is the thread that runs through the whole Bible. Here are just a few examples: *"But he stands alone, and who can oppose him?"* Job 23:13 (NIVUK)

"I know that you can do all things; no purpose of yours can be thwarted." Job 42:2 (NIVUK) "Our God is in heaven; he does whatever pleases him." Psalms 115:3 (NIVUK)

"Oh, the depth of the riches of the wisdom and knowledge of God! How unsearchable his judgments, and his paths beyond tracing out! 'Who has known the mind of the Lord? Or who has been his counsellor?' Romans 11:33-34 (NIVUK)

* * *

God knows what He's doing

Even in those times when we are not aware of God working in our lives, God never ceases to do so. We barely catch a glimpse of His works, and then we often mistake that small glimpse for the entire spectrum, forgetting how big our God is! We're like children who peep through the keyhole at the gift-wrapped presents on the other side of the door. At best we see an outline, and become excited and enthralled, or disappointed, depending on what we were hoping for, all the while forgetting that we are not seeing whole picture, as only the Lord does. And we mistake this partial picture for our whole reality.

He knows the measure of our days, He ordains every second of our existence, yet God Himself stands outside of time. Even though we use the term *Omnipotent* to describe the Lord, applying that label doesn't help our minds to understand the sheer vastness of Him. Our minds just can't do the maths, to comprehend this All-knowing, yet Knowable God, this cosmos creating indescribable God who is the knower of every thought. (Deuteronomy 29:29; Psalm 139)

There's no one like God

All through the Bible the rhetorical question arises, *'who is like the Lord?'* Of course it isn't a real question, because we know there's nobody like Him! (See: Exodus 15:11; Psalm 113:5) The New Testament continues with this theme. We see God manifest in flesh through Jesus, as He miraculously heals the sick, sees right into the hearts of broken, hurting people, and forgives sinners. It makes me smile to myself that the religious leaders, confused to encounter the *otherness* of God in the person of Jesus, unwittingly acknowledged His sovereignty when they said *"Who can forgive sins but God alone?"* Mark 2:7 (NIVUK)

In light of all this, how big is your God?

Is God truly your Sovereign? Do you believe that God is sovereign over all your problems, is He bigger than your future, bigger than your emotional and physical pain, bigger than your fears? Do you really believe that God is bigger than anything you are facing now, today? Or will ever face? If not, perhaps you need to swap your *god* for the Sovereign God of the Bible!

How Big Is Your God?

Monday - God's Gift Of Peace

God's Gift of Peace

"And the peace of God, which transcends all understanding, will guard your hearts and your minds in Christ Jesus." Philippians 4:7 (NIVUK)

Storms in life often seem to come suddenly and unexpectedly, don't they? You're happily trundling along, everything ticking over just the way it should, when seemingly out of nowhere, one small thing triggers another small thing and before you know it, your peace-filled little world is a typhoon! As Christians, we aren't exempt from problems, but we do have a 'secret weapon' that prepares and enables us through life's roughest storms - it's called *The Peace of God*

Peace is Jesus' gift to us.
This is what Jesus told his disciples, as he prepared himself and them, for his impending crucifixion: *"I am leaving you with a gift—peace of mind and heart. And the peace I give is a gift the world cannot give. So don't be troubled or afraid.* John 14:27 (NLT)

We need to note something very important about this peace that Jesus gives: It's the peace of God. God literally imparts His <u>own</u> peace to us; it's <u>His</u> - He shares the peace of His own heart with us. In Philippians chapter four, the scripture we opened with, Paul writes, *"And the peace of God, which transcends all understanding.."* Jesus said that it is a peace that the world <u>cannot give</u>. It's a supernatural peace that floods our hearts and minds when everything around us screams *hit the panic button!*

272

* * *

Peace isn't something we have to fight and struggle for, or pray and beg God for; <u>He has already given it</u> - peace of mind and heart is already freely available to the child of God.

Life happens - and of course we all know that just because we are Christians doesn't mean we will be exempt from the normal 'stuff' of life, but we have this gift of peace that enables us to stand, rock solid in life's storms!

How to find this peace in every storm

How can I experience peace when my world has turned upside down and inside out? - By fixing my thoughts on God. It sounds simple, but that's because it is.

I don't know about you, but when I'm in the middle of one of those times in life when everything seems to be kicking off at once around me, it feels as though I can't see past the great big looming problem. My thoughts start racing, I toss and turn at night. But Isaiah reminds us to take our thoughts off our issues and fix them with confidence on God. And when I do this, every time without fail, I am flooded with the *peace of God.*

"You will keep in perfect peace all who trust in you, all whose thoughts are fixed on you!" Isaiah 26:3 (NLT)

If you are facing a storm today and are wondering what happened to your peace, here are some steps you can take to refocus and fix your thoughts:

*Open and read your Bible, reminding yourself of God's promises, both to you and to his children collectively.

*Remember all the times He has come through for you.

*Focus on <u>His</u> greatness, <u>His</u> power, <u>His</u> might! - and watch those anxieties get smaller in comparison. I have added some scriptures below to help get you started.

"Our city is strong! We are surrounded by the walls of God's salvation."
"But for those who are righteous, the way is not steep and rough. You are a God who does what is right, and you smooth out the path ahead of them."
"Lord, you will grant us peace; all we have accomplished is really from you."
Isaiah 26:1,7,12 (NLT)
"I cried out, "I am slipping!" but your unfailing love, O Lord, supported me. When doubts filled my mind, your comfort gave me renewed hope and cheer"

Psalm 94:18-19 NLT

In closing, here's that scripture in Philippians once again, in another translation: *"Don't worry about anything; instead, pray about everything. Tell God what you need, and thank him for all he has done. Then you will experience <u>God's peace</u>, which exceeds anything we can understand. <u>His peace</u> will guard your hearts and minds as you live in Christ Jesus."* Philippians 4:6-7 (NLT)

Tuesday - *Don't Look At The Waves, Look At Jesus*

Don't Look At The Waves, Look At Jesus

"Yes, come," Jesus said. So Peter went over the side of the boat and walked on the water toward Jesus. But when he saw the strong wind and the waves, he was terrified and began to sink. "Save me, Lord!" he shouted. Jesus immediately reached out and grabbed him. "You have so little faith," Jesus said. "Why did you doubt me?" Matthew 14:29-31 (NLT)

I once decided I was going to try surfing. Not being very sporty (that's an understatement) and being about seven months pregnant with my first child at the time, both added up to this not being one of my finest ideas. There I was, in my red polka dot maternity swimsuit, far out from the shore, enjoying the peace and quiet. I floated on my board, waiting for a wave to come along, and, just as I was thinking how easy this was, the calm surface of the sea rippled and lifted on the horizon. A massive wave formed and started coming towards me. Knowing there was no way I was experienced enough to "ride" this wave, I panicked and scrambled off my board. I have to tell you at this point that back then I had developed a fear of water. My dad had drowned just eighteen months before, and I was still having terrible nightmares about it. This surfing try-out was an attempt to face the fear.

As the huge wave loomed over me, I froze, hanging onto my

board, waiting for impact. When the wave hit me, I lost my grip on the surfboard, went under the water, tumbled and rolled, felt my face scrape the sandy sea bottom, and eventually broke the surface again gasping for air.

In my sheer terror, I had forgotten that I was on a strong, solid surf board. All surfing instructions were forgotten, overshadowed by fear. Why? Because instead of looking at my secure position and remembering what I had been taught, I had looked at the size of the wave.

You will face deep waters

"When you pass through the waters, I will be with you; and when you pass through the rivers, they will not sweep over you." Isaiah 43:2 (NIVUK)

We looked at this scripture a couple of weeks back didn't we? But we can never read the same passage of scripture too many times! You and I will face deep waters in life, but we have by our side the One whose voice the wind and waves obey, so we have nothing to fear!

Don't look at the waves, look at Jesus

As you read this, maybe you are facing some deep waters. Perhaps big waves seem to loom on the horizon of your life, threatening to overwhelm and sink you. Remember your solid foundation. Remind yourself to Whom you belong. Hold fast to the truths that your heart knows.

Remember Peter, walking on water towards Jesus in a storm? He was doing it; he was actually walking on the surface of the water! It was only when he took his eyes off Jesus and looked at the size of the waves, and the strength of the wind, that he started to sink: *"So Peter went over the side of the boat and walked on the water toward Jesus. But when he saw the strong wind and the waves, he was terrified and began to sink. "Save me, Lord!" he shouted."* Matthew 14:29-30 (NLT)

But here's the important thing; the moment Peter called out to

Jesus in the midst of his fear, '*Jesus immediately reached out and grabbed him*' Matthew 14:31 (NLT)

Nothing is bigger than Jesus!

Some waves are very big, there's no doubt about that. But the One who made the wind and the waves is so much bigger! Some storms we face can <u>appear</u> terrifying, but the Lord will not let you drown! Don't Look at the size of the waves, look at Jesus. He never takes his eyes off you, not even for a second. "*When they call on me, I will answer; I will be with them in trouble. I will rescue and honor them*". Psalm 91:15 (NLT)

Wednesday - Exceedingly Abundantly

"Now to Him who is able to do exceedingly abundantly above all that we ask or think, according to the power that works in us."
Ephesians 3: 20 (NKJV)

He is able.

Whatever your situation, circumstances, or need today, our God is *able*. The Lord isn't subject to those things that limit us - those things we know and perceive as 'normal.' God is supernatural - and can do anything, for anyone, at any time. We can quickly forget this. And we expect God to act and move as we would, or according to the limitations our minds place on Him, because we can't comprehend His 'otherness' - His omnipotence. Who else do we know, after all, that is *All powerful?*

He is willing.

As well being able beyond our comprehension, God is *willing*. Most Bible scholars would agree that God is able; He's omnipotent, so of course He is able. But it isn't enough to have a head knowledge of God's ability. After all, what changes for us unless we personally know, and believe that He is also willing. In Luke chapter five, a leper came to Jesus and said, "Lord, if you are willing, I can be healed." Jesus replied, "I am willing." He says the same to you and me today.

Jesus *willingly* endured the cross, for our sake. *"I offered my back to those who beat me and my cheeks to those who pulled out my beard. I did not hide my face from mockery and spitting."* Isaiah 50:6 (NLT)

Above all that we ask or think.

God is bigger than our imaginations. I love the way the essence of this scripture is so beautifully captured in The Passion translation of the New Testament: "Never doubt God's mighty power to work in you and accomplish all this. He will achieve infinitely more than your greatest request, your most unbelievable dream, and exceed your wildest imagination! He will outdo them all, for his miraculous power constantly energizes you." Ephesians 3:20 (TPT)

Infinitely more, exceeding your wildest imagination! These are words of overflow and abundance, not lack; not or 'just enough to get by!' God is able to do, not just what our limited human imaginations can envision, He far exceeds that. He goes beyond that which we have the capacity to imagine!

The power that works in us

God's Spirit is at work both in and through us. It's this truth that makes impossible things, possible in our daily lives. His full potential is resident within us: *"And I will ask the Father, and he will give you another advocate to help you and be with you for ever – the Spirit of truth. The world cannot accept him, because it neither sees him nor knows him. But you know him, for he lives with you and will be in you."* John 14:16-17 (NIVUK)

We are the temple of the Holy Spirit (1 Corinthians 3:1-4,16) This means corporately, (as the Church) and as individuals. We have the Holy Spirit of God living in us! This is no small thing, it's absolutely mind boggling. Yet many still live as though they were just a B&B to the Holy Spirit, somewhere He's 'allowed' to visit now and then. Then they wonder why they feel powerless. God has plans and intentions, far beyond your greatest imagination and mine; if you are a follower of Jesus, His Holy Spirit *lives* in you, enabling you, giving you His supernatural strength as He works out those plans and purposes in and through you.

Thursday - The Hands That Bear Our Burdens

The Hands That Bear Our Burdens

"I love you, LORD, my strength." Psalms 18:1 (NIVUK)
David saw the Lord as not just his *source* of strength; as in, the
one who provided him *with* strength. David recognised that it
was *God Himself* that was his strength.

The mess

Have you ever tried to catch spilled water in your bare hands? I
tried the futile feat recently when I accidentally knocked over a
full jug of water. The jug seemed to tip in slow motion At first
and then as it fell onto its side, water gushed everywhere. I tried
to make a sort of wall with my hands, to stop the water from
touching the appliances on the kitchen worktop but it was no use,
my hands just weren't big enough, or fast enough. In seconds the
water had made its inevitable journey across the surface, wetting
everything in its path. It poured down the cupboard doors to form
a big puddle on the floor. I don't know what I thought I could
achieve. On some level, I knew I couldn't really catch the water
and was acting on instinct. I was fast, but not fast enough. I used
my initiative but it was no use. No amount of cupping my hands
'the right way' would have caught all that water - *my hands
simply weren't designed to hold that amount* of *water*. All I
ended up with was a mess and wet hands.

We can't - but God can!

I love the beautiful picture Isaiah presents as he asks this rhetorical question:"Who has measured the waters in the hollow of His hand, And marked off the heavens with a span [of the hand], And calculated the dust of the earth with a measure, And weighed the mountains in a balance And the hills in a pair of scales?" Isaiah 40:12 (AMP)

This is our God! Close your eyes for a moment and 'look' at the scale of His hands. These hands of His can measure all the waters of the earth in their palms - the rivers, springs, oceans, rainfall - not one drop escapes His notice. His hands can lift and gauge the height and weight of any mountain in the world. These hands are designed to carry great burdens, and they're the hands that carry your burdens and mine.

Whenever you're struggling or feeling overwhelmed by life, remember that all your striving to fix your problems is as futile as trying to catch running water in your fingers! But God says to you "release it all to me." Look at what He says in verses 25-31 of this chapter: *"To whom will you compare me? Or who is my equal?' says the Holy One. Lift up your eyes and look to the heavens: who created all these? He who brings out the starry host one by one and calls forth each of them by name. Because of his great power and mighty strength, not one of them is missing. Why do you complain, Jacob? Why do you say, Israel, 'My way is hidden from the LORD; my cause is disregarded by my God?' Do you not know? Have you not heard? The LORD is the everlasting God, the Creator of the ends of the earth. He will not grow tired or weary, and his understanding no-one can fathom. He gives strength to the weary and increases the power of the weak. Even youths grow tired and weary, and young men stumble and fall; but those who hope in the LORD will renew their strength. They will soar on wings like eagles; they will run and not grow weary, they will walk and not be faint."* Isaiah

40:25-31 (NIVUK)

God didn't design you to carry it yourself

At times life can feel a bit like that knocked over water jug of mine, where we find ourselves scrambling to try to catch hold of circumstances, to fix this problem, sort out that detail, stop this thing happening as a result of that other thing! Yet no matter how fast you move, or how hard you try, your hands just can't catch it all. There's just too much on your plate, and it seems something invariably slips through your fingers and you're left standing in a mess.

That's because God didn't design you to carry all that in your small hands.

We have an incomparable God, creator of every living thing. As we read earlier in the week He is beyond our wildest imagination; our (created) minds cannot even begin to comprehend His greatness and His power. And He cares for us intimately; He pledges to bear our burdens. All we need to do is hand them over! *"Praise be to the Lord, to God our Saviour, who daily bears our burdens."* Psalms 68:19 (NIVUK)

God-Directed Steps

"The Lord directs the steps of the godly. He delights in every detail of their lives. Though they stumble, they will never fall, for the Lord holds them by the hand."
Psalms 37:23-24 (NLT)

Picture this: a baby learning to walk, toddling on her wobbly little legs with her dad holding her hand. Suddenly, she loses her footing and stumbles! Her little heart races as the floor seems to rush up towards her. But she doesn't hit the ground; suddenly the strong hand that holds hers, becomes a little firmer, straightening her up, placing her on her feet again, with soft words of reassurance. This is exactly what our Father God does and how intimately involved He is with us, His children.

He directs my steps

Verse twenty three of this Psalm says that He directs the steps of the godly. Your Father, takes you by the hand and leads you, *directing* your steps. God both shows us and instructs us on where to put our feet. Sometimes, like toddlers, we try to assert our independence; we try to wrench our hands out of God's, thinking we can do it on our own, but we really can't. And neither do we have to. God takes delight in directing us and lovingly helping us, and He pays attention to the smallest details of our lives. Verse twenty three tells us this: *"He delights in every detail of their lives."* Psalm 37:23 (NLT)

Though I stumble I will never fall

When we listen to and walk according to our Father's direction, all clearly laid out for us in His written Word, then though we stumble, we will not fall. We will be coming back to this subject on the difference between a stumble and a fall in a later chapter of the book; for now let's just remember that there is a difference.

The word *fall* in verse twenty-four, is written as *'cast headlong'* in some translations of the Bible, and this captures more accurately the heart of this verse. Literally translated from the original language it means: *'hurled down at full length.'* Though we stumble; even trip over our own clumsy feet sometimes, God will never let allow us to be 'hurled down at full length.' He won't let you fall flat on your face.

Sometimes things happen in life that make us feel as though that has happened, but really, it's only a stumble, a slip; your Father has you by the hand and will always catch you before you hit the ground! 'He says I've got you!'

Trusting God to Lead

"Your own ears will hear him. Right behind you a voice will say, "This is the way you should go," whether to the right or to the left." Isaiah 30:21 (NLT)

When I was a child we used to play that party game blind man's buff. There were all sorts of variations of it, and the one we played went something like this: we got into pairs, or teams of two. One person in each team was blindfolded and then had to perform a task or work their way through an obstacle course relying completely on verbal instructions and guidance from their team mate, who could see everything because they weren't blindfolded. It sounds easy enough, but it requires a lot of trust.

There are times when life can feel a bit like blind man's buff. We want to know what's coming next; what's going to happen tomorrow, how is this or that situation going to turn out or how can we avoid these rough times in the first place. It's human nature to want to know what lies ahead, that's why people consult with fortune tellers and read their horoscopes, desperate for answers. But we, as God's children, don't ever need to do those things. We don't need to be afraid of the future, or the present for that matter! We have someone by our side, a Partner in life, for life, who sees everything and knows everything.

* * *

God doesn't promise to tell us what tomorrow holds, but He *does* promise that He holds all our tomorrows right in the palm of His hand. All we need to do is learn to trust Him; to listen to His voice telling us which way to go. *"Your own ears will hear him. Right behind you a voice will say, "This is the way you should go," whether to the right or to the left."* Isaiah 30:21 (NLT)

Ask God For Help

This wonderful promise comes with one small, simple 'condition:' *Ask*.

Verses eighteen and nineteen of that same chapter tells us: *"the Lord is a faithful God. Blessed are those who wait for his help. O people of Zion, who live in Jerusalem, you will weep no more. He will be gracious if you ask for help. He will surely respond to the sound of your cries."* Isaiah 30:18–19 (NLT)

Instead of panicking; trying to do it all on our own, all we need to do is humble ourselves, submit to God and ask Him for help. He *"waits to be gracious"* to us, and always responds to our prayer with love and mercy.

God My Strength

"I love you, Lord, my strength." Psalms 18:1 (NIVUK)

This is a Psalm that David sang to the Lord, who had delivered him from his enemies, particularly Saul, who had hounded David for many years.

I love you Lord

From the time of David's anointing as future king when he was still just a shepherd around twenty year before, David had known what it was to rely on the strength of the Lord. He had faced many battles and had been forced to live for years as a fugitive from Saul. Despite everything, David remained steadfast to the Lord and God, in His timing, delivered David from his enemies and fulfilled the promise of David's anointing. Time and time again, God had proven faithful to David. David had no doubts about the source of his strength and acknowledged that it was the Lord.

Now, in this Psalm, David tells God how much he loves Him. The word *love* David uses here, so plainly translated in our English language, is very special and unique in that this particular word isn't found anywhere else in Scripture. It speaks of a very special depth and tenderness; *a 'most tender affection.'*

It suggests a *binding, or knitting together in love.* And it reveals something of the nature of the relationship between David and the Lord.

The writers of the Passion Translation have captured this verse and the following one beautifully: "Lord, I passionately love you and I'm bonded to you, for now you've become my power! You're as real to me as bedrock beneath my feet, like a castle on a cliff, my forever firm fortress, my mountain of hiding, my pathway of escape, my tower of rescue where none can reach me. My secret strength and shield around me, you are salvation's ray of brightness shining on the hillside, always the champion of my cause." Psalms 18:1-2 (TPT)

My strength

It is God Himself that is our strength. It's more than just praying, asking Him to come and strengthen us, it is allowing our hearts to become bonded, fused together in agreement with the heart of God. He doesn't expect us to be strong; He knows we are not. David had a very firm understanding of this and declares it throughout the Psalms.

Have a look at what Psalm 28 tells us: *"You are my strength and my shield from every danger. When I fully trust in you, help is on the way. I jump for joy and burst forth with ecstatic, passionate praise! I will sing songs of what you mean to me! You will be the inner strength of all your people, the mighty protector of all, the saving strength for all your anointed ones."* Psalms 28:7-8 (TPT)

David knew that he was totally dependent on God; he relied on God in every battle and every hardship. He acknowledged God as his strength, his help and his victory. David had a reputation for greatness in battle from a young age and this grew as he matured. Other people could see too, that David's strength was in the Lord: A repeated theme throughout his life, in all these victories - the refrain on people's lips - was *"the Lord was with him"* (See 1 Samuel 16:18; 1 Samuel 18:14; 1 Chronicles 11:9)

My God

David *knew* God. He didn't only know about God, he knew God's character; He knew His love and had experienced His faithfulness. He trusted that God was who He said He was and that He would do as He had promised.

That's why David could write words like these: *"The eyes of the Lord are upon even the weakest worshipers who love him— those who wait in hope and expectation for the strong, steady love of God. God will deliver them from death, even the certain death of famine, with no one to help."* Psalms 33:18-19 (TPT)

David wasn't the only one who relied on God's strength. Have a look at these encouraging scriptures from some other strong-in-God's-strength worship-warriors!

"The Sovereign Lord is my strength! He makes me as surefooted as a deer, able to tread upon the heights. Habakkuk 3:19 (NLT)

"Don't be afraid, for I am with you. Don't be discouraged, for I am your God. I will strengthen you and help you. I will hold you up with my victorious right hand." Isaiah 41:10 (NLT)
"He gives power to the weak and strength to the powerless." Isaiah 40:29 (NLT)

"I can do everything through Christ, who gives me strength." Philippians 4:13 (NLT)
"Be strong in the Lord and in his mighty power." Ephesians 6:10 (NLT)

Whatever you are facing today, God does not expect you to be strong - He wants you to align your heart with His and find your strength in <u>Him.</u>

Jill McIlreavy

Gratitude and Joy

Monday - How Gratitude and Joy Are Linked

"It is not joy that makes us grateful; it is gratitude that makes us joyful." (David Steindl-Rast)

The 'theory' that a thankful attitude and approach to life is linked to joy, has been proven true by scientist. Funnily enough though, long before doctors and psychologists thought they'd hit on the newest self help-program, the Word of God taught us the same thing!

Joy

Real joy, has very little to do with our outward circumstances; how much money we have, what sort of car we drive or how many pairs of shoes we own. Joy, or the lack of it, has nothing to do with the great relationships in our lives. All the magazines and advertisements condition us to believe that we will find what we need in these things, but it's just not true. Of course having a beautiful new pair of sparkly shoes might bring a momentary *feeling* of happiness, but this isn't the kind of joy that the Bible speaks of.

How do we find joy?

We find joy through having an attitude of gratitude; Doctors have 'discovered' that in general, our approach to joy is the wrong way round. Most people believe that *joy leads to gratitude.* In other words, feelings of joy lead to feelings of being grateful. While this isn't necessarily incorrect, studies, have shown that it's the other way around - *gratitude, especially the verbal expressing of it, leads to joy!*

The king who counted his blessings

King David understood and practiced this concept long before our modern day scientists made their 'great discovery.' Psalm 103 is an outpouring of gratitude; David begins: "Let all that I am praise the Lord; with my whole heart, I will praise his holy name. Let all that I am praise the Lord; may I never forget the good things he does for me. He forgives all my sins and heals all my diseases. He redeems me from death and crowns me with love and tender mercies. He fills my life with good things. My youth is renewed like the eagle's!" Psalms 103:1-5 (NLT)

May I never forget

David tells his own soul, "don't forget all the things God has done for you!" We can so easily slip into a negative pattern of complaining, can't we? I'm sure David was no different. He may have been a king, but life was hardly a bed of roses - as a leader he faced many battles and as a father and husband, many personal hardships and heartaches. But David knew how to give himself a good talking to when he felt that cloud of complaint coming over. He had an attitude of gratitude.

I love this genuine, raw outpouring of David's heart in 2 Samuel: "Who am I, O Sovereign Lord, and what is my family, that you have brought me this far? And now, Sovereign Lord, in addition to everything else, you speak of giving your servant a lasting dynasty! Do you deal with everyone this way, O Sovereign Lord? "What more can I say to you? You know what your servant is really like, Sovereign Lord. Because of your promise and according to your will, you have done all these great things and have made them known to your servant. "How great you are,

O Sovereign Lord! There is no one like you. We have never even heard of another God like you!" 2 Samuel 7:18-22 (NLT)

David expresses complete awe and wonder mingled with gratitude, that God would be so faithful to him and would make such a weighty promise to him and his descendants. David's life may not have always been easy but he knew how to *count his blessings* and as a result he was a man filled with joy; Psalms of praise and joy flowed from him - many of which we still sing in our churches today.

Make a grateful list

I decided a few months ago to try listing three things every day that I'm grateful for, and to thank God for those things, early in the day before any grumbles grabbed hold. Try it, you'll be surprised, as I was, to see that there are always far more than three things. You'll find it hard to choose. For fun, I have made a grateful list from Psalm 103, entitled 'David's grateful list' because really, that's what it is!

David's grateful list (paraphrased by me)

1. You forgive all my sin
2. You heal all my sicknesses
3. You pulled me out of the deep pit I was in (and every out I get myself into!)
4. Your steadfast love and mercy is a crown on my head
5. Your goodness wraps around me like a warm, safe blanket
6. You renew me constantly; though outwardly I might be getting older, inwardly I'm growing stronger because of you.

What about you? What will you write on your grateful list?

Tuesday - Joy In The Moment

"As Jesus and his disciples were on their way, he came to a village where a woman named Martha opened her home to him. She had a sister called Mary, who sat at the Lord's feet listening to what he said. But Martha was distracted by all the preparations that had to be made. She came to him and asked, 'Lord, don't you care that my sister has left me to do the work by myself? Tell her to help me!' 'Martha, Martha,' the Lord answered, 'you are worried and upset about many things, but few things are needed – or indeed only one. Mary has chosen what is better, and it will not be taken away from her." Luke 10:38-42 (NIVUK)

Too busy for joy

Sometimes we can become so caught up in the busyness of life that we realise, too late, that we have missed the specialness of the moment. In our desire for everything to be 'just right,' we become performance driven, religion oriented, and forgot to choose joy.

I believe this is what happened to Martha. The Lord was in the house! She had to make sure everything was perfect. Martha became so consumed with her preparations, flapping about in the kitchen, that she didn't find time to just sit with Jesus and enjoy His company.

* * *

Every time we meet together as the Body - the Church, Jesus, the King of kings is *in the house*! He promised that where two or three are gathered in His name, He would be right there in the midst, didn't He? (Matthew 18:20) How do we respond? Are we like Martha, flapping about, going through all our religious rituals and man-made rules, hoping to make everything 'just right'? Why do we do these silly things, when Jesus is with us, <u>in</u> us, by choice?: He *wants* to be in our company, and it isn't because we have made things perfect, but because He did!

Jesus doesn't require the perfect scene, or aesthetically pleasing setting before He will come fellowship with us. All that is required is that we simply '*come*', exactly as we are, with hearts open and surrendered to Him. '*Mary chose the better',* Jesus very gently and kindly told Martha. Will we?

Being present

Mary was present in the moment. She knew how to simply find joy in Jesus' company; it didn't matter if the house was a bit messy, or the dinner wasn't perfect, *the Lord was in the house* and she didn't want to miss a thing!
Jesus is present, not only in our churches, but in our hearts and lives, twenty-four hours a day, seven days a week. (See Hebrews 13:5, Deuteronomy 31:6)
Will we live as though *the King is in the house,* and take joy from that truth as Mary did?

What an honour, that Jesus lives in me, and *wants* to have one-to-one fellowship with me! I want to learn to just come to Him exactly as I am, never missing an opportunity through my days to find special moments to sit with Him and find joy in His presence.
May I never become too busy, too distracted, and miss the special moments.

Wednesday - Three Reasons To Be Thankful

"give thanks in all circumstances; for this is God's will for you in Christ Jesus." 1 Thessalonians 5:18 (NIVUK)

I often see "Thankfulness Campaigns" on social media, the idea being that you should list reasons over a period of time, for being thankful. Please don't get me wrong, I'm not anti this idea. In fact I think it's a great one! Thanksgiving is a Biblical prescription for daily living. But there's a very subtle shift in focus in some of these social media threads, that if we aren't careful, can make our thankfulness *conditional*: depending on my circumstances, or *depending on what I perceive God to have done for me.*

The Psalmist wrote: *"Enter his gates with thanksgiving and his courts with praise; give thanks to him and praise his name." Psalms 100:4 (NIVUK)* I don't see any conditions here!

This is the truth

Our God is always worthy of our thanks and praise, in any season and every circumstance. We all have seasons in life when we allow our feelings to get in the way. Sometimes when we're in a prolonged Winter period, we can start to feel that we have to little to be thankful for, when nothing's going right for us.

The truth is, these hard seasons strengthen and refine our faith, and shape us to be more like Jesus.

It's easy to practice thankfulness when life's going well. But to express real thankfulness in hard times is faith-building and displays true character.

Psalm 100:4 is often quoted, but you know, it doesn't stop at telling us to enter *His gates with thanksgiving; the Psalm* goes on in the next verse to list some great reasons for thankfulness. Some people may be surprised to know that none of these reasons have anything to do with us or our circumstances!

I see nothing that mentions my job, my spouse, my great house, my income, my children, although of course it is good to be thankful for all of these things too. But they are not the main reason, or the conditions for thanking God.

Here's what the verse says: *"For the Lord is good and his love endures for ever; his faithfulness continues through all generations."* Psalms 100:5 (NIVUK)

Our thankfulness is about who God is! He is *good*, His *love endures* forever, He is *faithful*.

If you're in a Winter Season right now and finding it difficult to find a place of thankfulness, these three rich truths about our wonderful, matchless God listed in Psalm 100:5 are a good starting point. As you read through this verse slowly, think on the truths contained in the words, let them catch hold of your heart and mind and let thankfulness start to rise up in you again.

He is Good!

"How abundant are the good things that you have stored up for those who fear you, that you bestow in the sight of all, on those who take refuge in you."
Psalm 31:19 NIVUK

* * *

"Taste and see that the LORD is good; blessed is the one who takes refuge in him."
Psalm 34:8 (NIVUK)

"The LORD is good to all; he has compassion on all he has made." Psalm 145:9 NIVUK

His love endures forever!
"Give thanks to the Lord, for he is good; his love endures for ever." Psalm 107:1 NIVUK

Psalm 136 declares this very same thing, though the whole Psalm:"Because of the LORD's great love we are not consumed, for his compassions never fail. They are new every morning; great is your faithfulness." Lamentations 3:22-23 (NIVUK)

He is faithful!
"if we are faithless, he remains faithful, for he cannot disown himself." 2 Timothy 2:13 (NIVUK)

"Let us hold unswervingly to the hope we profess, for he who promised is faithful." Hebrews 10:23 (NIVUK) "

"The one who calls you is faithful, and he will do it."
1 Thessalonians 5:24 (NIVUK)

"He is the Rock, his works are perfect, and all his ways are just. A faithful God who does no wrong, upright and just is he."
Deuteronomy 32:4 (NIVUK)

This is our God! It would difficult to read these scriptures and not feel a stirring on the inside! He is so faithful, so good, His love endures, and bears us through the hardest Winter.

Thursday - An Attitude Of Gratitude

An Attitude of Gratitude

"Be thankful in all circumstances, for this is God's will for you who belong to Christ Jesus." 1 Thessalonians 5:18 (NLT)

From time to time I see "things I'm thankful for" type campaigns on social media. They're a nice idea and seem to be growing in popularity. I enjoy reading some of my friends' posts about what they're thankful for in their lives.

'An Attitude of Gratitude' has become a buzz-phrase in motivational skills, positive thinking, mindfulness and as a help for depression. Participants are encouraged to keep a "gratitude journal." This is a very good idea. But the important question is this, *Who are we grateful to?*

Who are we grateful to?

It's nice that people feel grateful, and definitely better than complaining. But I sometimes wonder, when I hear people who don't know or believe in God, who that is thankfulness directed *to.* While a grateful attitude in a general sort of way, could help a person to change negative thinking patterns, the kind of thankfulness the Bible teaches isn't an arbitrary, attitudinal, general gratitude. It is very specific.

Our deepest thankfulness belongs, first and foremost directed towards God: *"Give thanks to the Lord, for he is good! His faithful love endures forever."* 1 Chronicles 16:34 (NLT)

The will of God for you

At the end of his exhortation to give thanks in all circumstances, Paul writes, *"this is God's will for you who belong to Christ Jesus."* It isn't a case of *you must do this,* but rather, because it's God's will, you can do it in Christ Jesus (remember you can do <u>all</u> things through Christ who gives you strength)!

A thankful attitude isn't some great new form of mindfulness, discovered by modern psychologists. God, who formed us and knows us, knew from the beginning of time what our minds and hearts needed. That's why the Bible, from cover to cover, exhorts us to be thankful! When we redirect our focus from our circumstances to our ever present God, who is our hope and strength, we forget to grumble and complain.

Its a sacrifice to God

"Make thankfulness your sacrifice to God, and keep the vows you made to the Most High. Then call on me when you are in trouble, and I will rescue you, and you will give me glory." Psalm 50:14-15 (NLT) God takes our gratitude extremely seriously. He isn't interested in our rituals of sacrifice, the sacrifice He wants from us, God says here, is a heart that is thankful.

A thankful heart flows into a life of obedience and a living trust in the Lord. The reward, or blessing that results from this heart attitude is, God says, *"I will rescue you, and you will give me glory."*

It's <u>in</u> all circumstances that we are to give thanks, not <u>for</u>

We are to be thankful in all circumstances. This is not the same thing as being thankful <u>for</u> all circumstances. It may sound a bit like splitting hairs, but there is a difference. To give a very personal example, I miscarried twins a number of years ago, quite late into the pregnancy. Should I have given thanks to God *for* the loss of my babies? Of course not! What sort of cruel taskmaster would that make Him? But I could give thanks in those horrible circumstances. I could be grateful that He is the God who is near to the broken-hearted (Psalm 34:18) and that in those circumstances, possibly the deepest valley in my life, His presence never left me, even for a moment.

We can be thankful in all circumstances, because we recognise that God's Sovereign hand is in charge, and that He is with us, never leaving or forsaking us in our circumstances. We are not subject to fate or chance, we are *His*.

Life doesn't just 'happen'

There may be times when we feel that there's not a lot to be thankful for. "Life happens," doesn't it? But that's the thing, does life 'just happen?' Or does the Bible not tell me that I have a Heavenly Father who reigns Sovereign over everything, and with loving, intricate, personal care, directs my steps? Nothing in the life of a Believer is random!

Romans 8:28 tells me that God causes everything to work together for the good of those who love Him and are called according to His purpose. If I really believe this, then surely that means maintaining a grateful attitude even things don't *feel* so good at the time.

In closing, I love the way this Psalm expresses an outpouring of an "attitude of gratitude":
"Praise the Lord! Let all that I am praise the Lord . I will praise the Lord as long as I live. I will sing praises to my God with my dying breath. Don't put your confidence in powerful people; there is no help for you there. When they breathe their last, they

*return to the earth, and all their plans die with them. But joyful
are those who have the God of Israel as their helper, whose hope
is in the Lord their God. He made heaven and earth, the sea, and
everything in them. He keeps every promise forever. He gives
justice to the oppressed and food to the hungry. The Lord frees
the prisoners. The Lord opens the eyes of the blind. The Lord lifts
up those who are weighed down. The Lord loves the godly. The
Lord protects the foreigners among us. He cares for the orphans
and widows, but he frustrates the plans of the wicked. The Lord
will reign forever. He will be your God, O Jerusalem, throughout
the generations. Praise the Lord!" Psalm 146:1-10*

Friday - Joy In Uncertainty

"Always be full of joy in the Lord. I say it again—rejoice! Let everyone see that you are considerate in all you do. Remember, the Lord is coming soon. Don't worry about anything; instead, pray about everything. Tell God what you need, and thank him for all he has done." Philippians 4:4-6 (NLT)

Fear of the unknown can rob us of many things. Some might remain in a job that sucks the life out them because they are afraid to step out in faith into what God has called them to. Others might avoid going on an overseas mission trip because of a fear that the finances will run out. Still others will not step out of their comfort zones and try something new and different because *we've always done it this way'* and a fear of the unknown has them locked down. One of the most precious things we are robbed of when we allow fear to get hold of us in this way is joy; the joy that comes with obedient faith and the overflow that comes as a result.

Paul found joy in uncertainty

"For I fully expect and hope that I will never be ashamed, but that I will continue to be bold for Christ, as I have been in the past. And I trust that my life will bring honor to Christ, whether I live or die." Philippians 1:20 (NLT)

* * *

We can learn a lot about finding joy in uncertainty by looking at Paul's life. The book of Philippians is filled with exhortation to be joyful. Remember, Paul wrote his letter to the Philippians in prison awaiting trial! Paul was matter-of-fact about trials and suffering in life; but they were completely separate to his joy and therefore had no effect on his joy.

Paul wasn't defined by his circumstances - he didn't allow even prison bars to keep him from what God had called him to! Even though his future was uncertain, Paul did not allow himself to become debilitated by this. Instead he set about writing what we now know as the book of Philippians!
God was able to work in and through Paul while he was in prison, using his circumstances to bring letters of admonishment and encouragement to the churches. Many of the books in the New Testament are letters Paul wrote while in prison.

In Philippians chapter three Paul wrote: *"everything else is worthless when compared with the infinite value of knowing Christ Jesus my Lord. For his sake I have discarded everything else, counting it all as garbage, so that I could gain Christ"* Philippians 3:8 (NLT)

In other words, for Paul, knowing Jesus and experiencing fellowship with Him, was far more satisfying and reason for joy than any outward circumstance. Far be it from Paul to wait and see first if the conditions were 'right' before he would worship Jesus; or wait until God had 'worked everything out for his good' before being joyful! We can learn so much from Paul about joy in all circumstances!

Saturday - Joy In The Mundane

"So let's not get tired of doing what is good. At just the right time we will reap a harvest of blessing if we don't give up."
Galatians 6:9 (NLT)

Is God interested in the mundane?

Paul, in our verse for today challenges not to become weary in doing good, to keep up the practice of doing good, even when we don't feel like it. But how much does God care, really, about the mundane things of our day to day lives?

Does the Lord really care whether or not the fruit of the Spirit is overflowing in me while I wash the floors, vacuum the carpet, polish the car, groom the dog? I believe He does care. Everything we do in life is an opportunity for growth, and these mundane things often have much to do with our attitudes.

Years ago my sister told me a poignant story about a good friend of hers: He and his wife both worked full time, and then on Saturdays she would do all the household chores while he sat with his feet up watching television. She was annoyed and resentful of this, and let him know it in no uncertain terms by slamming the vacuum cleaner noisily into furniture, sighing loudly, and by her general grumpy demeanour. Eventually one morning, exasperated by his wife's muttering and grumpiness, the husband said, "would you please stop cleaning the house _at_ me!"

* * *

That little phrase has become something of a catchphrase in our house. My husband David and I remind each other from time to time to: 'stop washing the dishes at me', or stop cleaning the car at me.' In other words, if you're going to do something, do it out of love, and don't make the other person 'pay,' because you feel resentful.

So yes, when we look at it from that perspective, I believe that God is *very* interested in the mundane.

A harvest of extraordinary from 'mundane'

"If we don't give up" - some versions say, "if we don't lose heart.' We can often lose heart in seasons of mundanity, when it seems to our minds that we have been faithful in the small things forever. But even in these times we can find joy! There's the joy in the moment - enjoying the presence of God wherever we find ourselves, as we looked at yesterday. Then there's the anticipatory joy, expectant of the harvest that us to come.

If we wisely manage the resources God gives us, under the principle of sowing and reaping, we need add patience to the mix! A harvest never comes immediately after the seeds are sown.

It's dangerous to lose heart, and yet it's an easy heart-attitude to slide into. Here's a thought to ponder in closing. This phrase translated *lose heart* was used for the kind of fear and absolute weariness a woman experiences during labour.

There comes a moment- or a few moments - where nearly every woman in labour woman cries out, "I just can't go on!" But she can't simply stop labouring! It would be unthinkable: Besides, the moment she holds that brand new baby in her arms, the memory of hard labour begins to fade. To *lose heart* from a Biblical perspective describes a time when the work is difficult and painful, but at the same time, unfinished and unrewarded.

It's easy to lose heart when we feel that way, but these are the times when we need to push through, *not grow weary while doing good,* anticipate the joy of our labour, and see what God births!

Sunday - Joy In The Hard Times

'Consider it pure joy, my brothers and sisters, whenever you face trials of many kinds, because you know that the testing of your faith produces perseverance."
James 1:2-3 (NIVUK)

Consider it pure joy.
For James to tell us to consider it *pure joy* when we encounter the hard seasons of life sounds like a tall order and not much of an encouragement. But this depends on what 'spectacles' you are reading the scripture through. If you're a glass half-full person (as apposed to a glass half-empty one) you'll remember that James' wisdom, like Paul's, came from personally knowing Jesus' faithfulness through difficulty and trial. Of course he is not saying we should throw a party to welcome a tough season in life, but our joy is found in knowing that real growth and change can come through whatever we are experiencing in the season we find ourselves in. This sort of growth can't happen while we're sitting in comfort. Armchair Christianity doesn't work; it's a joyless existence.

Perseverance
"The testing of your faith produces perseverance." The more our lives are shaken up by trials, the more unshakable we become in our faith. Faith, just like muscle needs to be exercised, stretched-sometimes to its limits - built up, otherwise atrophy sets it and

our 'faith muscle' becomes weak. The more our faith muscle is tested and stretched to its limits, the greater our capacity to endure. And in this stretching and testing process, God will never allow us to be tested beyond our ability to bear (1 Corinthians 10:13)

I used to think our enemy Satan derived great pleasure from watching us suffer. But in recent years I've come to realise that while he might take some (limited) enjoyment, Satan dreads Christian suffering! He hates it because it draws people closer to Jesus. Suffering causes us to realise and remember our need of the Lord, and to cling all the more tightly to Him. For thousands of years our enemy has had to stand by and helplessly watch, while our good, All-Powerful, Wondrous God has taken all those twisted plots that Satan meant for our downfall and worked them all for our good! (Genesis 50:20 Romans 8:28)

Take Paul for example: Paul was imprisoned multiple times, stoned, beaten, often hungry and thirty, often in danger, living on the edge and falsely accused (see 2 Corinthians 6 and 2 Corinthians 11) Still, Paul said he was *"sorrowful, yet always rejoicing; poor, yet making many rich; having nothing, and yet possessing everything."* 2 Corinthians 6:10 (NIVUK)

People such as Paul are not limited to the Bible. I've personally known people who have endured suffering and hardship with a joy that could only have come from God. It's a supernatural joy. God hasn't changed, He's the same God today as in Biblical times and when we look to him in our seasons of suffering, He leads us beside those still waters, where we find peace, strength and hope again.

The Bridal Powder Room

Monday - Attending Versus Belonging

"so in Christ we, though many, form one body, and each member belongs to all the others." Romans 12:5 (NIVUK)

The Church was not a human idea, it was conceived in the heart of God: *"This people have I formed for myself, and therefore I do all this for them, that they may show forth my praise." Isaiah43:21 (NIVUK)*
The Church is the work of God's own hands. He formed her for Himself and she is being lovingly shaped according to His will. We do not go to church, we are the Church. You, as you read this, are a living stone, and so am I. (1 Peter 2:5) In the same way that He formed, led and cared for the children of Israel, our forefathers, God will always feed, lead and tenderly care for us.

Attending Versus Belonging

Do you attend church or do you belong? That might sound pernickety but there's an important difference. Church 'goers' are in danger of developing a consumerism approach to the Church, hopping from church building to church building, according to what suits their liking and personal tastes, but never putting down roots or making real connections.

Connected

"God decided in advance to adopt us into his own family by bringing us to himself through Jesus Christ. This is what he

wanted to do, and it gave him great pleasure." Ephesians 1:5 (NLT)

When you became a Christian, you became part of the Body of Christ; legally adopted by God *into His family.* In much the same way that you received the legal rights to your earthly family name at birth, when you were born again you received legal rights to the family name, *Christian.* That name belongs to you and nothing can take it away from you. You were designed to be connected and to belong. Romans 12:5 says that we belong to each other. This means: You share ownership, have a legitimate place, share responsibility, have a role, share in the corporate vision and common purpose and can let your guard down and be vulnerable. You are accepted, valued and significant.

A common purpose

Church is not all about getting together for a bit of worship, a sermon, and going home again till next week. We, the church worldwide, have a common purpose. King Jesus' purpose. "So be very careful how you live, not being like those with no understanding, but live honourably with true wisdom, for we are living in evil times. Take full advantage of every day as you spend your life for his purposes." (Ephesians 5:15-16 TPT)

Those who disconnect.

I hear people say, "I have no problem with God, it's the Church I have an issue with." They disconnect from church, and try to go it alone with God. The defence is often, "I still meet my Christian friends and read my Bible." But sadly, if I'm disconnected from church family, then meeting other Christians for coffee, watching the God Channel, or playing worship music till the walls vibrate doesn't demonstrate that I'm still a passionate follower of Jesus, all it shows is that I've become an ineffective and rather lonely one. We can't have a proper relationship with Jesus when we're out of relationship with His Church, His bride.

* * *

The Bible has no teaching of Solo Christianity. That's because we are designed to be joined to each other. God has gifted each member of His the body to serve one another; I will stick my neck out here and say that it is *impossible* to 'do' Christianity alone. To live a solo Christian life runs counter to everything the Bible teaches us: "*Whoever isolates himself seeks his own desire; he breaks out against all sound judgment. A fool takes no pleasure in understanding, but only in expressing his opinion*". Proverbs 18:1 (NLT)

"*Let us think of ways to motivate one another to acts of love and good works. And let us not neglect our meeting together, as some people do, but encourage one another, especially now that the day of his return is drawing near*" Hebrews 10:25-25 (NLT) Also see 1 Corinthians 12:12

The New Testament is filled with descriptions of church life. The early Church shared meals together, were hospitable, prayed and worshipped together, learned from their leaders, they didn't hold too tightly onto possessions but shared what they had with one other and they used their gifts outside in their communities. Were they perfect? Hardly! The New Testament is not a story of an idealised church where everything ran smoothly at all times; they weren't that different to us, except that in many ways life was so much harder for them.

Will we get hurt in church? The short answer is, yes. But we are still not given the option to go it alone. Any community has flaws, because people are flawed, but it's more personally damaging to separate ourselves from our flawed community, and flounder about trying to walk this Christian life alone, than be connected and committed to a flawed community. As Christians we are commanded to love one another, *bear with* one another, and The Holy Spirit has given us the tools we need to work through our interpersonal issues in order to 'do life' together. (See Galatians 5:22-23)

Jesus delights in His Church

"God's purpose in all this was to use the church to display his wisdom in its rich variety to all the unseen rulers and authorities in the heavenly places. This was his eternal plan, which he carried out through Christ Jesus our Lord." Ephesians 3:10-11 (NLT)

Jesus delights in His Bride. His grace runs through our imperfect, but redeemed lives. The Church is a community of imperfect people, made perfect through Christ. Community can be messy and painful; people sin. Even leaders sin. It's only because of God's incredible mercy that He chooses broken human beings like us to showcase his perfect grace.

Jesus started the Church with imperfect people and today it is still filled with imperfect people. I'm one of them, so are you. Each one of us is a work in progress; imperfect but made righteous in God's sight. There is *one* thing I would change about my home-church. *Me!* But thankfully God is doing that work!

If you are a Christian and don't belong to a local church family, I urge you to find one and put down roots there. If you have lost your sense of belonging, I would implore you to make every effort to reconnect to your church family. You belong!

Tuesday - What's The Point In Church Meetings?

We know that we don't 'go to church', we *are* the church. So if that's the case, then why do we need to bother with meeting a few times a week? Couldn't we just get on with our lives at home, at work, and meet other Christians for coffee now and then - perhaps have a big 'worship celebration' once a month at a church building? These are the sorts of things I often hear Christians say and it truly amazes me.

The Bible is very clear on why we need to be involved in a local church body. It isn't to score points with the Lord, or improve our Heavenly curriculum vitae. Skipping church is not going to keep us from going to heaven, but I do believe, as I have said before, that we are not given any option for solo Christianity - it doesn't work.

Encourage one another.

"Let us think of ways to motivate one another to acts of love and good works. And let us not neglect our meeting together, as some people do, but encourage one another, especially now that the day of his return is drawing near." Hebrews 10:24-25 (NLT)

How will we do this if we aren't in church? How can I motivate anyone to 'acts of love and good works' if I'm never in church? How could I encourage others if I had no idea what was going on in their lives? That's why Paul wrote, '*let us not neglect meeting together'*. The early church didn't meet just once a week, they 'did life' together.

In Galatians 6:2 we are commanded to *bear one another's burdens*. Do we? When God impresses someone on our hearts in need of an encouraging phone call, perhaps an invitation to coffee, are we too absorbed in our own issues to pay attention? Since the Church is so important to Jesus that He died for her, I would say that it's His *will* for us be part of Church - as in: roots deep, committed, heart-to-heart involved!

To worship God together

I hear people make statements such as, "I really enjoyed (or didn't enjoy) the worship today." This makes me smile; worship is not about us. It isn't a concert, to be critiqued! It is about taking our eyes off ourselves for a change, and standing in His presence to offer ourselves as an act of worship. We worship God, not for what He can or will do for us, but just because He is worthy. How privileged we are, to stand face to face with God. We can strip away everything hindering us and bare our souls to God - *'naked'* and unashamed. We can worship in Spirit and truth: *"But the time is coming—indeed it's here now—when true worshipers will worship the Father in spirit and in truth. The Father is looking for those who will worship him that way. For God is Spirit, so those who worship him must worship in spirit and in truth."* John 4:23-24 (NLT)

The heart-attitude of worship is more important than the *place* of worship, but at the same time, there is nothing more beautiful and special than worshipping God together, corporately with your Church family.

Fellowship together

Yesterday, we looked into how the Church is God's family. We are all looking for a place to belong, a place of acceptance. We 'mess up' and when we do, we need to know that there's a safe place, where we are loved; where forgiveness is not only taught but lived out. There's enough harsh criticism and nastiness out in the world, the Church should be a place where we are known by our love for one another. (John 13:35)

To use your spiritual gifts

We have each been given gifts and these are for sharing with others, and for building up and encouraging the body - the church. We are to be 'faithful stewards' of our gifts, as Peter wrote: "God has given each of you a gift from his great variety of spiritual gifts. Use them well to serve one another. Do you have the gift of speaking? Then speak as though God himself were speaking through you. Do you have the gift of helping others? Do it with all the strength and energy that God supplies. Then everything you do will bring glory to God through Jesus Christ. All glory and power to him forever and ever! Amen." 1 Peter 4:10-11 (NLT)

A shift of focus

Church life can be hard sometimes. But when we shift our focus just a little bit, when we put aside our excuses and make church about *God* instead of about *us*, we will see the Church the way He sees her. Beautiful!

* The Church is the body of Christ, your family forever.
* The Church is Holy, set apart for God.
* The Church place of rescue, healing and encouragement.

Wednesday - Peace Walls Or Offence Walls?

An offended friend is harder to win back than a fortified city.
Arguments separate friends like a gate locked with bars.
Proverbs 18:19 (NLT)

Peace walls or defence walls?

The Peace Walls were erected in the late sixties during The Troubles in Northern Ireland as separation barriers between Catholic and Protestant neighbourhoods. Initially, they were meant only as temporary structures but because of their effectiveness they slowly become wider, longer and more permanent, and have now been in place for fifty years. Today, long after the Troubles are over, and Northern Ireland tries hard as a community to put all of her painful, bitter history behind her and move forward, these so called Peace Walls remain, a permanent reminder, keeping divisions firmly in place, both figuratively and literally.

Choosing to live with the walls

If you like the work of Banksy, let me tell you we have a few aspiring 'Banksy's here in Northern Ireland! A blank gable wall seems to cry out for a mural, and our towns and cities are covered in colourful ones of every sort! Despite many of these being sectarian in nature, some of the murals are very striking, artistically speaking. In keeping with our culture's 'inner Banksy,' many of the Peace Walls have been beautified with murals and are now, ironically, a tourist attraction and part of an open-top bus tour of Belfast. Tourists come here from all over the world to gaze at the physical evidence of our ugly past.

It strikes me that we can be so very like this in our personal lives too. We become offended, so we put up walls to shut out those who have offended us. Then, our walls become so entrenched that it becomes easier to just live with them; we try to disguise them with attractive 'murals' of religiosity and 'Churchianity' - whitewash them with a coat of outer niceness and pretence, while inside we desperately long to tear the walls down and connect with people.

Forgive quickly

Offence destroys relationships. We need to learn how to forgive quickly to avoid building those so called 'Peace Walls' in our hearts and in our relationships.

"Bear with each other and forgive one another if any of you has a grievance against someone. Forgive as the Lord forgave you." Colossians 3:13 (NIVUK)

Offence has damaging consequences, no matter how slight that offence might seem. (There's actually no such thing as 'slightly offended')

Every person who has ever lived has been or will be offended at some time in their life. The words *offence, offended, offend, and offender* appear a total of seventy-three times in the Bible, which shows just how seriously God takes this 'heart condition.'

Watch yourself!

Jesus warns, *"So watch yourselves. 'If your brother or sister sins*

against you, rebuke them; and if they repent, <u>forgive them</u>."
Luke 17:3 (NIVUK)

Another version of the Bible translates the first part of this verse
as *"pay attention."* Jesus doesn't ask us to be doormats, but
warns what can happen in the life of the person who doesn't *'pay
attention'* to his or her own heart attitude. We become offended
so we build a wall. *Just a little one,* a temporary structure to
protect our offended heart from being hurt further. We tell
ourselves that we'll take the wall down as soon as the trouble
subsides. Then we realise that it's easier to just keep the wall up.
It feels safer hidden behind the wall, where we don't have to talk
through the painful issues that have hurt us. Slowly, that
temporary structure, just like that first wall in Belfast, becomes a
little more fortified. Before you know, your heart is 'walled in'.

The offender

Jesus doesn't allow the offender off the hook either. So serious is
He about this issue that he pronounces a solemn *'woe'* to those
who cause others to stumble in this way. (*see Matthew 18:7.
Luke 17:1*)
It isn't our job to concern ourselves with the person who has hurt
or offended us. That's God's job. Ours is to take care of our own
attitudes for the sake of our own relationship with God and
others.

*"Don't have anything to do with foolish and stupid arguments,
because you know they produce quarrels. And the Lord's servant
must not be quarrelsome but must be kind to everyone, able to
teach, not resentful."* 2 Timothy 2:23-24 (NIVUK)
*"At that time many will turn away from the faith and will betray
and hate each other,"* Matthew 24:10 (NIVUK)

Notice something here: Jesus is speaking about *believers*. I don't
want ever to be in this position, do you? Let's choose today, to

forgive quickly, to move past offence, to not allow that first defence structure - posing as a so-called 'Peace Wall', to go up. Otherwise we could find ourselves, like Northern Ireland, many years later, with those Walls entrenched and incorporated and accepted into our everyday life.

Thursday - A Grove of Trees

"Make every effort to keep yourselves united in the Spirit, binding yourselves together with peace. For there is one body and one Spirit, just as you have been called to one glorious hope for the future." Ephesians 4:3-4 (NLT)

Fused together, growing together

A few years ago, the Lord spoke to me through a vivid dream that still impacts me today in my thinking about church life. In the dream, I was walking through a grove of very tall trees, growing close together. Somehow, in the dream I knew they were Redwood trees, even though I've never seen a Redwood in real life.

All of a sudden my dream took me underground and I saw the root system of the trees. It was massive; complex and incredibly widespread. But what amazed me most was the way the roots of each tree was so entwined around the tree nearest to it that I couldn't tell which roots belonged to which tree. They were <u>fused together</u>, from years of growing together. *I knew immediately that this dream was a picture of the Church.*

Uprooting

Then I saw a tree being uprooted and it was a terrible thing to see what happened underground. Big chunks of the roots of the other trees broke off, as the beautiful tree wrenched itself away. A large gaping hole was left in the forest where the tree had been, with bits of broken root from that tree and the trees it had been entwined with, lying discarded in the dirt.

When people leave churches for the wrong reasons, such as unresolved conflict, or because they imagine they might find greener pastures elsewhere - in other word; for any other reason than God's leading and direction - they don't think about the very real truth that they are not only hurting themselves. That, 'uprooted' person leaves behind an an aftermath of bits of broken roots and a huge gaping hole where he or she once grew.

Planted in groves

Redwoods don't grow alone, they grow in groves or forests. They have a root system as wide underground as the trees are tall above ground. As their roots spread, they intertwine with the roots of the all the other Redwood trees. This interlocking root system is so strong that the trees literally hold one another up in storms and strong winds. The Redwood is created to resist drought, fire, insects, disease, mudslides, flooding, violent storms and strong winds. There are two reasons it can do all these things:

1. It has the ability to draw up and store thousands of gallons of water, enabling year round growth and even helping them survive through drought.

2. The fact that they grow in forests. That incredible root system is a formidable opponent - any outside threat such as storms, high winds, even fire has to 'take on' the whole forest together, not an individual tree!

This is a powerful picture of how we, the Church are created to be. As followers of Jesus, we are not meant to grow and 'do life' alone, but to allow our roots to grow deeper into Jesus, drawing constantly from Him, our life source. He has equipped us with everything we need to live for Him.

"But blessed are those who trust in the Lord and have made the

Lord their hope and confidence. They are like trees planted along a riverbank, with roots that reach deep into the water. Such trees are not bothered by the heat or worried by long months of drought. Their leaves stay green, and they never stop producing fruit. Jeremiah 17:7-8 (NLT)

(Also see 2 Peter 1:3, Psalm 1:2-3)

Like the Redwood, The Lord has created us with the capacity to 'draw up and store water' - *the Living Water of the Word of God, which is our source of life*. We can't survive without Him, but with Him we can face all the storms and droughts of life.

Lastly, we are to allow our roots to entwine with one another's. Put down roots in the Church family God has placed you in. Let your guard down and be vulnerable. Trust and be trustworthy.

When we see one of our number struggling, or under attack, let's show the enemy of our soul, the devil, that he's going to have to take on the *whole forest!*

"Then, by constantly using your faith, the life of Christ will be released deep inside you, and the resting place of his love will become the very source and root of your life."
Ephesians 3:17 (TPT)

Friday - Growing Up

"Someone who lives on milk is still an infant and doesn't know how to do what is right." Hebrews 5:13 (NLT)

Paul addresses the problem of perpetual immaturity in the Church, and those who were happy to remain just as they were, never moving on from the spiritual 'milk', intended for new believers to the 'meat' of God's Word. This is still a common issue in the church today.

How do we 'grow up'?
By learning to feed ourselves: A baby needs to be spoon fed until she can feed herself. When she's a toddler, she needs to be supervised in case she eats something dangerous. But if as an adult she expected her parents to purée food and spoon-feed her I say there was a problem!

Some Christians arrive at church having barely glanced at their Bibles all week, expecting their pastors to spoon feed them. Then off they go, hoping this week's sermon will be sufficient to get them through the week. As a result, many are spiritually 'undernourished.' Is this the pastor's fault? Is it my pastor's job to feed me, like an oversized baby, or do I just need to grow up and learn how to feed myself?

Have you noticed how, often God speaks to you from the Bible regarding something and that very same week, the sermon at your church 'just happens' to be on that very same subject? Why are we so surprised by this? As a parent, when I have something important to share, I tell it to all four of my children; how much more then would our Heavenly Father share His heart with *all* of us? Actually it happened quite a bit while I was writing this book and I found it encouraging to have God's words to me confirmed by Bible teachers I highly respect!

Of course, the teaching we receive in our churches is vital. But God can use what your church teaches as a 'springboard'; It's to pique your curiosity to study further, not to sit back feeling full, satisfied and 'fed' for the week ahead. If we rely <u>solely</u> on someone else's findings in scripture and the things that God has revealed and spoken them, we are living on someone else's leftovers - however rich or filling they may be in the moment.

This account in Acts is a great example of people who were teachable, but also knew how to feed themselves: *"Now the Berean Jews were of more noble character than those in Thessalonica, for they received the message with great eagerness and examined the Scriptures every day to see if what Paul said was true. As a result, many of them believed, as did also a number of prominent Greek women and many Greek men."* Acts 17:11-12 (NIVUK)

A table prepared for me

God invites me *personally,* to come. *"He prepares a table before me, in the presence of my enemies"* Psalm 23:5 (NKJV) My Bible doesn't say, 'He makes sure my pastor prepares a decent feast for me every Sunday.'

The imagery of a table is so beautiful; it reveals God as the attentive Host, showing foresight and loving care in preparation; and the words *'before me'* shows the personal, intimate connection; *me*, rather than *us*. God *knows* what each of us needs to nurture and feed us.

I am surrounded by a spiritual enemy, but I, God's child can sit down to the feast He has prepared, with perfect security. God has set his table right in *the presence of my enemies!* His care doesn't eliminate the <u>presence</u> of my enemies, but I enjoy God's goodness and bounty *even in their midst.*

Why Should We Grow up?

God has designed us to grow up and become mature, so that we can:

* Love, support and encourage others: Being a Christian isn't 'all about me.' Growing into spiritual maturity involves so much more than just my own joy and peace. I'm designed to grow in Christ's likeness, displaying the fruit of The Spirit, so that I can encourage and love others: "*You have been believers so long now that you ought to be teaching others. Instead, you need someone to teach you again the basic things about God's word. You are like babies who need milk and cannot eat solid food.*" Hebrews 5:12 (NLT)

"When I was a child, I talked like a child, I thought like a child, I reasoned like a child. When I became a man, I put the ways of childhood behind me." 1 Corinthians 13:11 (NIVUK)
So strongly does Paul want to emphasise the contrast between spiritual childishness and maturity that the words *child /childish* are used five times in this verse. And the context is all about relating to others in love. Paul comes back to this theme as he closes in chapter thirteen:
"Dear brothers and sisters, I close my letter with these last words: Be joyful. <u>Grow to maturity.</u> Encourage each other. Live in harmony and peace. Then the God of love and peace will be with you." 2 Corinthians 13:11(NLT)

* To Equip us for Life: *"Solid food is for those who are mature,*

who through <u>training</u> have the skill to recognize the difference between right and wrong". Hebrews 5:14 (NLT)

Mature Christians have 'trained themselves' on solid food. The word 'train' here, is the same word used in Proverbs 22:6 *"<u>Train</u> up a child in the way he should go, And when he is old he will not depart from it."* (NKJV)

It's also used here: *"He <u>trains</u> my hands for battle; he strengthens my arm to draw a bronze bow. You have given me your shield of victory; your help has made me great. You have made a wide path for my feet to keep them from slipping."* 2 Samuel 35-37 (NLT)

and here: "All Scripture is God-breathed and is useful for teaching, rebuking, correcting and <u>training</u> in righteousness," 2 Timothy 3:16 (NIVUK)
Why?
The next verse goes on to explain exactly - its: "so that the servant (that's us) of God may be thoroughly equipped for every good work." 2 Timothy 3:17 (NIVUK)

Additional reading: Jeremiah 17:7-8 and Psalm 1:2-3

Saturday - Love And Honour

Biblical competitiveness

Did you know that in one of his letters the the church at Rome, the Apostle Paul actually *tells* the church to compete against each other?; to actively go out of their way to outdo each other? He says: *"Be devoted to tenderly loving your fellow believers as members of one family. Try to outdo yourselves in respect and honor of one another."* Romans 12:10 (TPT)

Can you picture the Church filled with people who live by this Biblical principle? So many pastors would find their workloads reduced; freed at last to focus on what God has called them to, *pastoring* - The heavy burden lifted, of arbitrating in the petty squabbles and offences of believers who should have grown up years ago. Churches would be filled to capacity with more new people coming in, saying, "what is it that these people have?" Is this possible? I believe it is!

Blood is thicker than water

What is brotherly love? The first and main thing that unites me to my biological siblings is *blood*. We are joined by DNA; we are family and nothing can ever change that fact. No argument between us, no demographics, geographical distance, nothing. We don't always agree on everything, but we still love each other and would defend one another to the hilt. And even if we were to fall out, nothing could change the fact that we are family - it's written into our DNA.

Our church family is similar. The Church is united by blood; the blood Jesus shed for us on the cross. We *belong* to one another and nothing can ever change this fact. We love one another because we are family. It makes me sad when I see Christians ripping other Christians to shreds on social media and other public platforms. Why do we celebrate the downfall or demise of a *sibling,* joined to us forever by blood?

Here in Northern Ireland as anywhere else in the world, we have seen some very prominent Christians, and even whole churches get themselves into difficulties, and these sins, wrong choices or foolish decisions end up all over the tabloids and the national news. Sadly, rather than come to their aid and offer prayerful and practical support, warmth, and love, many of their own brothers and sisters from other church groups join their voices with the *'accuser of the brethren'* (Revelation 12:10). This saddens the heart of our Father.

Honour

Love and honour go hand in hand, they are compadres, joined at the hip. When you show honour to another person, you are letting them know that they matter and count. By your actions you demonstrate to those you honour that they are important and highly valued as an image bearer of Christ.

Other versions translate Romans 12:10 as *"prefer one another in love."* One example of preferring another could be standing back from something I really want for myself and allowing that other person to have it instead; not because they have earned it, or deserve it better than I do, but merely as an act of grace. Also see John 15:13

* * *

Here's a thought; I wonder if this account in Mark's Gospel is Jesus setting an example of preferring the needs of others over our own? Jesus had been working just as hard, in fact harder, than His disciples, yet He saw that they were tired and His concern was for <u>their</u> wellbeing, <u>their</u> rest: *"Come, let's take a break and find a secluded place where <u>you</u> can rest a while."* Mark 6:31 (TPT)

When we honour one another, we show through our actions that we are all equal before God. Not one of us is set higher than anyone else. Paul continues in his letter, *"Live happily together in a spirit of harmony, and be as mindful of another's worth as you are your own. Don't live with a lofty mind-set, thinking you are too important to serve others, but be willing to do menial tasks and identify with those who are humble minded. Don't be smug or even think for a moment that you know it all."* Romans 12:16 (TPT)

Of course there are times when, just as in any family we might not *feel* very loving, or indeed loved, but this is when we make the choice to grow up and 'do' love; Yes, I know that's terrible grammar, but I wrote it that way on purpose because love is a verb, not a *feeling;* it is a conscious act of the will! Let's love and honour one another today.

Sunday - What's So Special About The Church?

"But you are God's chosen treasure—priests who are kings, a spiritual "nation" set apart as God's devoted ones. He called you out of darkness to experience his marvellous light, and now he claims you as his very own. He did this so that you would broadcast his glorious wonders throughout the world. For at one time you were not God's people, but now you are. At one time you knew nothing of God's mercy, because you hadn't received it yet, but now you are drenched with it!" 1 Peter 2:9-10 (TPT)

The church is special because we are His

Jesus made special mention of the Church in the Gospel of Matthew. Interestingly, Matthew is also the only Gospel that makes direct mention of the church: *"Now I say to you that you are Peter (which means 'rock'), and upon this rock I will build my church, and all the powers of hell will not conquer it."* Matthew 16:18 (NLT)

'My Church.' We are His. The Church is special because Jesus died for her. The Church was worth everything to God; He was willing to give Heaven's greatest Treasure as a ransom for her - His own beloved Son Jesus. (John 3:16)

Jesus is the attentive, loving Bridegroom

Jesus cherishes His Church and takes loving, attentive care of her. Traditionally, when we read Ephesians chapter five, we take from it a view of Christian marriage, which is correct, but there's also a much deeper parallel thread running through this section of scripture; a picture of the relationship between Jesus and the Church. Let's have a look at it:

"Wives, submit yourselves to your own husbands <u>as you do to the Lord.</u> For the husband is the head of the wife <u>as Christ is the head of the church, his body, of which he is the Saviour. Now as the church submits to Christ,</u> so also wives should submit to their husbands in everything. Husbands, love your wives, <u>just as</u> Christ <u>*loved*</u> the church and <u>*gave himself up for her*</u> to make her <u>holy, cleansing her by the washing with water through the word, and to present her to himself as a radiant church, without stain or wrinkle or any other blemish, but holy and blameless. In this same way</u>, husbands ought to love their wives as their own bodies. He who loves his wife loves himself. After all, no-one ever hated their own body, but they <u>*feed and care*</u> for their body, <u>*just as Christ does*</u> the church – <u>for we are members of his body.</u> 'For this reason a man will leave his father and mother and be united to his wife, and the two will become one flesh.' <u>This is a profound mystery – but *I am talking about Christ and the church*</u>." Ephesians 5:22-32 (NIVUK)

The Church is the Father's gift His Son

We, the Church are God's gift to Jesus. Hard as this is to take in, it's true. We find it easier to accept that Jesus is the Father's gift to us - but that Jesus would be delighted to receive *us* as a gift? That's mind boggling; but it's true! In closing, we'll take a look at a few lines of Jesus' prayer for His disciples - those who walked with Him while He was on earth, and all future disciples:

"*You have already given me authority over all people so that I may give the gift of eternal life to <u>all those that you have given to</u>*

me. Father, I have manifested who you really are and I have revealed you to the men and women that you gave to me. They were yours, and you gave them to me, and they have fastened your Word firmly to their hearts.

And the very words you gave to me to speak I have passed on to them. They have received your words and carry them in their hearts. They are convinced that I have come from your presence, and they have fully believed that you sent me to represent you. So with deep love, I pray for my disciples. I'm not asking on behalf of the unbelieving world, but for those who belong to you, those you have given me. For all who belong to me now belong to you. And all who belong to you now belong to me as well, and my glory is revealed through their surrendered lives." John 17:2, 6, 8-10 (TPT)

No Place I Would Rather Be

Monday - Permanent Residence In God's Precence

"Those who live in the shelter of the Most High will find rest in the shadow of the Almighty." Psalms 91:1 (NLT)

(If you have a few moments, it would be a good idea to read through all of Psalm 91. It isn't very long)

Many other translations use the words *those who dwell.* The word *dwell* in this context, means, to *live in,* or *take up permanent residence in.* It's a conscious choice to draw near to God and to make his presence our permanent residence; and it is in doing so, that we find *'rest in the shadow of the Almighty.'* In verse seven the Psalmist declares, *"A thousand may fall at your side, And ten thousand at your right hand; But it shall not come near you."* Psalms 91:7 (NKJV)

How can he say this with such confidence? Because he has made God's presence his dwelling place. See verses nine and ten: *"Because you have made the Lord, who is my refuge, Even the Most High, your dwelling place, No evil shall befall you, Nor shall any plague come near your dwelling;"* Psalms 91:9-10 (NKJV)

Dwelling in God's presence sounds very high, lofty, and unattainable; only for the 'super spiritual.' But really that isn't the case. It is true that this devotional life of the spirit does seem to come more easily for some than for others, but *the secret place of the Most High* is for everyone who puts their trust in Him.

We often pray and 'invite' God to come, and I picture the Lord smiling and saying; 'I'm already here.' It's we who are are invited to 'come.' God's presence is always with us: *"I can never escape from your Spirit! I can never get away from your presence! If I go up to heaven, you are there; if I go down to the grave, you are there. If I ride the wings of the morning, if I dwell by the farthest oceans, even there your hand will guide me, and your strength will support me."* Psalm 139:7 (NLT)

Apart from special daily 'set aside time' with God, we can draw near to him all day, through the day, by just acknowledging His presence, talking to Him and including Him in everything we do. It sounds very simplistic, but that's because it is! It's we humans that complicate our relationship with God with all our religious trappings. He is there, beside us, all day, every day, and all we need to do is acknowledge this.

Make Him your permanent safe place

"This I declare about the Lord: He alone is my refuge, my place of safety; he is my God, and I trust him. He will cover you with his feathers. He will shelter you with his wings. His faithful promises are your armour and protection."
Psalms 91:2, 4 (NLT)

He will cover you with His feathers: David uses this beautiful imagery of a bird, probably an eagle, sheltering her young with her wings. There's a sense of great power combined with great gentleness. It would take a very bold (or stupid)! Individual to put a hand into that nest, braving those wings, those mighty talons in an attempt to drag the chicks from that warm hiding place under her wings! (Also see Psalm 61:4)

* * *

Jesus too, alluded to this theme, in Matthew's Gospel when He looked out over Jerusalem and His heart was wrenched: *"Jerusalem, Jerusalem, you who kill the prophets and stone those sent to you, how often I have longed to gather your children together, as a hen gathers her chicks under her wings, and you were not willing."* Matthew 23:37 (NIVUK)

Jesus longed to gather and shelter Jerusalem and its inhabitants, under His wings, but the people were just not willing. They just wouldn't come to him. They refused to 'dwell in the shelter of the Most High.' What about us today; are we willing?

Tuesday - The Shadow Of The Almighty

"Whoever dwells in the shelter of the Most High will rest in the shadow of the Almighty." Psalms 91:1 (NIVUK)

I love the thought of dwelling in the shadow of Most High. A shadow is a place of protection; If the direct heat of the sun becomes too much, we seek refuge in the cool of the shadows to escape the intensity. This is beautiful imagery of the shelter that God gives to His children. His shadow is the place of confidence, rest, protection, healing, peace and calm. It's where I want to be! Sometimes the 'heat' of life can become so intense. Pressures and stress can be as stifling and hot as the blazing sun, but those who dwell in the shelter of the Most High, will rest in the shadow of the Almighty.

Yesterday, we looked into the importance of dwelling permanently in God's presence. When we live permanently in God's presence, we abide - *live* - under His shadow, His *shade.*

We can't survive in the intense heat of life without the shade God's shadow provides. In His shadow we find a cool place to rest and recover our strength. His shadow shades us from the full blast of the 'sun'. Although God didn't ever promise that we would have a life free of hard times, He has provided a place of refuge, shade, shelter, comfort, peace, rest, renewed strength and so much more, when we *abide in - live in -* His shadow. That is, when we choose to make the shelter of His presence our lifestyle; *to keep company with Him.*

A Hiding Place

What do you picture when you think of a shady place? A canopy? A nice big gazebo or beach tent, shading you from the sun, yet allowing a cool breeze to waft through? That was what I used to think. But God's Shadow is *so much more* than that! He is a shelter for us, completely covering us and surrounding us on all sides.

God's Shadow is more than just some sort of canopy over our heads - God is our hiding place. Your enemy Satan cannot place even a toe into the fortified sanctuary that is yours and yours alone. So, when he comes with accusations and lies such as *"God couldn't love you, remember what you did last week?"* Then remember this from the Word of God: *"For you died, and your life is now hidden with Christ in God."* Colossians 3:3 (NIVUK)

The Psalms are filled with imagery of God as our Hiding Place. This sanctuary is a place of penitence, mercy, grace, forgiveness, safety, instruction, love, and refuge from our enemies:

"In his shelter in the day of trouble, that's where you'll find me, for he hides me there in his holiness. He has smuggled me into his secret place, where I'm kept safe and secure— out of reach from all my enemies." Psalms 27:5 (TPT)

"Keep me as the apple of your eye; hide me in the shadow of your wings" Psalms 17:8 (NIVUK)

"How abundant are the good things that you have stored up for those who fear you, that you bestow in the sight of all, on those who take refuge in you. In the shelter of your presence you hide them from all human intrigues; you keep them safe in your

dwelling from accusing tongues."
Psalms 31:19-20 (NIVUK)

"For in the day of trouble he will keep me safe in his dwelling; he will hide me in the shelter of his sacred tent and set me high upon a rock." Psalms 27:5 (NIVUK)

"You are my hiding-place; you will protect me from trouble and surround me with songs of deliverance."
Psalms 32:7 (NIVUK)

'For he will hide me in his shelter in the day of trouble; he will conceal me under the cover of his tent; he will lift me high upon a rock.' Psalm 33:19-20 (NLT)

What a beautiful picture of our God! Why would we ever want to be anywhere else but in the shelter God provides for us? In the shadow of the Most High is where we find all we need.

Wednesday - True Peace

"Peace I leave with you; my peace I give you. I do not give to you as the world gives. Do not let your hearts be troubled and do not be afraid." John 14:27 (NIVUK)

Do you need peace?

In today's world it can be hard to find, and maintain peace. Every time you lift a newspaper or turn on the television, the news headlines range from negative to terrifying.

Bombs, murders, paedophiles, sexual predators, terrorism, political mayhem, and more. And even if the *big stuff* isn't happening where you are, there are the confusing, conflicting reports that are a bit closer to home, such as our health and what may or may not affect it. One day they're telling you, 'eat plenty of this, it will stave off cancer,' and the next day, 'don't eat that, (very same thing) it will give you cancer.' If you aren't carefully 'guarding your heart' this could all make you feel a bit edgy, a sort of gnawing little uneasiness below the surface.

It would be easy to get swept up in it all. A little spark of fear, if not snuffed out immediately, can quickly become a big flame and then a wildfire!

Peace is Jesus' gift to us

"Peace I leave with you; my peace I give you. I do not give to you as the world gives. Do not let your hearts be troubled and do not be afraid." John 14:27 (NIVUK)

* * *

Shalom: Culturally this was a usual thing to say. (It still is) People would greet each other or say goodbye with "*shalom*" - 'peace be upon you', but it wasn't said with any special meaning. People used it in a similar way to how we use the word *goodbye*; did you know that *goodbye* literally means, *God be with you? - God-by-you.* Most people today don't mean it that way, it's just a word.

Jesus wanted His disciples to know that when He said, '*peace I leave with you,*' it wasn't in the casual, everyday way people usually said it. He took this everyday word and filled it with deeper significance, infused it with power, and gave it to all His followers as a gift: "*Peace I leave with you, My peace I give to you.*" My Peace.

Not as the world gives

It isn't the sort of peace we can find anywhere else. People practice yoga, 'mindfulness,' and all the other types of temporary so-called 'peace-giving' exercises the world tries to offer, but they are a mere facsimile of the *real* peace that Jesus gives. His is a peace beyond our ability to understand, because it's supernatural: "*And the peace of God, which transcends all understanding, will guard your hearts and your minds in Christ Jesus.*" *Philippians 4:7 (NIVUK)*

The peace Jesus gives, when we truly grasp hold of this incredible gift, causes us and others to look at our circumstances that *should* be causing us to have a complete melt down, and be amazed at the peace that floods our soul instead. Jesus described the peace He gives as '*My peace.*' Jesus' own peace was demonstrated in a heart that remained untroubled and unafraid in spite of all the suffering that He knew lay just ahead of Him. That's the kind of peace He said He was leaving us as a gift.

Unafraid, Untroubled - "Believe In Me!"

Having promised His peace that will be unlike anything the world has to offer, Jesus reiterates again the command "*Don't let your hearts be troubled and do not be afraid,*" which is where He started this farewell talk with the disciples. Right back in verse one of this chapter, Jesus starts off: *"Do not let your hearts be troubled. You believe in God; believe also in me."* John 14:1 (NIVUK).

I seem to be repeating this throughout the book, but I sense it's something the Lord would have me say, again: we *believe*, not just because we 'have faith,' but because we believe, trust and have faith in who we know Jesus to be. It's His character and nature that we believe - that He is faithful and true, and will do as He has promised.

When we put our faith in God, and receive the gift of peace that Jesus gives us through the person of the Holy Spirit, we can live fearlessly and untroubled in a fearful and troubled world.

Thursday - Seek The Giver Not The Gift

"I lie awake thinking of you, meditating on you through the night. Because you are my helper, I sing for joy in the shadow of your wings. I cling to you; your strong right hand holds me securely." Psalm 63: 6-8 (NLT)

I would suggest that you read Psalm 63 before reading this.

Trouble Sleeping?

Do you ever have trouble sleeping? Worries that keep you awake at night? Lying there, in the quiet, while everyone else is sleeping, the darkness seems darker. Problems are magnified out of all proportion. There's a solution. David discovered it. He was awake, but he wasn't dwelling on his troubles. I love reading Psalm 63 when I'm feeling overwhelmed, it reminds me of David's ability to refocus and shift his attention from his problems onto the Problem Solver, and that I can do it too.

Worship in the dark

This beautiful Psalm is attributed to David, written during his time in the wilderness, when he was fleeing from his enemies. Reading this, I wonder how I would react in the same situation. Admittedly, most of us will probably never have to go on the run from an enemy and camp out in a desert. But sometimes life can feel that way. And there are times when we face a spiritual wilderness.

* * *

When you wake up in the middle of the night, thinking about your child's plummeting school reports and worry that she might be being bullied, when your bank account is flat-lining again, when a loved one is waiting for test results from the doctor, when you're facing possible job loss, these modern-day issues are all very real and threaten to overwhelm us.

What did David do when life's problems threatened to overwhelm him? Rather than pleading with God for help, David pours out his longing for *God Himself.* I'm reminded of a song we used to sing in the 1990s that had the lyrics: *"I seek the Giver not the gift, My heart's desire is to lift you High above all earthly things, and bring you pleasure Lord."*

I believe this was David's motive in Psalm 63; to seek The Giver, not the gift. David longed for a deeper connection with God. He compares his soul to the desert he's hiding out in; dry, parched and weary; he tells The Lord how much he longs for refreshing and renewal. Then, incredibly, he begins to pour out his thanks to God and expresses his hope for the future. Isn't that amazing? In the middle of a desert! He declares his trust and confidence in the hand of God to hold him securely.

David's troubles were overshadowed by his remembrance of God's greatness
It strikes me that David was so involved in worship and thanksgiving that his troubles - very real, life threatening enemies - only receive a brief mention at the end, almost as an afterthought!

If you find yourself lying awake at night, mulling over problems, try shifting your focus from your problems to our All-Powerful, Faithful God; the One who promises never to leave you or forsake you. It's not that your problems will disappear, but they will certainly be diminished in comparison to God's greatness!

* * *

"Because you are my helper, I sing for joy in the shadow of your wings." Psalm 63:7 (NLT)

"Because you are my helper": Remind yourself who God is. How could we be afraid or overwhelmed with such a God by our side? ON our side!

"I will sing for joy in the shadow of your wings": David didn't wait till his circumstances improved before "singing for joy." In all the heat and dryness of the wilderness, still in the run, he found joy in God's presence and it just spilled out of him in worship; he couldn't contain it!

Friday - Have You Seen Him?

When they were alone, he [Jesus] turned to the disciples and said, "Blessed are the eyes that see what you have seen. I tell you, many prophets and kings longed to see what you see, but they didn't see it. And they longed to hear what you hear, but they didn't hear it." Luke 10:23-24 (NLT)

For centuries, the righteous among God's people had longed to see the arrival of God's Kingdom. Now here He was; Jesus, the long-awaited one. God become flesh. The God who stooped to touch us, Emmanuel, God with us. (See also Luke 2:25-32)

Have you seen Him? Have you seen His beauty and Majesty, His kindness and mercy? Some reading this might think I've lost the plot; 'of course we haven't seen Him, He's reigning in Heaven!' Sometimes, because we don't have Jesus with us in the flesh, and walking among us as a man today, we can forget that He is actually here with us and there are <u>many</u> ways to see Him.

How Do We See Him?

We see Him in so many ways, when we open our incredibly blessed eyes and just *see!*

*A perfectly timed word of encouragement from another Christian when we're feeling discouraged.

*A loving offer of practical help from an unexpected source.

*A warm smile from another person, just when you're feeling at

your most unloved and unlovable.
*An envelope with the exact amount of money you needed to pay that bill - slipped anonymously under your door.
*In the reading of a Bible verse that you have read countless times, that you 'suddenly' understand clearly for the first time. All these small things cause us to glimpse the face of Jesus, the One who draws near to us.

If you belong to Him, then the light of Jesus Christ shines in your heart: *"For God, who said, "Let there be light in the darkness," has made this light shine in our hearts so we could know the glory of God that is seen in the face of Jesus Christ." 2 Corinthians 4:6 (NLT)*

He prompts someone to come along and touch your hurting spirit as only Jesus could do, and *suddenly you see Him!* He quietly nudges you to discreetly pay for that lady's shopping, just ahead of you in the supermarket queue - you don't know her circumstances, but He does. Suddenly you're so aware of His presence that it seems tangible - *suddenly you see Him!*

These are just some of the many ways that we see Jesus, every single day, and the many ways we can reveal Jesus to someone else, every single day.

It's what the disciples did - they cause others to 'see' Jesus through their preaching, teaching, and lifestyle of ministering to others. And we can do the same!
"For we did not follow cunningly devised fables <u>when we made known to you</u> the power and coming of our Lord Jesus Christ, but were eyewitnesses of His majesty."
2 Peter 1:16 (NKJV)

Have you seen Jesus? Then don't keep Him all to yourself. Cause others to see Him through you.

Saturday - Wait For The Lord

"But those who wait on the LORD Shall renew their strength; They shall mount up with wings like eagles, They shall run and not be weary, They shall walk and not faint."
Isaiah 40:31 (NKJV)

The way God has designed an eagle to fly is such a beautiful picture of what He does in our lives when we put our trust in Him. The eagle knows when a storm is approaching. Before the storm breaks, she waits on a high mountain peak for the wind, and then, utilising the power of uplifting thermals to enable and empower her, she flies to those incredible heights that eagles are famous for without using up precious energy by flapping.

It takes a lot of energy to flap such large wings. Ornithological studies have shown that although eagles are perfectly capable of sustained flapping flight, they typically spend only an average of less than two minutes per hour doing so. The rest of the eagle's flight is spent soaring on the wind - essentially being carried by the wind. This reliance on the wind saves the eagle considerable energy. For mile after mile of her journey the eagle barely even has to flap her wings. What a picture of Isaiah 40:31!

Often we exhaust ourselves from rushing from this thing to that, trying to cope with every storm that comes our way all on our own. But God has not designed us for *flapping*, He created us to soar.

Perhaps there is a storm brewing in your life presently, or you feel that you are right in the in midst of a storm as you read this. In a similar way, but even better that the thermals carry the eagle and enable her to soar, the Wind of God; His Holy Spirit, will swoop you up empower you and carry you to incredible altitudes, enabling you to fly and for mile upon mile. God is ever ready to strengthen you and cause you to soar, but this only happens when you learn to stop flapping and wait for the wind of His Spirit.

Wait

What does it mean to wait on the Lord? The Hebrew word used for wait here is *qâvâh*, a verb meaning, *to await instruction, look eagerly for, linger, lie in wait for.*

Wait is not a passive word. It doesn't suggest a time of sitting about twirling our spiritual thumbs! Rather, we actively, consciously wait for the Lord with eager expectation and the *unshakable knowledge* that He will turn up. Wait for Him!

Sunday- Home Is Where The Heart Is

"Lord, through all the generations you have been our home!"
Psalm 90:1 (NLT)

I recently calculated that from the time I was born until eleven years ago I have moved house twenty-two times, across three continents. That's a lot of packing up! As a child, it was a lot of upheaval, at times very traumatic; I was always the new kid at school. I sometimes looked at people who had spent their entire lives in the same home and felt a little bit envious. I used to long for what I believed was the stability of a 'permanent home.'

That is, until I started to understand, a few years ago, that my home isn't made of bricks and mortar. We've all heard that saying 'home is where the heart is.' I used to think of it as meaning home is where family and loved ones are, no matter where in the world that may be. While there is a lot of truth to that, the saying has a new meaning for me these days, with three of my four children living abroad.

I've learned my Father God is my 'home.' He is that permanent home that I had always been longing for! If you belong to Him, then like me, you're just passing through. This world isn't our home:
"We are here for only a moment, visitors and strangers in the land as our ancestors were before us. Our days on earth are like

a passing shadow, gone so soon without a trace." 1 Chronicles 29:15 (NLT)

While I'm here, I can choose to make His presence my dwelling place, my 'safe place,' and my place of rest and shelter, as we have already looked at quite a bit this week in Psalm 91.
I can choose to follow wherever He leads me and trust Him when He says, *"I will never leave you or forsake you."* Wherever His presence is - that's my home!

God has made His home in us
The truth that God is my home is a huge comfort to me. However, that Almighty God, The One True God, The King of Kings, makes *His* home in *me* is both astounding and humbling. But it's the truth!

"Then Christ will make his home in your hearts as you trust in him. Your roots will grow down into God's love and keep you strong." Ephesians 3:17 (NLT)

"Don't you realise that your body is the temple of the Holy Spirit, who lives in you and was given to you by God?" 1 Corinthians 6:19 (NLT)

"I will live among you, and I will not despise you. I will walk among you; I will be your God, and you will be my people." Leviticus 26:11-12 (NLT)

"Jesus replied, "All who love me will do what I say. My Father will love them, and we will come and make our home with each of them." John 14:23 (NLT)

In God we have a permanent, forever home. Never displaced - we belong! Our roots are deeply, firmly planted, secure - we are established. We're citizens of The Kingdom of Heaven!

It really doesn't matter where we live, geographically or where God leads us to - as long as we remain rooted in Him, God will always, as *Psalm 90:1* says, be our home!

Seasons of Life

Monday - Winter

"We pray that you'll have the strength to stick it out over the long haul—not the grim strength of gritting your teeth but the glory-strength God gives. It is strength that endures the unendurable and spills over into joy, thanking the Father who makes us strong enough to take part in everything bright and beautiful that he has for us." Colossians 2:10-12 (MSG)

Everything tends to look dead in winter, doesn't it? Sometimes I look at our garden during the coldest, darkest days of winter and wonder whether I only imagined the beautiful, bright flowers that grew only a month or two ago - *will they ever grow again, will the bulbs and seeds I have planted ever break the soil and bloom?*

Spiritual seasons, particularly 'Winter;' can feel very similar. But Winter is a necessary, and important season. It gives plants time to build up strength for the next season. Those bulbs under the soil and the apparently dry, dead stalks on the shrubs and trees are, in fact, bursting with life and potential, just waiting for their 'appointed time.' Spring always follows Winter!

Are you presently in a Winter season of your life, spiritually speaking? Winter can seem as though it drags endlessly on, and we start to believe we are caught in some sort of personal Narnia - with no Spring in sight. If this describes your present season, find encouragement from the above passage in Colossians; this season is a precious time of growth, a time to rest, to let your roots go deeper into God, and grow stronger: *"Not the grim strength of gritting your teeth but the glory-strength God gives."*

God hasn't forgotten you. Winter has its purpose and it will pass. There will come a day when the Lord will take you by the hand and say to you, "Look, the winter is past, and the rains are over and gone. The flowers are springing up, the season of singing birds has come, and the cooing of turtledoves fills the air. The fig trees are forming young fruit, and the fragrant grapevines are blossoming. Rise up, my darling! Come away with me, my fair one!" Song of Songs 2:11-13 (NLT)

Prospering in Winter
"He has made everything beautiful in its time. He has also set eternity in the human heart; yet no-one can fathom what God has done from beginning to end." Ecclesiastes 3:11 (NIVUK)

God has created seasons of time on the earth. Similarly, with purpose and love, He divides our lives into seasons. If you are in a Winter season as you read this, remember that there is an appointed season for when your God-given dreams and promises will come to fruition - it is called *due season.*

In John chapter 2 Jesus told His mother, *"Jesus replied. "My time has not yet come." John 2:4* (NLT)
God had a specific season for Jesus' ministry to be fulfilled and Jesus understood this.

Abraham and Sarah tried to give God a helping hand in bringing about His promise of a child, not realising that God had a specific season already set for the fulfilment of the promise.

When we don't recognise the gift that a spiritual Winter is, we only see barrenness. That's because most of us view a prospering life God as the full, blooming tree in Spring, with fresh new leaves, or in summer, with branches groaning under the weight of sweet, ripe fruit. Winter is a gift; treasure it!

Tuesday - Refreshing Of God In A Dry Season

"He sat down under a solitary broom tree and prayed that he might die. "I have had enough, Lord," he said. "Take my life, for I am no better than my ancestors who have already died." 1 Kings 19:4 (NLT)

Have you ever found yourself suddenly and unexpectedly in a 'wilderness,'or what is commonly known as a *dry season*? In those times, if we aren't careful, we can start to lose perspective, and believe we've been in the wilderness for longer than we actually have, that no one cares, nothing *ever* goes right, and that even God has forgotten us. Once our thoughts head down that route, we feel overwhelmed and under-equipped. Fear starts to call through the crack of our previously resolutely closed door, whispering like an chilly wind: '*what if things are never going to get better?*' Elijah, mighty prophet of the Old Testament went through a period of feeling that way. He ran in fear into the wilderness and became so depressed that he begged God to let him die!

Faith filled

The amazing thing about this story is that if we just back up a little bit to the events prior to Elijah's 'meltdown,' see a very different Elijah, full of faith and fearless! He was obedient in taking God's message to King Ahab, and demonstrated his trust in God in the way he confidently addressed the king, confronting him about his idolatry. Incidentally, this same king had a death warrant out on Elijah! See 1 Kings 18:17-18 (NIVUK) Elijah demonstrated God's mighty supernatural power before Ahab and all the prophets of Baal.

Fear filled
What happened to this faith filled Elijah? It's quite simple, really. He let fear in, and, listening to the voice of fear, he obeyed it instead of faith: *"Elijah was afraid and ran for his life."* 1 Kings 19:3 (NIVUK)

Elijah had not been afraid of Ahab's threats, nor was he cowed by the four hundred and fifty prophets of Baal, yet this death threat from Jezebel found a chink in his armour. An unguarded moment, a crack in the door, and fear slithered it's way into his mind. So we find Elijah exhausted and at the end of his tether in the wilderness.

It's not sudden, it's a process.
If you find yourself in a position similar to Elijah's today, it may seem that this suddenly came upon you, but these feelings of despair, or spiritual exhaustion are seldom sudden. We can see from Elijah's experience that they are often the end result of a process; a sort of 'drip-feed attack.'

We are in a spiritual battle. Those negative and fearful thoughts are often a 'stealth operation' of the enemy in his attempt to rob you of peace and confidence in God. When you're tired and spiritually depleted you are 'running on empty,' and you're in danger of listening to the voice of fear. This is why, as followers of Jesus, it is vital that we *"take captive every thought to make it obedient to Christ."* 2 Corinthians 10:5 (NIVUK)

Refreshing in the wilderness

Elijah cried out to God as he sat there in his personal wilderness. Then exhausted from his anguish and self pity, he fell asleep. God's response to Elijah's cry demonstrates the heart of our gracious Father. God sent an angel to bring freshly baked bread and water to the sleeping Elijah.

Then God allowed Elijah to sleep some more, to be fully rested, prepared and strengthened for what lay ahead.
"Then he lay down and slept under the broom tree. But as he was sleeping, an angel touched him and told him, "Get up and eat!" He looked around and there beside his head was some bread baked on hot stones and a jar of water! So he ate and drank and lay down again." 1 Kings 19:5-6 (NLT)

God may not change your circumstances immediately, but He will give you the refreshment and strength you need in order to continue. Our daily fresh bread and water is the Word of God. Without it, we become spiritually depleted. God's Word is our source of life, sustenance and strength to enable us to rise above our circumstances and face anything.

"Then the angel of the Lord came again and touched him and said, "Get up and eat some more, <u>or the journey ahead will be too much for you.</u>" So he got up and ate and drank, <u>and the food gave him enough strength to travel</u> forty days and forty nights to Mount Sinai, the mountain of God." 1 Kings 19:7-8 (NLT)

Restoration

"What are you doing here, Elijah?" 1 Kings 19:13 (NIVUK)
I love this part of the story. It's as if the Lord says to Elijah, *'what's going on with you?'* When Elijah finally ends his fearful 'rant,' and the Lord can get a word in edgewise, He speaks.

God's voice is so mighty and powerful that, He *spoke* the whole cosmos into existence. His voice makes the mountains tremble and the seas roar. He could have spoken to Elijah's in thunder, lightening and fire, but instead He chose a *still, small voice*. It's not a voice of angry rebuke, it's the kind, loving voice of the Father. The Lord gives him instruction on where to go next, and Elijah's peace is restored.

Sometimes we engage our mouths more readily than our [spiritual] ears. We can't hear God over the noise of our own voices. Does God need to say to you today, *"what are you doing here?"* If you feel at the end of your tether, don't give up! Open the Word of God and ask God to feed you, to restore your strength, and to ready you for the road ahead. Allow Him to renew your hope and give you direction, just as He did Elijah.

Wednesday - A Season Of Change

"And the Lord—who is the Spirit—makes us more and more like him as we are changed into his glorious image. 2 Corinthians 3:18 (NLT)

"Don't copy the behaviour and customs of this world, but let God transform you into a new person by changing the way you think. Then you will learn to know God's will for you, which is good and pleasing and perfect." Romans 12:2 (NLT)

"And I am certain that God, who began the good work within you, will continue his work until it is finally finished on the day when Christ Jesus returns." Philippians 1:6 (NLT)

Diapause

At any stage during a caterpillar's development it can go into a period of dormancy called 'diapause.' Diapause is described as "a *period of arrested development"*. Simply put, this change resistant caterpillar puts transformation 'on hold' until further notice. This usually occurs when the caterpillar senses that the environment is not favourable to change. The caterpillar can remain suspended, putting off change, until the following Spring when the environment appears more favourable.

The change resistant Christian

Aren't we so like the caterpillar at times? Personally speaking, there have been times when I've known intellectually, that I could not remain in the cocoon of my comfort zone forever, but there was a *cost* to change; leaving the cocoon would alter my comfortable condition forever and I didn't that know what else the change might bring. So I clung to what felt familiar and secure.

Fear of the unknown causes *us to stay where we are.* We <u>talk</u> about change, we know that when God calls us to step out of our comfort zones it is in order to grow and develop us, sometimes we even clearly see the areas in our lives where God wants to bring the change. And then just as we are faced with the moment of choice, the opportunity to break free of the cocoon, a sort of 'spiritual diapause' invades our thoughts with excuses for why 'the time is not right.' Without understanding what it is that we are doing, we give up the wonderful things God wants to do in, for, and through us; forfeiting a life of flying for a cramped cocoon.

Moses the butterfly

Moses wasn't at all comfortable with the idea of going to speak to Pharaoh to tell him to free the Israelites. In fact when God told him to go, Moses pleaded with the Lord to send someone else: *"But Moses again pleaded, "Lord, please! Send anyone else."* Exodus 4:13 (NLT)

What a different historical picture we would have, had Moses decided to remain in his comfort zone! Of course God *could have* picked someone else, but He wanted *Moses* for the task, ineloquent as Moses believed himself to be. And history speaks for itself concerning Moses' transformation.

Live the life God intended for you

While the fat little caterpillar is happily chomping her way through life, the little creature has no idea just how very limited her life is in comparison to what lies ahead! Then, while she is tucked up in the safety and comfort of the cocoon, does she think (if caterpillars could think) "this is so wonderful, cool and comfortable. I never want to leave this place." If she only knew what God had in store for her!

When the butterfly emerges from the cocoon with her beautiful wings, she can flutter through the air - no more inching up prickly branches, no more confined, cramped space. She now can see everything from a whole new perspective because her view is no longer limited. The butterfly is now living the life God intended for her.

A cocoon is only ever meant to be a place of preparation. But diapause is another thing altogether! Let's not allow fear to feed us a *false sense of security,* to keep us in diapause, and prevent us from breaking out of that 'preparation place' once God says we are ready!

Thursday - A Season Of Planting

"For through the eternal and living Word of God you have been born again. And this "seed" that he planted within can never be destroyed but will live and grow inside you forever. For: Human beings are frail and temporary, like grass, and the glory of man fleeting like the blossoms of the field. The grass dries and withers and the flowers fall off, but the Word of the Lord endures forever! And this is the Word that was announced to you!" 1 Peter 1:23-25 (TPT)

This scripture brings to mind thoughts of Spring, and newly planted seeds. I'm not a very good gardener, but I've learned over the last few years, through trial and error, that when it comes to packets of seed you get what you pay for. Scrimp on price, and the seeds are often of lower quality and the resulting 'harvest' disappointing. Care and attention to detail such as the 'plant-by' date and the expiry date are very important to get the out of every packet. Seeds are perishable. The Word of God, however, is the richest quality seed you could ever imagine. It is imperishable and life-giving.

We are brought into this world through the perishable seed of our parents, which is subject to death. But by faith in the finished work of Jesus, we have now been born again through *imperishable seed,* through the power of the Holy Spirit.

God's Word is the incorruptible seed

"Don't lose sight of them. Let them penetrate deep into your heart, for they bring life to those who find them, and healing to their whole body." Proverbs 4:21-22 (NLT)

The Word of God is alive. As we read the Word of God, the Holy Spirit makes it alive *in* and *to* us. Don't you just love those moments when you are reading the Bible and you feel God's Word of truth become part of you, as though suddenly, the words you were reading deeply touched your heart.

Reading the Word of God is so much more significant that just agreeing with well-written words in a book. The written words in the Word of God are seeds, packed with life and truth, and God has a bespoke, 'plant-by' date on those seeds, for the garden of your heart, for specific seasons of your life.

Although I am writing this in the 'Seasons" chapter of the book, don't get me wrong; I'm not suggesting that these Rhema words only come to us 'seasonally." We can expect God to speak to us every time we open His Word.
I'm talking more about the wonderful way in which God has specific 'words in season' for you; and for me.

That moment when you feel the seed of a particular Word take root in your heart is the planting date God had in mind, long ago.The 'eureka' moment you had when the words on the page of your Bible seemed to become so clear suddenly - so loaded with meaning - that was the moment the incorruptible seed lodged in your heart and mind and took root.

It's a little bit like the moment of conception. The Word, which is the incorruptible seed of God, is planted into the soil of your heart, and life takes place. The more you meditate on that Word, the more it grows, and you realise the truth of it has forever changed something inside you. It is something no one can ever take from you!

Friday - A Season Of Waiting

"I wait for the LORD, my whole being waits, and in his word I put my hope. I wait for the Lord more than watchmen wait for the morning, more than watchmen wait for the morning." Psalms 130:5-6 (NIVUK)

Have you received a promise, or call, from the Lord that seems to be taking *forever* to come to fruition? Patience is not something most of us overflow with. We can be tempted to try to manipulate circumstances or people to get what we're longing for, forgetting that God doesn't share our perspective, sense of timing, or desires.

Babies are born impatient; they demand to be fed, changed and entertained - right now! Children have no concept of time and no sense of tomorrow or next week. When my children were little, I usually didn't tell them about an event until the day before, otherwise they would have asked me all day, every day, "how long now, until we go?" Waiting can come with maturity. It's something many of us work at and develop over years, and if the truth be told, it remains a work area for most of us.

Jesus couldn't get *even one* of his disciples to wait with him through that night of anguished prayer in the garden of Gethsemane. As much as they loved Him, they just couldn't muster up the self discipline or staying power to stay awake.

When I read the above verses in Psalm 130, a mental image of the lonely watchman comes to mind. I picture him, at the start of his shift, thinking, "this isn't so bad." By the time he's three or four hours into the shift, he longs for dawn to break, or at least for some action to break the monotony. But one thing the watchman knows with absolute surety is that dawn will come. As will the Lord, to the one who waits expectantly.

A time of expectancy

Waiting, in the Biblical sense, does not mean passivity or inactivity. The watchman couldn't afford to fall asleep while he waited, it was his job and responsibility to watch and to be on the lookout. He had to stay alert! When we are inactive or passive in our spiritual lives, we tend to drift in our commitment to wait and watch, and we are in danger of 'falling asleep on the job'.

When your own dream seems to be placed on hold, help others with theirs

Joseph is a true example of someone who had to wait. He waited for years, through very hard and trying circumstances for those dreams that the Lord had given him as a young man to come to fruition. But while he waited, rather than lying around in jail feeling sorry for himself, Joseph used his God-given gift of interpreting dreams. While awaiting the fulfilment of *his dreams*, he helped others by interpreting theirs. His good attitude and work ethic, even through great adversity, resulted in favour with the Egyptians, release from prison, and eventual promotion.

God is not inactive in our waiting

While we are waiting on God, we have no idea what He is working on behind the scenes, as He shapes all the pieces of our lives. Most importantly, He's working *in us*, moulding and shaping us, making us more like Jesus.

God is never inactive. When the religious leaders confronted

Jesus about healing people on the sabbath, Jesus told them, *"My Father is always at his work to this very day, and I too am working."*John 5:17 (NIVUK)
See also: Philippians 2:13 (NLT) *"For God is working in you, giving you the desire and the power to do what pleases him."*
Romans 8:28 (NLT) *"And we know that God causes everything to work together for the good of those who love God and are called according to his purpose for them."*

It's a time of patience

"Be still in the presence of the Lord, and wait patiently for him to act. Don't worry about evil people who prosper or fret about their wicked schemes." Psalms 37:7 (NLT)

If God has told you to wait, it is an opportunity for precious time between you Him. We all have a tendency at times to look at others who seem to be favoured, promoted or excelled, while we are not, and we start to take it personally. It seems so unfair! But another person's promotion, or time of favour doesn't imply your demotion or disfavour in God's plans. When our expectation and attention is fixed on the Lord and *no one else*, then we won't concern ourselves with these things.

Isaiah 40:31 (NIVUK) Tells us: *"but those who hope in the LORD will renew their strength. They will soar on wings like eagles; they will run and not grow weary, they will walk and not be faint."*

Those two words *'hope in,'* are taken from the root word in Hebrew that means, literally, *to bind together* (perhaps by twisting) and figuratively, *to expect.*
So, we see from this that the Psalmist is not writing about passively sitting around until the Lord comes and pours strength into us. We *expectantly* seek Him, binding our hearts in total devotion and obedience to Him, relying on His, strength instead

of our own. Nothing passive about it!

A time of expectancy, listening, hoping in God
"...and in his word I put my hope;" Psalm 130:5 (NIVUK)
Waiting is a time for infusing your heart with God's Word. If you're listening, God will speak to your heart through His Word. His leading will always be consistent with His written Word.

One day, all waiting will be over! *"And it will be said in that day: "Behold, this is our God; We have waited for Him, and He will save us. This is the LORD; We have waited for Him; We will be glad and rejoice in His salvation."* Isaiah 25:9 (NKJV)

Today, if you're waiting on God, keep close to Him, dwell in His presence, and trust Him. As surely as the dawn always follows even the longest night, so does our faithful God always come to those who wait for Him.

Saturday - A Season Of Discovery

"God conceals the revelation of his word in the hiding place of his glory. But the honor of kings is revealed by how they thoroughly search out the deeper meaning of all that God says." Proverbs 25:2 (TPT)

Perhaps I should not really have entitled today's devotional 'A season of discovery,' because the Lord is *always* discoverable, always available, constantly speaking to those who will listen. However, while all these are true, the Lord also has plans, which He reveals to those who <u>intentionally</u> seek Him. And He has incredible jewels of Truth, hidden in His word for us to discover (for those who take the time to discover them).

I have always loved this scripture in Proverbs, and would like to focus on it today. I used the Passion Translation to open with, but for the rest of the devotional I will switch to the NIVUK.

"It is the <u>glory</u> of God to conceal a matter; to search out a matter is the glory of kings." Proverbs 25:2 (NIVUK)

The Hebrew roots

The Hebrew word 'glory' in this verse is *"Kavod"* meaning, *glory, honour,* or *reverence.*
It can also mean abundance, or riches, or: *that which is of utmost value.*

376

The word translated as 'conceal' is the word *"Sa'tar"* which means, to *carefully hide,* or *carefully cover.* That's interesting, cover what? The translation I have used has the words 'a matter,' some translations say, 'a thing,' but in the original language it is the single Hebrew word *"Davar"* meaning, *an uttered message.* And <u>also</u>, very significantly, these words 'a matter' or 'a thing,' mean: *'that which is declared or promised' or 'a spoken instruction.'*

Why does God hide things and who can discover these hidden things?

We see from the first part of this Scripture, that the Lord says it is His honour, and reverence, to carefully hide or cover the words or instructions He has uttered. The question is, <u>why</u> would He want to carefully cover His uttered words, His spoken instructions?

We see why, as we read on. The verse continues, proclaiming that searching out a matter is the glory (honour, reverence and riches) of kings. 'Kings' is the Hebrew word *"Melech,"* meaning *to reign,* to be *inducted into royalty.* This word, literally translated means: the action of someone being ushered into royalty when making a covenant.

The words 'search out' in the Hebrew is just one word *"Chakar"* which means to *examine thoroughly,* to *explore intimately,* or to *press in, in order to find out* and to *receive the picture of revelation.*

They are hidden, not <u>from</u> us but <u>for</u> us!

So, by way of explanation, God's message, words, and promises are hidden in His Word, so that those who are *inducted or ushered into royalty* - that's us, every born again believer, every child of God - may seek out these truths. We *press in,* to explore His Word intimately, and as we do, we discover true reverence and revelation. God hid these truths, not <u>from</u> us, but <u>for</u> us!

Finding them will be true abundance and riches in the life of every believer who searches God's Word, longing for revelation from the heart of God the Father.

Unbelievers cannot fathom the Word of God. When they read it, it is dead to them. It was only when you became a Covenant Child of His that your spirit became alive to Him and to His Word. Don't you find that the more you read and study the Word of God, the more you *want* to study? It's no longer just an interesting book, but food for your spirit.

"The person without the Spirit does not accept the things that come from the Spirit of God but considers them foolishness, and cannot understand them because they are discerned only through the Spirit." 1 Corinthians 2:14 (NIVUK)

May we all hunger for God's Word and discover the abundance and riches of life in Him. Happy Treasure Hunting!

Sunday - A Season Of Sowing

"Farmers who wait for perfect weather never plant. If they watch every cloud, they never harvest. Just as you cannot understand the path of the wind or the mystery of a tiny baby growing in its mother's womb, so you cannot understand the activity of God, who does all things. Plant your seed in the morning and keep busy all afternoon, for you don't know if profit will come from one activity or another—or maybe both." Ecclesiastes 11:4-6 (NLT)

"For God is the one who provides seed for the farmer and then bread to eat. In the same way, he will provide and increase your resources and then produce a great harvest of generosity in you". 2 Corinthians 9:10 (NLT)

Sow!

Any farmer knows that there are set seasons for planting, sowing and harvest. No farmer who knows what he's doing will get these times mixed up. It would be a stupid farmer indeed who sowed a crop while all the other farmers were bringing in their harvest of that same seed. Similarly, gardening enthusiasts know there are specific times for planting each type of seed or bulb.

Now, imagine a farmer who has rich, fertile fields, but not a lot else - not even the money to buy seed. Then, suddenly, a kind and generous benefactor comes to his door and gives this farmer the gift of a lorry-loads of seeds! All the farmer has to do is sow them, and expect the harvest in due season. The farmer looks out of the window every day, anxiously watching the weather. The conditions just never look 'right' for sowing. And so the man never gets around to sowing, or reaping a harvest, but lives out the rest of his days in poverty and hunger, wondering why life was 'so unfair.'

Does this (completely fabricated) story remind you of anyone? Aren't we all like this farmer at times? The Lord gives us seed to sow, but we do nothing with this precious gift. We over analyse the 'conditions,' for example, God may require us to sow seeds in the workplace, but we feel the atmosphere in the office is not conducive to hearing about Jesus, so we 'put off' talking about Him, *"I'll do it tomorrow when that woman who speaks profanities all the time has her day off."* But then tomorrow brings something else that isn't 'quite right.' And so we become just like the farmer in Ecclesiastes, overly analytical of the wind and the clouds. And we end up never sowing.

When God gives us seed, it's for *sowing*, not for holding onto. If I look at the circumstances, before I'm willing to sow, I might as well be saying to God "I don't trust you to bring a harvest."

There's another kind of sower, the one who plants a crop of seeds a few and then just sits back and waits for the harvest, feeling they have done their 'bit.' But different seeds are planted all year round. God gives us the seed to plant at the appropriate time - *"a word in season."*(See Proverbs 15:23; Proverbs 25:11; Isaiah 50:4.)

We are never 'done' with the work of sowing and planting. We are commissioned by God to sow, whatever the circumstances might look like to us, even when it doesn't make sense to us, trusting that He knows the seasons, and will bring about a harvest in due season.

Expect a harvest

The sower can expect a harvest. This is promised throughout scripture. As I've written before, literal farmers of *real* seed are not always guaranteed a harvest; a season of bad weather or a plague of pests can wipe out all the fruit of their hard labour in a day. But when it comes to the Kingdom of God, it isn't for us to worry about the (spiritual) harvest. All we need to do is faithfully sow. God is the One who waters the seed, and we are promised harvest in 'due season'. (Deuteronomy 11:14; Galatians 6:9). The harvest might be next week, next month, in ten years time, or we might never see the harvest with our physical eyes. But when we stand before our Father in Heaven, I believe we will see the harvest of every seed we have obediently sown. Let's just keep faithfully sowing!

R.S.V.P

Monday - How God Responds To Us

"The righteous cry out, and the Lord hears them; he delivers them from all their troubles." Psalm 34:17 (NIV)

God responds to us with purpose

From Genesis to Revelation we see how God lovingly takes care of His children. So much about walking in our God-given destiny is about *us* responding correctly to God and His Word. God's intentions for us are settled. He is purposeful in His plans and responses towards us, not conflicted or confused. Jeremiah 29:11 tells us, "*I know* the plans I have for you."

Our walking in God's plan for our lives is more about our response than God's intentions. His intentions for us are always good, because <u>He is</u> good. His intentions are activated in our lives when we respond to Him 'correctly.' So, firstly, how does the Lord respond to us?

God responds to us with tenderness

Matthew 10: 29 tells us that not even one sparrow falling to the ground escapes God's notice. He sees you, responds to you, and is moved with compassion for you. He draws near to you in your tears. Psalm 56:8 describes how the '*God of all comfort' keeps watch over your weeping. He sees every single tear, and gathers them all, keeping them in his bottle.'*

* * *

We read earlier about how He responded to Hagar in the wilderness, drawing near to her in her sadness. He saw Hannah weeping in the temple for the longed for baby, and He responded to her and answered her cry. (1 Samuel 1:10-18.) When David was tired of his own groaning, God did not become weary of listening, and *responded* to David's cries. (Psalm 6:7-9)

In 2 Kings the Lord said to King Hezekiah *"I have heard your prayer and seen your tears; I will heal you."*2 Kings 20:5 (NIVUK)
Your anguish may well have gone unnoticed by others, but not for one moment has it escaped the attention of your Father, who *"never slumbers or sleeps."* Psalm 121:4 (NLT)

God responds to us with compassion
The tender mercy and compassion of God compels Him to draw near to the brokenhearted and bind up their wounds. See Psalm 147:3.

When Jesus saw a widow weeping over her son's body, He responded with compassion towards her. *"When the Lord saw her, his heart went out to her and he said, 'Don't cry."* Luke 7:13 (NIVUK)

The words, "don't cry," might seem a strange thing to say to a woman who has just lost a son. But of course we know that every word Jesus spoke had life and purpose. Jesus was about to put His compassion into action by raising this grieving woman's son from the dead!

When his friend Lazarus died, Jesus, *man of sorrows* wept (John 11:35). Lazarus' sister Mary wept too, but while Mary's were grief-stricken tears, Jesus' tears were from a place of deep compassion. Jesus knew that He was about to about to speak the words that would snatch Lazarus back from death, but His heart was moved with love and compassion for Lazarus' two sisters, who were feeling the loss of their brother so keenly.

This account of Jesus weeping is a wonderful example of how Jesus, the One who heals the sick and raises the dead, also takes time to linger with us in our grief and sorrow. He is right there with us in our valleys of tears, walking alongside us.

God responds to us. He is not a far-off God, up in the sky somewhere, but here with us, 'in tune' with His people. How will we, in turn respond to Him?

Tuesday - Jesus' Response and Response Of The Healed

"He looked at them and said, "Go show yourselves to the priests." And as they went, they were cleansed of their leprosy. One of them, when he saw that he was healed, came back to Jesus, shouting, "Praise God!" He fell to the ground at Jesus' feet, thanking him for what he had done. This man was a Samaritan." Luke 17:14-16 (NLT)

Jesus <u>looked</u> at them

"As he entered one village, ten men approached him, but they kept their distance, for they were lepers. They shouted to him, "Mighty Lord, our wonderful Master! Won't you have mercy on us and heal us?" When Jesus stopped to look at them, he spoke these words: "Go to be examined by the Jewish priests." They set off, and they were healed while walking along the way." Luke 17:12-14 (TPT)

The first thing that stands out in this story is the sentence, "[*they*] *approached him, but kept their distance, for they were lepers.*" It doesn't matter which version of the Bible you read it in, each gives a similar account, just with slightly different wording. The men cried out to Jesus *from a distance*. They were outcasts of society, called "unclean," forbidden by law and custom to go near people who were not infected.
(See Leviticus 13:46; Numbers 5:2; 2 Kings 15:5).

* * *

I find it interesting that verse 14 says Jesus *looked* at the lepers. Some versions say He *saw* them. Surely it would have made more sense to write "Jesus heard them"? After all, they had cried out to Jesus, and if you think about it, ten voices shouting together must have created quite a racket! Yet Luke doesn't write that Jesus heard their cry, or even, as one might imagine, that He was moved by the sound of their cry, but that *"Jesus looked at them."*

I believe that Luke's choice of words are both significant and purposeful. I think Luke wanted us to understand that, much more than merely hearing these men's voices, Jesus *saw* the men. He really *looked* at them, *properly*. He saw their plight and was moved to respond.

Jesus sees you and me that way too. Even when we try to stand at a distance from Him because we feel unworthy, ashamed or unclean, His loving gaze reaches right into the deepest places of our hearts, that we think are so well hidden. He doesn't recoil from us in disgust or horror, but looks at us with intent and purpose. He *responds* to our cries for help with compassion and mercy.

How did the lepers respond to Jesus?

Response 1. Obedient faith.

As was required practice, Jesus told the lepers to go and show themselves to the priests. When someone had recovered from a contagious disease, they had to be declared ceremonially clean by a priest, before they could rejoin society. What is interesting about this encounter however, is the *way* Jesus healed them. He didn't heal them first and then tell them to present themselves to the priests, but the other way around. Their healing required obedient faith. Nothing about the ten lepers' outer circumstances appeared to have changed. It was only as they began walking obediently away to carry out the instruction, that they suddenly noticed that they were healed.

On the many other occasions when Jesus miraculously healed people, He just did it, there and then. Even people with leprosy, such as the account recorded in Mark's Gospel. (Mark 1:40-45) We can get used to God doing things a certain way and then we expect Him to always do it that way. We try to box God into our neat little formulas and liturgies. But His ways are not our ways, His thoughts are so much higher that ours!

There's a lesson in this for all of us. Sometimes our outward circumstances may seem unchanged after we have prayed. These are often the times when God requires us to take a bold step of obedient faith.
For more scriptures on faith see: Matthew 21:22; 2 Corinthians 5:7; Mark 11:22; Matthew 9:29; Matthew 21:21 Luke 1:37; Romans 1:17; Romans 10:17; Hebrews 11:6; Mark 9:23

Response 2. Thankfulness (and a lack of it!)
One of them, when he saw he was healed, came back, praising God in a loud voice. He threw himself at Jesus' feet and thanked him – and he was a Samaritan.Then he said to him," Luke 17:15-16 (NIVUK)

Out of ten healed people, only *one* bothered to come back to thank Jesus. It seems they all found it easy enough to perform the external, religious ritual of going to the priests to be declared clean, but when it came to heart matters, only *one* out of ten took time to come back and seek Jesus out, and pour out his love and gratitude in praise.

Jesus said to him: *"Rise and go; your faith has made you well."* (Verse 19) The man was already physically well, so I believe Jesus meant that because of the man's *heart* response there was *extra* healing for him, not just of his body, as they had all received, but spiritual healing too.

Thankfulness is good for you

"Jesus asked, 'Were not all ten cleansed? Where are the other nine? Has no-one returned to give praise to God except this foreigner?" Luke 17:17-18 (NIVUK)

God doesn't need our thanks. Jesus wasn't offended by the nine who didn't thank Him. I think He was stating an observation. The one who was a 'foreigner,' was the only one who had made a heart connection, while the other nine who were 'of Israe,l' had not.

Here are 3 reasons why thanking Jesus is important.
* Thanking Him reminds us of His goodness in our lives.
* Our thankfulness encourages those around us.
* Thankfulness retrains our thinking. When we forget to be thankful it's easy to slip into a mindset of complaining, comparing, coveting and a lack mentality.

It's so easy to forget to simply say 'thank you,' to God, and to remember the source of every blessing. *"Every good and perfect gift is from above, coming down from the Father of the heavenly lights, who does not change like shifting shadows."* James 1:17 (NIVUK)

Wednesday - Our Response To God Can Determine Our Destiny

Today I'd like to look at how our response to God can determine our destiny. A large part - the most part - of walking in our God-given destiny is about our correct response to God and His Word. Are we obedient? Do we *believe* His Word? Or do we prefer to pick and choose the bits that suit us?

Mary's response

"Then Mary responded. "This is amazing! I will be a mother for the Lord! As his servant, I accept whatever he has for me. May everything you have told me come to pass." Luke 1:38 (TPT)

Imagine what a shock it must have been for Mary, a teenage girl, engaged to be married, merrily going about her everyday business, when suddenly the Angel Gabriel appeared to her. I find the conversation that took place interesting. Gabriel's first words to Mary were *"Grace to you, young woman, for the Lord is with you and so you are anointed with great favour."* Luke 1:28 (TPT)

Mary's initial response is so real, so human and so typical of most of us. *"Mary was deeply troubled over the words of the angel and bewildered over what this may mean for her."* Luke 1:29 (TPT)

* * *

How would you respond if the Angel Gabriel came to you and told you that you had caught God's eye, you had His special favour and anointing upon you and He was about to carry out a great plan through your life? Mary didn't know what this special favour and anointing was going to entail, just yet, and her first response was fear, and one of *"how is this going to affect my life?"* Isn't that so often the way we respond to God's call?

But it was as Gabriel reassured Mary, that something shifted in her heart. Fear left her and she responded to God's call and destiny for her life with faith and joy.
"The Angel reassured her, saying, "do not yield to your fear, Mary, for the Lord has found delight in you and has chosen to surprise you with a wonderful gift." Luke 1:30 (TPT) .

Something important to note is that Mary only became pregnant with her 'destiny' after she responded to God with a definitive, faith-filled yes. God doesn't force His plans on us. Mary's response is a beautiful example of how to respond to God's Word. Have a look at this song she sang later, when pregnant with Jesus the Messiah:

"My soul is ecstatic, overflowing with praises to God! My spirit bursts with joy over my life-giving God! For he set his tender gaze upon me, his lowly servant girl. And from here on, everyone will know that I have been favoured and blessed. The Mighty One has worked a mighty miracle for me; holy is his name! Mercy kisses all his godly lovers, from one generation to the next. Mighty power flows from him to scatter all those who walk in pride. Powerful princes he tears from their thrones and he lifts up the lowly to take their place. Those who hunger for him will always be filled, but the smug and self-satisfied he will send away empty. Because he can never forget to show mercy, he has helped his chosen servant, Israel, Keeping his promises to Abraham and to his descendants forever." Luke 1:46-55 (TPT)

* * *

Now, that's responding well, to God!

Thursday - Our Response To One Another

"Don't be quick to fly off the handle. Anger boomerangs. You can spot a fool by the lumps on his head." Ecclesiastes 7:9 (MSG)

Do you react or respond?

We can't control the events that occur in everyday life, and there are times when there may be little we can do about our circumstances, but there is one thing we do have control over, and that is what we *do* and how we *behave in* those circumstances. One such circumstance most of us will face is potential personal conflict.

Just when you think you're on top of your anger habit - your tendency to blow your top, and explode - and you're giving yourself a little mental hi-five, along comes that annoying person at work. Or some woman skips the queue in the supermarket, with her overflowing trolley, when all you have is one loaf of bread in your hand! You can bet your last penny some spotty teenager will cut right in front of you on your way to church, and it's going to be on the very morning that you're running late. And then, when you get to church, feeling out of sorts because you're later than you normally like to be, some insensitive person who should know better, makes a stupid joke about something deeply personal. What's your 'default,' do you react or respond?

* * *

The two may sound the same, but actually they are vastly different. Here are three differences between reaction and response:

* Reaction is usually quick, without thought, often tense or angry, while Response is measured, calm, carefully weighed, usually gentle, and non-threatening.

* Reaction provokes further reaction, and fast tracks into unnecessary and prolonged periods of disagreement and misery, with nothing accomplished. (Just think of all the senseless wars in this world); Response promotes discussion and conversation that leads to quick resolution, healing and moving forward.

*Reaction is emotion-filled and driven; Response is reason-filled, in fact response can <u>remove</u> heightened emotions.

Reaction

"Fools vent their anger," Proverbs 29:11 (NLT)

"Love doesn't force itself on others, Isn't always "me first," Doesn't fly off the handle, Doesn't keep score of the sins of others" 1 Corinthians 13:3 (MSG)

The person making this choice, and *it is* a choice, usually goes immediately into reply mode, firing off a tirade of words without a thought for the other person.

Some take a slightly different but just as damaging reactive measure - they go into 'silent treatment mode,' letting the other person know that they've definitely overstepped the mark. Reaction of either kind leads to ultimate damage to both parties. Have you ever sent an email or text message to someone in angry or upset reaction, only to regret it the moment your finger leaves the 'send' button? Just as we cannot re-call those regrettable emails and text messages, we can't unsay words, or undo actions. We can ask for forgiveness, but the words are still 'out there.' There's a better way, we can learn to respond instead.

* * *

Respond

"Fools vent their anger, but <u>the wise quietly hold it back</u>."
Proverbs 29:11 (NLT)
We can see from this Proverb that the wise person still *experiences* the emotion of anger; they aren't superhuman. The verse says, "fools vent their anger, but the wise quietly hold it back" - if the wise felt no anger there would be nothing to hold back would there? They feel, but they don't give vent to what they are feeling. They control the anger, rather than the other way around.

The person who *responds* is like someone who types their reaction in an email and then presses the delete button instead of 'send.' Mr or Mrs Responder lives and acts in *self control;* an aspect of the fruit of the Spirit that we all have the capacity to develop, and grow in, as followers of Jesus.

When someone does something that annoys Mr Responder, he temporarily removes himself from the heat of the moment, he might go outside for some fresh air, take fifteen minutes to consider an appropriate response, and *wait* before verbalising this, when emotions have settled down on *both* sides.

Have a look too, at Proverbs 10:19 (MSG) "The more talk, the less truth; the wise measure their words".
And: Proverbs15:1 (MSG) "A gentle response defuses anger, but a sharp tongue kindles a temper-fire."
Proverbs 15:8 (MSG) "Hot tempers start fights; a calm, cool spirit keeps the peace"

Friday - R.S.V.P To A Royal Invitation

"You search the Scriptures because you think they give you eternal life. But the Scriptures point to me! Yet you refuse to come to me to receive this life." John 5:39-40 (NLT)

"Come." It's just a little word, but it's one of the most profound words to come from the mouth of Jesus. It's an invitation, issued to people like you and me. People who struggle with everyday, life issues.

Come and be yoked with Him

In Matthew 11:28 (NLT) Jesus says: *"Come to me, all of you who are weary and carry heavy burdens, and I will give you rest."*

There's so much more to this invitation than just laying down our burdens (not that that's a small thing!) In the next verse Jesus goes on to say, *"Take my yoke upon you and learn from me, for I am gentle and humble in heart, and you will find rest for your souls."*

Matthew 11:29 (NIVUK)

To be yoked with Jesus doesn't mean laying down one burden, only to pick up another, and then try to carry that burden instead. *Jesus is the bearer of burdens*. Jesus invites us to take His *yoke* upon us. I love the imagery of the yoke.

When a young ox is being yoke-trained, he is coupled with an older, stronger, more experienced ox. The older ox takes the lead, shouldering most of the weight. When the younger one tries to pull in the wrong direction, the older one pulls him back on course, and keeps a steady pace.

This is a lovely picture of how Jesus works with us, keeping alongside us, taking the *weight* and burden out of life, setting the pace, keeping us on course.

Come and follow Him

The first time Jesus issued the invitation to "come," is found in Matthew four. *'Jesus called out to them, "Come, follow me, and I will make you fishers of men"'* Matthew 4:19 (NLT)

"I will *make* you fishers of men." It's Jesus who teaches and trains us, where we are willing to be taught and trained, to be 'fishers of men.'. I'm sure you have read or heard the well known saying - I'm not sure where it first originated - "God doesn't call the qualified, He qualifies the called" But we first have to <u>answer</u> the call.

Come on His Terms

What do we do when we receive an invitation? *We read the terms.* The date and time, whether we should bring anything, and, importantly, the dress code. So it is with Jesus' invitation.

<u>The time</u>: Now - it's always now! Often we believe we have to wait. This belief comes from all sorts of thinking patterns; One of the biggest things that holds us back from answering the invitation, is a feeling of unworthiness. Many feel that they need to be a better person first, nicer, more 'acceptable'. But even squeaky clean, by our standards, is like a pile of filthy rags, if we're trying to wheel and deal with the King of Kings on our terms. (See Isaiah 64:6)

Others feel they should know their Bible better first, maybe go to

Bible college so that they'd be 'more useful'. Some feel bogged down in young parenthood and think they need to wait till the children are a bit older. Some are afraid of what Jesus might ask them to give up. As if He wouldn't give us a thousand times more than any of our measly possessions. The time is always right now.

The dress code: Come as you are. Come unworthy, unclean, rejected by your peers, forsaken, abused, angry, outcast, overlooked, with all your pride, with your bad habits, your addictions, your striving, your empty religion. Jesus has the perfect clothing to exchange for all your old rags: *"a crown of beauty for ashes, a joyous blessing instead of mourning, festive praise instead of despair"* Isaiah 61:3 (NLT)
"he has dressed me with the clothing of salvation and draped me in a robe of righteousness. I am like a bridegroom dressed for his wedding or a bride with her jewels." Isaiah 61:10 (NLT)

RSVP: As with any invitation, Jesus' *daily* call to come to Him requires a response. How will you respond?

Saturday - Zacchaeus' Response To Jesus

"There was a man there named Zacchaeus. He was the chief tax collector in the region, and he had become very rich. He tried to get a look at Jesus, but he was too short to see over the crowd. So he ran ahead and climbed a sycamore-fig tree beside the road, for Jesus was going to pass that way." Luke 19:2-4 NLT

The tax collector:

I'm sure most of us have had times when we have felt rejected, or disliked, but imagine what it must have been like to be a tax collector for the Romans. Zacchaeus would have been despised by his peers. Tax collectors were viewed as traitors, and turncoats, because they worked for the Roman oppressors, rather than their own Jewish community. Many tax collectors were involved in the despicable practice known as 'tax farming.' While the Romans turned a blind eye, the tax collector made his profit on whatever *extra* he could get away with charging his victims. A particularly greedy tax collector would make the taxes as high as possible while he got rich on his community's misery and heartache. (See Luke 13:3)

He recognised his need of Jesus

I wonder had Zacchaeus heard of Jesus, the one who was going about the region teaching and healing people. He must have already started to believe that Jesus was no ordinary man and that His message was something very special, because he made sure he had positioned himself to hear and see Jesus.

Zacchaeus must have known, deep inside, that he needed Jesus. He must have got to the point in his life where he knew, '*I can't go on living this way*'. Why else would a wealthy, well dressed, government official, throw all dignity to the wind, tuck up his clothing, and clamber up a tree like a child in order to see over the crowds? To do what Zacchaeus did was an extremely undignified act for a grown man. My guess is that there was a gnawing emptiness inside Zacchaeus. Why? Because it's there in the heart of every person who tries to 'do' life without Jesus. Deep down, there's a sense of *what's the point in all this?* No matter how powerful, rich, or successful we are, without Jesus, we are are nothing, and life is empty. (see John 15:5)

Zacchaeus put aside his pride and climbed a tree, risking ridicule. What sort of man who wants to be taken seriously by his peers climbs a tree? This action reveals a man who was really *desperate* to see Jesus, and didn't care what anyone thought. In climbing that tree like a little boy, it is my belief that Zacchaeus, without even knowing it, fulfilled Jesus' words that unless we become like little children, we will not see the Kingdom of God (Matthew 18:3).

Thoughts little to ponder

<u>Do I let the crowd stand in the way?</u>
When you feel the Lord leading you to do something that will bring you closer to Him, are you willing to wholeheartedly follow Him? Perhaps it might be something as simple as raising your hands in worship, sharing a prophetic word, praying with someone. Maybe it's something far more personally stretching. Do you let fear of what the crowd will think, hold you back? Or are you so desperate to 'see' and connect with Jesus, that no crowd could stand in the way?

* * *

<u>Is the 'tree' I need to climb the one of pride</u>.

Do you need to go back to the church you left in a huff, a few years ago, and make right with the people who hurt you, and those you hurt? Do you need to let go of the pain and anger that you have held onto so long towards an ex-spouse, a friend, a parent, who hurt or rejected you?

Zacchaeus' response was to make reparation for what he had done.

"But Zacchaeus stood up and said to the Lord, 'Look, Lord! Here and now I give half of my possessions to the poor, and if I have cheated anybody out of anything, I will pay back four times the amount." Luke 19:8 (NIVUK)

Perhaps it's time to make reparation by forgiving, and, in your heart, letting go. It's interesting to me, that Jesus had already gone to Zacchaeus' house. Zacchaeus was already accepted by Jesus. Zacchaeus could have responded by leaving it at that. But Zacchaeus *wanted* to make right with people.

Everything changed in his life the day Zacchaeus responded to Jesus. He was prepared to swallow his pride, ignore any jibes that might come about a grown man climbing a tree, surrender everything to Jesus, take Jesus into his home, and make reparation. We can learn a lot from this plucky and tenacious tax collector's response to Jesus.

Sunday - Jesus' Response to Zacchaeus

"When Jesus came by, he looked up at Zacchaeus and called him by name. "Zacchaeus!" he said. "Quick, come down! I must be a guest in your home today." Luke 19:5 (NLT)

Jesus Saw Him

Jesus was, as usual, surrounded by throngs of people, pushing and jostling to get a better view of Him, wanting to touch Him, hear Him speak, maybe even see a miracle. Zacchaeus, who was small in stature, and couldn't see, had run ahead of the crowds and climbed a tree. Jesus got to where the tree was, looked up and saw him in the tree. *Jesus saw him,* and didn't pass him by. Zacchaeus *stood out* to Jesus, from all the crowd. And Jesus connected with him.

Jesus was God incarnate, He was *Immanuel God with us.* I have no doubt that if Zacchaeus had been hiding at the back of the crowd, and God the Father had directed Jesus to call him out, Jesus could easily have seen him where he was and done just that. An important lesson we see in this encounter is that Jesus responds to our moving towards Him. Zacchaeus wanted to know who Jesus was, so he had taken action by climbing the tree. And Jesus responded.

Wherever you are, at this very moment, Jesus sees you. He knows all your secret fears, hurts, hopes and the sins that you think are so well hidden. In Isaiah 30 we are told that God "waits to be gracious" to us. *"Therefore the Lord waits [expectantly] and longs to be gracious to you, And therefore He waits on high to have compassion on you. For the Lord is a God of justice; Blessed (happy, fortunate) are all those who long for Him [since He will never fail them]."* Isaiah 30:18 (AMP)

He waits, but action is required on our part, because our moving towards Him shows our willingness, our desire for encounter with Him. Zacchaeus took action by climbing a tree. I believe Jesus responded as He did because He knew that Zacchaeus' actions were a sincere attempt to move towards Him. We saw yesterday that it would have cost a man his pride and dignity to hitch up His clothing, run, and climb a tree like a little boy. Jesus sees right into our hearts; He would have spotted right away any falseness in Zacchaeus. But His response to Zacchaeus was immediate and loving.

Jesus called him by name

Jesus looked directly at Zacchaeus and called him by name. A person's name is so important. I've no doubt Zacchaeus was called many things, and known by many names, few of them very nice! Maybe this was the first time, in a very long time, that Zacchaeus heard someone other than his mother say his name with kindness. Calling someone by name makes all the difference to a conversation doesn't it? By using his name, Jesus was saying to Zacchaeus, *"I know you."* Jesus was fully aware of the importance and significance of a name. Remember, Jesus said that He calls His sheep by name (John 10:3).

Jesus went to Zacchaeus' home

Jesus could have stood where He was and preached to Zacchaeus, along with everyone else. But Jesus was acting in response to Zacchaeus' heart-revealing tree-climbing expedition.

* * *

Jesus wasn't after a 'religious conversion,' but quality time with Zacchaeus, building a real relationship with him. Jesus wanted to go to Zacchaeus' house and share fellowship with him. He called Zacchaeus to Himself, and Zacchaeus was excited and joyful in his response. Luke 19:6 (NLT) tells us that he got down quickly and *"took Jesus to his house in great excitement and joy"*

We aren't privy to the whole conversation that took place at Zacchaeus' house, between Jesus and Zacchaeus but we can clearly see that there was repentance and a life-turnaround through the encounter.

Everything changes when you know that you're loved
Whatever took place between Jesus and Zacchaeus, changed this man, deep inside, and made him *want* to live differently. Zacchaeus was probably as amazed as everyone else, when Jesus said He wanted to go to his house. The onlookers were shocked and critical of Jesus' actions: *"the people were displeased. "He has gone to be the guest of a notorious sinner, "* they grumbled." Luke 19:7 (NLT)

But Jesus didn't care about the opinion of others. I believe just saw He saw a man who had wanted 'a better view of Jesus' and *positioned himself* to get that view. I believe Jesus' heart was moved by this, and He responded by saying, *"the Son of Man came to seek and to save the lost."* Luke 19:10 (NIVUK). Jesus sought out, and befriended, people who were lost. He came precisely to save people like Zacchaeus, who recognise their need of Him.

The funny thing is that Zacchaeus sought Jesus, but as it turns out, Zacchaeus was the one who needed to be found! Zacchaeus was living a lost life. He had lost his community and any friends he may have once had. But he was not lost to Jesus. Jesus had found him!

* * *

Zacchaeus had woken up that morning a taker. He went to sleep that night a giver, and, as Jesus called him, *"a true son of Abraham."* Only a personal encounter with Jesus can so fundamentally change a person. *Everything changes when you know you're loved!*

Jesus knows *your* name. He sees you in your 'tree.' Your move towards Him doesn't go unnoticed. And just as Jesus called Zacchaeus by name, He calls *you* by name. He calls you into relationship with Himself, as He did Zacchaeus. A relationship of friendship, dialogue, intimacy and discipleship. Will you invite Him into your 'home,' that is, your everyday life, or will you stay up there in your personal tree, observing Him from a distance?

"If you look for me wholeheartedly, you will find me." Jeremiah 29:13 (NLT)

This Is Our God!

Monday - He's The God Who Is Willing

"A man with leprosy came and knelt in front of Jesus, begging to be healed. "If you are willing, you can heal me and make me clean," he said. Moved with compassion, Jesus reached out and touched him. "I am willing," he said. "Be healed!" Mark 1:40-41 (NLT)

The God who is willing

What would you consider to be the three most impactful words anyone could ever say to you? "I love you?" It's true that many people long to hear those words. Jesus said three words to a man that I would venture to say were the most impactful words anyone had ever said to him in his life: "I am willing." Those three words changed the man's life forever.

The man had leprosy. In Biblical times leprosy was a deeply misunderstood disease and sufferers were banned to the outer limits of the town, declared unclean. Imagine the loneliness and rejection these people must have felt, cast out from their families, friends and society. As their bodies went through the terrible physical ordeal of leprosy, no one would come near them, let alone touch them. *No one, that is, except Jesus.*

This man was used to people turning away from him in revulsion. His words to Jesus reveal what was in his heart: an expectation of further rejection, a hope that this man with burning compassion in His eyes might see past the outward appearance.His fear of rejection was overridden by faith that

Jesus was the One who could bring healing. If, that is, Jesus would be willing.

Three impactful words

Jesus was moved with compassion for the man. He answered "I am willing." Jesus did what no one else would have been willing to do. He reached out and touched a leper. The next verse tells us that the man was instantly healed.

I believe that what moved Jesus' heart was the man's faith and courage in coming to Him, despite the rejection by the townspeople and their fear of the man's disease. He stepped out of hiding, and pushed down his own fear that Jesus might reject him. Faith that Jesus could heal him propelled him forward. He expressed his faith from the start, "*you can heal me and make me clean,*" Mark 1:40 (NLT)

The man came to encounter Jesus and didn't go away disappointed! When we draw near to Jesus, rather than hiding in the shadows, Jesus more than meets us halfway. We don't even need to utter those words "if you're willing," Jesus is always willing to heal, emotionally, physically and spiritually.

Physical Healing

Jesus still heals today. I have seen it with my own eyes, and I have personally experienced healing."*Jesus Christ is the same yesterday, today, and forever". Hebrews 13:8 (NLT)*

Although Jesus is exalted to the highest place, enthroned in Heaven, He is still the same Jesus who healed and delivered people two thousand years ago. His Holy Spirit indwells every child of God. He still touches and transforms hearts and lives. Every drop of blood that trickled down His bruised and battered body as he hung there, dying for you, conquered death and won your healing. "*he was pierced for our transgressions; he was crushed for our iniquities; upon him was the chastisement that brought us peace, and with his wounds we are healed." Isaiah*

53:5 (NLT)

Emotional Healing

"He was despised and rejected, a man of sorrows, acquainted with deepest grief. We turned our backs on him and looked the other way. He was despised, and we did not care. Yet it was our weaknesses he carried; it was our sorrows that weighed him down." Isaiah 53:3

Every time you feel the sting of rejection, the hurt of betrayal, the heartache of grief, remember that Jesus faced these things too. He found refuge in the presence of His Father, by drawing close to Him, by communing with Him, setting an example for us to do the same.

Spiritual Healing

Sometimes, even as Christians, we feel like that leper. We tell ourselves we can't come to Jesus with our hidden, secret sins and shameful habits. But like the leper, there is nothing about us that will ever make us repulsive to Jesus, or exclude us from his presence. Come to Him in humility, confess your sin to Him, and He promises to forgive and cleanse you, (see John 1:9)

The question we need to ask is not, "Lord are you willing?" He is always willing. The question is rather, "Am I willing?" Are you willing, today, to step out of the shadows and trust Jesus with those things you keep hidden? Are you willing to trust Him to heal your physical ailment, your depression, the grief you have buried so deeply that it has almost become a part of you? Are you willing? He is.

Tuesday - God Is Good

"Taste and see that the LORD is good; blessed is the one who takes refuge in him." Psalms 34:8 (NIVUK)

It might seem strange that the Bible uses the word *taste* when inviting us to experience God's goodness, but actually it isn't really. In the English language we use these sort of words every day, to speak about our life experiences. We talk about *savouring* every moment. We describe people as *sweet, bitter, or sour.*

Goodness is God's nature

We commonly use the word *good* to describe people; "he's such a good man." But the truth is there is *no one* good, not one. We can of course *do* good. We can do kind acts, but the only good *in* us is God, and only God is truly good. (See Mark 10:18)

God's goodness is an inherent part of who He is. He is blamed by those who do not know His nature for every world disaster - officially called 'an act of God' on insurance claims! He is accused of inflicting family tragedy and personal heartache, yet the Bible is filled with scripture declaring His goodness, and gives accounts of His goodness in the lives of His people - and sometimes even in the lives of people who were not His. He is the same God today, still demonstrating His goodness in our lives!

You may be finding it hard to see the goodness of God in your life at present. Romans 8:28 tells us *"we know that for those who love God all things work together for good, for those who are called according to his purpose." (NLT)*

All things work together for good

My Auntie Ilse makes an incredible cherry crumble using soured cherries. I don't usually like cooked cherries, *or* crumble, but hers is irresistible. Who would have thought that shudder inducing sour cherries could be turned into something so mouth-wateringly delicious? It requires just the right combination of skill and ingredients to create something so good!
This is what God does with our lives, when we surrender to His all-knowing, skilled hands. He is able to take those things in our lives that seem 'sour,' hard, bitter, unpleasant, and turn the whole mix around to work for our GOOD.

Going Forward Remembering God's Goodness

Here are some reminders of God's goodness.

"How abundant are the good things that you have stored up for those who fear you, that you bestow in the sight of all, on those who take refuge in you." Psalms 31:19 (NIVUK)

"Surely your goodness and love will follow me all the days of my life, and I will dwell in the house of the LORD for ever." Psalms 23:6 (NIVUK)

"no good thing does he withhold from those whose way of life is blameless." Psalms 84:11 (NIVUK)

"You are good, and what you do is good; teach me your decrees." Psalms 119:68 (NIVUK)

"Give thanks to the LORD, for he is good; his love endures for ever." Psalms 107:1 (NIVUK)

* * *

There are dozens more, but I'm sure by now you have the picture - our God is good! His heart is kind and overflows with abundant goodness, mercy and love. It's just who He is!

Wednesday- He's The God Who Carries Us

I recently watched a television programme, in which antiques dealers competed against each other to buy antiques at knockdown prices, and then sell them at auction, to see who made the biggest profit.

One of the dealers bought a bronze god for fifty pounds Sterling. It sold at auction for three thousand eight hundred pounds Sterling, the biggest ever profit in the history of the programme. The auctioneer said something interesting, *"people are prepared to pay big money for deities."*

I was really struck by the truth and tragedy of this statement. How sad, that someone would pay all that money for a great ugly lump of bronze - a fake god - when they could know the *real* God, One who is alive, the One who speaks, loves, and transforms lives.

The man-made god has to be carried

"To whom will you compare me? Who is my equal? Some people pour out their silver and gold and hire a craftsman to make a god from it. Then they bow down and worship it! They carry it around on their shoulders, and when they set it down, it stays there. It can't even move! And when someone prays to it, there is no answer. It can't rescue anyone from trouble." Isaiah 46:5-7 (NLT)

* * *

When we think of idols, we usually picture the idols of the Old Testament, or statues in temples in foreign countries, dedicated to false deities. But not all man-made gods are statues. Anything that we turn our attention to instead of God, becomes a false god. Anything, or anyone, who occupies more of our attention and thought-life that the Lord our God, is an idol. We might not pay huge monetary value for these false gods, but the cost becomes evident in other ways. It takes its toll on our lives as we strain to get by, carrying our own burdens, because, of course, our worthless idols cannot help us. And so our bodies become weary, and our hearts become worn out and hardened, as our false gods become heavier and heavier.

Throughout history the One true God has issued the invitation to mankind to *come,* to make Him their refuge, to cast all their burdens upon Him. And man persistently looks away.

The God who made us carries Us

"I have cared for you since you were born. Yes, I carried you before you were born. I will be your God throughout your lifetime— until your hair is white with age. I made you, and I will care for you. I will carry you along and save you. Isaiah 46:3b-4 (NLT)

This is our God! And the best thing of all is that The One True God is not going to cost you thousands of pounds. His love is free. His mercy, forgiveness, grace, loving kindness, goodness and peace are absolutely free to you and me, because the price has already been paid. All we have to do is "come."

"And let the one who hears say, "Come." And let the one who is thirsty come; let the one who desires take the water of life without price." Revelation 22:17 (NLT)

When we are His, we need not look anywhere else, or to anything else. God really is our absolute 'all -in-all', the One who satisfies every need, the One who carries us through life, caring for us, our Shelter, our Shepherd, our Defender. What a God!

Thursday - Ever Faithful God

"Understand, therefore, that the Lord your God is indeed God. He is the faithful God who keeps his covenant for a thousand generations and lavishes his unfailing love on those who love him and obey his commands." Deuteronomy 7:9 (NLT)

There was a song we used to sing as children, with the words, "*My God is so big, so strong and so mighty, there's nothing that He cannot do.*"

It's good to know that nothing, and no one can match the wondrous power of our God. I know with all my heart that this is true. However, I have learned that because of God's very nature, there is, in fact, something He cannot do. Actually it is something that is *impossible* for Him to do.

Wait! Before you put the book down, deciding I'm a heretic, it says so in the Bible. "*So God has given both his promise and his oath. These two things are unchangeable because it is impossible for God to lie. Therefore, we who have fled to him for refuge can have great confidence as we hold to the hope that lies before us.*" Hebrews 6:18 (NLT)

God cannot and will not, lie.

For God to lie would be to go against His very nature and character. God will never break a promise. Every covenant He has made has been, and will be kept. Did you know that accounts of covenants between God and His people can be found approximately two hundred and seventy-seven times in the Bible? That means testimony after testimony of God's faithfulness. His faithfulness is still proven in the lives of His children today.

His Faithfulness is unending

When we say God is faithful, it means He is totally trustworthy and perfectly faithful. Isaiah wrote: "O Lord, you are my God; I will exalt you; I will praise your name, for you have done wonderful things, plans formed of old, faithful and sure. Isaiah 25:1 (NLT)

Jeremiah wrote: "The faithful love of the Lord never ends! His mercies never cease. Great is his faithfulness; his mercies begin afresh each morning." Lamentations 3:22-23 (NLT)

God keeps His promises

We can trust Him, because He is the only one who is totally trustworthy. As human beings, however well intentioned, we are, after all, only human. We all, at some time, break promises, tell the occasional 'white lie' (there's no such thing, by the way. A lie is a lie) *"there is no-one on earth who is righteous, no-one who does what is right and never sins."* Ecclesiastes 7:20 (NIVUK)

God is Faithfulness personified!

It is impossible for God to fail you. It is impossible for God to break His promises to you. It is impossible for God to let you down, or lie to you. God is utterly faithful, completely trustworthy, absolutely truthful.

"For the word of the Lord holds true, and we can trust everything he does." Psalms 33:4 (NLT)

Additional reading: Titus 1:2, Hebrews 10:23, Hebrews 11:11, 2 Thessalonians 3:3, Daniel 9:4, 1 Cor 1:9

Jill McIlreavy

Friday - Matchless God

It's all a matter of perspective. When you remember how big God is, you see how small your problems are in comparison.

I've been thinking about what keeps me strong, in times when everything around me seems to be falling apart. It's certainly not that I'm a strong person - I'm not. It's because my life is built on these truths: God is Sovereign, He loves me, and His goodness, faithfulness, and mercy towards me will never end. There is no Name higher, no power greater, no one wiser than my God. Let's have a look through Isaiah chapter forty today and remind ourselves how Great our God is!

There is no name greater or higher
"To whom can you compare God? What image can you find to resemble him? "To whom will you compare me? Who is my equal?" asks the Holy One." Isaiah 40:18,25 (NLT)

He is All-Knowing
He knows everything, and because of this, He never misses a beat. He never falls asleep, He see everything, knows every tiny detail of every life. That's incredible, and so comforting: "O Jacob, how can you say the Lord does not see your troubles? O Israel, how can you say God ignores your rights? Have you never heard? Have you never understood? The Lord is the everlasting God, the Creator of all the earth. He never grows

weak or weary. No one can measure the depths of his understanding." Isaiah 40:27:28 NLT

His Wisdom is absolute

"Who is able to advise the Spirit of the Lord? Who knows enough to give him advice or teach him? Has the Lord ever needed anyone's advice? Does he need instruction about what is good? Did someone teach him what is right or show him the path of justice? No, for all the nations of the world are but a drop in the bucket. They are nothing more than dust on the scales. He picks up the whole earth as though it were a grain of sand." Isaiah 40:13-15 (NLT)

He is All-Powerful

"Look up into the heavens. Who created all the stars? He brings them out like an army, one after another, calling each by its name. Because of his great power and incomparable strength, not a single one is missing." Isaiah 40:26 (NLT)

His Word is all that will stand

God has the last word, the final say. "The grass withers and the flowers fade beneath the breath of the Lord. And so it is with people. The grass withers and the flowers fade, but the word of our God stands forever." Isaiah 40:7-8 (NLT)

He is bigger than any mountain you may face

"Who else has held the oceans in his hand? Who has measured off the heavens with his fingers? Who else knows the weight of the earth or has weighed the mountains and hills on a scale?" Isaiah 40:12 (NLT)

Even though God is so great, so all-powerful and awesome, that should He want to, He could wipe out entire nations in seconds with His thunderous voice, the Lord our God takes tender care of His children, as a loving shepherd cares for his sheep:

* * *

"He will feed his flock like a shepherd. He will carry the lambs in his arms, holding them close to his heart. He will gently lead the mother sheep with their young." Isaiah 40:11 (NLT)

Whatever sort of month, week, or day, you might be having as you read this, is it not wonderful to just close your eyes for a moment and remember this God is *your* God, and He is right by your side?

Saturday - King Of kings

"Yes, God will make his appearing in his own divine timing, for he is the exalted God, the only powerful One, the King over every king, and the Lord of power!" 1 Timothy 6:15 (TPT)

"On his robe and on his thigh he had inscribed a name: King of kings and Lord of lords."
Revelation 19:16 (TPT)

Jesus is King of **all** kings. He's the King of Righteousness, King of the ages, King of Heaven, King of Gory. No name is higher than the name of Jesus Christ!

David an earthly king, wrote:"I will exalt you, my God and King, and praise your name forever and ever. I will praise you every day; yes, I will praise you forever. Great is the Lord! He is most worthy of praise! No one can measure his greatness."Psalm 145:1-3 (NLT)

Matchless King

King Jesus is beyond our ability to describe, though I have tried here. There are no means to measure or define His limitless love and mercy. Man has developed the Hubble telescope, which can see far into outer space, but even such a far-seeing and powerful implement cannot bring into our line of vision the horizon of the shores of His bountiful supplies.

There is no distance or barrier that can hinder Him from pouring out His blessing where He wills. Nothing can oppose Him. King Jesus is eternally steadfast, enduringly strong, entirely true. He is matchless in power and impartially merciful. He is God's Son. He is also <u>fully</u> God. He is Jesus: He is unique, unparalleled, unprecedented, supreme and pre-eminent!

He's the only one able to supply <u>all</u> the needs of all His people simultaneously, giving strength to the weak, help to the tempted and encouragement to the one facing trials.

Strong Defender

He's the Saviour of sinners, Healer of the sick, Breaker of the chains of oppression. He's the Defender of the widow and Provider for the poor. He regards the elderly, makes beautiful the humble and rewards the diligent.

He is the Key of knowledge and Wellspring of all wisdom. He's the Doorway of deliverance and the Pathway of peace. He's the Roadway of righteousness, the Highway of holiness, the Gateway of glory. He's the Good Shepherd.

No Name Higher

King Jesus is the Leader of the legislatures; high over every government. There is no name higher; He's the Master of the mighty, the Captain of conquerors. He's the Head of heroes. He's the Overseer of the overcomers. He's the Governor of governors. He's the Prince of princes. He's the King of kings and He's the Lord of lords!

His light shines brighter than anything we could imagine - matchless! Brighter than ten thousand suns. His goodness is limitless. His mercy is everlasting. His love never changes. His Word never fades. His grace is sufficient. His reign is righteous. His yoke is easy and His burden is light. He's the incomprehensible, invincible, irresistible Conqueror of hearts and I hope you know Him!

He's unstoppable

The religious leaders of His day were threatened by Him, but to their great consternation they couldn't stop Him. Pilot could find no fault in Him. The witnesses for the prosecution couldn't get their testimonies to line up against Him. Satan thought he had Him, but death couldn't handle Him! The grave simply couldn't hold Him!

The Romans had thought it was funny to put a sign on his cross stating "King of the Jews." They meant it as a mockery, but they had no idea how close to the truth they were!
Now, exalted to the highest place in Glory, He reigns forever and ever. One day every knee will bow, every tongue will confess, that He is Lord. He is, and always will be, my King. Is He yours?

Sunday - The Way God Loves

"But anyone who does not love does not know God, for God is love." 1 John 4:8 (NLT)

God's love permeates everything - all He is, and all He does, is *from* love. God cannot and <u>does</u> not do wrong. He loves *perfectly* (1 John 4:18). God's love is the purest and truest form there is. No one loves as God does. He loves completely, not in part - giving one hundred percent of His love to every one of His children, even though we are incapable of reciprocating such great love.

Our salvation is an expression of God's love.
The greatest demonstration of God's love was in the sacrificial gift of His only Son, Jesus. (John 3:16) He did this, not as any reward to hearts that were obedient, but as a ransom for hearts that were rebellious, hearts that were at enmity with Him. *"But God showed his great love for us by sending Christ to die for us while we were still sinners."* Romans 5:8 (NLT)

We clearly see Jesus' love demonstrated throughout the Gospels as He compassionately touched people, spoke tenderly to the grieving, healed the sick, fed five thousand hungry people, poured Himself out, with genuine humility and kindness, without requirement of gratitude. Even as He hung dying on the cross, Jesus asked God the Father to forgive the ones who crucified

Him.

Our ability to love is only because of God's love

"So now I am giving you a new commandment: Love each other. Just as I have loved you, you should love each other. Your love for one another will prove to the world that you are my disciples." John 13:34-35 (NLT)

'As I have loved you.' This seems like a tall order, but because we are made in God's image, and much more importantly, because we have been born again and the fruit of the Spirit is now part of our spiritual make-up, God has equipped us to love as Jesus has commanded. To love our neighbours as ourselves requires a love that does not come naturally to us, but flows from a life rooted in the Holy Spirit. It's a radical, supernatural love. We couldn't possibly love like that without Him.

Jesus set the example for us: *"We know what real love is because Jesus gave up his life for us. So we also ought to give up our lives for our brothers and sisters."* 1 John 3:16 (NLT)

We might never be required to literally give up our lives, as in, to die, for our brothers and sisters, but we can certainly die to *self*. When Jesus washed His disciples' feet, He took on the role of a servant, dying to self, and placing others above His own dignity. He instructs His followers to do the same.

God's love is steadfast true

To remind yourself of this, just read through Psalm 136 from beginning to end, slowly. Notice the repeated refrain is, *"His steadfast love endures forever"*. That means His love will never, ever, come to an end. He loved you from before the beginning of time, He loves you now, and He will continue to love you for all eternity!

* * *

The importance of understanding God's love

Paul wrote in his letter to the Ephesians, "may you have the power to understand, as all God's people should, how wide, how long, how high, and how deep his love is. May you experience the love of Christ, though it is too great to understand fully. Then you will be made complete with all the fullness of life and power that comes from God." Ephesians 3:18-19 (NLT)

Until we understand and grasp that we are completely loved by God, we will never really live the incredible, complete, full, abundant power-filled life that He intends for us.

I Love Your Ways, Lord

Monday - God Knows

I often hear people say, as a throwaway comment, *"God knows."* For example, *"God knows how long I'm going to have to wait in this queue."* It sounds strange, even profane to my ears, when these words are spoken out of the context of celebrating God's omniscience. I wonder do people realise what they're saying? Do they realise that they're stating a truth? *God does know.* He knows absolutely everything there is to know!

God knows everything

The word used to describe this complete knowledge is o*mniscient*, meaning, 'infinite awareness, understanding and insight.'God knows everything about the past, present and future. Nothing could ever take Him by surprise. Nothing is new to Him. His knowledge is absolute. *"Oh, the depth of the riches of the wisdom and knowledge of God! How unsearchable his judgments, and his paths beyond tracing out! 'Who has known the mind of the Lord? Or who has been his counsellor?"* Romans 11:33-34 (NIVUK)
"Great is our Lord and mighty in power; his understanding has no limit." Psalm 147:5 (NIVUK)

God knows everything about *you*.

It is such a comfort, in our increasingly crazy world, to know that we have a God who knows us and cares for us. Contrary to common belief - and that song "From a distance" - God is not watching this world, uninvolved and detached, from a distance, but is intimately involved. *"The eyes of all look to you, and you give them their food at the proper time. You open your hand and satisfy the desires of every living thing."* Psalms 145:15-16 (NIVUK)

One hears of people who have such a close bond that they finish each other's sentences. Well the Lord does even better than that - He knows you so well, that before a word is even properly formed on your lips, He knows what you're thinking, and what you're going to say. In fact He knew what you were going to *think* before you thought it!

"You have searched me, LORD, and you know me. You know when I sit and when I rise; you perceive my thoughts from afar. You discern my going out and my lying down; you are familiar with all my ways. Before a word is on my tongue you, LORD, know it completely." Psalm 139:1-4 (NIVUK)

God knows exactly what you need, and when
"And my God will meet all your needs according to the riches of his glory in Christ Jesus." Philippians 4:19 (NIVUK)

So, the next time you hear someone who doesn't personally know God casually say, "Ah, God knows," just smile to yourself, and thank Him that He really does!

Tuesday - Our Place In God's Story

How do you see your life? If your life were a book, who would the main character be, and the story be all about? I had a Christian teacher in primary school, who taught our class that *"history is more than just the story of man, it is His-story."* Those wise words have always stayed with me.

My purpose, and yours, is not to fit God into our own life stories, but to understand the incredible truth that God has made a place for *us* in His story! This radical about-turn in our thinking can make all the difference in our spiritual growth, and our daily walk with Him. The story of life is all about Jesus, from creation to the present day. And we, His children, are invited to be a part of His story!

We tend to turn it all around. We make it all about us. We think we're making great sacrifices by laying down our lives, picking up our crosses, and following Jesus, finding a place for God in our stories. This way of thinking can cause us to miss out on being part of <u>His</u> incredible story! Many Christians settle for 'churchianity,' rather than vibrant Christianity.

'Churchianity'

'Churchianity' accepts that Jesus Christ is the only way to salvation, but once 'saved' adopts a works attitude, a sort of *"thank you for saving me Jesus, but I'll take it from here,"* mindset, and then looks for ways to fit God into their story, by religiously applying Biblical principles without *life*. But we know, don't we, that the Bible is not some sort of religious self-help guide?

The Bible is the story of Jesus! He is present from Genesis to Revelation, and His story is relevant to everyday Christian life. The Bible is <u>living</u> and active, it pulses with the very heartbeat of Jesus Christ and it has the power to change lives!

His story is about His glory, and we - puny as we are - are invited to join Jesus in His story. We are invited to partner with the Living God in His great purposes, plans far greater than our human minds could ever dream up. Isn't is strange then, that we, the created ones, think we should invite our Creator to join us, and partner with us?

"When I gaze at your moon and your stars, mounted like jewels in their settings, I know you are the fascinating artist who fashioned it all! But when I look up and see such wonder and workmanship above, I have to ask you this question: Compared to all this cosmic glory, why would you bother with puny, mortal man or be infatuated with Adam's sons? Yet what honor you have given to men, created only a little lower than Elohim, crowned like kings and queens with glory and magnificence. You have delegated to them mastery over all you have made, making everything subservient to their authority, placing earth itself under the feet of your image-bearers." Psalms 8:3-8 (TPT)

Wednesday - Be Still and Know

"Be still, and know that I am God; I will be exalted among the nations, I will be exalted in the earth." Psalm 46:10 (NIVUK)

Be still - cease working, stop striving, relax, be calm
Many of us, when life's craziness hits, feel the urge to do our 'headless chicken impersonation.' Our survival instinct kicks in and we're either immobilised by panic, or we go into 'fix-it mode,' where we drive ourselves to distraction trying sort the problems out by ourselves.

I really like this scripture in the Passion Translation: *"God, you're such a safe and powerful place to find refuge! You're a proven help in time of trouble— more than enough and always available whenever I need you. So we will never fear even if every structure of support were to crumble away. We will not fear even when the earth quakes and shakes, moving mountains and casting them into the sea. For the raging roar of stormy winds and crashing waves cannot erode our faith in you. Pause in his presence"* Psalms 46:1-3 (TPT)

The worst may happen - we might be hit by an earthquake, the very mountains might crumble to nothing and collapse into the sea. But let them! Let the worst happen because we, God's people have something so precious, so indestructible inside us, that when we look to Him in our time of trouble, we can 'be still' and trust Him. Why?

Because He is The Lord our God!
Here's what the Psalm says occurs after the mountains may
crumble and fall into the sea, here's how that precious gift inside
us becomes evident. "God has a constantly flowing river whose
sparkling streams bring joy and delight to his people. His river
flows right through the city of God Most High, into his holy
dwelling places. God is in the midst of his city, secure and never
shaken. At daybreak his help will be seen with the appearing of
the dawn. When the nations are in uproar with their tottering
kingdoms, God simply raises his voice and the earth begins to
disintegrate before him. Here he comes! The Commander! The
mighty Lord of Angel Armies is on our side. The God of Jacob
fights for us! Pause in his presence" Psalms 46:4-7 (TPT)

Our enemies are also still before Him
Here's another thought; I have always read verse one of this
Psalm, *"be still and know that I am God,"* from the perspective
of God's people being still, and waiting for Him to act, to move,
to speak. But when our God is on the move, when He speaks,
everyone, including our enemies are silent before Him. He says
to those circumstances that threaten to overwhelm you, "be still -
be silent, and know that I am God!"

We can know a calm confidence in our God. We don't need to
devise and strategise to fix our problems. They may be very big,
but our God is bigger! We only need to rest in Him. Be still.
Know - remember - that He.Is.God.

Thursday - Omnipotent God

Let's just think about God's power for a few moments.
All power belongs to our God. His power is infinite and can never, and will never, diminish. Unlike us, God doesn't expend energy that needs to be replenished. When He carries out His mighty works none of His power is depleted. To put it simply, one could say God runs at one hundred percent power at all times. Completely self-sufficient, He doesn't need to look outside of Himself for renewal of energy. All the power God requires for anything and everything He does comes from His own infinite self, and remains in undiminished fullness. When it says in Genesis that God rested on the seventh day, it was to set an example for us to rest, not because God was tired or needed to recover power. And it was only from creating the world that He rested, not from *working,* because God *never* ceases to work. (See John 5:17)

There is no power or authority in heaven or on earth greater than our God

"Now he is far above any ruler or authority or power or leader or anything else—not only in this world but also in the world to come. God has put all things under the authority of Christ and has made him head over all things for the benefit of the church."
Ephesians 1:21-22 (NLT)

His omnipotence was demonstrated in creation

"This is what the Lord says— your Redeemer and Creator: "I am the Lord, who made all things. I alone stretched out the heavens. Who was with me when I made the earth?"
Isaiah 44:24 (NLT)

His omnipotence is shown in salvation
"Now all glory to God, who is able to keep you from falling away and will bring you with great joy into his glorious presence without a single fault. All glory to him who alone is God, our Savior through Jesus Christ our Lord. All glory, majesty, power, and authority are his before all time, and in the present, and beyond all time! Amen." Jude 1:24-25 (NLT)

He is limitless!
"How great is our Lord! His power is absolute! His understanding is beyond comprehension!"
Psalms 147:5 (NLT)

How do we apply this knowledge?
God is all powerful, the Bible leaves no room for doubt on that. So how do we apply this knowledge in our day-to-day living?

1. <u>We look to Him, and Him only</u>: *"I look up to the mountains— does my help come from there? My help comes from the Lord, who made heaven and earth!"*Psalms 121:1-2 (NLT); *"The name of the Lord is a strong fortress; the godly run to him and are safe."*
Proverbs 18:10 (NLT); "For I can do everything through Christ, who gives me strength."
Philippians 4:13 (NLT).

2. <u>Believe God:</u> Believe that He is who He says He is. First, you need to <u>know</u> His character. Many people say they believe <u>in</u> God. They might know a lot <u>about</u> God, but they don't really know Him. Jesus addressed this issue in John's Gospel. These religious leaders were Biblical scholars, yet their hearts were so

closed to God, their spiritual eyes so blinded that they could not see that He was standing right in front of them! *"You study the Scriptures diligently because you think that in them you have eternal life. These are the very Scriptures that testify about me, yet you refuse to come to me to have life."* John 5:39-40 (NIVUK)

3: <u>Trust God</u>: *"Some trust in chariots and some in horses, but we trust in the name of the LORD our God. They are brought to their knees and fall, but we rise up and stand firm."* Psalms 20:7-8 NIVUK. We start by believing that He is all-powerful, and then we cease striving to fix our problems ourselves. As the Psalmist says, *'lift your eyes to the maker of heaven and earth'.* Ask the Omnipotent God to help and strengthen you and He will. God said these words to us through Isaiah: *"Don't be afraid, for I am with you. Don't be discouraged, for I am your God. I will strengthen you and help you. I will hold you up with my victorious right hand."* Isaiah 41:10 (NLT)

Sometimes, in my Bible reading I like to focus on just one of our Father's attributes. It's one of the many ways we can get to know Him better. Did you ever have that age-old playground squabble, 'my daddy's stronger than your daddy?' How comforting to know, as God's children, that our Daddy's strength truly is matchless, therefore we can face anything.

Friday - My Strength and Shield

"The Lord is my strength and shield. I trust him with all my heart. He helps me, and my heart is filled with joy. I burst out in songs of thanksgiving. The Lord gives his people strength. He is a safe fortress for his anointed king." Psalms 28:7-8 (NLT)

Yesterday we looked at God's omnipotence. Today, I'd like to think about how shares His strength with us. God doesn't expect us to be strong. He knows we are not. He wants us to find our strength in Him.

David looked to the Lord for strength

David had a reputation for greatness in battle from a young age and this grew as he matured. But there's a common thread running through David's life, he was victorious because <u>the Lord was with him:</u> *"And David became more and more powerful, because the Lord of Heaven's Armies was with him."* 1 Chronicles 11:9 NLT (Also 1 Samuel 18:7)

In spite of all David's victories, instead of becoming arrogant or proud, revelling in people's high opinion of him, David acknowledged that it was *God.* He knew that the Lord was his source of strength and the one who brought the victories. David knew that he was completely dependent on God and he relied on Him in battle and hardship and poured out his gratitude and worship in Psalms, acknowledging God as the Victor. Psalm eighteen is a beautiful example, (also see 2 Samuel 22)

David knew God

"I love you, Lord; you are my strength. The Lord is my rock, my fortress, and my saviour; my God is my rock, in whom I find protection. He is my shield, the power that saves me, and my place of safety." Psalms 18:1-2 (NLT)

David knew God, not just about God, he knew God's character. "I love you Lord, you are my strength". This reflects a relationship that is deeply personal, and built on trust. David trusted that God was who He said He was, and that He would do as He had promised. David demonstrates this belief in these words in Psalm 33: "The best-equipped army cannot save a king, nor is great strength enough to save a warrior. Don't count on your warhorse to give you victory— for all its strength, it cannot save you. But the Lord watches over those who fear him, those who rely on his unfailing love. He rescues them from death and keeps them alive in times of famine." Psalms 33:16-19 (NLT)

Whatever you are facing today, God doesn't expect you to be strong, only to remember who He is, and to find your strength in Him, as you trust in Him to be all that He says He is.

Saturday - You Can Run But You Can't Hide

"Where could I go from your Spirit? Where could I run and hide from your face? If I go up to heaven, you're there! If I go down to the realm of the dead, you're there too! If I fly with wings into the shining dawn, you're there! If I fly into the radiant sunset, you're there waiting! Wherever I go, your hand will guide me; your strength will empower me. It's impossible to disappear from you or to ask the darkness to hide me, for your presence is everywhere, bringing light into my night." Psalms 139:7-11 (TPT)

The questions '*where could I go from your Spirit,*' and *where could I run and hide from your face?,*' are rhetorical, they do not express any intent on David's part to run from God, but are infused with awe and wonder at God's relentless, loving, pursuit of him.

You can't outrun God

Wherever you are in life, literally, and figuratively speaking, you can never outrun God. There's nowhere in this world that His presence cannot find you. You are never too far gone or too backslidden, for God to reach you. You are never too angry, even with with Him, for His love to reach you and uphold you. If you're in a 'good place,' you'll know that all it took was a heartfelt move towards God in humility, and repentant response to His voice, and there He was!

You can try to move across entire continents, but He will be there, waiting for you when you arrive - in fact, He'll accompany you all the way there too, because His presence never leaves you. He is omnipresent- He's here with me now as I write this, and there with you now, as you read it. He never ceases, in His pursuit of deeper relationship with His children.

God doesn't do shotgun weddings

We are created for relationship with God. Nothing, and no one can ever fill that gap in our hearts. You'd think then, that we would all respond by running into His presence, with the boldness, and confidence, that He has freely given us as His children, (Ephesians 3:12) holding nothing back from Him. But we have also been given free will. God doesn't do 'shotgun weddings,' or 'arranged marriage.' He won't force us into relationship with Himself. He invites us, calls us, woos and pursues us.

Taste and see that He is good!

Sadly, many Christians spend their lives with just an acquaintanceship with God. Some are happy with just a salvation experience, and never really grow much past that, to get to know God, up close and personally. As I write this, these words come to mind: *"Taste and see that the Lord is good. Oh, the joys of those who take refuge in him!"* Psalms 34:8 (NLT)

Do you run <u>from</u> God rather than <u>to</u> Him? When we 'taste and see,' we will see that He is a good God, not the God many picture in their minds, but the One who loves us with an everlasting love. He is Good, and everything He does is good. Once we have tasted, let us not be satisfied with just a taste - but *take refuge in Him* and make Him our fortress, our refuge, our <u>permanent</u> resting place, and, as we read about earlier in the book, our *home.*

Sunday- God of All Hope

"May the God of hope fill you with all joy and peace as you trust in him, so that you may overflow with hope by the power of the Holy Spirit." Romans 15:13 (NIVUK)

The word translated into English as *'overflow'* (with hope) is closer to *"abound,"* in the original language, meaning: *to be present in great quantity, to be prevalent, to be richly supplied with.* How many of us can truthfully say that we live as though we *believe* that our lives are anchored by this kind of hope? Would your family and friends describe you as a person *'filled* with *all* joy, and peace, in believing and *abounding* in hope?' Would mine?

Paul writes, 'may the God of all hope fill you' (with these qualities) therefore I conclude that it must be <u>possible</u> for us to grow in, and continue to increase in, joy, peace, trust and hope, and this in itself should give hope to the one who feels hopeless! Even among Bible believing Christians, not many could claim to be filled with '<u>all</u> joy and peace, to be 'abounding in hope.' How can we go about becoming filled with these qualities?

The God of hope.

By 'the God of all hope,' Paul means that God is both the source or <u>giver</u> of hope, and the <u>Object</u> of our hope. God is the one who shapes our character, and gives us the qualities we need, in order

443

to love others, endure all things, have unwavering hope, and persevere where the world would give up.

In Romans 15:5 Paul describes God as *"the God of perseverance and encouragement."* This is in the context of loving others; God *gives* those qualities to those who seek Him.

In Romans 15:33 and 16:20, Paul describes God as *"the God of peace."* Again, it is God who *gives peace* to His people. It would make sense then, that if we lack hope, or peace, that we should turn to the One to who is the *'God of all hope,'* the Source of true hope!

The hope God gives is not merely a wishful thinking sort of hope, as in, "I hope such-and-such going to happen." The hope God gives is *sure*; it is a precious hope that helps us endure trials, and it gives our lives meaning. We don't merely hope everything *might* work out in the end, but ours is a confidence that God *will* work everything together for our good. (Romans 8:28). It's because of this Hope that we don't give up, we don't lose heart, and we can say as the Psalmist did: *"Yet I am confident I will see the Lord's goodness while I am here in the land of the living."* Psalm 27:13 (NLT)

The 'steps' towards hope

Paul's prayer is that you would be filled with all joy and peace as you trust in Him (Jesus), so that you may overflow with hope, by the power of the Holy Spirit. This *hope* comes as a product, or result of, being filled with joy and peace.

<u>Joy</u>: Paul prays, not only that God will fill you with joy, but with *'all joy.'* Joy is so much more than a feeling. It is the ability to be content and joyful in every circumstance.

* * *

There has never been anyone more full of joy than Jesus; He was anointed with the *'oil of joy'* (Hebrews 1:9, Psalm 45:7). As we are His, it makes sense that we can also be filled with joy, for this life.

Peace: Peace is harmony in our relationships, its a treaty or agreement to 'cease hostilities.' And the peace of God is these things and then more! It's a supernatural peace that makes no sense to us; a peace that enables us to 'be still and know [that He is God]' when everything thing seems to be falling down around us: "And the peace of God, which transcends all understanding, will guard your hearts and your minds in Christ Jesus."Philippians 4:7 (NIVUK)

When we are filled with these first two qualities, and as they grow in us, we learn trust; The further we walk in fellowship with God, growing to know him and understand His desires concerning us, hope grows and abounds in our hearts and overflows from us.

For those 'Dory' Days

Monday - Dory Days

Dory, in the film Finding Nemo, has a problem. She suffers from short term memory loss. She can't remember things, just minutes after they've been told to her. Sometimes in our walk with God, we can be like Dory. We feel so blessed. Anchored. Safe and secure. Then, trouble comes to our door, and we forget. Again!

The memory lapse

Seemingly out of nowhere, a hard time comes knocking. It always seems to come just as we are feeling 'on top of the world.' We forget the faithfulness of God. The very same God we were praising just days, or hours before, for His goodness to us.

Has God forgotten you?

"Never. Not for one moment. Look at what God says about you: "Jerusalem says, "The Lord has deserted us; the Lord has forgotten us." "Never! Can a mother forget her nursing child? Can she feel no love for the child she has borne? But even if that were possible, I would not forget you! See, I have written your name on the palms of my hands. Always in my mind is a picture of Jerusalem's walls in ruins." Isaiah 49:14-16 (NLT)

I love this depiction of God as the tender, loving parent. What mother, even in our human frailty, could ignore the cries of her hungry baby? The Lord never forgets us, we are always at the forefront of our Father's mind, and He is moved at the sound of our cry.

"In panic I cried out, "I am cut off from the Lord!" But you heard my cry for mercy and answered my call for help." Psalms 31:22 (NLT)

"But in my distress I cried out to the Lord; yes, I prayed to my God for help. He heard me from his sanctuary; my cry to him reached his ears." Psalms 18:6 (NLT)

There are so many verses throughout the Bible that speak of God hearing when we cry out to Him, but I chose those two specifically, because of how they start off - 'In panic' 'In my distress'

Here was King David, a man after God's own heart, a 'hero' of the faith, admitting that he had just had a 'Dory moment.' He had a temporary memory lapse, and had allowed his emotions to get the better of him in his circumstances.
David, hounded and pursued by Saul, had not only felt distress, but had panicked. In these intense emotions David cried out to God, and God instantly responded. *"He heard me," "my cry reached His ears."* And then David remembered! He remembered who God is, so much bigger than anything, or anyone who comes against his Beloved ones.

If you had your Bible open to read that last scripture in Psalm 18, read on down through the Psalm, and see how God responded! Here's a taste. "He reached down from heaven and rescued me; he drew me out of deep waters. He rescued me from my powerful enemies, from those who hated me and were too strong for me. He led me to a place of safety; he rescued me because he delights in me." Psalms 18:16-17, 19 (NLT)

Help when we most need it

Sometimes, when life feels chaotic, we plead with God for what He has already <u>promised</u> us, as if He didn't already know our situation; as if we weren't His precious children!

"So let us come boldly to the throne of our gracious God. There we will receive his mercy, and we will find grace to help us when we need it most." Hebrews 4:16 (NLT)

Where is God in the crises and stresses of our lives?
"God is our refuge and strength, A very present help in trouble." Psalms 46:1 (NKJV)
He's right there, with you, "very present." He hasn't changed. His love for you hasn't waned, nor has His faithfulness, and they never will.

"Why do you say, O Jacob, and speak, O Israel, "My way is hidden from the Lord, and my right is disregarded by my God"? Have you not known? Have you not heard? The Lord is the everlasting God, the Creator of the ends of the earth. He does not faint or grow weary; his understanding is unsearchable. He gives power to the faint, and to him who has no might he increases strength." Isaiah 40:27-29 (NLT)

Be encouraged, if you are having a Dory moment today. You aren't alone in your temporary memory lapse. But <u>don't stay there</u>. Remind yourself, as David did, of who God is, who you are to God, and in God! Say to your heart as David did, "Why are you cast down, O my soul? And why are you disquieted within me? Hope in God; For I shall yet praise Him, The help of my countenance and my God." Psalms 43:5 (NKJV)

Tuesday - Do You Know?

"You intended to harm me, but God intended it all for good. He brought me to this position so I could save the lives of many people." Genesis 50:20 (NLT)

As you may have noticed, I love the story of Joseph. I love how God, in His great faithfulness, took hold of the evil plots that Joseph's own brothers had hatched against him, and Joseph's subsequent years of hardship, slavery, and imprisonment, and worked all these into unimaginable favour and blessing.

Do you find yourself in a tough season presently?

In many ways you and I have something in common with Joseph. Joseph's brothers hated and resented Him because he had his father's love, affection and favour. We too have an enemy who hates us because we have <u>our</u> Father's love, affection and favour, lavished generously upon us, His children.

From the moment we put our faith in Jesus, Hell took up arms against us, 'intending evil' against us. But this is not a frightening prospect, because we know that no matter what comes our way, our God, in His unfailing love and faithfulness, can, and will, turn every situation around for our good. *"And we know that God causes everything to work together for the good of those who love God and are called according to his purpose for them."* Romans 8:28 (NLT)

* * *

This is possibly one of the most quoted and preached about scriptures. It's one of my staple 'go to' passages to read, whenever I'm facing hard times. But I've noticed that people often focus on the second part - the Lord working things together part - which is wonderful, and true, but bear with me and let's have a look again at the first three words of the verse, "*and we know*..."

And We Know

Do you? Do you really, really, know it? I have to ask myself that same vital question. Do you truly know, in other words, believe, *absolutely*, that God will do this: take your upside-down, 'messed up,' confusing, sad, lonely, misunderstood, anger-filled, or anxiety riddled situation, and turn it completely around, causing it to work together for your good?

Why would He do that for you? Well, firstly because He loves you beyond measure, and secondly, because He says in His Word that He will do this, and our God keeps His promises. We *can* know, and be assured of, this great truth!

I'm sure as the years went by, Joseph must have felt, at times, that he would be a slave forever. As he lay in prison, I wonder did he think he'd never get out. And all the while, God was working out His great plan for Joseph - setting the scene.

God will lead you through this time you are in. You will step out of the other side of your valley, difficult season, or time of waiting, in God's perfect timing. Don't doubt for a moment that our Great God is working out His perfect plan, even right now as you read this. And who knows what lives may be touched for His Kingdom's sake, because of your faithfulness, and steadfastness, in your difficult season? And you will be able to say, like Joseph: "*You intended to harm me, but God intended it all for good. He brought me to this position so I could save the lives of many people.*" Genesis 50:20 (NLT)

Wednesday - This I Call To Mind

"Yet this I call to mind and therefore I have hope: Because of the LORD's great love we are not consumed, for his compassions never fail. They are new every morning; great is your faithfulness. I say to myself, 'The LORD is my portion; therefore I will wait for him.'" Lamentations 3:21-24 (NIVUK)

In this, Jeremiah's book of deep lamentation, he writes all about the reason for Israel's affliction, their sin and repeated spiritual adultery. Jeremiah understood the reasons for this dreadful period, but still, it must have been heartbreaking for him to witness the fall of Jerusalem, the enslavement of his people and the destruction of the Temple. In spite of whatever inner turmoil Jeremiah may have felt at witnessing such destruction, he was able to stand firm in these truths: that it was only because of the Lord's great love, that they were not totally consumed. That God's compassions never comes to an end. That the Lord Himself is the inheritance of His people. And for these reasons Jeremiah would wait for Him.

This I call to mind

"This I call to mind." In other words, "I will remind myself." Jeremiah reminds himself, and the reader, of God's great love and compassion, without which we would surely be consumed by our circumstances. He recalls God's faithfulness in renewing His mercies every morning, offering reproof, instruction, direction in righteousness, and hope for the future.

Therefore I have hope

Because of all these things, namely, God's love, compassion, mercies, and faithfulness in renewing those mercies daily, Jeremiah says, "I have hope!" And he declares that he will patiently wait for God. *"I say to myself, 'The LORD is my portion; therefore I will wait for him."* Lamentations 3:24 (NIVUK)

Someone else in the Bible who was no stranger to this principle of talking to himself about God, reminding his own heart of God's faithfulness, recalling God's goodness and mercy, was David: *"Why, my soul, are you downcast? Why so disturbed within me? Put your hope in God, for I will yet praise him, my Saviour and my God."* Psalms 43:5 (NIVUK). Also see 1 Samuel 30:6

What truths do you need to call to mind today regarding God's goodness, love, mercy, and faithfulness? No matter what you may face in this transitory life, remember, *"God is faithful; he will not let you be tempted beyond what you can bear. But when you are tempted, he will also provide a* way out *so that you can endure it."* 1 Corinthians 10:13 (NIVUK)

Paul said, even in the face of incredible hardship and suffering, *"I know whom I have believed, and am convinced that he is able to guard what I have entrusted to him until that day."* 2 Timothy 1:12 (NIVUK)

'I know whom I have believed.' Remember, Paul was not one of the original disciples. He never actually knew Jesus, the man; he only ever knew Him the same way you and I do, through salvation, by putting his faith in Jesus Christ, as his Lord and Saviour. But Paul absolutely knew, and trusted in the nature of

Jesus. So remind yourself that <u>you know Him too.</u> Like Paul, you *know* His character and His nature. He is good. His heart is kind. He has always been, and always will be, faithful to you. He is for you, not against you!

As you begin to recall and remember, your heart will resonate with the words of Jeremiah: *The Lord is my portion - therefore I have hope in Him.*

Thursday - Does My 'But' Look Big In This?

Are you affected by the size of your but? No, I have not made a spelling error, I really did mean to spell the word *but* with only one 't.' The age-old question '*does my butt look big in this,?*' has become fodder for comedians the world over. A *perceived* large derrière can be a real and debilitating psychological problem, and often reflects deeper body-image issues. However there is a different type of 'big-but-perception' issue we all face at times that can be even more debilitating.

In Exodus chapter four, we read about one of the biggest buts in the Bible. "*Then Moses answered and said, "<u>But</u> suppose they will not believe me or listen to my voice; suppose they say, 'The LORD has not appeared to you."* Exodus 4:1 (NKJV)
Moses argues with the Lord, eventually exposing the huge 'but' that he sees standing in his way, his own unworthiness, so he says: "*Pardon your servant, Lord. Please send someone else.*" Exodus 4:13 (NIVUK)

Is your but too big?
Sometimes, when God calls us to move forward, we find ourselves stuck, unable to move, because, like Moses when God first called him, we are more focused on the size of our *but*.

'*But*' is one of the smallest words in the English language and yet it speaks volumes. Spoken from our lips, it is often an excuse.

However it doesn't have to be! With just a little bit of a heart-shift, we can start to see, and use the word *but* from the Lord's perspective, and turn it into something powerful! Today we will look at how, when we place the word *but* in its proper place in a sentence, we completely change not just the sentence structure, but the structure of our thought patterns, and ultimately our heart attitudes.

How?

It isn't difficult, however it will take discipline and training. You can start by replacing 'but I' statements with 'but God' statements. For example, instead of saying "I want to forgive that person who hurt me but I can't," change your statement to something like: "I want to forgive that person who hurt me, it isn't easy, but God will enable me"

How different our outlook would be, our family and church relationships, if we would only shift our thinking, just that tiny bit to end our statements with *but God*.

But God
The Bible is filled with examples of but God statements. Here are a few to encourage you!
"Jesus looked at them and said, 'With man this is impossible, but with God all things are possible." Matthew 19:26 (NIVUK);

"Not many of you were wise by human standards; not many were influential; not many were of noble birth. But God chose the foolish things of the world to shame the wise; God chose the weak things of the world to shame the strong." 1 Corinthians 1:26-27 (NIVUK);

"My flesh and my heart may fail, but God is the strength of my

heart and my portion for ever." Psalms 73:26 (NIVUK);
"The grass withers and the flowers fall, <u>but</u> the word of our God endures for ever." Isaiah 40:8 (NIVUK);

"If the God of my father, the God of Abraham and the Fear of Isaac, had not been with me, you would surely have sent me away empty-handed. <u>But God</u> has seen my hardship and the toil of my hands, and last night he rebuked you." Genesis 31:42 (NIVUK);

"You intended to harm me, <u>but God</u> intended it for good to accomplish what is now being done, the saving of many lives." Genesis 50:20 (NIVUK);

"You killed the author of life, <u>but God</u> raised him from the dead." Acts 3:15 (NIVUK);

"To the roots of the mountains I sank down; the earth beneath barred me in for ever. <u>But you, Lord</u> my God, brought my life up from the pit." Jonah 2:6 (NIVUK)

"Day after day Saul searched for him, but God did not give David into his hands." 1 Samuel 23:14 (NIVUK);

"People look at the outward appearance, <u>but</u> the LORD looks at the heart." 1 Samuel 16:7 (NIVUK)

"Very rarely will anyone die for a righteous person, though for a good person someone might possibly dare to die. <u>But God</u> demonstrates his own love for us in this: while we were still sinners, Christ died for us." Romans 5:7-8 (NIVUK)

Let us determine today to no longer allow our puny little buts to be bigger than God, nor shrink back from what He calls us to because we are focused on but I, rather than but God!

Jill McIlreavy

Friday - A Retune

One morning recently, I stood in the kitchen, waiting for the kettle to boil for my morning coffee, and happened to glance at our old retro-style radio. It occurred to me that I haven't switched it on for ages. It has sat there, gathering dust, for the best part of two years. Does that mean radio broadcast have stopped? Not as far as I know!

The radio itself is just a cleverly put together box with the right wires and receivers inside it to enable it to pick up a signal. But unless the 'on' button is pressed, the radio has as much capacity to receive transmissions as the biscuit tin.

Radio broadcasts are constantly going on, day and night, whether we 'believe' in them or not, and whether we choose to tune in and listen to them or not. There are radio waves continually being transmitted - into homes, cars, hospitals, places of work - even aeroplanes - all over the world. People are being comforted, cheered, soothed, informed, and even and provoked, by radio programmes. Whether my radio is switched on or not doesn't factor into the equation.

The goodness of God is true, whether we 'tune in' to that truth or not

You and I have the correct 'wiring and receivers' inside us to know, see, hear and experience the goodness of God. But sometimes, things happen that cause us to doubt His goodness, especially towards us as individuals.

God is good, whether we choose to believe this or not. The Bible is filled with references to God's goodness. Here's just a glimpse: *"You, Lord, are forgiving and good, abounding in love to all who call to you."* Psalm 86:5 (NIVUK)
"the Lord is good and his love endures for ever; his faithfulness continues through all generations." Psalm 100:5 (NIVUK)
"Give thanks to the LORD, for he is good; his love endures for ever." Psalm 106:1 (NIVUK)
1 Chronicles 16:34 says exactly the same.

God never ceases to be good

Whatever your current circumstances may seem to say, God's goodness never fails - His goodness towards you, never fails. Sometimes, especially when things aren't going according to our own hopes and plans; when we're struggling through hard times in life, we fail to recognise the goodness of God. But does that mean His goodness towards us has stopped? Of course not. It's impossible. God does not withhold His goodness. He's good because it's His nature. Not only is God good *in* Himself, but He is good *to* His children. We can't earn it. We don't deserve His goodness; yet He is still good to us anyway. That's why David wrote: *"Surely your goodness and love will follow me all the days of my life, Psalms 23:6 (NIVUK)*

Switch on and tune in

Radio broadcasts continue, even through the times when I haven't had the time, or the inclination, to tune in and listen to what used to be my favourite station. Perhaps, if you are no longer recognising the goodness of God in your life, you might want to check your 'on' switch. It can easily be switched back on by opening up your Bible and reminding yourself of who He is.

* * *

God's goodness is unfailing, His mercies are new every morning. His faithfulness endures forever! Whether you and I tune in to Him or not, those truths remain!

As you read through scriptures about Him, ask God to open your eyes to see that no matter how dire your situation may seem, or how low you feel, God is, always has been, and will always be, good!

Saturday - When 'Be Still' Means Be Quiet!

"He says, 'Be still, and know that I am God; I will be exalted among the nations, I will be exalted in the earth." Psalms 46:10 (NIVUK)

Have you ever prayed one of those desperate "Help me Lord!" sort of prayers, and then instead of waiting for God to answer, gone ahead and tried to help yourself? I have. One particular occasion will stay with me, because it taught me another aspect of what it can mean to *be still.*

I was about to go on a much looked-forward to mission trip with a team from my church. The very day before we were due to go, I couldn't find my passport, which also had the necessary visas in it for the country we were to visit. After a thorough search, I phoned some friends and asked them to pray. I prayed too. My prayer went something like this: "Lord you know exactly where my passport is, so I'm not going to panic, I'm just going to wait and trust you." Immediately Psalm 46:10 came to mind *"Be Still and know that I am God"* For a few minutes I felt calm, and peace flooded my soul. "It's going to be Okay, the Lord, will remind me where I put my passport". So I waited. A whole three minutes.

And then I spent the next seven hours (not an exaggeration) tearing the house apart, alternately searching and praying. As the hours ticked by, I became increasingly panicked.

At around five in the evening I finally sat down, for the first time that day, and wept. There were no places left to search, I'd looked in them all, at least three times. Then, in the quiet, a small thought came to me, *"what about that little blue travel wallet you bought the other week?"*

I immediately dismissed the thought because I'd already looked there. In fact I had emptied the wallet out. But the thought grew so strong, it was *compelling*. I got up, went over to the place I had last seen the wallet. I picked it up, my heart racing, and looked inside. It looked empty. Then I noticed a concealed zip compartment that I hadn't remembered. With hope starting to rise, I unzipped it, and there was my passport!

Why had I not remembered that I had put it in there? I'd looked in the wallet during my search, and had even impatiently shoved the wallet out of the way several times to look behind it! The truth is, if had I just *been quiet* for a few minutes, if I had just said to my racing thoughts and my own mouth "shush!" then the Lord could have got a word in edge-ways! With hindsight (hindsight a great thing) the Lord had kept bringing that little blue wallet to my attention and I had merely glanced inside, and tossed it aside, all the while praying increasingly desperate prayers!

Sometimes the answer we seek is right in front of us all along, but we're so busy trying to fix what we've asked God to fix that we don't see it! Sometimes we're making so much noise with our desperate prayers, that we drown out the still, small, voice of God as He answers us. Sometimes 'be still,' means *be quiet!*

God always answers prayer!

Remember who He is. There's no one else like Him, no name mightier, nothing, and no one can oppose Him, or stand in the way of His purposes. And He loves you.

"Then you will call on me and come and pray to me, and I will listen to you." Jeremiah 29:12 (NIVUK)

"And I will do whatever you ask in my name, so that the Father may be glorified in the Son. You may ask me for anything in my name, and I will do it." John 14:13-14 (NIVUK)

"This is the confidence we have in approaching God: that if we ask anything according to his will, he hears us. And if we know that he hears us – whatever we ask – we know that we have what we asked of him." 1 John 5:14-15 (NIVUK)

Sunday - Heartburn

"They said to each other, "Didn't our hearts burn within us as he talked with us on the road and explained the Scriptures to us?" Luke 24:32 (NLT)

Two disciples of Jesus were on the road to Emmaus after the crucifixion of Jesus. They were very low in spirits as they trudged along, discussing their griefs, and confusion. As they walked, Jesus caught up with them, and began walking with them, but God prevented them from recognising Jesus.

The disciples' sadness was etched on their faces, see (Luke 24:17) and Jesus asked them what was wrong. Still not realising who He was, they poured their hearts out. "We had hoped…" they said sadly.

We had hoped

Have you ever been so caught up in your troubles, sorrows, and dashed hopes, that you haven't recognised Jesus walking right beside you?

"We had hoped." What were *you* hoping for? What hopes and dreams didn't turn out the way you thought they were going to, leaving you heavy-hearted, and feeling distant from the Lord?

As the two disciples told Jesus their story, this stranger-who-was-not-a-stranger started to explain the scriptures to them. *"There's something about this man,"* must surely have been the though going through their minds. Yet still they didn't make the connection.When the time came to go their separate ways, they felt so drawn to this man, assured by his company, and his teaching, perhaps a stirring of hope again, that they begged him to stay with them. They wanted to stay in his presence a bit longer.

Jesus stayed with them. As they sat down to share a meal, Jesus took the bread, blessed it and broke it. It would seem that the realisation dawned on both of the disciples at once. It's Jesus! Suddenly, it all made sense. Then Jesus vanished. The two friends marvelled at how they hadn't recognised him. *"Didn't our hearts burn within us as he talked with us on the road and explained the Scriptures to us?"* Even though their physical eyes had not recognised Jesus, their hearts had recognised him all along! Except, they had ignored the "heartburn," that deep, inner nudge, while they walked along the road.

Sometimes during those times in life when we can't see past our pain, and problems, we fail to recognise Jesus. We don't see that He is walking right beside us, loving and encouraging us. As they had walked, Jesus kept reminding those two distraught disciples of what the scriptures say. He does the same for us. In our dark, difficult, times His Holy Spirit, draws alongside, our Comforter, our Teacher. We know He's there, but often we ignore the 'heartburn.' We feel that inner nudge of the Holy Spirit, reminding us of this scripture, and that, calling and drawing us to come close. But we fail to recognise Him, until we look back and see clearly that He was there all along.

Holy Heartburn

After the Lord has led you through yet another dark time when you felt no hope, how often have you looked back and marvelled that you hadn't recognised Him, right there, with you through it all, working all things together for your good? (Romans 8:28). Not for one moment did He leave your side, or forsake you! (Deuteronomy 31:6)

We all - disciples of Jesus that is - feel that 'heart-burn.' It's a knowing, deep down in our "knower," that place in the deepest part of the heart, where we store truth. We *know* that He is who He says He is. Even in those times when you feel far from Him, a bit lost, dry, empty, or without hope. You know that none of these scenarios are true for you, because living in you, causing your heart to burn, is The Spirit of the Living God! He's the Alpha and Omega, the same yesterday, today, and forever. He is Jesus, Emmanuel, God with us!

Growing Pains

Monday - Forgiveness

"And when you pray, make sure you forgive the faults of others so that your Father in heaven will also forgive you. But if you withhold forgiveness from others, your Father withholds forgiveness from you." Matthew 6:14-15 (TPT)

It's Jesus command

Part of Jesus' commandment to love, is to *forgive*. Why is it then, that we search endlessly for justification not to do so? Admittedly it isn't always easy to forgive, but its a vital part of our spiritual growth, and as with other Biblical commands, the Lord equips and enables us, we don't have to try to do it on our own. All He requires is the *willingness* to forgive; a heart submitted to Him in obedience.

Regain perspective

When we remember how much we have been forgiven it changes our perspective. Remember the 'unmerciful servant' in Matthew 18? Jesus told the parable in response to Peter's question, *"How many times do I have to forgive my fellow believer who keeps offending me? Seven times?"* Matthew 18:21 (TPT) Jesus told Peter that actually it was more like *seventy* times seven, and then went on to tell the story of a man who had been forgiven so much, yet he, in turn, could not forgive the smallest of debts owed to him.

We all like the *concept* of forgiveness. Oh and of course we're more than willing to *be* forgiven; but often the thought of forgiving the perpetrators of the hurts we carry seems to cause us deeper pain than the original hurt! The truth is, in a strange way, we <u>like</u> taking those hurts and offences out of the hidden places of our hearts and re-playing them in our minds. We think it makes us feel better. Perhaps it's that it gives us a chance to 're-write' the story. We imagine facing the person who hurt us, exept <u>this</u> time, we won't be such victims, oh no; this time we will have the words to say that will put them right in their place! But Jesus says, "Forgive them."

Forgive always

"Tolerate the weaknesses of those in the family of faith, forgiving one another in the same way you have been graciously forgiven by Jesus Christ. If you find fault with someone, release this same gift of forgiveness to them." Colossians 3:13 (TPT)

We are simply commanded to forgive, not to wait until we feel like it, or until the dust has settled, and we've allowed ourselves the 'luxury' of bearing a grievance for a while, or even until the other person has <u>asked</u> for forgiveness. In fact that person may never apologise or ask for forgiveness. They might even believe we are in the wrong. But we are still required by God to forgive them.

We forgive, simply because Jesus says so. If that seems 'unfair,' we can remind ourselves of this great unfairness: the One who was guiltless was scorned, mocked, spat upon and endured unspeakable suffering on a cross in our place (see 1 Peter 2:22) Yet with His dying breaths He asked His Father in Heaven to <u>forgive</u> very ones who had done these things to Him.

* * *

"Freely you have received the power of the kingdom, so freely release it to others." Matthew 10:8 (TPT).

Often we simply *choose* not to forgive those who have sinned against us, even though we continually sin against the One who has forgiven all our sin. It seems we are quick to forget how much we have been <u>freely</u> forgiven. When we have been wounded, rather than focusing on how much God has done *for* us, all we can see is what others have done *to* us.

That person may never even know that you have forgiven them. Forgiveness is for <u>your</u> spiritual wellbeing. I'm sure you have heard this a hundred times, but it's always good to remind ourselves - there's a saying that goes something like this: unforgiveness is like drinking poison and expecting your neighbour to die. Unforgiveness is a killer. Let's be a people free of this lethal poison!

Tuesday- All Tangled Up

"I'll say it again—it is easier for a camel to go through the eye of a needle than for a rich person to enter the Kingdom of God!"
Matthew 19:24 (NLT)

I don't know about you, but growing up I heard many sermons on this verse. At face value, it almost seems as though Jesus is saying that it is a sin to be rich, and that if you are rich, it will be virtually impossible for you to get into heaven. But this would make no sense when you study the Bible and read about people such as Abraham, and Kings such as David, Solomon and Hezekiah, who were rich men and <u>also</u> lived lives of intimacy with God. Their wealth was a *blessing* from God, it didn't keep them from true, deep, relationship with God.

Let's look then, at the context in which Jesus spoke about camels and eyes of needles. A rich young man came to Jesus and asked Him what good thing he could do, so that he could have eternal life. Jesus' reply is quite surprising, until we realise *why* He answered as He did: Jesus started listing the ten commandments. Think about this for a moment. Remember the question was regarding how to have eternal life. In the light of this, it seems odd that Jesus starts talking about the law. We know we cannot *earn* salvation through our own deeds or our own righteousness. (Ephesians 2:8-10) But that's not what Jesus was suggesting.

* * *

Not what he expected

The young man seemed to misunderstand too, as his reply shows. He told Jesus he had kept *all* the commandments from a young age. Jesus didn't accuse him of lying, so it's possible that the man really was obedient to the Word of God, but then Jesus delivered the real, hard-hitting request. It cut right to the heart of this man's true issue: *"go and sell all your possessions and give the money to the poor, and you will have treasure in heaven. Then come, follow me."* Matthew 19:21 (NLT)

The young man walked away sadly because he was very rich. He just couldn't do it - he could not bring himself make that big a sacrifice.

It was then, that Jesus said to His disciples: *"I tell you the truth, it is very hard for a rich person to enter the Kingdom of Heaven. I'll say it again—it is easier for a camel to go through the eye of a needle than for a rich person to enter the Kingdom of God!"* Matthew 19:23-24 (NLT).

Difficult - not because he was rich, but because he could not surrender his riches to the One from whom they came in the first place.

Needles, Camels and ropes.

When we look at aspects of this verse in the languages of Hebrew and Aramaic, an amazing picture comes to life. The Hebrew word for 'needle' simply describes *"a needle as used by tailors."*

It's when we get to the word *camel* that it's interesting: the word 'camel' used here is of Hebrew origin – *gamal* – which means *beast of burden.* However ..when you look at the original Hebrew text of Matthew 19, it is the Aramaic word *"gamla"* that is used – which actually means *'thick rope,'* the sort of rope used to anchor ships or boats in Biblical times.

Splitting hairs, or untangling?

I didn't know this about the *thick rope*, until I read Matthew 19 in the Passion Translation recently, and then did a little bit of research on the topic. Here it is in the Passion Translation: "*In fact, it's easier to stuff a heavy rope through the eye of a needle than it is for the wealthy to enter into God's kingdom realm!*" Matthew 19:24 (TPT)

Now, we could think this is just semantics, splitting hairs, after all, does it matter whether it's a camel or a thick rope trying to get though the eye of a needle? It's still extremely difficult!

Then, as I continued to study, the Lord showed me some things about this thick-rope concept that it made it all so much clearer to me.

A rope of any thickness is made up of many small threads, tightly woven together. The thicker the rope, the more threads - sometimes *hundreds* of tiny threads. It would, of course, be impossible to push this rope through the eye of a needle. But if you were to *unravel* the rope - untangle all those tightly woven threads from each other, then the smaller threads would fit through.

The rich man wanted to do all the deeds of obedience, to follow the law to the letter, but he was not willing to untangle his heart from his material things. Jesus had simply called him to follow and be His disciple, but the man was so tightly bound, like a thick rope, too tightly tangled up in the worldly goods he had set his heart upon. There was no way, unless he *untangled* himself that he was getting into the Kingdom.

Many people need to untangle and unravel themselves from those things that so tightly bind and prevent a wholehearted following of Jesus. Those of us who are in the Kingdom can learn from this too - we can submit to Jesus and allow Him to work in us, to unravel us, and keep unraveling us, from those things that bind us. Yes, we are part of

His Kingdom and nothing can remove us - but we are still, and will be until we go to be with Him, works in progress!

Wednesday - Unbelief, The Hidden Enemy

"I say to you, if you have faith as a mustard seed, you will say to this mountain, 'Move from here to there,' and it will move; and nothing will be impossible for you." Matthew 17:20 (NKJV)

Why is it that some people just seem to have more faith than others? When comparing faith portions to seeds, some have faith the size of a pumpkin seed, others have faith that resembles a peach pit, and some really do have the smallest measure of faith, just like the mustard seed that Jesus spoke of. However we need to remember it isn't the *size* or measure of faith that matters; what is important is that you *have* faith, even mustard-seed faith is enough to move mountains!

Some may read this and be discouraged, wondering why the 'mountains' in their lives never seem to move. After all, they do have faith the size of a mustard seed.

Mustard seed faith

It's always important to look at scripture in context. The mustard seed verse is in the context of a real life story, which is found in Matthew 17:14-21. A man had come to Jesus' disciples for help for his son, who was tormented by a demonic spirit. The disciples hadn't been able to cast the demon out, and they asked Jesus why they had been unsuccessful.

Jesus told them in no uncertain terms, *"Because of your*

unbelief;" Jesus <u>then</u> went on to say, in the same context (it's part of the same verse) *"for assuredly, I say to you, if you have faith as a mustard seed, you will say to this mountain, 'Move from here to there,' and it will move; and <u>nothing will be impossible for you.</u>"* Matthew 17:20 (NKJV)

Nothing will be impossible for me? With faith the size of a *mustard seed?* That in itself seems impossible to most of us if we're completely honest. So what is the problem, really? What hinders people who have faith the size of a mustard seed from seeing those mountains move?

Unbelief - the hidden enemy

Read through the story in Matthew, it's only a few verses long. At first glance one could understandably be of the opinion that the focal point of this account is the demon that the disciples could not cast out. Not so. That demon was nothing. It was, as we say in Northern Ireland 'wee buns' to Jesus! He cast it out without batting an eyelid, as any disciple of Jesus has the authority to do. The *real* antagonist, cleverly hiding itself (though not from Jesus) is <u>the spirit of unbelief</u>. Unbelief counteracts faith.

While the disciples were concerned about the demon in the boy, Jesus was more concerned with the unbelief in His disciples! The disciples asked Jesus about casting out demons, and Jesus' reply was about casting out doubt. That's because Jesus knew that once unbelief has been cast out, demons, mountains, and anything else that comes our way would be 'wee buns,' easy peasy - mustard-seed faith sized easy peasy!

Believe!

Believe - it's as simple as that; either we do or we don't. Believe *what?* Belief and faith are not quite the same thing. It isn't about believing that our faith is big enough, nor is it believing in ourselves. To *believe* is simply, to completely accept with my heart and mind that God is who He says He is. It's believing that God will be true to His nature, that He is faithful, will always do as He has promised, and that His word is absolute, final and true.

Jesus repeatedly told people, *"believe."* I have listed just a few of these:

"The kingdom of God has come near. Repent and <u>believe</u> the good news!" Mark 1:15 (NIVUK)

*"If you <u>believe</u>, you will receive whatever you ask for in prayer."*Matthew 21:22 NIVUK

"Do not let your hearts be troubled. You believe in God; <u>believe</u> also in me." John 14:1 (NIVUK);

Mark 5, records the account of Jesus raising Jairus' daughter from the dead. But before doing so, Jesus put unbelief in its place - outside. Then Jesus told the girl's father, *"Don't be afraid, just <u>believe</u>."* Mark 5:36 (NIVUK)

I believe that the valuable life-lesson Jesus wanted us to grasp from all of this, is that the size of our faith matters not one jot; all we need is the tiniest measure of faith combined with *belief;* then, truly nothing will be impossible!

Thursday - God's Workbench

As a maker of costume jewellery, I have to use particular tools. Some of these are surprisingly powerful, when you compare the size of the tool to the task it is designed for. For example, to cut sheet metal, I use a tool that looks like nothing more than a large pair of strangely shaped scissors, yet this simple tool, operated by hand, glides through metal like a hot knife through butter.

The thing is, none of my my tools would be of any use on their own. They are designed to fit into, and work in the hands of a crafts-person. Out of my hands, my tools are merely interesting looking tools, lined up on my workbench.

We can do nothing without God

So it is with us. God has perfectly designed us to fit into, and work in, His hand. Apart from Him we can do nothing (John 15:4). Our God takes the weak, and makes them strong. He takes the hopeless, and transforms them into beacons of eternal hope! God desires to pick you up in His strong hands, and accomplish through you the incredible calling for which He created you. God sees your potential (in His hand).

I love the story of Gideon's calling, which you can read in Judges 6:12-18 (NKJV). The angel of the Lord appeared to Gideon and said these words to him, *"The Lord is with you, O mighty man of valour."* God called Gideon a 'mighty man of valour,' before

Gideon had actually done any 'mighty' acts. But God knew that He had *designed* Gideon to be a mighty man of valour - in His hand.

1 Corinthians 1:27-29 (NLT) tells us,"God chose things the world considers foolish in order to shame those who think they are wise. And he chose things that are powerless to shame those who are powerful. God chose things despised by the world, things counted as nothing at all, and used them to bring to nothing what the world considers important. As a result, no one can ever boast in the presence of God."

Something important to remember is that, although God said He chose the powerless and the weak, we don't remain weak; <u>no tool in the hands of God is weak</u>. His strength makes us strong! Everything we accomplish is in His strength, not in our own.

Fit for purpose

Another thought is this. I maintain my tools, I sharpen them regularly, oil them, tighten them where necessary, and generally make sure they stay in good condition. God does the same with us. God calls us to a life of eternal significance. We were created to live a life that changes the world. In order to accomplish the life to which we were called we need to spend time in His presence, being honed, oiled, and sharpened by Him. God maintains us, to keep us fit for purpose. This happens when we immerse ourselves in His Word, when we remain faithful in trials, and worship Him through all circumstances.

God is always near, ready and able you, to lift you up in His mighty hand, and empower you.

Friday - I Don't Feel Ready!

Have you been putting off something you know God has called you to do, because you don't feel ready? I think we've all done that from time to time. When God first called Moses to go and speak to Pharaoh, Moses didn't feel ready. He protested and argued that surely the Lord had picked the wrong man for the job.

It isn't about whether we feel ready

If we always waited until we felt ready, nothing would ever get done! I'm not just talking about going as a missionary to some far-off country. When do you *ever,* really, feel ready to approach a complete stranger in your local supermarket and talk to them about Jesus? Or tell your work colleagues that you're a Christian, and start *living* as one in the workplace when you haven't really done so in the past? Or pray with your sick aunt who has always scoffed at your beliefs in God? Should we wait until we <u>feel</u> ready before we do the these things, or should we just do them out of obedience to the Lord?

God didn't ask Moses if he *felt* ready to lead the Israelites out of Egypt. Moses definitely didn't feel ready, and was very vocal in letting God know this. *"But Moses protested to God, "Who am I to appear before Pharaoh? Who am I to lead the people of Israel out of Egypt?"* Exodus 3:11 (NLT)

God calls ordinary people to do extraordinary things
The Bible is filled with examples of ordinary people, called by
God to do extraordinary things. Things that they didn't feel ready
to do and they told The Lord so. Here are two other examples.

Gideon: *"But Lord," Gideon replied, "how can I rescue Israel?
My clan is the weakest in the whole tribe of Manasseh, and I am
the least in my entire family!" Judges 6:15 (NLT)*
Jeremiah: *"O Sovereign Lord," I said, "I can't speak for you!
I'm too young!"Jeremiah 1:6 (NLT)*
That the Lord went ahead and led these (reluctant) heroes of the
faith to do His work, despite their protests, isn't a demonstration
of a lack of care on the Lord's part for how they felt. It was
because God knew them inside out and He knew that He had
prepared their hearts for the task at hand – therefore, as far as He
was concerned, they were ready!
God doesn't ask if us if we feel ready, He knows when we are
ready. If He has called you to something, then you can be sure
He has prepared you for it, He knows that you are ready! He will
provide everything you need, so you don't have to be afraid. He
will accomplish through you, plans that seem impossible by your
own standards.

God doesn't ask you to fly solo, He is with you!
*What was God's reply to Moses' protests? "God answered, "I
will be with you."Exodus 3:12 (NLT).*

*And this was God's response to Gideon's fears: "The Lord said
to him, "I will be with you. And you will destroy the Midianites
as if you were fighting against one man."
Judges 6:16 (NLT).*

*To Jeremiah -I love this!"The Lord replied, "Don't say, 'I'm too
young,' for you must go wherever I send you and say whatever I
tell you. And don't be afraid of the people, for I will be with you*

and will protect you. I, the Lord, have spoken!" Then the Lord reached out and touched my mouth and said, "Look, I have put my words in your mouth!" Jeremiah 1:7-9 (NLT) See that? The Lord even gives the very words to say!

And lastly, Jesus to his disciples – those present with Him then and all future disciples, such as you and me: "And be sure of this: I am with you always, even to the end of the age." Matthew 28:20 (NLT)

Even as the excuses start to form on our lips God is saying "*I will be with you!*" God doesn't expect us to go it in our own strength, but offers His, and where we lack the words, He will even give us those. God doesn't search for the heart that is ready. He looks for the heart that is willing. Are you willing?

Saturday- There's Purpose In The Wilderness

"They refused to give up their evil practices and stubborn ways."
Judges 2:19 (NIVUK)

The Wilderness

The Israelites *had* to go through the wilderness, there was no other way to get to the Promised Land, but it was never God's intention for them to spend forty years in the wilderness. That long, arduous journey, that should only have taken a matter of weeks, was a result of their own stubbornness and disobedience. I see two important lessons that the Lord had for the Israelites through their wilderness experience.

Obedience versus stubbornness

I have always found maths difficult. It was a struggle at school, I just couldn't seem to get the formulas into my head.When I was ten years old I had a really kind teacher, who took time to sit with me and tried to help me with maths, even giving me extra work to take home and practice, but I still never really got the hang of 'school maths.' The problem was, my teacher's help fell on deaf ears. By then, I had already worked out my own system that kind of worked - with my method I still arrived at the correct answer, but it took a little longer to get there.

As my teacher sat with me and patiently explained, my mind was stubbornly closed to what he was saying, because I'd already decided that it was too difficult, and that my method was easier, and better. Instead of seeing my teacher's actions as kindness, and for my ultimate good, all I could see was the hours of extra work he was giving me to take home, the unfairness of having to do maths worksheets while everyone else was outside playing. Eventually, when I repeatedly returned to school with the worksheets completed by my own methods, my teacher gave up.

At the time, my ten year-old self secretly thought I'd won that battle of wills. But decades later, I now see why I should have listened and obeyed. I was unable to help my own children with their maths homework, and now, even my grandson knows better than to ask me!

Worship in the wilderness:
God's intention all along had been to take His people to the Promised Land. But He had a purpose for the wilderness as well. Notice what He told Moses to say to Pharaoh, before their journey even began: '*The Lord, the God of the Hebrews, has sent me to tell you, "Let my people go, so they can worship me in the wilderness.*" Exodus 8:16 (NLT)

God did not tell Moses to say "*let my people go so that they can go to the Promised Land and live happily ever after.*" Or even "*So that they can worship me in their own new land.*" It was the Lord's intention to take them through the wilderness, so that they would learn to worship Him *in* the wilderness. The wilderness is tough. It's a place where we are honed. The wilderness times we go through are opportunities to draw near to God, for our relationship with Him to be strengthened, our dependence upon Him heightened. It's easy to worship God when everything is 'flowing with milk and honey,' isn't it? Not just as easy in the midst of a hot, dry, wilderness. The purpose of the wilderness was to deepen their relationship with the Lord.

Living by God's Instruction Manual

God's Word is our instruction manual for every aspect of life.
We have a teacher, the Holy Spirit, who promises to *"guide you
into all truth."* While we might not blatantly disobey God as the
Children of Israel did, when they practiced idolatry, disobedience
doesn't always look like that. There is such as thing as *passive
disobedience*, or *passive stubbornness.* This is much subtler, but
equally damaging as blatant disobedience. It's an underlying
attitude of, *"I can do it my way."* It's a bit like the ten-year old
me, in my attitude towards my maths teacher. Technically, I was
still doing maths, but I was relying on *my* way of doing things to
get me through, and, mathematically speaking at least, you could
say I'm still wandering in the desert forty years later!

Don't wander in the wilderness

Every child of God has a 'wilderness experience,' at some point
in our walk with God, however, not everyone has to <u>wander</u> in
the wilderness. When I find myself in a wilderness time
spiritually, I can have two choices.
* Allow God to use the experience, to draw me closer to
Himself, to teach me to rely completely on Him, and to worship
Him through the experience, trusting Him to lead me out again.
*Lazily let old attitudes of self reliance kick in. Stubbornly try to
carry my own heavy load, despite God having said that *He* is the
One who daily bears our burdens. (Psalm 68:19)

Self reliance is not 'being strong,' it is being pridefully stubborn!
Obedience, on the other hand, is trusting God to be God, and
allowing Him to have His way.

Sunday - Obedience

"But Samuel replied, "What is more pleasing to the Lord: your burnt offerings and sacrifices or your obedience to his voice? Listen! Obedience is better than sacrifice, and submission is better than offering the fat of rams." 1 Samuel 15:22 (NLT)

I well remember the old hymn with the words: "Trust and obey, for there's no other way to be happy in Jesus, but to trust and obey." To my pre-teen mind, it brought images of a very austere God, who required unquestioning obedience. Well, the thing thing is, God *does* require unquestioning obedience. Not because He's austere, and harsh, but because He loves His children with an everlasting love, has a perfect plan, far greater than we could ever imagine, and wants us to be part of that plan.

Difficulty in obedience

Why is it that obedience is one of the greatest areas of difficulty for so many children of God? Is He unfair? Unkind? Has God not proven His goodness to us, time and time again? We are like sheep, prone to wandering, and our Shepherd constantly has to nudge us with His staff, to keep us on the right path. We are quick to rationalise away His clear commands, slow to obey them. We have learned to be masters of excuses and procrastination, while simple obedience remains so difficult to master.

Trust in God

"And you must always obey the Lord's commands and decrees that I am giving you today for your own good." Deuteronomy 10:13 (NLT).

God's commands are not given to make us unhappy. He says clearly that they are for our <u>own good.</u> God is omniscient. He knows exactly what the future holds. He knows the past. He knows every detail of every life on the planet! He is all-wise. God has the insider-knowledge of what is going to happen economically, and politically, in every county and nation across the world. Remember how He spoke to Elisha, and gave him prophetic, 'insider information' regarding the plots of the enemies of Israel? (2 Kings 6) He's still the same God! He speaks to those of His children who are willing to listen and obey, giving clear instruction, guidance, and prophetic insight. To obey God is best thing the Child of God can do, for ourselves, our families, our churches, our nations and our world.

Obedience costs but the benefits are out of this world!

In chapter six ('Seen and Known') do you remember we looked at how, because of their obedience, God provided for both Elijah, and a widow who was living in extreme poverty? Let's think about this story again for a moment.

We could look at it and question why God didn't send Elijah to a rich home, but when you really consider it, God *did*! The woman may not had much by way of material possessions, but she was rich in obedience! She was willing to sacrifice what little she had in obedience to God.

Elijah didn't really need this woman's food, God could have provided for Elijah in any number of ways. God sent Elijah to the widow, not in order to provide for Elijah, but so that He could provide for the widow!

What might have seemed, in the moment, to be an extreme and costly sacrifice, was in fact for her own good! Her obedience unlocked a fountain of provision far beyond that which she could have ever have imagined: *"She went away and did as Elijah had told her. So there was food every day for Elijah and for the woman and her family. For the jar of flour was not used up and the jug of oil did not run dry, in keeping with the word of the Lord spoken by Elijah."* 1 Kings 17:15-16 (NIVUK)

Walking The Walk

Monday - The Man Who Walked With God

"After he became the father of Methuselah, Enoch walked faithfully with God 300 years and had other sons and daughters. Altogether, Enoch lived a total of 365 years. Enoch walked faithfully with God; then he was no more, because God took him away." Genesis 5:22-24 (NIVUK)

The Man Who Walked With God

A few short lines sum up Enoch's life. No great stories of battles fought, and won. No memorable sermons preached and quoted from years later. Just those few words in Genesis 5:22, but what a way to be remembered - for your life to be recorded and read about centuries later as the man who walked with God!

Walking with God equals a life of blessing

God created us for the enjoyment of relationship that involves intimate conversation, companionship, and *walking together.* God longs to walk with you. He constantly seeks to draw you into a closer walk with him. Galatians 5:16-26 instructs us to *'walk by the Spirit'* and to *'keep in step'* with the Spirit.

In Psalm 119:1-2 we are told: "You're only truly happy when you walk in total integrity, <u>walking in the light of God's word.</u> What joy overwhelms everyone who keeps the ways of God, those who seek him as their heart's passion!"
Psalms 119:1-2 (TPT)

* * *

Those who keep company with God are truly blessed. I'm not talking about a "name it, claim it, and frame it," kind of blessing, but the blessing of God's presence, guidance, friendship and provision. As we draw closer to God, He reveals the beauty of his face to us through his Word, and lights up our way, one step at a time: *"Your word is a lamp to guide my feet and a light for my path."* Psalms 119:105 (NLT).

And, when we walk with God, He teaches us the secrets of his Kingdom. He confides in those who walk closely with Him. *"The Lord is a friend to those who fear him. He teaches them his covenant."* Psalms 25:14 (NLT)

God wants to walk with us before He works through us.
God works with his friends. Yes, of course, God can use anyone He chooses, or speak through anything. I frequently hear people say "if God can use a donkey (as in Balaam's donkey) He can use me." But this always makes me think, 'why be a donkey when you can be God's friend and walking companion instead?' Jesus told us that He confides his Kingdom purposes to his friends: John 15:15 *"I no longer call you slaves, because the slave does not understand what his master is doing. But I have called you friends, because I have revealed to you everything I heard from my Father."*

That tiny paragraph in Genesis, summing up Enoch's life, contains a huge legacy. And it's a legacy that is attainable for any one of us who chooses to walk with God!

Tuesday - Stumbling and Getting Back Up

We've all stumbled at one time or another in our Christian walk. If you're in a place today where you've stumbled, I hope today's devotional encourages you.

What can cause us to stumble?
James 3 tells us: *"We all stumble in <u>many</u> ways. Anyone who is never at fault in what they say is perfect, able to keep their whole body in check."* James 3:2 (NIVUK)

It's amazing how a stumble always seems to be just when you're in full stride. You're confident, feeling good about life, when suddenly there's a bump in the road that causes you to stumble. But where do those 'bumps' come from, that we trip over?

Bumps in the path

<u>Pride and Haughtiness:</u> If we are carrying a bag-load of pride, nothing empties it out faster than a good stumble!

"So, if you think you are standing firm, be careful that you don't fall!" 1 Corinthians 10:12 (NIVUK)

"Pride goes before destruction, and haughtiness before a fall." Proverbs 16:18 (NLT)

<u>An Unbridled Tongue:</u> James 3:2, describes how our tongue can

be likened to the rudder of a ship - so small, yet it has the ability to determine the direction of a large vessel. Our tongues, if we don't have control over them, can cause us to stumble.

Recovering from a stumble

Acknowledge, repent, move on, don't blame-shift. Have you ever sat in a coffee shop and people-watched? If you have, then you will have observed what people usually do when they trip. They almost always look back, with puzzlement on their faces, at the pavement, as though something had tripped them! It's as if there's something instinctive in all of us to want to 'save face,' when we stumble; *it couldn't possibly be my own clumsy feet!*

We need someone, or something, to blame. Adam, did this in the garden. Instead of just acknowledging his sin to God, he blamed Eve, saying *"The woman you put here with me – she gave me some fruit from the tree, and I ate it."* Genesis 3:12 (NIVUK) So, to Adam's mind, it was God's fault for giving him the woman in the first place, and it was Eve's fault for enticing him with the fruit.

Another thing we do when we stumble, is to surreptitiously glance around to see who might have seen. We feel *shame,* we're embarrassed. Sometimes rather than shame, it's fear that grabs hold of us, a fear rooted in pride. We're fearful of acknowledging that we've tripped up, in case we lose favour with people, or worse, with the Lord. Let's have a look at what John writes about all of this: *"If we claim we have no sin, we are only fooling ourselves and not living in the truth. But if we confess our sins to him, he is faithful and just to forgive us our sins and to cleanse us from all wickedness. If we claim we have not sinned, we are calling God a liar and showing that his word has no place in our hearts."* 1 John 1:6-10 (NLT)

Many hundreds of years before John, Isaiah, prompted by the Spirit of God, wrote these words:

"Even youths grow weary and tired, And vigorous <u>young men stumble badly</u>, But those who wait for the Lord [who expect, look for, and hope in Him] Will gain new strength and renew their power; They will lift up their wings [and rise up close to God] like eagles [rising toward the sun]; They will run and not become weary, They will walk and not grow tired. Isaiah 40:30-31 (AMP)

Usually when I read this much loved, much quoted scripture I'm focused on the last part of the verse; I want to soar like that eagle! But look at what it says at the beginning: "*<u>even youths grow weary and tired <u>and vigorous young men stumble badly</u></u>.*"

Those who consider themselves too mighty and strong in the Lord to ever stumble, are just as susceptible, if not *more* so, to 'stumble badly.' Tomorrow, we will have a look at the difference between a stumble and a fall.

Wednesday - A Stumble and A Fall Are Not The Same

"The steps of the God-pursuing ones follow firmly in the footsteps of the Lord, and God delights in every step they take to follow him. If they stumble badly they will still survive, for the Lord lifts them up with his hands." Psalms 37:23-24 (TPT)

Have you ever made such a mess of things that you are left wondering whether you'll ever recover? Yesterday we looked at how to recover from a stumble: Acknowledge your sin, repent, get back up and keep walking! God isn't waiting to beat us with a big stick when we stumble; He knows we will stumble, but He also promises that His right hand will be holding us that we won't *fall flat on our faces: "The Lord directs the steps of the godly. He delights in every detail of their lives. Though they stumble, they will never fall, for the Lord holds them by the hand"* Psalm 37:23-24 (NLT)
Your stumble might <u>feel</u> very much like a fall, but it isn't, its a stumble.

A stumble and a fall are two different things
A person who stumbles gets straight back up again, and keeps walking. A fall is something more serious. This applies spiritually, as well as literally.
I had a very bad (literal) fall around three years ago; I took a tumble down a full flight of stairs, knocked myself, unconscious

497

broke my arm in two places, and a had a nasty concussion. Somehow I don't think this scripture means no Christian would ever fall and hurt themselves. But....did God have me by the hand? Absolutely! Several doctors and nurses told me repeatedly while I was in the hospital how "lucky" I was, not to have broken my neck, spine, or worse, to have died. One nurse told me of a neighbour of hers who had died from falling down just three steps and breaking his neck. *Lucky?* We know better, don't we?

In addition to that, I soon saw God work that circumstance together for my good (Romans 8:28). My broken bones led to my conscientious GP insisting on a bone density scan, which I would not have had for at least another ten years, had I not fallen. The result was a very early diagnosis of osteoporosis, which is completely treatable and even reversible if caught soon enough!

"They will never fall, for the Lord holds them by the hand." Our modern translations simply use the word *'fall;'* In the original language the word actually means *"utterly cast down"* - to 'fall headlong'; rather like me, falling down the stairs, knocking myself out - really doing a <u>proper</u> job of it!

Sometimes we can feel as though, spiritually, we have taken a tumble down a full flight of stairs and just might never get up again. Not so! The 'benefit' and favour on the one who walks with the Lord and allows the Lord to direct his or her steps, is that though they may at times 'stumble badly' in the sense they will not fall *away* - that is, not be *utterly cast down.* This is not because of their own internal strength or goodness, but because the LORD has them by the hand and upholds them,

Verse 23 says - in our more traditional translations - *"the Lord directs the steps of the godly."*
The original word, where we have 'godly,' or 'righteous' is *Geber,* which in its proper use signifies *a strong man,* a

conqueror or *hero*. It would seem then, to be saying that even the most powerful still need to be supported, and directed, by the Lord.

Often, when we stumble it can feel a like a bad fall, but in truth it isn't, it is merely a 'bad stumble.' *"even youths grow weary and tired and vigorous <u>young men stumble badly</u>."*
God, in His loving kindness and mercy makes provision recovery and restoration, through repentance and forgiveness.

Thursday - Stand!

"Therefore put on the full armour of God, so that when the day of evil comes, you may be able to stand your ground, and after you have done everything, to stand." Ephesians 6:13 (NIVUK)

In this chapter all about walking, I want to look, briefly today, at an important part of our walk - standing. Paul wrote (above) *"and after you have done everything, <u>stand"</u>*

When the day of evil comes

Paul doesn't say, *"if* a day of evil comes, but *when."* Even though we know that Satan is a defeated enemy, and that Christ has triumphed over him, we need to remember that we are still in a battle, and will be, until the day we leave this mortal body behind to be with the Lord, or Jesus returns. Paul wrote *"our struggle is not against flesh and blood, but against the rulers, against the authorities, against the powers of this dark world and against the spiritual forces of evil in the heavenly realms." Ephesians 6:12 (NIVUK)*

Whether you or I care to acknowledge, or believe it, the Bible is clear about this. We are in a spiritual battle. Sadly, many Christians choose to remain in a state of ignorance or disbelief. An indication that this person is probably taking quite a few unnecessary beatings.

The struggle

Our struggle is not against flesh and blood. We aren't fighting against people, whatever they may have done, or we perceive them to have done, against us.

I have to be honest, and say, when I have been hurt by someone's actions or words, my first thoughts are not always that it might be the enemy at work. It sometimes takes me a little while to arrive at that conclusion!

Have you ever become hurt or - the dreaded *'O'* word, [offended] rears its ugly head. The other person may be entirely innocent, not even realising, and certainly not intending to hurt you. The lies of the enemy to start to infiltrate your mind and take hold of your heart, in a vice-like offence-grip. Satan and his cohorts thrive on causing disharmony. They know that God has commanded us to love one another, and *why* God has commanded this. The Word of God tells us to get rid of all these attitudes, laid out in Ephesians 4:31.

Another tactic of Satan is drip-feeding worldly thinking, and false doctrine into the church. Paul warned the church at Colossi to guard their thinking, against "elemental spiritual forces." *"See to it that no-one takes you captive through hollow and deceptive philosophy, which depends on human tradition and the elemental spiritual forces of this world rather than on Christ."* Colossians 2:8 (NIVUK)

The wiles of the devil

In Ephesians 6:11 Paul writes: *"Put on all of God's armour so that you will be able to <u>stand firm</u> against all strategies of the devil."* Ephesians 6:11 (NLT)

The 'devil's wiles' are intimidation and insinuation, and the mind is his chief playing field. Satan is clever at playing the role of both good cop and bad cop - he can be both a bully, and a beguiler, in his battle campaign against Christians. He is described as "like a roaring lion, seeking whom he may devour," and on the other hand "a liar and the father of lies". Now, if someone is going to con you with lies, are they going to try to beguile you with things you would not be interested in? Of course not. Sin is attractive. Offence feels quite nice, if we're honest. We feel we are right and the other person is wrong. We tell ourselves *"they had no right to treat me like that. I have a right to be angry!"*

Paul wrote to the church at Corinth: *"We are human, but we don't wage war as humans do. We use God's mighty weapons, not worldly weapons, to knock down the strongholds of human reasoning and to destroy false arguments. We destroy every proud obstacle that keeps people from knowing God. We capture their rebellious thoughts and teach them to obey Christ."* 2 Corinthians 10:3-5 (NLT)

The full armour of God

God provides every believer with a full set of armour. It is *the armour of God,* both in the sense that comes *from* Him, and that it's God's *actual* armour. In Isaiah we see the Lord depicted as wearing the very armour that He now graciously clothes us in. *"He put on righteousness as his breastplate, and the helmet of salvation on his head; he put on the garments of vengeance and wrapped himself in zeal as in a cloak."* Isaiah 59:17 (NIVUK.) According to the book of Ephesians, this armour is available to you and me.

That you may be able to stand

In any other army, a soldier is dressed for battle and then sent out into battle, to take part in hand-to-hand combat, involving blood and gore. But Paul repeatedly says, put on the full armour of God and then.....STAND. Or, that you may be *"able to stand"* In verse 11, he writes, *"so that you can take your stand against the*

devil's schemes." (NIVUK)
In verses 13 and 14, he says, *"so that when the day of evil comes, you may be able to <u>stand your ground, and after you have done everything, to stand. Stand firm then..</u>"* Ephesians *6:13-14 (NIVUK)*

Stand, is the operative word, throughout Ephesians chapter six, not *fight.* I We are not told to put on the armour of God and enter into mortal combat, but to <u>stand</u>. The schemes of the devil that rage against us come to nothing when we stand against him dressed in the armour of our Conquering King, in the power and name of our victorious Jesus, who has already won the battle.

Friday - Keep In Step

"Since we live by the Spirit, let us keep in step with the Spirit."
Galatians 5:25 (NIVUK)

I saw a little 'drama' of this verse, played out in front of me one morning, as I drove through our town. I had indicated to turn right, off the main road, and as I slowed to a stop, I saw a man and his little boy, out for their morning run together.

They were about to cross the road I intended to turn into. The man saw me, and slowed his pace, instinctively putting a protective hand on his son's shoulder, to draw his attention to the potential danger. All in one smooth movement, the man, with one hand now resting on his child's shoulder, looked over his own shoulder, to see if any more cars were coming in the other direction. When he saw that the road was clear and that I was obviously going to let them cross the road before turning, he gave his son's shoulder a gentle tap and the two of them continued with their run.

This scene only lasted a few seconds, but it has imprinted itself on my memory, because in the moments following, as I drove away, the Holy Spirit said to me; *"that's how I work in your life, to help you to keep in step with me."*

"Whether you turn to the right or to the left, your ears will hear a

voice behind you, saying, 'This is the way; walk in it." Isaiah 30:21 (NIVUK)

Joined with Him

That little child and his father were running 'as one.' Similarly, but a thousand times better, we run as one with our Father, because His Spirit dwells in each and every one of us, individually as well as corporately - as in, the Church:

"Don't you realize that all of you together are the temple of God and that the Spirit of God lives in you?" 1 Corinthians 3:16 (NLT);

"For we are the temple of the living God. As God said: "I will live in them and walk among them. I will be their God, and they will be my people." 2 Corinthians 6:16 (NLT)

"Don't you realize that your body is the temple of the Holy Spirit, who lives in you and was given to you by God? You do not belong to yourself," 1 Corinthians 6:19 (NLT)

If you are born again, then the Spirit of God lives in you. That's all there us to it. You dont have a diluted version of Him, but the same Spirit that raised Christ from the dead (Romans 8:1). The Holy Spirit will not force His desires on us, He simply calls us to keep in step with Him, to do as He does. His power is freely available to us, but this will make no impact in our lives, unless we acknowledge His presence, yield to Him by faith, and trust His leading.

That little boy could have run on - his dad didn't grab him by the arm, but just put a warning hand on the boy's shoulder, applying the gentlest, guiding pressure, and the boy chose to trust his dad and keep in step with him.

* * *

Let's make a daily commitment to uphold our union with God by being obedient to His voice, and by keeping in step with His Holy Spirit. Our lives don't belong to just ourselves anymore, we are His. Let's walk surrendered:

"Be imitators of God in everything you do, for then you will represent your Father as his beloved sons and daughters. And continue to walk surrendered to the extravagant love of Christ, for he surrendered his life as a sacrifice for us. His great love for us was pleasing to God, like an aroma of adoration—a sweet healing fragrance."
Ephesians 5:1-2 (TPT)

Saturday - Enjoy The Journey

I recall a four-day hike my sister and I did in the mountains, many years ago with a group of friends. It had seemed like a fun idea, before we set out out. For the first few miles, we had laughed as we shared funny stories, and made up silly songs to keep up morale. By day two though, it was all starting to get a bit much. My whole body ached, and frankly, I was bored with the scenery, which at first had looked so beautiful, now stretched on and on, relentless and seemingly unchanging, giving the impression that we weren't getting anywhere.

Sadly, I was so consumed with reaching our final destination so that I could rest, that I couldn't enjoy the incredible mountain views, the miles of natural beauty stretched out on the landscape below, or the camaraderie of my companions.

The thing is, if I had only remembered that I was going to reach my destination eventually, perhaps I could have enjoyed the journey, instead of pushing myself so hard. I might have picked some mountain flowers to press, taken photos of the stunning scenery, and revelled in the quiet beauty of the place, away from all the rush of life. But I didn't.

Does Your Christian Walk Currently Feel More Like a Hike?

Jesus came so that we would have abundant life! (John 10:10). Our Christian walk is about so much more than being headed for a final destination - it's about enjoying the journey, <u>in</u>

partnership with Jesus. We're going to reach our destination anyway, that's a promise, sealed and held in surety for us!
We can experience times in life when our walk with God feels more like a hike, and the road feels rocky and steep. We put our head down, and plod on, praying that God will bring the change, only to lift our head again and see what appears to be the same scenery! It seems as if we are just not making any headway.

A journey, not a destination

Like me on that hike, we can become so focused on getting to our final destination that we forget about the importance of the journey - the wonder and awe that we are walking in partnership with the King of Kings! How quickly we start to question God's goodness when the terrain becomes tough or unchanged to *our* liking.

We can so quickly forget *why* we're actually on this walk, and that it's not all about us, but about reaching otherr, touching other people's lives with the truth of the Gospel. *"Therefore see that you walk carefully [living life with honor, purpose, and courage; shunning those who tolerate and enable evil], not as the unwise, but as wise [sensible, intelligent, discerning people], making the very most of your time [on earth, recognizing and taking advantage of each opportunity and using it with wisdom and diligence], because the days are [filled with] evil."* Ephesians 5:15-16 (AMP)

Here are three great truths about our walk with God, that I remind myself of if I'm tempted to start complaining about the "scenery" of my life, or circumstances.

I'm not walking on my own
God has me firmly by the hand, leading and empowering me: "Wherever I go, your hand will guide me; your strength will empower me." Psalms 139:10 (TPT)

* * *

"He <u>leads</u> me beside peaceful streams. He renews my strength.
He <u>guides</u> me along right paths, bringing honor to his name.
Even when I walk through the darkest valley, I will not be afraid,
for <u>you are close beside me</u>." Psalms 23:2-4 (NLT)

God has a road map for my life

God isn't lost. He knows what He's doing, and I can trust Him to
do it! "You saw me before I was born. Every day of my life was
recorded in your book. Every moment was laid out before a
single day had passed." Psalm 139:16 (NLT)

He has empowered and equipped me for the journey

"God, the Lord, is my strength; he makes my feet like the deer's;
he makes me tread on my high places. "The Sovereign Lord is
my strength! He makes me as surefooted as a deer, able to tread
upon the heights. (For the choir director: This prayer is to be
accompanied by stringed instruments.)" Habakkuk 3:19 (NLT)
"He makes me as surefooted as a deer, enabling me to stand on
mountain heights." Psalms 18:33 (NLT)

In both of these scriptures the words *"tread upon the rocky
heights,"* in the original language, is: *"he enables me to negotiate
the rough/rugged terrain."* God has equipped us to walk
confidently over the roughest terrain, not in our own strength, but
with our hand firmly in His. Enjoy the journey, with Him!

Sunday - Walk By Faith

"For we walk by faith, not by sight" 2 Corinthians 5:7 (NKJV)

Readjust your perspective

Years ago, I had a friend who was a very talented artist. Her house was once featured in a magazine, because of the very detailed murals she had painted on the ceilings and floors of almost every room.

I'll never forget the first time I visited the bathroom in her house. The walls and ceiling were a mural of the sky, with white fluffy clouds. One wall had a sideways, level view, of a flying Second World War Spitfire, as if you were looking at it from another plane. Then I looked at the floor. It was painted from the perspective an aeroplane, high in the sky. 'Far below,' was a patchwork of green fields, dotted with tiny sheep, cattle, and the rooftops of houses.

This played such a trick on my mind. Even though I knew it wasn't real, my eyes perceived the altitude, and my mind told me that I would fall if I stepped over the threshold. So I stood there, frozen, for at least a minute before I managed to readjust my thinking. My fear was irrational. But my eyes saw something that looked so realistic, and they told my mind and my feet not to move!

There are times when God calls us to do, or say things, when our eyes deceive us, our 'logic' tells us, *'this isn't going to work,'* and our minds scream "don't move!"

See it from God's perspective

As children of God, we are called to walk by faith, not by sight: "for we walk by faith, not by sight [living our lives in a manner consistent with our confident belief in God's promises]" 2 Corinthians 5:7 (AMP)

We are commanded, just like Joshua, to be strong and courageous:*"I promise you what I promised Moses: 'Wherever you set foot, you will be on land I have given you— No one will be able to stand against you as long as you live. For I will be with you as I was with Moses. I will not fail you or abandon you. "Be strong and courageous, for you are the one who will lead these people to possess all the land I swore to their ancestors I would give them. This is my* command*—be strong and courageous! Do not be afraid or discouraged. For the Lord your God is with you wherever you go."* Joshua 1:3,5-6,9 (NLT) Joshua, who was not a young man at this time, had spent many years as the assistant of Moses, and now here he was finding that it was his own time to lead. Was Joshua afraid? I'd say he probably was, why else would God have issued this command? God sees deep inside our hearts, while man looks at the outside. Of course God knew Joshua was afraid, he was about to step out into unknown territory and lead the people into the promised land.

What Joshua was about to do required unwavering faith in the promise that God had given, which was this: *"Wherever you set foot, you will be on land I have given you."* Firstly, Joshua had to believe, without doubt, that this land was theirs as God had promised. Secondly, his

faith required action - walking! "Wherever you set foot,"

* * *

Entrust the future you don't know to the God you do know.

Walking by faith means not only trusting in the things God has said, but trusting God Himself. It is having faith in the character and nature of our God.

For example, to go back to my friend's mural, my eyes and my temporarily skewed perspective, told me that it wasn't safe to step forward. But in spite of what my eyes told me, that floor was solid, immovable and safe. Whatever your eyes and human logic might tell you today, about your life circumstances, remember the God that you know! The Faithful One who bears you up; your Solid Rock!

In the book of Proverbs we read: *"A man's heart plans his way, But the LORD directs his steps."* Proverbs 16:9 (NKJV) God directs our steps. He cannot do this if we are not walking, if we stand rooted to the spot in fear. All we need to do is take that first step of faith, followed by another, and before we know it, we're walking!

Are We There Yet?

Monday - Get Up And Walk!

"Now there is in Jerusalem near the Sheep Gate a pool, which in Aramaic is called Bethesda and which is surrounded by five covered colonnades. Here a great number of disabled people used to lie – the blind, the lame, the paralysed. One who was there had been an invalid for thirty-eight years." John 5:2-3, 5 (NIVUK)

You might know that *Bethesda*, means 'House of mercy.' I read this passage and it struck me that this man had gone to this so called House of mercy, lain all day beside what was reputed to be the 'healing waters,' watching others go in and receive their healing, and had left again in the same condition. He did this for *thirty eight years*! I wonder how he felt, to have got so close to being healed only to go home disappointed again and again, year in, year out, while others were healed.

Our churches are filled with people like this. If we're honest, we ourselves can sometimes be just like this man. Some are the 'walking wounded,' with wounds inflicted by past relationships, that bleed a little when inadvertently pressed on by others. Many suffer from debilitating financial worry, that grips them so tightly that they literally cannot move forward. And others are in need of physical healing, but have struggled with their ailment for so long, that deep down, they don't really believe God will heal them. And they come to God's house, His *real* House of mercy, week after week, watching others receive their healing, spiritually, emotionally, and physically, while they go home disappointed. That is not what God wants for His precious children!

No one will help me

"When Jesus saw him lying there and learned that he had been in this condition for a long time, he asked him, 'Do you want to get well?' 'Sir,' the invalid replied, 'I have no-one to help me into the pool when the water is stirred. While I am trying to get in, someone else goes down ahead of me." John 5:6-7 (NIVUK) The man's response to Jesus' question is so revealing of his state of mind and heart. Jesus asked the simple question *"do you want to get well?"* Instead of saying, with relief, 'yes!' The man immediately launched into a tirade about why he hasn't been healed. He blamed other people - 'no one will help me' and 'someone always gets there before me.' Isn't that so typical of us all?

Just get up and walk!

Jesus was having none of it, He didn't entertain this tirade. Instead He said "Get up! Pick up your mat and walk:" *"At once the man was cured; he picked up his mat and walked."* John 5:8-9a (NIVUK)

When we belong to Jesus, we have full access to the REAL House of Mercy, God's throne room. Yet we so often sit at the side of the water, nursing age-old emotional hurts and wounds, battling sickness, and fear. We point the finger of blame at other people for where we find ourselves, when Jesus simply says to us, "Do you *really* want to be healed, or are you going to sit here blaming? Get up and walk!"

It's as simple as that; just roll up those 'sleeping mats' of wrong beliefs, doubts and blame shifting, and start walking, by faith, in the truths God's Word! Jesus didn't mince His words, did He? Not then and not now. Do we want to be healed, today? If so, we know what to do!

Tuesday - Love Letters

"My child, never forget the things I have taught you. Store my commands in your heart. If you do this, you will live many years, and your life will be satisfying. Never let loyalty and kindness leave you! Tie them around your neck as a reminder. Write them deep within your heart. Then you will find favor with both God and people, and you will earn a good reputation. Trust in the Lord with all your heart; do not depend on your own understanding. Seek his will in all you do, and he will show you which path to take. Don't be impressed with your own wisdom. Instead, fear the Lord and turn away from evil. Then you will have healing for your body and strength for your bones."
Proverbs 3:1-8 (NLT)

Unopened Love Letters

Elizabeth Barrett had spend most of her life as an 'invalid,' lonely, and isolated, with only her writing as a comfort, until Robert Browning appeared on the scene. They fell in love, and because of Elizabeth's father's tyrannical control over her life, ran away together to get married and settled in Italy.

Elizabeth still loved her father, and for years sought to rebuild their relationship. She faithfully wrote letter after letter to him, expressing her affection, describing her life with Robert. He never once responded. One day, years later, Elizabeth received a large parcel in the post. Excited when she recognised her father's handwriting, she tore open the package. Her heart broke as she saw that inside was every letter she had written to her father, each one unopened.

Elizabeth and her father remained estranged, and when she died in her husband's arms in Italy it was too late for reconciliation. The originals of Elizabeth's letters are on display in a museum, and are considered to be among the most beautiful writings in English literature.

How very tragic that the letters were never read by the person they were meant for. Had Elizabeth's father opened just one letter, would his his hard heart have softened towards his daughter, and would they have reconciled in time?

The Father's love letters

God has written a series of love letters. His letters are filled with His outpourings of love, direction, instruction for our everyday living, and His Fatherly hopes and dreams for us, His children. In the Bible, we discover the Father's true character. He makes Himself known to us as we absorb and apply His words.

The Bible is the most quoted-from book in the world. Like Elizabeth's letters, it sits displayed like a museum piece on coffee tables, in hotels rooms, and other public places. Some churches even have huge, ornamental copies on display on plinths at the front, meant only for looking at, as though it were an art exhibit. Sadly, many people are like Elizabeth's father. They have never read, and possibly never will read, God's love-filled letters.

Think of your own loved ones who don't know your Father, God. Don't you just long to say to them, *"if you would just read some of His written words, you would catch a glimpse of God's nature; how incredible He is; how much He loves you, then maybe your stubborn, hardened heart would melt a little so that His love could get through to you."* But, sadly, like Elizabeth's father, many people never will soften. They will never read, or hear, God's words and never be reconciled to Him.

* * *

There's another type of person. The Christian who 'skim-reads' their Bible; just the 'nice bits,' the sanitised, attractive sounding verses that can be posted on social media without offending anyone. But don't ask these people to engage in any sort of study programme, or to put God's Word into practice in a way that might be life-changing.

The Bible is so much more than mere words written on pages; His Word is life giving. It is food to our souls and life to our bones. What will you do with your Father's love letters to you, today?

Wednesday - What A Friend We Have In Jesus

"You perceive every movement of my heart and soul, and you understand my every thought before it even enters my mind. You are so intimately aware of me, Lord. You read my heart like an open book and you know all the words I'm about to speak before I even start a sentence! You know every step I will take before my journey even begins". Psalm 139:1-3 (TPT)

Pour all your worries on Him

Can you imagine having a friend, who loved you so much that they said to you, "give me all your worries, all those things that are weighing heavily on your mind, and keeping you awake at night. I will bear the weight of them all for you." The wonderful truth is, that as friends of Jesus we don't have to imagine it, this is exactly the kind of friend we have in Jesus.

"Pour out all your worries and stress upon him and leave them there, for he always tenderly cares for you." 1 Peter 5:7 (TPT) Most other versions use the word *cast*, here rather than *pour*: *Casting* suggests throwing your burdens away from you, with force, and purpose (onto Jesus). When you throw something away from you in that way, you're less likely to try to retrieve it later, aren't you? I quite like the Passion Translation's idea of "pouring out," for the same reason. Once you have poured out something, it's *gone*, expended. These analogies imply a relief from our burdens that is far more permanent than just gently

laying our burdens at Jesus' feet, where we are likely to pick them back up again later!

There are very few friends on whom we could pour out all our worries, and if we were to make a habit of doing so I think we would quickly find ourselves a bit 'lonesome,' to say the least. No matter how well intended, kind, or caring, friends are when they say 'I'm always here for you', the truth is most of us have our own issues, stresses, worries and cares. Even the best of friends, who love one another dearly, can become wearied by the other person's problems. Jesus will never become weary of you.

He cares _for_ you, not just about you.

It's nice to have someone who cares about you; Jesus doesn't only care *about* you, He cares *for* you. There's a vast difference between caring about and caring for. The word for 'cares' in the original language in this scripture means, "He *'takes tender care'* of you." Jesus loves you so deeply, that He *takes tender care of you*. He knows your next words, before you will speak them, in fact He even knows what you're going to think next! (Psalm 139:1-3) And He says to you: *"Indeed, the very hairs of your head are all numbered. Don't be afraid; you are worth more than many sparrows."* Luke 12:7 (NIVUK)

He chooses to call you His friend

"I no longer call you servants, because a servant does not know his master's business. Instead, I have called you friends, for everything that I learned from my Father I have made known to you." John 15:15 (NIVUK)

As Jesus' friends, we are to follow the example He sets for us; to walk in step with Him and learn from Him. Jesus takes the carrying of burdens very seriously, so seriously that we, too, are commanded to bear each other's burdens: *"Carry each other's*

burdens, and in this way you will fulfil the law of Christ."
Galatians 6:2 (NIVUK)

Thursday - This Is Who Walks Beside Me

"David sang to the LORD the words of this song when the Lord delivered him from the hand of all his enemies and from the hand of Saul." 2 Samuel 22:1 (NIVUK)

This chapter is a beautiful worship song, by David, expressing love, honour, and thanksgiving to God, who had rescued him from all his enemies.

David's enemies were very real and some of them had the potential to make his life very miserable, to say the least. But David knew that God was his Victory, and he regularly, loudly, proclaimed his thankfulness and poured out his worship to God, reminding himself, and everyone within earshot, of God's great, incomparable attributes. Was David ever discouraged and low? Of course he was. But he knew how to 'encourage himself in the Lord.' He focused on who God is, rather than who his enemies were.

Whenever circumstances threaten overwhelmed me, a good scripture to 're-set' my heart is 2 Samuel chapter 22. I like to read through it all, slowly, letting the words wash over me, reminding me (again) just who it is that I have on, and by my side!

The God who Hears (and responds to) your distress call
"In my distress I called to the LORD; I called out to my God. From his temple he heard my voice; my cry came to his ears." 2

Samuel 22:7 (NIVUK)

The One True God
"As for God, his way is perfect: the Lord's word is flawless; he shields all who take refuge in him. For who is God besides the Lord? And who is the Rock except our God?" 2 Samuel 22:31-32 (NIVUK)

David says, 'As for God.' I like the way the NET version translates it: '*The one true God,*'
We may not have the false gods of Old Testament times, but often, when our backs are against the wall, we put our trust in our modern-day false gods of overeating, self medicating, religious ritual, self-help books, or complaining incessantly about our problems; just about anything or everything, before we think of looking to *The One True God* who, David declares, 'is a *shield for all who take refuge in him*!'

The One Who Enables
"It is God who arms me with strength and keeps my way secure. He makes my feet like the feet of a deer; he causes me to stand on the heights." 2 Samuel 22:33-34 (NIVUK)
The literal meaning of this is, in the original language is: "He removes the obstacles in my way. He gives me the agility of a deer and enables me to negotiate the rugged terrain."

Habbukuk was a man who could have let himself slide down the slippery slope into despair, after all he'd been through. But he made a choice. In the midst of chaos, he chose to rejoice in the Lord. In the midst of disaster, he celebrated God's faithfulness.

The 'secret' to Habakkuk's joy was worship. His thanksgiving wasn't dependent on external things, it was firmly established in Habbakuk's confidence in who God is.
In Habakkuk chapter three we find almost the exactly the same wording as in 2 Samuel 22:34: "Though the fig-tree does not bud

and there are no grapes on the vines, though the olive crop fails and the fields produce no food, though there are no sheep in the sheepfold and no cattle in the stalls, yet I will rejoice in the LORD, I will be joyful in God my Saviour. The Sovereign LORD is my strength; he makes my feet like the feet of a deer, he enables me to tread on the heights. Habakkuk 3:17-19 (NIVUK)

We touched on this combination of two scriptures on Saturday of last week's devotionals - God designed the deer, specifically the *hind*, to walk the high rocky, mountain terrain; treacherous to other animals and humans. This deer can <u>negotiate the rugged terrain</u> confidently, without even thinking about it, because it's *created* to do so.

He has uniquely designed you too, Child of God, to negotiate the rugged terrain of life! There will often be times in life when the terrain is 'rugged.' God has designed and enabled you to walk with confidence over that terrain! And in addition to that, you <u>can</u> rejoice, because you don't have to negotiate that rugged terrain on our own, He walks with you.

Friday - God is So Much Bigger Than Formulas

"My thoughts are nothing like your thoughts," says the Lord. "And my ways are far beyond anything you could imagine. For just as the heavens are higher than the earth, so my ways are higher than your ways and my thoughts higher than your thoughts." Isaiah 55:8-9 (NLT)

God's perfect number seven

The Bible contains some very interesting symbolism. For example the number seven, the has much significance. It is the symbol of completion and of Divine perfection. God told Naaman to bathe himself in the Jordan seven times to be cleansed of leprosy. Joshua was told to march around the walls of Jericho seven times on the seventh day, and on that day, seven priests were to blow seven trumpets, to bring those walls down!

Putting the Lord in a box

We often see patterns like this in scripture, and then think to ourselves, "Ahah! So this is how God works, I have the Lord all figured out now!" We try to box God into our *ideas* of Him, and how He should do things. The problem with this way of thinking is that when God doesn't act as we believe He 'ought to,' we tell Him by our attitudes, "you can't do that Lord, that isn't how you do things!" And we end up with schisms and factions within the Body of Christ, that Jesus Himself is refused entry to: "Sorry Lord, but we don't do it that way in our church!"

* * *

I wonder if Jesse had this subconscious attitude when Samuel told him to bring his sons, so that the new King could be chosen, and anointed from amongst them. Jesse brought <u>seven</u> sons and stood them before Samuel. Perhaps I'm reading too much into this, but I can't help wondering if Jesse, once blessed with his seventh son, felt complete; satisfied. Notice: "*all seven of Jesse's sons were presented to Samuel. But Samuel said to Jesse, "The Lord has not chosen any of these.*" 1 Samuel 16:10 (NLT) <u>All seven</u>. Jesse had eight sons!

It's almost as if his eighth son is of no consequence. If seven was *perfection*, to that mindset then an eighth son would have been superfluous - extra, surplus to requirements. Whether that's what went on in Jesse's mind is only an interesting theory, however, what *is* true is that although David *was* the youngest, the *baby, he was still Jesse's son,* and his own father did not consider him worth bringing before Samuel.

God's perfect number eight, nine, ten....
Many people go through life with an 'eighth son mentality.' They have a deep-seated belief that they are unwanted, overlooked, and forgotten. But in God's eyes none of His sons and daughters are these things. There is no 'pecking order' in God's family. Each and every one of His children, in God's eyes, is cause for celebration; He rejoices over you with loud singing! (Zephaniah 3:17) Every single one of us has a God-ordained future.

You may not always be the first choice by your church leaders, or your boss. You might still be waiting for a life partner. Perhaps you feel ignored, unseen, and undervalued by your peers. But you have not been forgotten by the Lord. Eighth-son David just quietly obeyed his father and kept the sheep. There may be long periods where you feel that's all *you* do; exist in the background, barely noticed, hardly making an impact, until suddenly you are chosen and everything changes!

Samuel said to Jesse, 'Er, hang on a minute, isn't there another son?' (my paraphrase) and eventually David was fetched: "*as David stood there among his brothers, Samuel took the flask of olive oil he had brought and anointed David with the oil. And the Spirit of the Lord came powerfully upon David from that day on.*" 1 Samuel 16:13 (NLT)

If you feel forgotten and overlooked today, I hope this will encourage you. Or perhaps you could encourage someone else who you know feels that way. Be patient and wait for God. Don't let persistent *no's* discourage you, or keep you from your God-given dreams. If God has a plan for you, *He* will make it happen. And lastly, remember what Samuel said, that while man looks at the outside, God looks at the *heart*. He sees the *real* you. Under David's humble, rough, shepherd's robes beat the heart of a Godly King, a man after God's own heart. What's the *condition* of your heart?

Saturday - The Mountain Top

"People from many nations will come and say, "Come, let us go up to the mountain of the Lord, to the house of Jacob's God. There he will teach us his ways, and we will walk in his paths." For the Lord's teaching will go out from Zion; his word will go out from Jerusalem." Micah 4:2 (NLT)

The Christian life is likened to *walking.* At various times we find ourselves, spiritually speaking, in a valley. At other times on a mountain top. Neither of these metaphorical places are for dwelling in, they are periods of time, part of a journey, or a season in the Christian experience.

The mountain top

People often use the term *Mountain Top,* to describe where they 'are,' in their walk with God, when things are going well. The mountain top is a place of awe, and wonder. It's a place of insight and inspiration. In the Bible, Mountains are often recorded as places of powerful, personal encounters with God.

Abraham's faith was tested on a mountain; He took his son up the mountain with him, and did as the Lord had told him to. Just as he was preparing to do the *unthinkable,* God stepped in, powerfully, and miraculously. You can read this account in Genesis 22.

It was on Mount Ararat that Noah's ark came to rest after the

Flood, and God made a covenant with Noah there.

In Luke's Gospel chapter nine, Peter, James, and John had the greatest Mountain Top experience ever, when Jesus took them up the mountain with him to pray. Suddenly the veil of Jesus' humanity dropped away, revealing all His Glory and majesty.

When Moses received the Ten Commandments on the mountain, his encounter with God was so powerful that when he came back down from the mountain his face radiated the glory of God's presence. You can read about this in Exodus 20.

The mountain top prepares us for the valley

Our Christian life could be compared to a series of valley and mountain top experiences. In the same way that we are not meant to set up camp and dwell in the valley - we walk *through* it, and God's presence is with us - the mountain-top is *part* of our journey. We don't live on the top of the mountain all the time. I believe God leads us there to encounter Him. The mountain top experiences we have just looked at in the Bible were all powerful, dramatic and life-changing. When we encounter God in this way it changes us, and it prepares us for the valley, where 'real life happens.'

Jesus often separated Himself from others and went up a mountain to be alone with His Father; these intimate encounters with God the Father enables Jesus to 'keep-on-keeping-on' in His daily life, of ministering to others. See Luke 6:12; Matthew 14:23-24.

To encounter God isn't all about a warm fuzzy feeling. God uses the mountain top to teach us His ways, to shape our thinking, and ultimately, the way we live. I believe this was Jesus' purpose in choosing a mountain on which to preach His greatest sermon, known to us today as "the sermon in the mount," in which He teaches us how to walk in a way that pleases God.

* * *

Does God expect us to run out and find a literal mountain to climb? The short answer is no. But He does want us to find time, in the daily grind of our valley-walking, to find some alone time with Him. He constantly calls us to *'come up higher,'* which may seem a bit like a slog and a hike, especially if you are bogged down with cares and worries. But when you respond to this call, you will discover something: think of the last time you were at the top of a mountain or high place. Your perspective was so much 'bigger,' wider and far reaching. So it is when you throw off those heavy burdens and 'come up higher,' to spend time on the mountain top with God; you start to see things from His perspective. That view will remain with you, in your mind's eye, when you are walking through the valley!

Sunday - A Sacrifice Of Praise

"So we no longer offer up a steady stream of blood sacrifices, but through Jesus, we will offer up to God a steady stream of praise sacrifices—these are "the lambs" we offer from our lips that celebrate his name!" Hebrews 13:15 (TPT)

Have you ever had a letter containing bad news that made you fearful, anxious, or kept you awake at night with worry? Perhaps it was bad news from your doctor? Or maybe your position at work was hanging in the balance? What would your reaction be, if someone were to say to you in those moments following bad news, *"what about worshiping God right now, and giving thanks to Him just because He's so good?"*

The thing is, that hypothetical friend, irritating as they may be, would be right. God *is* worthy of our worship whatever our circumstances. We may not *feel* thankful, we may not particularly *want* in the midst of trying circumstances, to start praising God, but that's exactly why it's called a sacrifice. A sacrifice is *costly.*

For many of us, our first response to bad news is *'panic now, pray later, and worship when the dust has settled.'* To respond with faith in fearful circumstances, and trust God when everything seems to be crumbling around us, is quite literally a sacrifice. It is laying our fears and doubts on the alter and giving God the praise and worship due to Him, *just because of who He is.* There's a great story in 2 Kings where King Hezekiah did just that.

Because you prayed

"Then Isaiah son of Amoz sent this message to Hezekiah: "This is what the Lord, the God of Israel, says: Because you prayed about King Sennacherib of Assyria, the Lord has spoken this word against him: "The virgin daughter of Zion despises you and laughs at you. The daughter of Jerusalem shakes her head in derision as you flee." Isaiah 37:21-22 (NLT) The whole story can be found in 2 Kings 18.

The Assyrian King Sennacherib's very name instilled terror. Known for his brutality, he and his army had plundered, raped, and brutally murdered their way across that entire region. Now he had sent a threatening message to King Hezekiah of Judah to say that he was preparing to destroy Jerusalem.

One of Sennacherib's evil tactics was to break down the morale of the people he planned to conquer with a barrage of threats, striking fear in their hearts and causing them to believe they had no hope. He tried this with Hezekiah, but it didn't work. Hezekiah continued to trust in the Lord. Eventually Sennacherib sent a message to King Hezekiah to say he was on his way! His message read a bit like this: "just to let you know, Hezekiah, all the other nations I've killed and pillaged also claimed that their gods would help them. So you needn't think your God will save you!" (my paraphrase)

Spread it out before the Lord

Hezekiah took the message to the temple in Jerusalem, and there he "spread it out before the Lord" 2 Kings 19:14 (NLT) But Hezekiah started with worship before he asked the Lord for help: *"O Lord, God of Israel, you are enthroned between the mighty cherubim! You alone are God of all the kingdoms of the earth. You alone created the heavens and the earth."* 2 Kings 19:15 (NLT)

Then he prayed, "Now, O Lord our God, rescue us from his power; then all the kingdoms of the earth will know that you alone, O Lord, are God." 2 Kings 19:19 (NLT)

God responded immediately. He sent a prophetic word to Hezekiah through Isaiah, bringing comfort, hope, strength and reassurance, of The Lord's continued presence and help. It's the beginning of The Lord's words that so captivate my heart; *"Because you prayed."* Isaiah 37:21 (NLT)

When we read on, we see that Hezekiah's prayer was answered that very night. God intervened, conquering the enemy forces outside the city gates. Not only did the Assyrian army not set foot in Jerusalem, they never even got to shoot a single arrow (2 Kings 19:32). Sennacherib, having skulked back to his own land, met with a sticky end at the hands of his own sons, while he worshipped in the temple of his fake god.

Whatever you might be facing today, this week or this month, take it to the Lord our God, "spread it out before Him," worship Him with a sincere heart for His faithfulness to you, His unfailing goodness and mercy that will follow you all the days of your life, and ask Him for his help.

Hungry And Thirsty?

Monday - Come To Me

"Then Jesus said, "Come to me, all of you who are weary and carry heavy burdens, and I will give you rest. Take my yoke upon you. Let me teach you, because I am humble and gentle at heart, and you will find rest for your souls. For my yoke is easy to bear, and the burden I give you is light." Matthew 11:28-30 (NLT)

Come to Me

These words of Jesus' sounded shocking to the religious leaders of the time; they were angered and riled by the 'audacity' of it. No one had ever dared to say anything like this. An invitation such as this - *"come to me"* - was unthinkable, unless it came from the mouth of God Himself. Jesus' invitation reveals His Divinty.

All of you who are weary and carry heavy burdens

I love the way the Message Bible captures the heart of the invitation. "Are you tired? Worn out? Burned out on religion? Come to me. Get away with me and you'll recover your life. I'll show you how to take a real rest. Walk with me and work with me—watch how I do it. Learn the unforced rhythms of grace. I won't lay anything heavy or ill-fitting on you. Keep company with me and you'll learn to live freely and lightly." Matthew 11:28-30 (MSG)

And of course other translations use the better known words, 'weary and heavy laden.'

All who are weary

The invitation is to those who are labour. We could read this and think, 'well, I'm pretty weary at the moment. I work hard, but aren't we supposed to work?' However, I believe Jesus was addressing the issue of weariness from trying to live a life of religious ritual; of self effort, and self-sufficiency, and constantly falling short. The word Jesus uses here for 'weary' is *kopiao*, meaning "*to labour, toil, expend great effort in hard and disagreeable work, to grow weary, tired, labor to the point of exhaustion.*" The word is in the present continuous tense; it describes man's desperate, fruitless, efforts to deal with sin, guilt, and personal misery by religious legalism and human strategy, both of which do nothing but add to our burden and weariness! (Colossians 2:16-23)

The heavy workloads we carry are self-imposed and not at all what God has required of us. Weariness comes from the heavy burdens we pick up and carry and the labours and toils we burden ourselves with. God doesn't ask us to run ourselves ragged until we collapse from exhaustion!

I think of Martha, running about, fussing over making Jesus a meal. Jesus had not askeded her to do that. *"But Martha was distracted by all the preparations that had to be made. She came to him and asked, 'Lord, don't you care that my sister has left me to do the work by myself? Tell her to help me!"* Luke 10:40 *(NIVUK)*

I love the way Jesus gently chided her: *"Martha, Martha,' the Lord answered, 'you are worried and upset about many things, but few things are needed – or indeed only one. Mary has chosen what is better, and it will not be taken away from her."* Luke 10:41-42 (NIVUK)

Heavy laden

Heavy laden is phortizo, in the original, meaning 'to place a burden upon; to load as when placing a load upon the back of an ox.'

In Matthew 23:4 Jesus addresses the issue of the heavy burdens of religious ritual and laws, placed upon the people by religious leaders with their own agendas.

"The teachers of the law and the Pharisees sit in Moses' seat. So you must be careful to do everything they tell you. But do not do what they do, for they do not practise what they preach. They tie up heavy, cumbersome loads and put them on other people's shoulders, but they themselves are not willing to lift a finger to move them." Matthew 23:2-4 (NIVUK)

In Luke 11:46 Jesus uses very strong words "And you experts in the law, <u>woe to you</u>, because you load people down with burdens they can hardly carry," Luke 11:46 NIVUK

The word for burdens in both, is phortizo, and Jesus uses it to compare the oppressive legal burdens placed on the people.

Gentleness and humility is Jesus' leadership style

One of the things I love about this scripture is that Jesus tells us directly, a little bit about Himself; about His nature and personality. Most of what we know about Him is from personal experience (through knowing Him) and through reading the Bible, especially the four Gospels. But here, Jesus describes Himself. He assures us through His words that we don't need to fear His yoke or His burden, because He is not like our previous masters. *"I am gentle and humble,"* He says.

In other words; your previous masters, of religious ritual without relationship, your own sin, Satan, and the world's system; these placed heavy burdens upon you. Whereas, the yoke I give you, Jesus tells us, "is easy to *bear, and the burden I give you is light." Matthew 11:28-30* (NLT)

* * *

Jesus leadership style is gentleness, love and humility. We see His humility when He, the King of all glory, washed His disciples' feet, and when He rode into Jerusalem on a donkey. We see His gentleness where He touches lepers that no one else would go near, and a woman with "an issue of blood," regarded as unclean by everyone else. His gentleness is evident wherever He took time to speak to, smile at, look into the eyes of, people on the fringes; unwanted, unloved, despised by their peers. That's our Jesus. That's *my* Jesus.

What is Jesus' yoke and burden?

There is still a yoke, but Jesus' yoke is easy. We will be looking at the concept of the yoke tomorrow, but just in brief, "easy" is *chrestos*. It is from a verb which means *"useful, manageable, serviceable, that which fills a need and is well fitting."* In other words, it is designed to fit our needs, it is custom-made just for us.

There is still a burden, but the burden Jesus gives us is *light*. "Light" is *elaphros*, *"light in weight, agile, not burdensome, or overbearing."* It is about discipleship with relationship, rather than religion, with liturgy and rules, but lacking intimacy. Does this qualify as a' burden'? It does, in that there is a cost to discipleship, it doesn't *just happen*. There are spiritual disciplines, such as actively seeking God, prayer, a lifestyle of worship, cultivating thankfulness, being joyful, encouraging others, showing love, and so much more. But these things should not *feel* burdensome. If they do, it could be an indication that we have set down Jesus' light burden and picked up our own again. We carry Jesus light burden of discipleship out of love and devotion to Him, not out of an overbearing sense of obligation, people pleasing, or an attempt to please God.

Paul exhorted Timothy; *"Have nothing to do with godless myths and old wives' tales; rather, train yourself to be godly."* He *continues, "That is why we labour and strive, because we have put our hope in the living God, who is the Saviour of all people, and especially of those who believe."* 1 Timothy 4:7-8, 10 (NIVUK)

Tuesday - Blessing and Favour

"Seek the LORD and His strength; Seek His face continually [longing to be in His presence]."1 Chronicles 16:11 (AMP)

It was a very significant day; David had just restored the Ark of the Covenant, the symbol of the presence and glory of God to its rightful place. It's no wonder then that there was such a celebration going on! David wrote a worship song especially for the occasion. We see it in its entirety in I Chronicles 16, and then repeated in parts through the book of Psalms, (Psalm 105:1-15; Psalm 96:1b-13a; Psalm 106:1-47 and 48).
In 1 Chronicles 16:11 David reminds the people of the importance, always and forever of seeking God's face and His strength.

God's face equals favour and blessing
I believe that to 'seek the Lord's face,' in this context means to seek His favour and blessing. In the Book of Numbers, the Lord told Aaron and the priests to pronounce to the following blessing on the people:

"The LORD bless you, and keep you [protect you, sustain you, and guard you]; The LORD make His face shine upon you [with favor], And be gracious to you [surrounding you with

lovingkindness]; The LORD lift up His countenance (face) upon you [with divine approval], And give you peace [a tranquil heart and life]." Numbers 6:24-26 (AMP)

And Paul wrote these words to the church at Corinth: *"And God is able to make all grace [every favor and earthly blessing] come in abundance to you, so that you may always [under all circumstances, regardless of the need] have complete sufficiency in everything [being completely self-sufficient in Him], and have an abundance for every good work and act of charity."* 2 Corinthians 9:8 (AMP)

"The Lord *make*, His face to shine on you," implies that God's face doesn't shine on everyone. I believe that the Lord causes His face to shine on those who intentionally seek His face and want to be a blessing to Him.

There are a number of Biblical references to where the people of God ask Him not to hide His face from them: *"Do not hide Your face from Your servant, For I am in distress; answer me quickly."* Psalm 69:17 (AMP)

Also see: Job 13:24, Psalm 27:9, Psalm 44:24, Psalm 88:14, Psalm 102:2, Psalm 143:7.

I firmly believe that God has always wanted to bless His children; it is His desire to protect and sustain us, to be gracious to us, to give us His favour and fill us with peace, and this was why He commissioned the priests with that wonderful blessing to speak over the people.

God's Strength

We are exhorted to continually seek both the Lord's <u>strength</u> and his <u>face</u>. The two are different, yet so closely linked that it comes as one exhortation; 'seek His face and His strength.' To seek His strength is self explanatory; God is all-powerful, the Bible is filled with references to His strength, and the truth that He is more than willing to arm and enable us with His strength. In every circumstance the strength of God is always available to us, and in everything we do we should seek His strength, rather than attempting to go it alone.

I believe that when I start to attempt to do things in my own strength, rather than seeking, and relying on the Lord's strength, God takes His hands off and says "go ahead." He knows we can't do it alone, but He doesn't *force* His strength on us. He does, however, lavish it upon us when we seek Him!

Paul was a man who truly knew how to practically live out this verse in 1 Chronicles, and in his letters frequently spoke about his own weakness versus God's enabling strength. He wrote to the church at Philippi: *"I can do all things [which He has called me to do] through Him who strengthens and empowers me [to fulfill His purpose—I am self-sufficient in Christ's sufficiency; I am ready for anything and equal to anything through Him who infuses me with inner strength and confident peace.]"* Philippians 4:13 (AMP)

Wednesday- The (Real) Real Thing

*"Do not love this world nor the things it offers you, for when you love the world, you do not have the love of the Father in you. For the world offers only a **craving** for **physical pleasure**, a craving for everything we see, and **pride** in our achievements and possessions. These are not from the Father, but are from this world. And this world is fading away, along with everything that people crave. But anyone who does what pleases God will live forever." 1 John 15-17 (NLT)*

There's a slogan - "The real thing" - for a certain carbonated beverage has been well known for decades, even by people who don't drink it! Whether you like fizzy drinks or not, one has to admit that whoever came up with the catchphrase was a very clever marketing strategist. In truth though, there's only one 'real thing;' only One who brings true satisfaction, hope, joy and peace; and that is the person of Jesus Christ. Psalm 107:9 (NLT) tells us, *"he satisfies the thirsty and fills the hungry with good things."*

The opposite of the real thing

Psalm 107:9, outlines for us what the Lord fills our hungry souls with. By contrast, John lays out in our opening Scripture exactly what this world has to offer us, and shows how *empty* it all is. He ends with the words, *"And this world is fading away, along with everything that people crave. But anyone who does what pleases*

God will live forever."

The world only offers more craving

We crave, so we look for ways to fill our cravings, and end up feeling emptier than when we started, because we look in the wrong places. When we feel empty, lonely or unloved, it's tempting to think we can fill our emptiness with temporary physical pleasures, such as food, television, sports, drink, new clothing, shoes, household goods; perhaps even a new romance. But the things we consume will eventually consume us. What starts out as a small thing, can become something we can't get enough of. When watching the next episode of that box-set we are following on television becomes more important to us than time alone with God, I think we could say we have a problem.

Lust: Lust doesn't only apply in a sexual context; anything that pulls us away from our true, first love - Jesus - is lust. When our eyes see that shiny thing that someone else has; a promotion at work, a ministry position in church, an annual holiday, or material things, and we start to believe that if we only had what they have then our lives would become as good as theirs. And we become so focused on that 'shiny thing,' that it outshines, and eclipses Jesus. Before we know it, we're hooked and will to go to any lengths to have the thing we want!

Boasting: We've all done it, at times, and we've all seen others do it. We feel rejected, left out, hard done by, 'less-than,' so we feel the need to blow our own trumpet a bit, to make ourselves feel better. Some do it in rooms filled with other people, some on a platform, others on social media. When it comes to social media, the 'likes' and complimentary comments seem to pour 'healing balm' on the sting of rejection. *But it's a lie! Its a temporary fix.* Like one of those fake creams that can be bought online; it has all the right packaging of an expensive ointment but is a cheap copy of the real thing.

The REAL thing

Only God offers something REAL to heal our hearts and fill every emptiness we may feel and in him there is **no** lack. And the best thing of all? It's God's free gift to us.

"Is anyone thirsty? Come and drink— even if you have no money! Come, take your choice of wine or milk— it's all free! Why spend your money on food that does not give you strength? Why pay for food that does you no good? Listen to me, and you will eat what is good. You will enjoy the finest food. "Come to me with your ears wide open. Listen, and you will find life."
Isaiah 55:1-3 (NLT)

Thursday - A River of Life!

"Anyone who believes in me may come and drink! For the Scriptures declare, 'Rivers of living water will flow from his heart." John 7:38 (NLT)

(If you get a chance, I would recommend that you read Ezekiel 47:1-12.)

I love this powerful and graphic account Ezekiel gives of his vision. It's edge of your seat stuff! Ezekiel describes seeing, in his vision, a trickle of water coming from under the door of the temple, flowing across the court, and under the main outer wall. As the stream headed east, it quickly grew wider and deeper until it rapidly became a mighty river.

There's a vast, and dense population of lush, fruit-bearing trees growing along the banks of the river. (This brings to mind Psalm 1:1-3!) The river flowed towards the Dead Sea, and in its path, everywhere it went, it brought life to previously dead places; stagnant waters started to teem with life! The trees that grew on the banks of this amazing river, provided a constant supply of food, and their leaves brought healing to the sick.

There are several places in scripture where God's 'River of delights' is mentioned. Here are two examples: *"you give them drink from your river of delights. For with you is the fountain of life; in your light we see light." Psalms 36:8-9 (NIVUK)*

"There is a river whose streams make glad the city of God, the holy place where the Most High dwells." Psalms 46:4 (NIVUK).

To think Ezekiel actually got to see the river in action, albeit in a vision. What a powerful vision!

In the book of Revelation, John describes a similar vision as wonderful as Ezekiel's: *"Then the angel showed me the river of the water of life, flowing with water clear as crystal, continuously pouring out from the throne of God and of the Lamb. The river was flowing in the middle of the street of the city, and on either side of the river was the Tree of Life, with its twelve kinds of ripe fruit according to each month of the year. The leaves of the Tree of Life are for the healing of the nations. And every curse will be broken and no longer exist, for the throne of God and of the Lamb will be there in the city. His loving servants will serve him;"*
Revelation 22:1-3 (TPT)

Healing for the nations

Just as in Ezekiel's vision, the trees along the riverbank, soaking up the water from this precious river, had healing in their leaves.

Jesus spoke of something similar, in his conversation with the woman at the well: *"but if anyone drinks the living water I give them, they will never thirst again and will be forever satisfied! For when you drink the water I give you it becomes a gushing fountain of the Holy Spirit, springing up and flooding you with endless life!" John 4:14 (TPT)*

The wonderful and incredible thing is, we don't have to wait until some day in the future to see this River of Life at work. And it's not just some hard to understand 'thread,' running through the Bible. That very same River of Life flows through every single follower of Jesus, today!

Jesus said, *"If anyone thirsts, let him come to me and drink. Whoever believes in me, as the Scripture has said, 'Out of his heart will flow rivers of living water."* John 7:38 (NLT) that's you. That's me!

Jesus invites all who are thirsty to come to Him and be refreshed. He IS the Living Water. The supply is never ending - it will never run dry. But it doesn't end there; there's a second, vitally important part. It isn't all about us. We have a responsibility to continually drink from the River of Life - Jesus - and to "remain in Him - the True Vine; we are the branches. We *need* Him. Without Him to sustain us, we can do nothing. We have a mandate to let Him to flow through us, to bring His refreshing water everywhere we go, like the river in Ezekiel's vision; bringing life to dead places, hope where Hope has gone, and healing to our parched world.

In what ways are we going to allow that River of life to flow out of us today?

Friday - Thirsty For Rain

"Ask the Lord for rain in the spring, for he makes the storm clouds. And he will send showers of rain so every field becomes a lush pasture." Zechariah10:1 (NLT)

In Biblical times, rain was viewed as a tremendous blessing; in their desert-like places, a rainy day was a wonderful day! In the Bible rain is also often used as a metaphor for blessing.

Rain is a promise, a blessing and a gift
"I will bless my people and their homes around my holy hill. And in the proper season I will send the showers they need. There will be showers of blessing." Ezekiel 34:26 (NLT)

"The Lord will send rain at the proper time from his rich treasury in the heavens and will bless all the work you do. You will lend to many nations, but you will never need to borrow from them." Deuteronomy 28:12 (NLT)
Also see Deuteronomy 32:2; Job 5:10; Psalm 147:8

God sometimes blesses us in ways we don't recognise
Have you ever prayed for the 'rain' of the Spirit upon your church or town? I always picture an outpouring of the Holy Spirit, like a deluge; a monsoon of healing, joy, renewed faith, strength and hope, all resulting in a deeper, stronger walk with God and each other.

551

* * *

I want that! I want it for myself, my church, my family, my town! And that's often how the 'rain' we ask for does fall. But something I've discovered is that sometimes my idea of what blessing looks like and God's are two very different pictures. And what do people instinctively do when it starts to rain? We put up our umbrellas! We grumble and complain, about the *very thing* that the Lord has given us to refresh us, and water our dry and thirsty places, to bring growth. We put up the metaphorical umbrellas of our old 'default settings', failing to recognise God's blessing.

But God has a way of not always doing things the way we we think He ought to.
"My thoughts are nothing like your thoughts," says the Lord. "And my ways are far beyond anything you could imagine. For just as the heavens are higher than the earth, so my ways are higher than your ways and my thoughts higher than your thoughts." Isaiah 55:8-9 (NLT)

Think Before You Put Up That Umbrella !

Have you ever thought that the 'rain' of those difficulties and challenges you're facing are actually a blessing? The rain isn't falling on you because God <u>doesn't</u> love you. It's because He <u>does</u>!
The greatest blessing of this kind of rain is that in your difficulties you will draw you closer to God, and learn to rely solely on Him. And your intimacy and closeness with God will deepen, far beyond that which you have ever known. That is; if you do not put up that umbrella, and you draw close to Him instead. Trust your Father; after all, He promises to be:
* Your Provider: Philippians 4:19
* Your Strong Tower and Refuge: Psalm 18:10
* Your Peace: John 14:27

Saturday - Hungry And Thirsty For Righteousness

"Blessed are those who hunger and thirst for righteousness, for they will be filled." Matthew 5:6 (NIVUK)

"As the deer pants for streams of water, so my soul pants for you, my God. My soul thirsts for God, for the living God." Psalms 42:1-2 (NIVUK)

Hunger and thirst are incredibly powerful forces; there's nothing like a dry, parched throat or a rumbling stomach to compel a person to take prompt, decisive action in seeking food and something to drink. In the same way, those who are hungry for *righteousness,* are compelled to take action, to have those hunger pangs satisfied.

If you ever have experienced genuine, ongoing physical hunger then you'll know that it can't be ignored - it consumes your every waking thought until you <u>do</u> something about about it. Genuine hunger for God's righteousness has the same effect. It's a profound , gnawing hunger, a constant 'rumbling' of the soul that could never be satisfied by a quick snack - a two minute read of a scripture, here and there, but demands a proper, substantial meal!

God's righteousness not ours
Notice that Jesus said that it is those who *hunger and thirst after*

righteousness who are blessed; He didn't say, blessed are the *righteous*.

The kind of righteousness that has been imputed to us because we are born again, pertains to our legal standing before God. However we are now called to <u>live</u> by God's righteousness. Jesus said:
"For I tell you that unless your righteousness surpasses that of the Pharisees and the teachers of the law, you will certainly not enter the kingdom of heaven." Matthew 5:20 (NIVUK)

"Be perfect, therefore, as your heavenly Father is perfect." Matthew 5:48 NIVUK

It sounds unreachable and impossible doesn't it? But we know that Jesus wasn't talking about striving to 'be good,' 'better,' or 'nicer' and it is not righteous in our own strength, by our own standards, because if that were the case we could easily slip into <u>self</u>-righteousness. (See Luke 18:9)

Jesus continued by telling the parable of the Pharisee and the Tax collector, to illustrate that self-righteousness - the establishment of our own standards of righteousness - means nothing in God's eyes (Luke 18:10-14).
On the other hand, when we are hungry <u>to know Jesus more</u> deeply, and to grow in His righteousness, we will be filled, that's a promise! (See Isaiah 55:1-3).

When we ask God to fill us, He will answer way beyond our expectations: *"Ask and you'll receive. Seek and you'll discover. Knock on heaven's door, and it will one day open for you. Every persistent person will get what he asks for. Every persistent seeker will discover what he needs. And everyone who knocks persistently will one day find an open door: "Do you know of any father who would give his son a snake on a plate when he asked for a serving of fish? Of course not! Do you know of any father who would give his daughter a spider when she had asked for an egg? Of course not! If imperfect parents know how to lovingly take care of their children and give them what they need, how much more will the perfect heavenly Father give the Holy Spirit's fullness when his children ask him."* Luke 11:9-13 (TPT)

Are you hungry and thirsty, longing to be filled with His righteousness? It is not some lofty, unattainable thing, reserved for only the few. Just ask Him.

"for he satisfies the thirsty and fills the hungry with good things." Psalms 107:9 (NIVUK)

Sunday - Evergreen Faith!

"I am still as strong today as I was in the day that Moses sent me; my strength now is as my strength was then, for war and for going and coming." Joshua 14:4 (NLT)

Many people refer to the later years of life as the 'Winter of life'. I deliberately didn't write this devotional in the 'Seasons' chapter, because I believe that this an incorrect way of looking at this rich, and beautiful time of life. Sadly, so many older people are overlooked, and undervalued, not only by society in general but in our churches. Retirement and beyond is seen as a time to 'put out to pasture,' and just while away the hours. *Why*? It can be the cause of deep discouragement, loneliness and fosters a feeling of having been discarded. The Lord has a very different view of 'old age' - He never ceases to refresh, replenish, and strengthen, until the day we go to be with Him! Let's have a look, for a few moments, at the life of Caleb.

Caleb's faith was evergreen

As a younger man, Caleb was one of the spies sent on the important mission to The Promised Land, before the Israelites were to go in and conquer it. While the other spies had returned with fear-filled reports on the land, that disheartened, and struck fear in the hearts of the people, Caleb remained resolute in his faith that God would help them to defeat the Canaanites who lived in the Land, promised to them by the Lord: *"but my brothers who went with me frightened the people from entering the Promised Land. For my part, I wholeheartedly followed the Lord my God."* Joshua 14:8 (NLT)

Caleb had never lost faith in the promise of the Lord and we find him, forty five years later, age eighty five saying: *"Now, as you can see, the Lord has kept me alive and well as he promised for all these forty-five years since Moses made this promise—even while Israel wandered in the wilderness. Today I am eighty-five years old. I am as strong now as I was when Moses sent me on that journey, and I can still travel and fight as well as I could then. So give me the hill country that the Lord promised me. You will remember that as scouts we found the descendants of Anak living there in great, walled towns. But if the Lord is with me, I will drive them out of the land, just as the Lord said."* (Joshua 14:10-12 NLT)

Now this does not sound to me like an elderly man asking for his newspaper and slippers! Nor is it the reminiscing, sentimental ramblings of an old man. This is a man who has remained man fit and strong in the Lord, through every season, and now in the supposed Winter of his life, he can say *"I am still as strong today as I was in the day that Moses sent me."*

Who gets to define 'old' anyway?

I see so many 'older' people become discouraged. They feel they have no real purpose anymore and they fade into the background in our churches. I don't see *anywhere* in the Bible that tells me to slow down, take a back seat, or give up on my God-given dreams when I grow older.

The Bible has quite a lot to say about the elderly. None of it even hints at any form of being put out to pasture! Just remind me, at what age did God call Moses? Oh, and what age was Sarah when she had her first baby?

* * *

We often focus on prayer for the younger generation. And so we *should* pray for our young people, they are a precious part of the Church, but we should not neglect to pray for our elderly. The truth is, we need each other, young, old and in between! Here's what King David had to say on the matter: *"God, now that I'm old and gray, don't walk away. Give me grace to demonstrate to the next generation all your mighty miracles and your excitement, to show them your magnificent power!"* Psalms 71:18 (TPT)

Remember

You will never be 'too old' to worship God, It's is what we were created for. God isn't interested in what we can *do* for him, He just wants our hearts; our complete devotion, because He is devoted to us. Even if your body is frail, and you can't physically do much, you can still draw near to God and enjoy His presence. You can still be a prayer warrior!:

"In the last days,' God says, 'I will pour out my Spirit upon all people. Your sons and daughters will prophesy. Your young men will see visions, and your old men will dream dreams." Acts 2:17 (NLT)

Would the Lord give the elderly (prophetic) dreams, for them to just sit in their rocking chairs and mull over all alone? I hardly think so!

This is God's promise to you, so be encouraged today, if you feel in that 'certain age' group! *"I will be your God throughout your lifetime— until your hair is white with age. I made you, and I will care for you. I will carry you along and save you."* Isaiah 46:4 (NLT)

This *richness* comes from being *deeply planted* by that stream we can read about in Psalm 1:2-4, which is the Word of God. Whatever age you are, keep your roots in that river!

Who Do You Think You Are?

Monday - Spiritual Identity Theft

Cyber crime, and identity theft, has become a widespread and common problem in our modern society. Imagine the feeling of discovering that someone out there has stolen your identity; your bank account cleared out in a few clicks of a keyboard, your social media and online shopping accounts hacked. In just a few minutes a whole life can be 'stolen,' and even with the help of the police, the mess identity theft leaves can take months to untangle.

Spiritual identity theft

There's such a thing as 'spiritual identity theft.' In a similar way to online identity theft, which can take place in minutes, spiritual identity theft happens quickly. It usually starts with a small thought; something that might sound like 'does God *really* love me?' Entertained and encouraged to linger, this thought invites others to follow, and this results in a messy, impromptu 'party' in your mind, of all manner of negative, self destructive thoughts, such as self-dislike, comparison, rehashing of the past, doubts and fears. Before you know it you've forgotten who you are as a Child of God! Countless Christian men and women are daily robbed of their spiritual identity.

The spiritual identity thief

We all know that it's important to protect our private, personal details from cyber criminals, to avoid identity theft. In much the same way, it's vital to know our identity and to guard our true identity from another kind of thief. The Bible warns us to be on our guard against this thief, who Jesus describes in John 8:44 as not just as a liar, but *'the father of lies'*.

Like the cyber criminal, all it takes is a few moments of unguardedness, or sloppiness, and he has a foot in the door. One lie believed and agreed with and it could be likened to handing over your banking password to a thief! *"You're unworthy of God's love,"* he whispers. *"God could never forgive you for what you did today."* Jesus tells us in John's Gospel *"The thief comes only to steal and kill and destroy; I have come that they may have life, and have it to the full."* John 10:10 (NIVUK)

This enemy of ours constantly tries to convince men and women of God that we don't quite measure up, or make the grade, that surely there must be something *more* we need to do to please God. It is a constant drip-feed, *'night and day,'* of lies, accusation and condemnation from this thief and liar. He is furious, because he knows what lies ahead for him: *"Now salvation and power are set in place, and the kingdom reign of our God and the ruling authority of his Anointed One are established. For the accuser of our brothers and sisters, who relentlessly accused them day and night before our God, has now been defeated —cast out once and for all! They conquered him completely through the blood of the Lamb and the powerful word of his testimony. They triumphed because they did not love and cling to their own lives, even when faced with death."* Revelation 12:10-11 (TPT)

The thief wants to rob you of your identity, because he fears the Bible believing Christian who grasps hold of the Truth of who he or she is and begins to live out that truth.

Secure in your identity.
If you had a multi million pound inheritance in your bank

account would you ignore it and live a life of scrimping and scraping, worrying about tomorrow? How silly that sounds. Yet it's exactly how many of us live our Christian lives. We exist, struggling along from day to day like spiritual paupers. You and I have an immeasurable inheritance in our spiritual bank accounts, given to us by our lavishly generous Father. We are children of God, forgiven and declared righteous because of Jesus' incredible sacrifice. We have free access to His presence - His throne of mercy. He crowns us with steadfast love and mercy. He has blessed us with *'every spiritual blessing'*, He has equipped us with spiritual gifts, He lavishes His love upon us. He has freed us from fear and He empowers us to touch and effect to lives of those around us. We belong to Him, and nothing can ever separate us from His love.

In closing, remind yourself afresh of your true identity (below).

"For it was always in his perfect plan to adopt us as his delightful children, through our union with Jesus, the Anointed One, so that his tremendous love that cascades over us would glorify his grace—for the same love he has for his Beloved One, Jesus, he has for us. And this unfolding plan brings him great pleasure! Every spiritual blessing in the heavenly realm has already been lavished upon us as a love gift from our wonderful heavenly Father, the Father of our Lord Jesus—all because he sees us wrapped into Christ. This is why we celebrate him with all our hearts! And he chose us to be his very own, joining us to himself even before he laid the foundation of the universe! Because of his great love, he ordained us, so that we would be seen as holy in his eyes with an unstained innocence.

Since we are now joined to Christ, we have been given the treasures of redemption by his blood—the total cancellation of our sins—all because of the cascading riches of his grace. This superabundant grace is already powerfully working in us, releasing within us all forms of wisdom and practical understanding. And through the revelation of the Anointed One,

he unveiled his secret desires to us—the hidden mystery of his long-range plan, which he was delighted to implement from the very beginning of time."
Ephesians 1:3-9 TPT

Tuesday - We Are God's Inheritance

"But the Lord's portion is his people," Deuteronomy 32:9 (NLT)
"The Lord is my portion," says my soul, "therefore I will hope in him." Lamentations 3:24 (NLT)

Simply translated, the word *portion* in both of these scriptures means *inheritance*. If you are a follower of Jesus, are the Lord's *inheritance*. You are His very own, chosen, set apart one, on whom He has set his affections, goodness and mercy.

His by choice. (His choice)
You might believe you chose Him; 'found Him,' as many of our modern worship songs declare, but it's the other way around. He chose *you*.

His By Purchase
"your lives were ransomed once and for all from the empty and futile way of life handed down from generation to generation. It was not a ransom payment of silver and gold, which eventually perishes, but the precious blood of Christ—who like a spotless, unblemished lamb was sacrificed for us". 1 Peter 1:18-19 (TPT).

He loved you so much that He willingly paid the highest price possible for you. There can be no dispute about whether or not you belong to Him. If you have surrendered your life to Jesus Christ, then you are His. It's a legally binding contract. The Lord's portion - that's you and me - has been fully paid for and redeemed.

2 Timothy 2:19 (NLT) tells us that "the Lord *knows those who are his."* Jesus knows and recognises His own. He knows exactly who you are, how many hairs are on your head, how many breaths you've taken since you opened your eyes this morning, what you're going to think next! He knows you. He has not forgotten you and never will. You are sealed by, and for, Him.

His by conquest!

Of course we know that Jesus conquered sin, death and our enemy Satan, on the cross. But there's a battle we sometimes forget about. The battle He won *in* us! How long did Jesus have to lay siege to your heart before you surrendered? Do you remember the day Jesus conquered your heart? I remember the day He conquered mine. How could I ever have thought I my life had any meaning before He found me?

Do you remember when His love broke down the ramparts surrounding your heart, and your conquering King staked His everlasting claim on you? Like the Mighty Conqueror that Jesus is, He planted the Conqueror's flag of His Omnipotent love and mercy into His claimed ground - your heart. You're His, and nothing will ever change that.

How God cares for His inheritance

"He found them in a desert land, in an empty, howling wasteland. He surrounded them and watched over them; he guarded them as he would guard his own eyes. Like an eagle that rouses her chicks and hovers over her young, so he spread his wings to take them up and carried them safely on his pinions." Deuteronomy 32:10-11 (NLT)

Our lives were a wasteland before the Lord found us. Not only did He conquer us, and purchase us, but because we are His inheritance He takes tender loving care of us. It makes sense - we are His priceless inheritance!
Remember the comparison earlier in the book of the Lord to an

eagle, sheltering us under His wing? Have you ever been up close to an eagle? She is a huge, magnificent and fearsome bird, especially when she has young In her nest. Her eyes are piercing, her massive talons look as though they could snap a man's neck in seconds, if he dared to touch her precious little ones. This is how the Lord watches over you, His inheritance.

Wednesday - God Is Our Inheritance

"I say to myself, 'The LORD is my portion; therefore I will wait for him.'" Lamentations 3:24 (NIVUK)

Yesterday we looked at how God's people are His portion and that the word *portion* means inheritance. The New Living Translation puts it this way: "I say to myself, *"The Lord is my inheritance; therefore, I will hope in him!"* Lamentations 3:24 (NLT)

Maybe because English is, in many way,s such a limited language, the word portion brings to my mind a <u>bit</u>, or <u>slice</u> ,of something; as in a slice of pie. I picture a family sitting round a table dividing the pie up - *"That's your little bit"* and squabbling over who might have got more than someone else. But this word in, context, in the original language, means nothing like that. In fact it's the complete opposite. "*Portion*" here means *everything*, "my entire inheritance." The <u>lot</u> - the whole pie! God, quite literally, is our everything.

God Himself is our inheritance

In our churches we speak, sing, and preach a lot about God's love, grace, mercy, faithfulness, and goodness; how He provides for our needs, heals us and delivers us. All these are true, of course they are, but these things that God does <u>for</u> us, and the things He gives <u>to</u> us are not our inheritance. If that were so, it would make the relationship all about us.

What Jeremiah is saying here in that one little word *'portion,'* is that <u>God Himself,</u> is the sum total of his soul's inheritance. In God is everything Jeremiah possessed or desired.

The Psalmists also recognised this

Lord, <u>you alone</u> are my inheritance, my cup of blessing. Psalm 16:5 (NLT).
There are two schools of thought as to whether David or Asaph was the author of the following Psalm, however the heart of the Psalm is the same; God is everything I have, need and could ever need: *"Whom have I in heaven but you? And earth has nothing I desire besides you. My flesh and my heart may fail, but God is the strength of my heart <u>and my portion for ever.</u>"* Psalms 73:25-26 (NIVUK)

What is an inheritance?

When you inherit something, you take possession of it. It becomes fully yours. Please don't get me wrong here, I'm not going to say that we *own* the Lord. But what I am saying is that if you are His, through faith in Jesus Christ, then you own the right to be called His child: *"to those who believed in his name, he gave the right to become children of God –"* John 1:12 (NIVUK)

Our inheritance is to be enjoyed now and the future

The resources God makes available to us are limitless, as is His love - God doesn't love in part. He doesn't hold back. He isn't sparing, stingy, or partial in His love, God gives one hundred percent of Himself to all of His children:
"I pray that from his glorious, unlimited resources he will empower you with inner strength through his Spirit. Then Christ will make his home in your hearts as you trust in him. Your roots will grow down into God's love and keep you strong. And may

you have the power to understand, as all God's people should, how wide, how long, how high, and how deep his love is. May you experience the love of Christ, though it is too great to understand fully. Then you will be made complete with all the fullness of life and power that comes from God." Ephesians 3:16-19 (NLT)

It's mind boggling but true; God is not only knowable but He is everything we need. God Himself, not what He can give us or do for us, but He is the inheritance of His children.

Thursday - You Gave Them To Me

"I have revealed you to the ones you gave me from this world. They were always yours. You gave them to me, and they have kept your word." John 17:6 (NLT).

Do you ever wonder what Jesus <u>really</u> thinks of you? All you need to do in those times is to open your Bible and read Jesus' prayer for us, His disciples, in John 17.

Remember whose you are

If you ever have moments, as most of us do, when you feel alone in the world, or unloved, this prayer of Jesus' is so powerfully 'perspective changing'.

I'd encourage you to read it all, it's only 26 verses long, yet in it we catch a glimpse of the heart of Jesus towards His disciples. Jesus looks at us and says, *"You're mine. My Father gave you to me."*

In John 17 see Jesus, soon to face crucifixion, His heart filled not with terror at his imminent torture and death, but with the deepest love and concern for His disciples, how <u>they</u> were going to feel, and what <u>they</u> were going to face. *"You gave them to me,"* He says to The Father.

This prayer was not for the whole world, but for all Jesus'

disciples who would carry His message of love and redemption *to* the world. And it was not only the twelve who had walked with Jesus that were heavily on His heart in those moments, but all disciples, then and the ones that were to come: *"I am praying not only for these disciples but also for all who will ever believe in me through their message.* John 17:20 (NLT).

You're part of an incredible, unbreakable union

"I pray that they will all be one, just as you and I are one; as you are in me, Father and I am in you." John 17:21a (NLT).
"I am in them and you are in me. May they experience such perfect unity that the world will know that you sent me and that you love them as much as you love me." John 17:23 (NLT)

The intimacy, and familiarity, with which Jesus speaks to the Father is clearly evident throughout this prayer. From before the foundation of the world, Jesus, God the Father and Holy Spirit have shared a perfect, loving union. The most incredible thing is that God made a way, through Jesus, for us to be part of this perfect union.

We have that same loving intimacy with God the Father; the same familiarity. We call Him '*Abba*' - Daddy: *"you received God's Spirit when he adopted you as his own children. Now we call him, "Abba, Father." For his Spirit joins with our spirit to affirm that we are God's children.* Romans 8:15-16 (NLT)

Next time you feel lonely or unloved, do your heart a world of good by reading John seventeen slowly, taking in and savouring every word.It doesn't matter whether you have known Jesus for five weeks, five years or fifty years, we all need to remind ourselves of these basic truths from time to time!

Friday - Know Who You Are! -1

"Anyone who listens to the word but does not do what it says is like someone who looks at his face in a mirror and, after looking at himself, goes away and immediately forgets what he looks like." James 1: 23-24 (NIV)

The Word of God repeatedly affirms our identity in Christ, yet we so quickly and easily forget. James perfectly sums up this spiritual malady. Let's have another look in the mirror today, and remind ourselves of what we look like to God.

Part of a much bigger picture

When you feel insignificant, lonely, sad, discouraged or any of those other emotions we all struggle with from time to time, remember that God is building something unshakable and unstoppable and that as His child, you are part it!

"Come and be his "living stones" who are continually being assembled into a sanctuary for God. For now you serve as holy priests, offering up spiritual sacrifices that he readily accepts through Jesus Christ. For it says in Scripture: Look! I lay a cornerstone in Zion, a chosen and priceless stone! And whoever believes in him will certainly not be disappointed. As believers you know his great worth—indeed, his preciousness is imparted to you. But for those who do not believe: The stone that the builders rejected and discarded has now become the

cornerstone" 1 Peter 2:5-7 (TPT)

A work in progress

Paul wrote to the Philippians,"I pray with great faith for you, because I'm fully convinced that the One who began this glorious work in you will faithfully continue the process of maturing you and will put his finishing touches to it until the unveiling of our Lord Jesus Christ!" Philippians 1:6 (TPT)

A child of God

"For it was always in his perfect plan to adopt us as his delightful children, through our union with Jesus, the Anointed One, so that his tremendous love that cascades over us would glorify his grace—for the same love he has for his Beloved One, Jesus, he has for us. And this unfolding plan brings him great pleasure!" Ephesians 1:5-6 (TPT)

"You have been adopted into God's family. It's a legally binding contract; you are now His child. Nothing can undo that fact.

"You have all become true children of God by faith in Jesus the Anointed One!" Galatians 3:26 (TPT)

"Look with wonder at the depth of the Father's marvelous love that he has lavished on us! He has called us and made us his very own beloved children. The reason the world doesn't recognize who we are is that they didn't recognize him." 1 John 3:1 (TPT)

"Now we're no longer living like slaves under the law, but we enjoy being God's very own sons and daughters! And because we're his, we can access everything our Father has—for we are heirs of God through Jesus, the Messiah!" Galatians 4:7 (TPT)

Bought at a great price

You belong to Jesus, paid for with His own blood. He bought you with all your baggage, bad habits and hang ups, and your purchase is complete. He will not decide at some later date that, actually He's disappointed with you would like to 'return' you.

"You were God's expensive purchase, paid for with tears of blood, so by all means, then, use your body to bring glory to God!" 1 Corinthians 6:20 (TPT)

Chosen and dearly loved
"You are always and dearly loved by God! So robe yourself with virtues of God, since you have been divinely chosen to be holy." *Colossians 3:12a (TPT)*

Jesus' friend
I no longer call you servants, because a servant does not k"now his master's business. Instead, I have called you friends, for everything that I learned from my Father I have made known to you." John 15:15 (NIVUK)

A purpose filled life
Do you long to know what God's plan is for your life? It's written in scripture, plain as day. "For we are God's handiwork, created in Christ Jesus to do good works, which God prepared in advance for us to do." Ephesians 2:10 (NIVUK)
"So be very careful how you live, not being like those with no understanding, but live honorably with true wisdom, for we are living in evil times. Take full advantage of every day as you spend your life for his purposes. And don't live foolishly for then you will have discernment to fully understand God's will." Ephesians 5:15-17 (TPT)

Christ's ambassadors
You are His image bearer; His representative to everyone you meet. As the saying goes, "your life might be the only Bible some people ever read."
"We are ambassadors of the Anointed One who carry the message of Christ to the world, as though God were tenderly pleading with them directly through our lips. So we tenderly plead with you on Christ's behalf, "Turn back to God and be

reconciled to him." 2 Corinthians 5:20 (TPT)
"For when you demonstrate the same love I have for you by loving one another, everyone will know that you're my true followers." John 13:35 (TPT)
"Live honorable lives as you mix with unbelievers, even though they accuse you of being evildoers. For they will see your beautiful works and have a reason to glorify God in the day he visits us." (1 Peter 2:12 TPT)

Commissioned

"You didn't choose me, but I've chosen and commissioned you to go into the world to bear fruit. And your fruit will last, because whatever you ask of my Father, for my sake, he will give it to you!" John 15:16 (TPT)

"Now wherever you go, make disciples of all nations, baptizing them in the name of the Father, the Son, and the Holy Spirit. And teach them to faithfully follow all that I have commanded you. And never forget that I am with you every day, even to the completion of this age." Matthew 28:19-20 (TPT)

Saturday - A New Name

"Jesus looked at him and said, 'You are Simon son of John. You will be called Cephas' (which, when translated, is Peter))." John 1:42 (NIVUK)

Jesus never did or said anything, just for the sake of it. Everything action and word was purposefu,l and led by His Father. (John 5:19). I believe Jesus looked at Simon and, seeing supernaturally, deep into his soul, named Simon who he was *to become* - the man that God *already saw him as.* A bit like Gideon, when God called him "mighty man of valour," long before Gideon had outwardly lived up to such a name.

Jesus has a way of doing that! His piercing gaze sees right into the heart, shining light into every little 'corner.' He knows us inside out. Just before this encounter with Simon, Jesus met Nathaniel, and we see how He summed up Nathaniel's character from just a glance (a distant glance at that!): *"When Jesus saw Nathanael approaching, he said of him, 'Here truly is an Israelite in whom there is no deceit."* John 1:47 (NIVUK)

What's in a Name?

I had a godly teacher when I was nine years old who called me a "born artist." I still feel the impact of his words now, all these years later and they still have the power to make me feel ten feet tall. I was only a child, I hadn't yet painted, or created anything of much significance, but my teacher saw potential in me that no one else had seen, and his words made me feel validated, noticed and appreciated. I *wanted* to become what he had called me, *and eventually I did, although it was many years later.* I wonder if, in a much bigger way, was this how Simon felt when Jesus called Him by his new name.

A New Name

Jesus looked right into Simon's soul, and He didn't recoil when He saw Simon's tendency towards impetuousness that frequently got him into trouble. He didn't focus on Simon's failures; Jesus saw and validated something deeply true about him that Simon himself probably hadn't recognised, and Jesus spoke that over Simon, giving him his true name - Cephas -Peter-<u>Rock</u>. Simon wasn't living as that person just yet. But Jesus *knew* his true potential and spoke that over him. He spoke it again in Matthew sixteen: "*Jesus replied, 'Blessed are you, Simon son of Jonah, for this was not revealed to you by flesh and blood, but by my Father in heaven. And I tell you that you are Peter, and on this rock I will build my church, and the gates of Hades will not overcome it.*" Matthew 16:17-18 (NIVUK)

Did Peter live up to his new name?

We all know the awful thing Peter did. I don't think we need to dwell on it. We know too, the affirming words that Jesus had spoken over Peter in Matthew 16. It's clear that at the time of Peter's three-time denial that, although he had grasped who *Jesus* was, Peter still hadn't grasped who *he*, Peter, was.

Fast forward to the book of Acts though, and we find a transformed Peter! Here he is boldly preaching and teaching, filled with the Holy Spirit and power. In Acts chapter four, Peter and John preach to a crowd and *five thousand* people become believers! They were both arrested and hauled before the religious leaders, who asked, "by whose authority" they had been preaching and healing people. Peter answered that it was by the authority, and in the name of Jesus Christ. You might want to go and read this chapter in Acts again for yourself, because the interaction between the religious council and Peter and John is truly inspiring!

This is what happens to someone who grasps hold of their true identity in Christ - someone who begins live up to the way <u>Jesus</u> sees them: "The members of the council were amazed when they saw the boldness of Peter and John, for they could see that they were ordinary men with no special training in the Scriptures. They also recognized them as men who had been with Jesus." Acts 4:13 (NLT).

The council recognised Peter and John as men who had been with Jesus. Do people look at you and me and recognise us as men and women who have been in the company of Jesus?

Defined by Jesus

Jesus looks at you with His eyes of fire and sees right inside you, deep inside your soul, where no one else sees. He knows all your flaws, weaknesses, and failures; all your deepest secrets, and guess what? He doesn't recoil from you. Jesus sees past those things you try to keep hidden, to who you truly are, in Him. Here are just some of the things you are called by the One who created you and loves you more than you beyond measure:

Forgiven: Colossians 3:13

Child of God: 1 John 3:1

Justified and Reconciled: Romans 5:9-10

Royal, Holy, *His Own*: 2 Peter 2:9

Chosen: Colossians 3:12

Dearly Loved: also Colossians 3:12

Chosen and Faithful: Revelation 17:14

He spoke everything that lives into being, so surely His words about you matter. These Living Words spoken and written about you define who you *are*, not only today but every day, and for all eternity!

Sunday - A Royal Priesthood, A Holy Nation

"But you are a chosen people, a royal priesthood, a holy nation, God's special possession, that you may declare the praises of him who called you out of darkness into his wonderful light. Once you were not a people, but now you are the people of God; once you had not received mercy, but now you have received mercy." 1 Peter 2:9-10 (NIVUK)

So many Christians go through life completely missing this incredible truth - the wonder of the great honour bestowed upon us, God's people. Being a Christian is so much more than going to church meetings once or twice a week for the rest of our lives, waiting to one day be with Jesus in glory. We are His chosen people. A royal priesthood. A holy nation. God's special possession. All of these things are *now,* while we live here in the earth.

A chosen people, His own special possession

The special privilege that once belonged exclusively to Israel; their 'chosen-ness,' by God, the priesthood and holiness, are now bestowed by God upon every believer in Jesus Christ, His Son. It's *because* we belong to Jesus that we are special, it wasn't because we are special that Jesus chose us. An ordinary, everyday item becomes *greatly* significant, even precious, when it is treasured by the person to whom it belongs. Jesus treasures us, His people. Once ordinary people now have great significance and value because we belong to Him. Jesus was prepared to pay the highest price for us, so highly did He value us, and want us.

A royal priesthood and holy nation

The offices of *royalty* and *priesthood* were once jealously separated in Israel. But Jesus, who is our King, and Priest, has brought them together in, and for His people.
Ordinary people under the Old Covenant could not go into the presence of God; it was unthinkable! Only a ritually clean priest could offer sacrifices on behalf of the people. And only the High Priest could go behind the *veil*, into the holy of holies, the place where the Ark of the Covenant resided, the symbol of God's presence and glory.

As Jesus sighed His last triumphant breath on the cross, the veil was torn in two! *"At that moment the curtain of the temple was torn in two from top to bottom."* Matthew 27:51 (NIVUK). The significance of this is huge for us. Now sanctified by His grace, we are welcomed with open arms into the presence of God. No more curtain. We can freely come before God and minister to His heart by offering up our spiritual sacrifices of worship, praise and prayer.

I frequently hear people talk about 'finding your tribe,' in the sense of finding a group of likeminded people to 'run with'. But Believers don't need to do that. We have found our 'tribe!' We once were without these privileges, we had no hope of obtaining them. But God In His incredible mercy, has set us apart for Himself. We, who had no sense of belonging, now belong to a whole new people group, a new Kingdom: *"and with your blood you purchased for God persons from every tribe and language and people and nation. You have made them to be a kingdom and priests to serve our God, and they will reign on the earth.'"* Revelation 5:9-10 (NIVUK)

* * *

The entire focus and purpose of our lives changes with this knowledge. We are *in* this world, but not *of* it; we are merely passing through. We belong to a Kingdom that will never end, ruled by the King of kings, whose word is the final authority. We are not only His subjects, but His sons and daughters. As such, we have been set apart from this world for relationship with Him and to fulfill His purposes.

This simply means that we <u>choose</u> to be people of obedient faith, honour and love, reflecting Jesus in our daily lives and our own spheres of life; "making the most of every opportunity" to live out our high calling as priests of the Most High God, as Ephesians 5:16 tells us:
"So be very careful how you live, not being like those with no understanding, but live honorably with true wisdom, for we are living in evil times. <u>Take full advantage of every day as you spend your life for his purposes.</u>" Ephesians 5:15-16 9TPT)

His Purposes

His purposes. In the mundane, in the everyday, ordinary things of our lives; we are to live out our King's purposes. That's an honour beyond words. What are His purposes? Jesus said it quite plainly, several times.

"The Spirit of the Lord is on me, because he has anointed me to proclaim good news to the poor. He has sent me to proclaim freedom for the prisoners and recovery of sight for the blind, to set the oppressed free, to proclaim the year of the Lord's favour."Luke 4:18-19 (NIVUK)

"I have not come to call the righteous, but sinners." Mark 2:17 NIVUK

He has called, anointed and commissioned every single one of us to get out there and "spend our lives for His Kingdom purposes," in partnership with Him.

Living On Purpose

Monday - Choose this day....

"But if you refuse to serve the Lord, then choose today whom you will serve. Would you prefer the gods your ancestors served beyond the Euphrates? Or will it be the gods of the Amorites in whose land you now live? But as for me and my family, we will serve the Lord." Joshua 24:15 (NLT)

You were created for more!

Do you suffer from spiritual inertia? Perhaps you would love to serve the Lord with enthusiasm but you feel your ideas are never taken seriously, you're always overlooked, you applied to Bible college and were not accepted, you auditioned for your church's worship team and didn't 'make it.' Perhaps you dreamed of being a missionary to a needy country on the other side of the world but circumstances didn't allow for this to happen.

Many Christians feel that their lives are purposeless and yet deep down there is an ongoing, unrelenting nudge on the inside that whispers, *"You were born for this."* What is the *'this'* that people long for?

You are not wrong, you definitely *were* created for more! You have a God-designed assignment, written into your very DNA. Maybe you have been waiting for a sign, a confirmation, an affirmation, someone or something to establish you, empower you, or give you permission to step-up. You may have had to wrestle doubt and disappointment, but don't *settle,* don't give up, and don't be deterred. There's a simple principle that you need to follow, and it's this: *"choose this day whom you will serve,"* will it be the God of the Bible, who created you <u>with</u> purpose, <u>for</u> a purpose, or the gods you served before you knew Him? Those ones of defeatism and "what's the point?"

You have been created with purpose, for a purpose
The purpose you were created for was first, and foremost, <u>for His good pleasure</u>. God made us to enjoy intimate relationship with Him. These words of Jesus' say it as plain as day: *"Teacher, which is the most important commandment in the law of Moses?" Jesus replied, "You must love the LORD your God with all your heart, all your soul, and all your mind.' <u>This is the first and greatest commandment.</u>"* Matthew 22:36-38 (NLT)

Notice, the 'first and greatest commandment,' the greatest thing that God's heart yearns for, is that we would love Him. He could have said, 'serve me,' first, but He said 'love me.'
Our desire to serve God will grow stronger, when the truth of His immeasurable love for us sinks in and takes root in our hearts. God loves us with an *everlasting love!* (Jeremiah 33:3). We are in a two-way love relationship with the King of kings. We could never love Jesus as much as He loves us, its impossible, but He wants our willing devotion.

If you are going to *choose this day to serve <u>Him</u>,* then choose, as well, to <u>believe</u> what He says about you, in spite of what your present circumstances may tell you. Don't wait for years, until you feel better, or circumstance fit better, or fame and fortune come your way, before you serve Him. You could just miss out on some of your best years with God!

Choose *this day* - today - whom you will serve. When you do, and you start walking in your God-given purposes, the joy, peace, and relief that fills your soul is indescribable. You'll find that you can't quite remember where your own dreams start and end; where God's begin, because they're so intermingled.

How do we serve Him?

Everyone wants to make their mark in the world, it's instinctive; nobody wants to just live, die and be forgotten. But we believers in Jesus are here to make His mark on the world, not our own. We are to be His image bearers and ambassadors - to impact our own little spheres of influence for His name's sake, wherever we are, and whatever we do. Some are called into 'full-time' Christian ministry but this has nothing to do with status, or value in God's eyes. Those people are not more called that you or me. We are in fact *all* called to full time ministry, in whatever regular job we do - and even when we are out walking the dog, shopping, doing the school run, going to the gym. We are never 'off duty.'

Every day, each one of us is one very small decision away from a life of mediocrity, or a potent, Spirit-filled, magnificent one! The decision is this: choose *this day* whom you will serve.

Tuesday - Sowing Weeds

"I said to myself, "I will watch what I do and not sin in what I say. I will hold my tongue when the ungodly are around me. Psalm 30:1 (NLT)

A problem halved?

A problem shared is a problem halved. Have you ever heard this 'wise' urban proverb? I believe that in the church, we have to be extremely careful of certain kinds of sharing. Problems shared carelessly, without due diligence, may well will be problems *multiplied,* rather than halved.

There are times we might feel that we just *have to* share with someone how we are feeling. But its important to remember that once said, our words can never be unsaid. The words we release are seeds sown. They take on a of life of their own, bringing either life or death. (Proverbs 18:21). I may be struggling with negative thoughts, doubts, or fears, but the moment those thoughts are released from my lips, they will multiply, so that it is no longer only me that has the problem. There's a saying *"don't make your problems mine!"* That is literally what we do when we are not careful with our words. We make our problems everybody else's.

Weed spreading.

The negative seed 'harvest' may not be immediate. The fertile heart-soil of your friend's heart will be too busy listening, trying to offer comfort. Then, as she goes away and thinks about what you've shared, those words of discouragement, doubt, fear, anger, maybe just plain gossip, start to take root.

Your words might niggle at your caring friend's heart; shake her own faith a little, or cause her to call into question the integrity of the person you have a grievance against. You might feel better because you have unburdened yourself, but in truth, all you have done is sow a load of weed-seeds into the heart of the one listening. The poor, unsuspecting friend will soon have a crop of weeds growing in her own heart, until at some point she feels the need to unburden herself of them. And so the weeds spreads further.

Zip that lip

Psalm 39 (see above) opens with David trying hard to not speak. It is clear that he had got to a point where he was struggling to understand God's work in his life and was perhaps finding it hard to see God's justice in it all. He really wanted to let rip; to give vent to all his hurt and pain.

But David knew that his thoughts at that moment were too dark and painful to utter out loud. Especially within earshot of *"the ungodly."* However he might be feeling, David had the spiritual maturity to know that it was temporary, and he was not going to expressed it in front of unbelievers. We can easily forget that unbelievers watch us with interest, and not necessarily because they are interested in knowing God, but because they are looking for ways to pick holes in the claims we have made about God in the good times. What do we say about God's faithfulness, goodness, love, and mercy when the pressure is on? Do we bad-mouth God? We don't have to actually take His name in vain to do so. Just stating our negative emotions, doubts, and fears, in company speaks volumes. We're saying, essentially, "I don't *really* believe God - I don't trust Him." Those words will have a lasting impression on the people listening to. *Let's not sow be weed sowers!*

David sensed in his spirit that he should be silent. In the following verse, he writes about how the harder he tries to remain quiet, the greater the turmoil grows inside him. *"But as I stood there in silence, not even speaking of good things he turmoil within me grew worse.The more I thought about it, the hotter I got, igniting a fire of words"* Psalm 39:2-3 (NLT)

Don't we all experience this at times? We feel the urge to defend ourselves, stand up for our rights, give someone a piece of our mind. We simmer and boil as we struggle to keep silent. That's when we're in danger of sowing weeds.
David may well have found momentary satisfaction, had he spewed out all the negativity that was boiling away inside him, all over anyone unfortunate enough to be nearby. But I'm so glad he didn't. Because God teaches us a valuable lesson through this.

When David eventually <u>did</u> speak, it was not the words he had been fighting to keep down. Instead, David chose words that edified both himself and us today as we read this Psalm.

He begins by remembering who he, a puny man is in comparison to God, in all his goodness, justice and loving discipline. Then David goes on to look at how fleeting life is, and how futile it is to waste it in rebellion and complaint. David's words begin to put his circumstances and his thoughts back into perspective. *"Lord, <u>remind me </u>how brief my time on earth will be. <u>Remind me</u> that my days are numbered - how fleeting my life is. You have made my life no longer than the width of my hand. My entire lifetime is just a moment to you, at best, each of us is but a breath." Psalm 30:4-5 (NLT)*

* * *

God is the One we need to pour our hearts out to, <u>not</u> in a barrage of negativity, and complaint, but following David's example. In Psalm 141 we find another example from David: *"I call to you, Lord, come quickly to me; hear me when I call to you. May my prayer be set before you <u>like incense;</u> may the lifting up of my hands be like the evening sacrifice."* Psalm 141:1 (NLT)

How could my prayer be 'incense' to God if it reeks of negativity and complaint against Him and His people? David continues in the next verse with the words, *"Set a guard over my mouth, Lord; keep watch over the door of my lips"* Psalm 141:3 (NLT)

Let this be our prayer today and always.

Wednesday - Well Meant Words

"Wise words satisfy like a good meal; the right words bring satisfaction. The tongue can bring death or life; those who love to talk will reap the consequences." Proverbs 18:20-21 (NLT)

Sowing life or death

The tongue is like a seed dispenser. Every single word we speak has the potential to take root and grow. A few fertile words into just the right soil conditions are similar to scattering seeds to produce an entire harvest in season. This is a sobering thought and an awesome responsibility!

We choose the words we speak, or don't speak; a wise person, keeping in step with the Holy Spirit, will learn when to speak and when to keep silent. When we understand the creative and destructive power of our words, great things can start to happen in the everyday situations we face, and the people we come into contact with.

In the above verse, we are warned that the tongue has the power of life and death. Our words have the power to build people up or destroy them. Many of us may have used our mouths for demolition at some time in our lives, but as disciples of Jesus we have a responsibility to master our mouths; to sow life, and hope, with our words and to ensure that our words build up, rather than tear down.

Well intentioned (but misinformed) words

There's an account in Luke's Gospel where Jesus rebuked His disciples for their words. Here, we find Jesus on route to Jerusalem to face His ultimate calling. But although Jesus knows what's awaits Him in Jerusalem, He hasn't lost focus on the here and now. He's still listening to, and obeying His Father. For Jesus to take that particular route to Jerusalem was unusual; and to attempt to find hospitality in a Samaritan village was still more unusual, but Jesus "sent messengers ahead" to enquire, probably seeking accommodation, and somewhere to rest, and eat. The town sent back word rejecting Him! James and John, were aghast. *"Lord, if you wanted to, you could command fire to fall down from heaven just like Elijah did and destroy all these wicked people."* Luke 9:54 (TPT)

Yes, if He had wanted to, Jesus could have done just that. But, firstly Jesus knew the power of words, so He was hardly going to start uttering 'fiery' ones! Jesus hadn't taken the rejection personally. Secondly, He *didn't* want to, (they had said 'if you wanted' to) because that was neither Jesus' nature or His calling from God. The reason He came, Jesus explained to them, was not to destroy life, but to bring life! *"Jesus rebuked them sharply, saying, 'Don't you realize what comes from your hearts when you say that? For the Son of Man did not come to destroy life, but to bring life to the earth."* Luke 9:55 (TPT)

This teaches us that we need to watch <u>even</u> those words of ours that are well intentioned. James' and John's words were well meant, but they didn't *think* before they spoke, or perhaps they were too caught up in their righteous indignation, and fervour, their sense that they should 'take a stand for Jesus.'

Knowing when to zip it

Sometimes we say silly things, that can damage people. The husband of a friend of mine was facing a cancer scare a few

years ago, and had been to the hospital for a series of tests.
During their long wait for the results, many people prayed.
Others spoke encouraging, and prophetic words to him. All fine,
good things to do, if directed by the Lord to do so. But my
friends had to contend with *some* people who spoke *well meant,*
but *unwise* words. Words such as; *"ah he'll be fine, God is
good"*. Those were 'idle words.' They were not untrue, because
yes, God *is* good, but those people had not been given any
revelation from God that my friend was going to be healed. So to
equate 'he'll be fine,' with the goodness of God is walking in
thin ice.
That couple know, and believe with all their hearts that God is
good. But what if that man had not received the all-clear from his
doctor? Would that have called into question the goodness of
God in the hearts and minds of other people who had observed,
and listened to, those idle words? Many a New Christian has
been caused to stumble by such foolish, well intended words.

All those well-meaning people needed to do was to phrase their
words something like this: *"I'm praying for your husband,
trusting in God's goodness for his healing."*
It isn't as difficult as it sounds, to change our speech habits, and
we can ask God to teach us, when to speak, when to be silent,
and how to speak words that come straight from His heart.

Thursday - Tending Your Heart-Garden

"The LORD will guide you always; he will satisfy your needs in a sun-scorched land and will strengthen your frame. You will be like a well-watered garden, like a spring whose waters never fail." Isaiah 58:11 (NIVUK)

I lived with a noxious weed in the 'garden of my heart,' for over twenty years, because I had chosen to take to heart something hurtful said to me in my mid twenties. As we know, our words are seeds, and I had let those words go right into the depth of my heart, and take root. Every time I mulled over the words, even though I paid lip-service to having forgiven that person, I watered those seedling words, and they grew a bit more in significance, until they became a fully fledged weed crop, with sharp thorns. It didn't matter how many sermons I listened to on my identity in Christ, how many books I read about who God says I am. It didn't matter how often friends, or family told me I was loved, and accepted, because just below the surface, those thorns were constantly stabbing into my soul, again, and again. That's is, until a few years ago, when the Holy Spirit showed me that until I *genuinely* forgave, I was not going to be free.

Forgiveness is a powerful weed killer!

I have always loved that scripture in Isaiah that I opened this devotional with; God promises: *"You will be like a well-watered garden, like a spring whose waters never fail."* But … there arecertain conditions to be met, before that promise. We sometimes like to quote encouraging verses, and forget the context. Before the Lord would satisfy my needs 'in a sun scorched land' there were some things in my life I needed to attend to.

A lack of Obedience

This is how the chapter starts: *"Shout with the voice of a trumpet blast. Shout aloud! Don't be timid. Tell my people Israel of their sins! Yet they act so pious! They come to the Temple every day and seem delighted to learn all about me. They act like a righteous nation that would never abandon the laws of its God. They ask me to take action on their behalf, pretending they want to be near me.*

"No, this is the kind of fasting I want: Free those who are wrongly imprisoned; lighten the burden of those who work for you. Let the oppressed go free, and remove the chains that bind people." Isaiah 58:1-2, 6 (NLT).

The last part of verse six, in The Message Translation says: *"free the oppressed, cancel debts."* (MSG)

Yes, an injustice had been committed against me, but by holding onto this, by rehashing it in my mind, along with all the accompanying unfavourable thoughts towards that person, *I was now the unjust one.* My own great debt has been cancelled, and I was being just like the unmerciful man in the parable Jesus told in Matthew 18:21-35.

The moment I made the choice to *really* forgive that person, and to say the words out loud, "Lord I am cancelling his debt, as you have so graciously cancelled mine," that thorny weed was ripped from my heart, and the light of God's Love was able to get to the fledgling seeds trying to grow in my heart - all *His* truths about me. My heart become, once again, a 'well watered garden.'

Keep On Top of The Weeding

"Keep vigilant watch over your heart; that's where life starts. Don't talk out of both sides of your mouth; avoid careless banter, white lies, and gossip." Proverbs 4:23-24 (MSG)

The spiritual diligence we need to apply to our hearts, is a bit like keeping ahead of the weeds in a garden. Weeds will spring up; untended, they choke the life out of the good plants. Sometimes, as we pull them out, just the stalk breaks off, leaving the root in the soil, so we need to make sure the whole thing is uprooted, and replaced with the truths of God's good seeds instead: *"My child, pay attention to what I say. Listen carefully to my words. Don't lose sight of them. Let them penetrate deep into your heart, for they bring life to those who find them, and healing to their whole body."* Proverbs 4:20-22 (NLT)

Tearing out and re-planting

Whatever particular type of weed is growing in your heart-garden, remember, these don't stay small and innocuous. We don't always spot the weeds, but we can ask God to highlight them with the truth and light of His Word. And we can humbly submit to one another, Godly friends, and leaders, to help us to see those weeds in our lives. Here are three common 'heart weeds' and powerful weed killer to pour on them:

Guilt and unworthiness: *"So now there is no condemnation for those who belong to Christ Jesus."* Romans 8:1 (NLT)
God doesn't love me: *"I have loved you with an everlasting love; I have drawn you with unfailing kindness."* Jeremiah 31:3 (NIVUK)
I can't forgive: *"I can do all this through him who gives me strength."* Philippians 4:13 (NIVUK)

Here are a few seeds to plant and cultivate instead, concerning who you are and Who He is:
You are His friend: John 15:15

You're adopted as His Child: Galatians 4:7
You are a citizen of heaven: Philippians 3:20-21
You are a branch of the True Vine *(Jesus):* John 15:5

His Love endures forever: 1 Chronicles 16:34; Psalm 118:1-4
His Faithfulness Endures forever: (Psalm 117:2
His Name is a Strong Tower: Proverbs 18:10
He is Tender Hearted: Matthew 6:26,30 Luke 1:78,79
He is Just: Psalm 97:7-8
He is slow to anger and compassionate: Psalm 103:8
He abounds in mercy and love: Psalm 103:8
He provides for your every need: Philippians 4:19

Friday - Dead, or Comatose?

"Take advantage of every opportunity to be a blessing to others, especially to our brothers and sisters in the family of faith!"
Galatians 6:9-10 (TPT)

A shocking fake news story

A fake news report did the rounds of social media a few years ago. It was actually based on a fake news report in a Newspaper from January 2001. The headline and story went something like this:

<u>Office worker dead at desk for 5 days!</u>

"Bosses of a publishing firm are trying to work out why no one noticed that one of their employees had been sitting, dead, at his desk for five days, before anyone asked if he was feeling okay. George Turklebaum, 51, who had been employed as a proof-reader at a New York firm for 30 years, had a heart attack in the open-plan office he shared with twenty three other workers. He quietly passed away on Monday, but nobody noticed until Saturday morning when an office cleaner asked why he was working during the weekend.

His boss Elliot Wachiaski said: "George was always the first guy in each morning and the last to leave at night, so no one found it unusual that he was in the same position all that time, and didn't say anything. He was always absorbed in his work and kept much to himself."

A post mortem examination revealed that he had been dead for five days after suffering a coronary. Ironically, George was proofreading manuscripts of medical textbooks when he died."

A shocking true news story

This story, at the time, was really shocking, and made quite an impact. People were outraged and saddened, imagine the loneliness the poor man must have felt - the isolation. What heartless coworkers. It was probably a relief then, when it turned out to be a hoax.

But do you know what the great tragedy is? A similar story, and one that is not fake news; not a hoax, happens every day in our churches, all over the world. You could have a 'co-worker' who sits right beside you every week in your church, who is slowly slipping into a coma, while nobody notices or cares. Perhaps you are that person. Maybe you feel 'dead' on the inside, (you are not, really if you truly have new life in Jesus Christ).

"Share each other's burdens, and in this way obey the law of Christ." Galatians 6:2 (NLT)

Are we not commanded, to love one another? To bear one another's burdens? When did you or I honestly look into the eyes of the person we usually sit next to at church and see past the facade that we all wear? Sometimes we need to push past the hurried "how are you," I'm fine thanks," conversations we have at church and take time to ask, 'but are you fine, really?"

Remember that River of life we have, flowing out of us? Let's allow it to really flow, and affect those around us with the life of Jesus.

Saturday - Not Quitters!

"Let us not become weary in doing good, for at the proper time we will reap a harvest if we do not give up." Galatians 6:9 (NIVUK)

Not too bad

We have some ways of greeting each other in Northern Ireland that would sound funny, or strange, to people from outside. One of these is "what about you?" - meaning 'hello, how are you?' all rolled into one. The usual response to this is, "not too bad." The amusing thing is, that whether the responder is over the moon with happiness, or in the pit of despair, the response remains the same. *Not too bad.*

The Quitters Club

Some Believers have a "not too bad" approach to Christian living. Some have never risen above the level of 'all right,' and mediocre. Ask them the question "how are you?" and they'll tell you, I'm fine, but in truth, they are not really. Underneath, there is the nagging feeling that *there's more.* The problem is, they have become weary, and given up on their God-given dreams.

I've heard it said that the one of the biggest organisations in the world is the Quitter's Club. All quitters are welcome to join. The club never actually meets, there'd be no point; the members would only quit coming! There are no fees, the members quit paying them long ago. The Quitter's Club is comprises of people who, faced with a tough job, a hard situation, or a tough failure, have lost heart, thrown in the towel, and quit.

Norman Vincent Peale, author of "The Power of Positive Thinking" said: *"It's always too soon to quit."* A very thought provoking quote; but actually the Holy Spirit spoke the 'original version' of it through Paul, in Galatians 6:9!

Don't grow weary

Paul says don't grow weary. This is both an admonishment and a warning. What does Paul mean by *don't grow weary*? That's a tall order; surely we all get tired? Paul isn't talking about the normal, physical tiredness we all experience. He's speaking of another kind of tiredness; a weariness of heart and mind, which results in a ministry that is merely a dull, lifeless, routine. A same-old-same-old, joyless approach to the work of God. We could put Paul's admonition this way: *It is one thing to grow weary in serving God, but watch that you don't grow weary of serving God.* When the first happens, we can rest and replenish our strength. But the latter is a far more dangerous thing. It's a heart attitude that starts to seep out of the weary one.

The priests in Malachi chapter one had developed this kind of attitude to the work of Lord. (I'd recommend reading it.) We see, from the Lord's response to their offerings, how He feels about a half-hearted approach to Him, as though we were doing Him a favour! *"My name will be great among the nations, from where the sun rises to where it sets. In every place incense and pure offerings will be brought to me, because my name will be great among the nations,' says the LORD Almighty. 'But you profane it by saying, "The Lord's table is defiled," and, "Its food is contemptible." And you say, "What a burden!" and you sniff at it contemptuously,' says the LORD Almighty. 'When you bring injured, lame or diseased animals and offer them as sacrifices, should I accept them from your hands?' says the LORD."*

Malachi 1:11-13 (NIVUK)

<u>We</u> are priests: *"To him who loves us and has freed us from our sins by his blood, and has made us to be a kingdom and priests to serve his God and Father "* Revelation 1:5-6 (NIVUK)
When we cease to serve God from a heart filled with love and worship, we cease to be joyful 'co-workers' with God, and become, instead, menials and slaves. We are miserable, and we make everyone around us miserable.

The promise of a harvest

If there is one labourer in this life who understands persistence, endurance, and patienc,e it's the farmer. First, he has to prepare the soil. Then sow the seed, then he has to contend with weeds, and pests, all the while waiting patiently for the harvest. The natural farmer is not always guaranteed a harvest. Bad weather conditions can change everything in a day. But you and I are promised a harvest "in due season" (Galatians 6:10)

Know the season you're in

There are seasons to the Lord's work, a time of preparation and ploughing of the fields, a time of planting. A time of caring for the seedlings, and then, time of reaping!
We may not see the results of our labours today, next week, or even next year. But we will see them. Some of the results of our labour will only be evident on that day when we stand before the Lord. But, just like the farmer, we keep sowing, and trusting God to do as He has promised, in His time. Let's not be quitters.

We are more than "not too bad!" - so much more than "okay." We are expectant!!

Sunday - Just Do It!

"Saul said to David, 'Go, and the LORD be with you.'"
  1 Samuel 17:37 (NIVUK)

There's a particular famous brand of sportswear, with the bold slogan, *"just do it!"* I like that slogan! Some of us could do with applying a statement like that to Biblical principles, for example <u>obedient faith</u>, and in doing so, the landscape of our lives would look very different.

In our reading today in 1 Samuel, we see a young David going out to fight Goliath. David had absolute faith that he would win this battle, even though, 'logically speaking,' all the odds were stacked against him. Why? Because David had developed a habit of reminding himself of who God is.
Do you ever feel at a place in life where you are' stuck' and can't seem to move forward? For whatever ever reason, be it fear of the unknown, circumstantial set backs, demotivation, or plain old lack of faith, for some reason you seem to have lost your 'mojo.'

Just Go!
Take that first step of obedient faith, make that first tiny move forward, write the first lines of that job application, say those first opening words in telling your [scary] boss about Jesus, face your particular 'giant.' Any journey, whatever its length or the terrain it covers, has to start with that first step. We have to just, well, ... *'go!'*

* * *

If we listen to the inner voice that tells us "you're crazy, you can't do that!," then fear and discouragement gets hold of our hearts, and inertia sets in.

That *could* have happened to David, when he went to fight Goliath and the story would have had a very different ending. Actually the story might never have even happened! But David didn't allow himself to be distracted by the voice of discouragement.

Single minded

When David let it be known that he intended to fight the giant, his brothers were dismissive and mocking. Then King Saul tried to talk him out of it, *"Don't be ridiculous!" Saul replied. "There's no way you can fight this Philistine and possibly win! You're only a boy, and he's been a man of war since his youth."* 1 Samuel 17:33 (NLT)

But David remained single minded, his eyes fixed on God. Faithful obedience was David's default response to God; <u>David activated his faith in God, by recalling God's faithfulness</u> to him, describing to Saul all the ways that God had delivered him from powerful predators in the past:*"I have done this to both lions and bears, and I'll do it to this pagan Philistine, too, for he has defied the armies of the living God! The Lord who rescued me from the claws of the lion and the bear will rescue me from this Philistine!"* 1 Samuel 17:36-37 (NLT)

God said it - Case closed

I love the way David's declaration of God's faithfulness just settled the argument, right there and then. There was nothing more to say on the matter. Case closed! It brings to mind a song the children used to sing in kids' church back in the 1980's, that had the lines, *"God said it, I believe it, and that's good enough for me."* I want to have that sort of faith!

* * *

If you're feeling 'stuck' today, unable or afraid to move forward, start to remember and declare out loud all the times God has been faithful to you. Remind yourself that God has equipped you with everything you need. (2 Peter 1:33)

And remember, you aren't slogging it out on your own, God calls you to partner with Him, to work alongside Him. Just do it! Take that first step of faith, put one foot out and let the other foot follow, and keep walking, remembering that "*the Lord your God is with you*". Suddenly you'll realise it's happening- you're "GOING!!"

So we come to the end of the chapter, and the book. Thank you friend, for travelling part of this journey with me! I hope that you have been encouraged, and reminded of what can happen in the life of an ordinary person, wholly surrendered to our Extraordinary God.

.